THE WORLD'S GREAT
ATTACK
AIRCRAFT

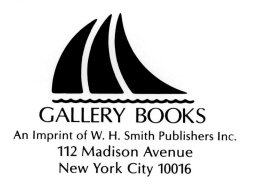

GALLERY BOOKS

An Imprint of W. H. Smith Publishers Inc.
112 Madison Avenue
New York City 10016

THE WORLD'S GREAT
ATTACK
AIRCRAFT

ISBN: 0 8317 9675 8

Pictures were supplied by:

Assoc Press, British Aerospace, Bob Archer, J W Bennett, Patrick Bunce, Philip Chinnery, COI, Dassault-Breguet, David Donald, General Dynamics, Flygvapen Nytt, Peter R Foster, Grumman, Rene J Francillon, Denis Hughes, International Defence Review, Paul A Jackson, A Johnson, Robert L Lawson, Letectvi & Kosmonautika, McDonnell Douglas, Peter R March, MOD, Bob Munro, Lindsay Peacock, RAF, RAF Germany, RAF News, Tomask Rodak, SAAB, Robbie Shaw, Swedish Air Force, Rockwell International, USAF, US Dept of Defense, US Navy, Vought Corporation.

Production editor: Roy Wilkinson
Design: Millions Design

Title page: The spacious cockpit of the Grumman Intruder

CONTENTS

The PANAVIA TORNADO IDS

Panavia Tornado GR.Mk 1
No. 617 Squadron
Royal Air Force

Rain dispersal ducts
Pressurized air bled from the air-conditioning system is ducted forward of the windscreen panels to disperse rain/sleet/snow

Windscreen
Comprises flat centre panel and two curved side panels, all armoured and incorporating Sierracote electrically conductive heating for both anti-icing and demisting; in the event of electrical failure can be demisted by engine bleed air

HUD
Pilot's electronic head-up display/weapon-aiming computer is of the 6/50 Series developed by Smiths/Teldix/OMI; provides a multi-purpose display for a variety of air-data and navigation tasks and performs the weapon-aiming computations

Canopy
Rear-hinged and upward opening one-piece canopy is by Kopperschmidt/AIT; it is demisted by engine bleed air

Accommodation
Pilot (forward) and navigator/weapon's officer (aft) on tandem Martin-Baker Mk 10A zero-zero ejection seats that provide safe escape at zero altitude and at speeds up to 630 knots

Transmitter
Angle-of-attack transmitter, sensing angle of the wing chord in relation to oncoming undisturbed airstream, and providing vital information in conjunction with the air data probe for the onboard flight control system

Aerial
IFF aerial for the Cossor SSR-3100 IFF transponder, which provides identification friend or foe with extensive and sophisticated interrogation capability

Radome
AEG-Telefunken radar-transparent nose-cone, incorporating the air data probe and a lightning conductor strip, houses antennae for the Texas Instruments multi-mode forward-looking ground mapping radar and terrain-following radar; radome and small fuselage section hinges to the right on the ground to provide access to radar equipment and antennae

Inflight-refuelling
There are provisions for a detachable retractable inflight-refuelling probe on the right side of the fuselage, near the cockpit, as well as for the use of a buddy-buddy refuelling pack

Cannon
IWKA-Mauser 27-mm cannon, one each side, with 180 rounds of ammunition per gun

Aerial
UHF/Tacan aerial; the Marconi Avionics AD2770 Tacan navigation and homing aid provides range and bearing from any Tacan ground station or suitably equipped aircraft

BOZ-107 Chaff and flare dispenser
The Swedish-designed BOZ-107 is a sophisticated self-contained, microprocessor-controlled, reprogrammable ECM dispenser carried on Tornado to augment the British Sky Shadow.

Air-to-air missiles
On the inner side of each inboard swivelling pylon is a launch rail for an AIM-9L Sidewinder; the third-generation variant of this extensively built missile, it has an active infra-red proximity fuse for greater lethality and incorporates double-delta nose fins for much improved manoeuvrability

Auxiliary fuel
The subsonic external fuel tanks, one beneath each inboard swivelling pylon, are of 1500 litres (330 Imp gallon) capacity; there is provision for auxiliary drop tanks to be mounted beneath the fuselage, and lower capacity tanks can also be carried

Landing gear
Of hydraulically retractable tricycle configuration, there is a nitrogen gas emergency extension system, Goodyear anti-skid units, and the Dunlop wheels with multi-disc brakes carry low-pressure heavy-duty tyres that allow for operations from and to semi-prepared surfaces

Underfuselage ram-air intake
Feeds air to bootstrap cold air unit which in conjunction with Normalair-Garrett air cycle system, provides cool air to the cockpit and pressurization system; maximum pressurization differential 0.37 kg/cm² (5.25 lb/sq in)

Tornado IDS: Striker Supreme

In dirty weather, at night, flying at supersonic speed 50 feet above the rocks and trees of a German valley, carrying a knockout punch to the heavily-defended enemy; it can only be the Panavia Tornado IDS, the world's most advanced strike aircraft.

One of the pillars of democracy which NATO exists to defend is the freedom of its members to purchase disparate military equipment. Thus, though they supposedly must be able to fight shoulder-to-shoulder in the event of war, alliance members find even peacetime away-from-base operations a potential nightmare of non-standardization. Narrow national interests perpetuate this state of affairs, but occasionally NATO members take a bold step along the road already familiar to their rigorously uniform Warsaw Pact counterparts. In the realm of aviation, such a challenging move was the Panavia Tornado, now establishing itself as an interdictor and strike (IDS) aircraft par excellence.

Product of a late-1960s pact between the UK, West Germany and Italy, the variable geometry Tornado IDS serves with the air forces of all three consortium members, and with the West German navy. A further model, the Tornado ADV (Air Defence Variant), has been specially produced to meet RAF long-range fighter specifications and so warrants separate mention. By all accounts, the Tornado story has been a triumph technically and politically in an arena where intransigence and prejudice can so easily provoke tragedy. Well up to expectations and only slightly above cost (but some years behind the optimistic schedule announced at its conception) the aircraft is being welcomed by air and ground crews alike in its four operator air arms.

Development

When Panavia GmbH was formed in Munich to oversee the programme on behalf of the aerospace firms which are now known as BAe, MBB and Aeritalia, the project was designated MRCA (Multi-Role Combat Aircraft). Six principal operational roles were identified for the aircraft to fulfil (some of them shared by more than one customer): these were close air support and battlefield interdiction; interdiction/counter-air strike; naval strike; reconnaissance; air superiority; and interception/air defence. (The two last are specific to the ADV.) At that point the NATO members' collective nerve failed them, and instead of proceeding to standardize their armaments, they called for the MRCA to be able to carry every appropriate offensive weapon.

Panavia has succeeded in satisfying this daunting requirement, with the result that equipment on some of the aircraft's three underfuselage and four underwing attachment points varies considerably from country to country. Within the airframe, however, it is a different story, with all employing the two purpose-designed IWKA-Mauser 27-mm cannon. Equipment variations between operators are otherwise restricted to such items as different radios and IFF equipment, so that each nation is able to make use of the aircraft's remarkable all-weather, low-altitude terrain-following capability and phenomenally accurate navigation and weapon-delivery system. Without doubt, the Tornado is the most efficient strike aircraft available to East or West, and will not be rivalled until the Rockwell B-1 is in use.

Between July 1976 and January 1984, six production contracts were placed with Panavia for a total of 805 Tornados, 165 of them ADVs. Four additional aircraft are required for service, to be produced by refurbishing some of the nine prototypes and five pre-series aircraft which made their initial flights between 14 August 1974 and 26 March 1979. Half the 809 aircraft had been delivered by the end of 1984 from production lines at Warton (UK), Manching (West Germany) and Turin (Italy).

The first three squadrons to form within the RAF (Nos 9, 617 and 27) are home-based at Honington and Marham, taking the place of Avro Vulcan B.Mk 2 units. Considerable modification work was undertaken at these airfields in preparation for the Tornado, notably in the provision of hardened shelters and personnel accommodation. Eight Tornado GR.Mk 1 squadrons are assigned to RAF Germany, replacing BAe Buccaneer S.Mk 2Bs and SEPECAT Jaguar GR.Mk 1s. The first unit, No. 15 Squadron, formed on 31 October 1983. The timetable calls for six squadrons to have converted by October 1985, after which one (probably No. 9) will transfer from the UK. The last is to be No. 2 Squadron, due to replace its Jaguars by reconnaissance-configured Tornados in 1986-7. A reconnaissance unit will also be established in the UK.

Armament

For its strike/attack role in British service the Tornado operates with a wide range of weaponry, including a single 431-kg (950-lb) nuclear store of up to 500-kiloton yield. Conventional armament is carried on the three hardpoints beneath the fuselage, with the two outboard positions mounting up to eight Mk 13/1 454-kg (1,000-lb) bombs in two sets of tandem pairs, in which case a fuel tank may be carried in the centre. When the 626-kg (1,380-lb) Mk 13/15 'Paveway' laser-guided bomb is used, the maximum is one per weapon rack, i.e. three per aircraft.

◄ Low-level strike is the name of the game, and there is none better than the Tornado. No. 9 Sqn was among the first RAF units to receive the aircraft, and has since demonstrated its effectiveness against all NATO units.

▼ The Tornado is a very well equipped aircraft bristling with complex avionics.

► The Tornado will be able to knock out enemy radars using BAe ALARM anti-radiation missiles. Seven are shown here, but a service configuration would be fewer, mixed with cluster bombs to take out the remnants of the SAM site.

◄ JP233 is one of the special weapons of the RAF's Tornados. It is an airfield denial weapon, emitting hundreds of mines to damage runways. Among these mines are delayed-reaction weapons which lie in the rubble and explode when moved.

▼ The Luftwaffe operates the Tornado for much the same ground attack duties as the RAF. Some of their units have adopted a new 'lizard' paint scheme, while others are still flying the original grey/green combination.

Operational range with this warload can be extended by inflight refuelling via a 'clip-on' retractable probe unit which rests flush with the starboard side of the fuselage, forward of the cockpit, when not in use. The probe is not normally fitted to the Tornados of RAF Germany, because no tanker aircraft are assigned to this force.

An important wartime task of the Tornado will be counter-air strike: disabling the enemy's airfields. For this two Hunting JP233 bomblet dispensers, each of 2335-kg (5,148-lb) weight, will be mounted beneath the fuselage and activated as the aircraft makes a low-level pass over the target. A JP233 pod contains 30 SG367 parachute-retarded runway-cratering munitions and 215 HB875 area-denial mines to dampen the enthusiasm of repair parties, and is automatically jettisoned when empty. JP233 deliveries began in the spring of 1985, and to assist attack precision with this and all other weapons, the Tornado has a Ferranti LRMTS.

Offensive weaponry is of little value if the carrier is shot down before reaching the target, and it is for this reason that the Tornado is well equipped with defensive aids to augment the inherent advantages of small size and terrain-following flight. High on the fin are the twin antennae for an RWR, while other equipment is stowed beneath the wing. On the port outer pylon is a Marconi ARI 23246/1 Sky Shadow programmable active jammer pod to disrupt enemy radars, and on the opposite side a Philips BOZ-107 chaff and flare dispenser as a decoy for both radar-guided and heat-seeking missiles. The inboard pylons are equipped to carry a 1500-litre (330-Imp gal) fuel tank, but there are subsidiary attachment points on both the pylons' sides for a self-defence AIM-9L Sidewinder AAM (inboard) and a BAe ALARM (outboard). ALARM, ordered in 1983 for service entry four years later, is an anti-radiation missile which homes on enemy radars, forcing them to switch off or be destroyed. If assigned to the defence-suppression role, a Tornado could carry nine ALARMs on its fuselage and inner-wing attachments.

In the Federal German Luftwaffe roles parallel those of the RAF but employ different equipment. Area attacks are made using the 4600-kg (10,141-lb) MBB-Diehl MW-1 belly-pack dispenser, which contains 112 horizontal storage tubes for a variety of bomblets optimized for destroying runways, aircraft and armoured vehicles or for hampering personnel movement. Different combinations of bomblet are carried according to whether the target is an airfield or land battle zone. Long-term plans call for German attack aircraft to be fitted with a stand-off dispenser similar in operation to the MW-1, this weapon sporting 'pop-out' wings and an optional motor for increased range. Following indefinite postponement of contracts for the Rockwell GBU-15 glide bomb, Germany will procure the Hughes AGM-65 Maverick as a precision attack missile, and could well adopt the Texas Instruments AGM-88 HARM for anti-radiation attack.

Self-protection is provided by AIM-9L Sidewinders, aided by an AEG Cerberus jamming pod and a BOZ-101 chaff and flare dispenser. However, a more potent jamming version of the aircraft is under consideration in the form of the Tornado ECR (Electronic Combat and Reconnaissance), which is intended to have a performance similar to that of the USAF's Grumman (General Dynamics) EF-111A Raven. West Germany requires some 40 Tornado ECR aircraft over and above the 324 Tornados on order for its armed forces, the breakdown being 96 (including 10 dual control) for the Marineflieger (naval air arm) and 226 (including 53 trainers) in Luftwaffe service, plus two refurbished pre-series aircraft.

In service

Tornados are replacing Lockheed Starfighters in both West German flying services, the naval aircraft having a different weapons fit for their role of anti-shipping operations in the Baltic. Two MBB AS-34 Kormoran missiles are carried beneath the fuselage (plus one optionally on each inboard pylon for short-range missions), with ECM equipment on the outer pylons. Deliveries are under way of 26 MBB-Aeritalia reconnaissance pods equipped with IR Linescan and visual spectrum cameras. The navy formed the first operational Tornado wing in West Germany during July 1982, while the Luftwaffe waited a further year before JBG 31 was established as the first of four to convert. Weapons training for both forces was handled first by the Waffenausbildungskomponente (WaKo), formed at Erding in February 1982, until this was re-designated JBG 38 at Jever in August 1983.

Italy is having much the same equipment as the Luftwaffe for its 99 production Tornados (including 12 dual-control aircraft) and single refurbished pre-series model. Of these, 54 are assigned to the front line, 36 to reserve and 10 to type conversion with the TTTE in the UK. Acquisition is planned or under way of MW-1 pods, AGM-65 Mavericks, AS-34 Kormorans and 20 MBB-Aeritalia pods to provide ground-attack, anti-ship and tactical reconnaissance capabilities within three squadrons. Production of the Tornado in Italy began slightly later than in the other two countries, with the result that the 154° Gruppo (squadron) of the 6° Stormo (wing) did not commission until February 1983 to serve as both a weapons unit and a combat force. Next, in 1984, the 156° Gruppo was formed in the 36° Stormo, including a flight assigned to anti-shipping operations with AS-34 Kormorans, while the 155° Gruppo of the 51° Stormo followed in 1985 to complete the programme. The last 11 Italian Tornados are due to be delivered in 1986.

Clearly, the Tornado is living up to the expectations of those who drafted the requirements for a Multi-Role Combat Aircraft back in the 1960s. Representing the best in aeronautical expertise available from three of Europe's leading aircraft companies and a host of ancillary firms, the aircraft is justifiably hailed as a milestone in combat aircraft development and international collaboration. Carrying its formidable range of weaponry, it will be a familiar sight for years to come.

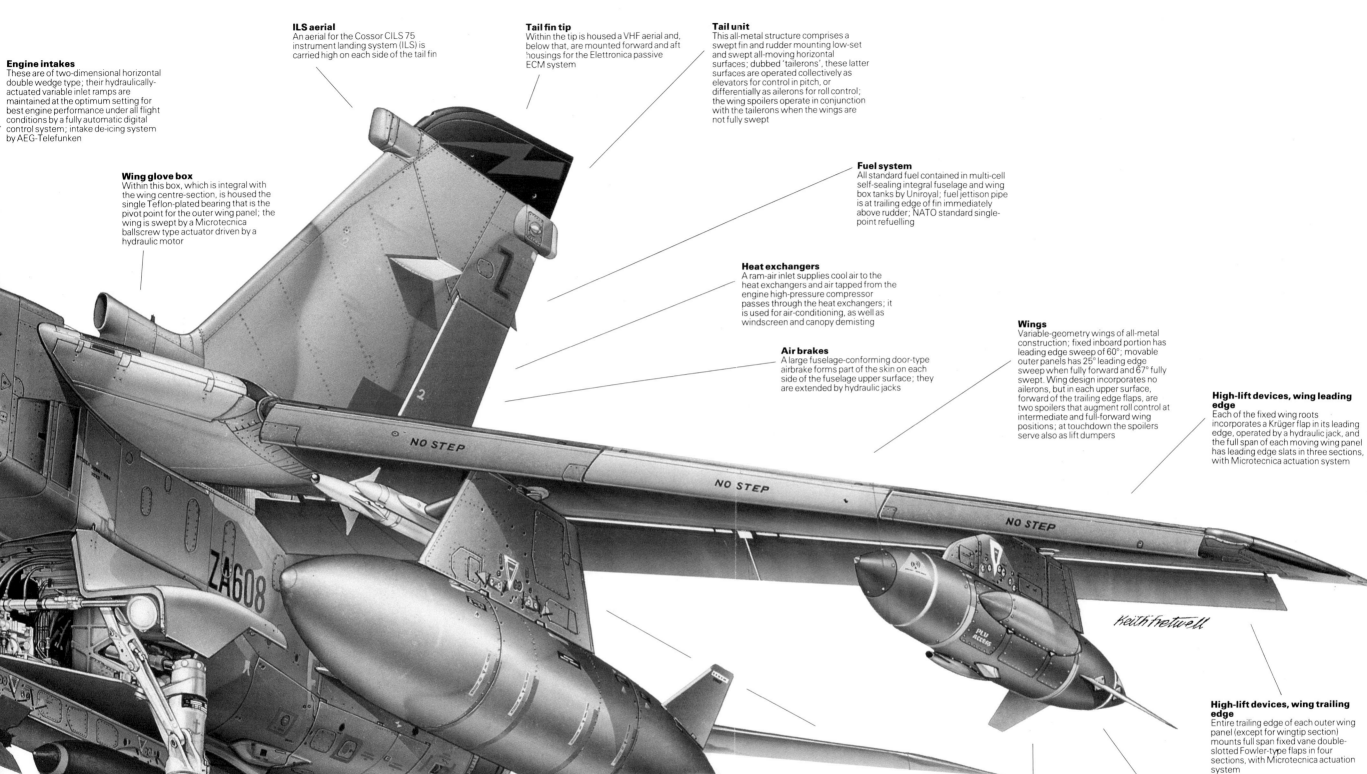

Engine intakes
These are of two-dimensional horizontal double wedge type; their hydraulically-actuated variable inlet ramps are maintained at the optimum setting for best engine performance under all flight conditions by a fully automatic digital control system; intake de-icing system by AEG-Telefunken

ILS aerial
An aerial for the Cossor CILS 75 instrument landing system (ILS) is carried high on each side of the tail fin

Tail fin tip
Within the tip is housed a VHF aerial and, below that, are mounted forward and aft housings for the Elettronica passive ECM system

Tail unit
This all-metal structure comprises a swept fin and rudder mounting low-set and swept all-moving horizontal surfaces; dubbed 'tailerons', these latter surfaces are operated collectively as elevators for control in pitch, or differentially as ailerons for roll control; the wing spoilers operate in conjunction with the tailerons when the wings are not fully swept

Fuel system
All standard fuel contained in multi-cell self-sealing integral fuselage and wing box tanks by Uniroyal; fuel jettison pipe is at trailing edge of fin immediately above rudder; NATO standard single-point refuelling

Wing glove box
Within this box, which is integral with the wing centre-section, is housed the single Teflon-plated bearing that is the pivot point for the outer wing panel; the wing is swept by a Microtecnica ballscrew type actuator driven by a hydraulic motor

Heat exchangers
A ram-air inlet supplies cool air to the heat exchangers and air tapped from the engine high-pressure compressor passes through the heat exchangers; it is used for air-conditioning, as well as windscreen and canopy demisting

Air brakes
A large fuselage-conforming door-type airbrake forms part of the skin on each side of the fuselage upper surface; they are extended by hydraulic jacks

Wings
Variable-geometry wings of all-metal construction; fixed inboard portion has leading edge sweep of 60°; movable outer panels has 25° leading edge sweep when fully forward and 67° fully swept. Wing design incorporates no ailerons, but in each upper surface, forward of the trailing edge flaps, are two spoilers that augment roll control at intermediate and full-forward wing positions; at touchdown the spoilers serve also as lift dumpers

High-lift devices, wing leading edge
Each of the fixed wing roots incorporates a Krüger flap in its leading edge, operated by a hydraulic jack, and the full span of each moving wing panel has leading edge slats in three sections, with Microtecnica actuation system

High-lift devices, wing trailing edge
Entire trailing edge of each outer wing panel (except for wingtip section) mounts full span fixed vane double-slotted Fowler-type flaps in four sections, with Microtecnica actuation system

ECM pod
The ARI 23246/1 Sky Shadow ECM pod, for which Marconi Space and Defence systems was the prime contractor, incorporates both active and passive electronic warfare systems, an integral transmitter/receiver, a processor and a cooling system

Underwing pylons
Both inboard and outboard pylons are swivelled as the wing is swept to maintain correct fore and aft position; only the inboard pylons are plumbed to carry fuel tanks. Maximum external stores load, including underfuselage stations, is approximately 9000 kg (19,842 lb)

Powerplant
Two Turbo-Union RB199-34R Mk 101 turbofan engines, mounted side-by-side in the rear fuselage, and each developing 7257 kg (16,000 lb) thrust plus with reheat; each engine has an integral target-type thrust reverser with buckets attached to the jet-pipe; large downward-opening doors in the underfuselage simplify servicing and engine change

Arrester hook
For short-field landings a runway arrester hook is incorporated in the rear fuselage structure and can be lowered as and when required

Fuselage pylons
Fuselage shoulder pylons, two, each mounting here two Mk 83 454-kg (1,000-lb) HE bombs; a wide range of alternative weapons can be carried on the underfuselage and underwing pylons and include air-to-surface missiles; fire, flare, general purpose, retarded, runway penetration, and smart bombs; rockets; and air-to-surface missiles

ZA608

Keith Fretwell

Tornado in service units and example aircraft

International
Tri-national Tornado Training Establishment
Commissioned: 29 January 1981
Base: RAF Cottesmore
Task: Aircrew conversion (airframe)
Aircraft: (RAF) ZA320 'B-01', ZA322 'B-50', ZA356 'B-07', ZA548 'B-10', ZA602 'B-13'; (Luftwaffe) 4306 'G-25', 4311 'G-30', 4316 'G-32', 4324 'G-74', 4335 'G-38'; (AMI) MM7002 'I-92', MM7004 'I-90', MM55000 'I-42', MM55001 'I-40', MM55004 'I-44'

Royal Air Force

No. 2 Squadron
Forming: 1986-7
Base: Laarbruch, West Germany
Task: Strike/attack/reconnaissance
Aircraft: none yet delivered

No. 9 Squadron
Formed: 1 June 1982
Base: Honington
Task: Strike/attack
Aircraft: ZA368 'Y', ZA543 'T', ZA559 'U', ZA587 'B', ZA591 'F', ZA596 'L'

No. 14 Squadron
Forming: 21 October 1985
Base: Brüggen, West Germany
Task: Strike/attack
Aircraft: still converting from Jaguar; some Tornados on strength, including ZD842 'BZ'

No. 15 Squadron
Formed: 31 October 1983
Base: Laarbruch, West Germany
Task: Strike/attack
Aircraft: ZA392 'EK', ZA410 'EX', ZA448 'EB', ZA453 'EG', ZA455 'EJ', ZA472 'EE'

No. 16 Squadron
Formed: 29 February 1984
Base: Laarbruch, West Germany
Task: Strike/attack
Aircraft: ZA412 'FZ', ZA458 'FB', ZA460 'FD', ZA465 'FK', ZA466 'FH', ZA468 'FN'

No. 17 Squadron
Formed: 1 March 1985
Base: Brüggen, West Germany
Task: Strike/attack
Aircraft: ZD717 'CD', ZD743 'CZ', ZD789 'CE', ZD791 'CC', ZD792 'CF', ZD793 'CA' (remainder in process of delivery)

No. 20 Squadron
Formed: 29 June 1984
Base: Laarbruch, West Germany
Task: Strike/attack
Aircraft: ZA452 'GK', ZA461 'GA', ZA463 'GL', ZA491 'GC', ZD709 'GJ', ZD741 'GT'

No. 16 Sqn was the second RAF Germany unit to receive the Tornado GR.Mk 1, based at Laarbruch.

No. 27 Squadron
Formed: 12 August 1983
Base: Marham
Task: Strike/attack
Aircraft: ZA365 '14', ZA395 '06', ZA562 '12', ZA600 '07'

No. 31 Squadron
Formed: 1 November 1984
Base: Brüggen, West Germany
Task: Strike/attack
Aircraft: ZD707 'DB', ZD710 'DC', ZD720 'DF', ZD739 'DE', ZD745 'DH', ZD746 'DJ', ZD747 'DK', ZD748 'DG', ZD790 'DL'

No. 45 Squadron — Tornado Weapons Conversion Unit
Formed: 1 January 1984
Base: Honington
Task: 'Shadow' squadron for TWCU
Aircraft: ZA366, ZA371, ZA397, ZA400, ZA407, ZA612

No. 617 Squadron
Formed: 16 May 1983
Base: Marham
Task: Strike/attack
Aircraft: ZA367 'T', ZA541 'S', ZA561 'J', ZA605 'O', ZA607 'P', ZA608 'Z'

Tornado GR.Mk 1T dual-control trainer of the TWCU based at Honington.

Luftwaffe

Jagdbombergeschwader 31
Formed: 1 August 1983
Base: Norvenich
Task: Strike/attack
Aircraft: 4392, 4400, 4409, 4422, 4429, 4441

Jagdbombergeschwader 32
Formed: August 1984
Base: Lechfeld
Task: Strike/attack
Aircraft: 4436, 4437, 4438, 4439, 4440, 4450 (deliveries continuing)

Jagdbombergeschwader 33
Formed: August 1985
Base: Büchel
Task: Strike/attack
Aircraft: none yet delivered

Jagdbombergeschwader 34
Forming: 1987
Base: Memmingen
Task: Strike/attack
Aircraft: none yet delivered

Jagdbombergeschwader 38
Formed: 26 August 1983
Base: Jever
Task: Aircrew conversion (weapons system)
Aircraft: 4319, 4322, 4328, 4338, 4340, 4410, 4411

Marineflieger

Marinefliegergeschwader 1
Formed: 2 July 1982
Base: Schleswig/Jagel
Task: Maritime attack
Aircraft: 4342, 4349, 4351, 4352, 4365, 4373, 4383, 4386

Marinefliegergeschwader 2
Forming: 1986
Base: Eggebeck
Task: Maritime attack/reconnaissance
Aircraft: none yet delivered

Tornado of Marinefliegergeschwader 1 based at Schleswig/Jagel.

Aeronautica Militare Italiana

The Italian air force's 36° Stormo based at Gioia del Colle is continuing its re-equipment with Tornados, having flown Aeritalia F-104S Starfighters. The unit is tasked with both conventional strike and maritime duties.

154° Gruppo/6° Stormo
Formed: February 1983
Base: Ghedi
Task: Attack and crew conversion (weapons system)
Aircraft: MM7006 '6-01', MM7012 '6-11', MM7017 '6-14', MM7021 '6-30', MM7027 '6-32', MM55009 '6-16'

156° Gruppo/36° Stormo
Formed: 1984
Base: Gioia del Colle
Task: Attack/maritime attack
Aircraft: MM7046 '36-34', MM7050 '36-44', MM7051 '36-43', MM7053 '36-45' (deliveries continuing)

155° Gruppo/51° Stormo
Forming: 1985
Base: Treviso/Istrana
Task: Attack/reconnaissance
Aircraft: none yet delivered

© Pilot Press Limited

Panavia Tornado GR.Mk 1 cutaway drawing key

Panavia Tornado IDS

1 Air data probe
2 Radome
3 Lightning conductor strip
4 Terrain following radar antenna
5 Ground mapping radar antenna
6 Radar equipment bay hinged position
7 Radome hinged position
8 IFF aerial
9 Radar antenna tracking mechanism
10 Radar equipment bay
11 UHF/TACAN aerial
12 Laser Ranger and Marked Target Seeker (Ferranti), starboard side
13 Cannon muzzle
14 Ventral Doppler aerial
15 Angle of attack transmitter
16 Canopy emergency release
17 Avionics equipment bay
18 Front pressure bulkhead
19 Windscreen rain dispersal air ducts
20 Windscreen (Lucas-Rotax)
21 Retractable, telescopic, inflight refuelling probe
22 Probe retraction link
23 Windscreen open position, instrument access
24 Head-up display, HUD (Smiths)
25 Instrument panel
26 Radar 'head-down' display
27 Instrument panel shroud
28 Control column
29 Rudder pedals
30 Battery
31 Cannon barrel
32 Nosewheel doors
33 Landing/taxiing lamp
34 Nose undercarriage leg strut (Dowty-Rotol)
35 Torque scissor links
36 Twin forward-retracting nosewheels (Dunlop)
37 Nosewheel steering unit
38 Nosewheel leg door
39 Electrical equipment bay

40 Ejection seat rocket pack
41 Engine throttle levers
42 Wing sweep control lever
43 Radar hand controller
44 Side console panel
45 Pilot's Martin-Baker Mk 10 ejection seat
46 Safety harness
47 Ejection seat headrest
48 Cockpit canopy cover (Kopperschmidt)
49 Canopy centre arch
50 Navigator's radar displays
51 Navigator's instrument panel and weapons control panels
52 Foot rests
53 Canopy external latch
54 Pitot head
55 Mauser 27-mm cannon
56 Ammunition feed chute
57 Cold air unit ram air intake
58 Ammunition tank
59 Liquid oxygen converter
60 Cabin cold air unit
61 Stores management system computer
62 Port engine air intake
63 Intake lip
64 Cockpit framing
65 Navigator's Martin-Baker Mk 10 ejection seat
66 Starboard engine air intake
67 Intake spill duct
68 Canopy jack
69 Canopy hinge point
70 Rear pressure bulkhead
71 Intake ramp actuator linkage
72 Navigation light
73 Two-dimensional variable area intake ramp doors
74 Intake suction relief doors
75 Wing glove Krüger flap
76 Intake bypass air spill ducts
77 Intake ramp hydraulic actuator
78 Forward fuselage fuel tank

79 Wing sweep control screw jack (Microtecnica)
80 Flap and slat control drive shafts
81 Wing sweep, flap and slat central control unit and motor (Microtecnica)
82 Wing pivot box integral fuel tank
83 Air system ducting
84 Anti-collision light
85 UHF aerials
86 Wing pivot box carry-through, electron beam welded titanium structure
87 Starboard wing pivot bearing
88 Flap and slat telescopic drive shafts
89 Starboard wing sweep control screw jack
90 Leading-edge sealing fairing
91 Wing root glove fairing
92 External fuel tank, capacity 330 Imp gal (1500 litres)
93 AIM-9L Sidewinder air-to-air self-defence missile
94 Canopy open position
95 Canopy jettison unit
96 Pilot's rear view mirrors
97 Starboard three-segment leading-edge slat, open
98 Slat screw jacks
99 Slat drive torque shaft
100 Wing pylon swivelling control rod
101 Inboard pylon pivot bearing
102 Starboard wing integral fuel tank
103 Wing fuel system access panels
104 Outboard pylon pivot bearing

105 Marconi 'Sky-Shadow' ECM pod
106 Outboard wing swivelling pylon
107 Starboard navigation and strobe lights
108 Wing tip fairing
109 Double-slotted Fowler-type flaps, down position
110 Flap guide rails
111 Starboard spoilers, open
112 Flap screw jacks
113 External fuel tank tail fins
114 Wing swept position trailing edge housing
115 Dorsal spine fairing
116 Aft fuselage fuel tank
117 Fin root antenna fairing
118 HF aerial
119 Heat exchanger ram air intake
120 Starboard wing fully swept back position
121 Airbrake, open
122 Starboard all-moving tailplane (taileron)
123 Airbrake hydraulic jack
124 Primary heat exchanger
125 Heat exchanger exhaust duct
126 Engine bleed air ducting

127 Fin attachment joint
128 Port airbrake rib construction
129 Fin heat shield
130 Vortex generators
131 Fin integral fuel tank
132 Fuel system vent piping
133 Tailfin structure
134 ILS aerial
135 Fin leading edge
136 Forward passive ECM housing
137 Fuel jettison and vent valve
138 Fin tip antenna fairing
139 VHF aerial
140 Tail navigation light
141 Aft passive ECM housing
142 Obstruction light
143 Fuel jettison
144 Rudder
145 Rudder honeycomb construction
146 Rudder hydraulic actuator (Fairey Hydraulics)
147 Dorsal spine tail fairing
148 Thrust reverser bucket doors, open

149 Variable area afterburner nozzle
150 Nozzle control jacks (four)
151 Thrust reverser door actuator
152 Honeycomb trailing edge construction
153 Port all-moving tailplane (taileron)

161 Tailplane hydraulic actuator
162 Hydraulic system filters
163 Hydraulic reservoir (Dowty)
164 Airbrake hinge point
165 Intake frame/production joint
166 Engine bay ventral access panels
167 Engine oil tank
168 Rear fuselage fuel tank
169 Wing root pneumatic seal
170 Engine driven accessory gearboxes, port and starboard (KHD), airframe mounted
171 Integrated drive generator (two)
172 Hydraulic pump (two)
173 Gearbox interconnecting shaft
174 Starboard side Auxiliary Power Unit, APU (KHD)
175 Telescopic fuel pipes
176 Port wing pivot bearing
177 Flexible wing sealing plates
178 Wing skin panelling
179 Rear spar
180 Port spoiler housings
181 Spoiler hydraulic actuators
182 Flap screw jacks
183 Flap rib construction
184 Port Fowler-type double-slotted flaps, down position
185 Port wing fully swept back position
186 Wing tip construction
187 Fuel vent
188 Port navigation and strobe lights
189 Leading-edge slat rib construction
190 Marconi 'Sky-Shadow' ECM pod
191 Outboard swivelling pylon
192 Pylon pivot bearing
193 Front spar
194 Port wing integral fuel tank
195 Machined wing skin/stringer panel
196 Wing rib construction
197 Swivelling pylon control rod
198 Port leading-edge slat segments, open
199 Slat guide rails
200 External fuel tank
201 Inboard swivelling pylon
202 Inboard pylon pivot bearing
203 Missile launch rail
204 AIM-9L Sidewinder air-to-air self-defence missile
205 Port mainwheel (Dunlop), forward retracting
206 Main undercarriage leg strut (Dowty-Rotol)
207 Undercarriage leg pivot bearing
208 Hydraulic retraction jack
209 Leg swivelling control link
210 Telescopic flap and slat drive torque shafts
211 Leading-edge sealing fairing

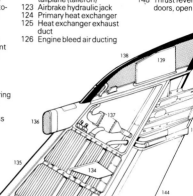

AVIAGRAPHICA

154 Tailplane rib construction
155 Leading-edge nose ribs
156 Tailplane pivot bearing
157 Tailplane bearing sealing plates
158 Afterburner duct
159 Airbrake hydraulic jack
160 Turbo-Union R.B.199-34R Mk 101 afterburning turbofan engine

212 Krüger flap hydraulic jack
213 Main undercarriage leg breaker strut
214 Mainwheel door
215 Landing lamp
216 Hunting JP 233 Airfield Attack Weapon (two, side-by-side)

217 Submunitions compartments (30 SG357 runway penetration bombs and 215 HB876 area denial weapons in each JP 233)
218 Port shoulder pylon
219 Fuselage shoulder pylon (two)
220 ML twin stores carriers
221 Hunting BL 755 cluster bombs (eight)
222 Mk 83 high speed retarded bomb
223 Mk 13/15 454-kg (1,000-lb) HE bomb

Tornado IDS warload

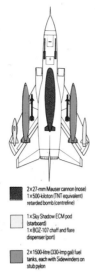
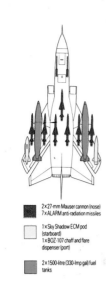
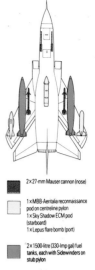
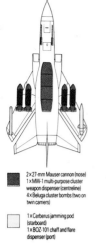
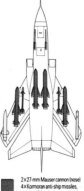

RAF tactical nuclear strike
- 2 × 27-mm Mauser cannon (nose)
- 1 × 500-kiloton (TNT equivalent) retarded bomb (centreline)
- 1 × Sky Shadow ECM pod (starboard)
- 1 × BOZ-107 chaff and flare dispenser (port)
- 2 × 1500-litre (330-Imp gal) fuel tanks, each with Sidewinders on stub pylon

An artist's impression shows the probable configuration of a nuclear-armed Tornado GR.Mk 1, with a single weapon on the centre pylon. Having a yield of up to 500 kilotons, this could be carried over a hi-lo-lo-hi combat radius of some 1290 km (800 miles) without inflight-refuelling. The aircraft would be employed for tactical strike against targets behind the battlefield.

RAF airfield denial
- 2 × 27-mm Mauser cannon (nose)
- 2 × Hunting JP 233 airfield denial weapon packs (underfuselage)
- 1 × Sky Shadow ECM pod (starboard)
- 1 × BOZ-107 chaff and flare dispenser (port)
- 2 × 1500-litre (330-Imp gal) fuel tanks, each with Sidewinders on stub pylon

One of the prime tasks for the Tornado is to destroy enemy airfield installations, especially runways and taxiways. The potent JP 233 airfield-suppression weapon dispenses a range of cratering charges, delayed-action and tremble-activated mines, and a mix of anti-personnel bomblets.

RAF anti-radiation
- 2 × 27-mm Mauser cannon (nose)
- 7 × ALARM anti-radiation missiles
- 1 × Sky Shadow ECM pod (starboard)
- 1 × BOZ-107 chaff and flare dispenser (port)
- 2 × 1500-litre (330-Imp gal) fuel tanks

The Tornado can attack enemy radars using a maximum of nine ALARMs, but it would be more normal to carry a smaller number (perhaps four) in addition to an attack payload.

Luftwaffe reconnaissance
- 2 × 27-mm Mauser cannon (nose)
- 1 × MBB-Aeritalia reconnaissance pod on centreline pylon
- 1 × Sky Shadow ECM pod (starboard)
- 1 × Lepus flare bomb (port)
- 2 × 1500-litre (330-Imp gal) fuel tanks, each with Sidewinders on stub pylon

In the reconnaissance role the Tornado combines agility with good range and low-level performance. The lack of an internal equipment bay precludes the use of cameras with long focal lengths, but nonetheless tactical reconnaissance can be undertaken with a variety of photo or infra-red sensor pods.

Luftwaffe anti-armour
- 2 × 27-mm Mauser cannon (nose)
- 1 × MW-1 multi-purpose cluster weapon dispenser (centreline)
- 4 × Beluga cluster bombs (two on twin carriers)
- 1 × Cerberus jamming pod (starboard)
- 1 × BOZ-101 chaff and flare dispenser (port)

The MW-1 is a multi-purpose cluster weapon which can dispense any combination of six sub-munitions, three of them designed for the anti-tank role. Some 4,700 anti-armour projectiles can be deployed from the pod's 224 apertures, being ejected from both sides without recoil effects. The width of the pattern can be preset, and its length can be adjusted in flight.

Marineflieger anti-shipping
- 2 × 27-mm Mauser cannon (nose)
- 4 × Kormoran anti-ship missiles, plus one Sidewinder on stub pylon of each inboard pylon
- 1 × Elettronica EL/73 ECM jammer pod (port)
- 1 × BOZ-101 chaff and flare dispenser on starboard wing

Aircraft of the Marineflieger typically carry the German Kormoran anti-ship missile, while their RAF equivalents are equipped with Martel or Sea Eagle. Operating in pairs or as singletons, they are capable of ultra-low-level approach over the sea.

Specification and performance

Wings
Span, unswept	13.91 m	(45 ft 7.5 in)
swept	8.60 m	(28 ft 2.5 in)
Sweep on outer panels, unswept		25°
swept		67°

Speed at sea level
- Tornado GR.Mk 1 Mach 1.2
- General Dynamics F-111F Mach 1.2
- Su-24 'Fencer' Mach 1.2
- MiG-27 'Flogger-D' Mach 1.1
- SEPECAT Jaguar Mach 1.1
- Mirage 2000 Mach 1.1

Take-off run
- SEPECAT Jaguar 3,085 ft with tactical load
- F-111F 3,000 ft with tactical load
- Tornado GR.Mk 1 2,900 ft
- MiG-27 'D' 2,625 ft max 'clean' weight

Fuselage and tail unit
Length overall	16.72 m	(54 ft 10.25 in)
Height overall	5.95 m	(19 ft 6.25 in)
Tailplane span	6.79 m	(22 ft 3.5 in)

Landing gear
Wheelbase	6.20 m	(20 ft 4 in)
Wheel track	3.10 m	(10 ft 2 in)

Weights
Empty	14091 kg	31,065 lb
Maximum take-off, 'clean' with full internal fuel	20412 kg	45,000 lb
Maximum take-off with external stores	27216 kg	60,000 lb
Maximum external fuel	5851 kg	12,900 lb
Maximum weapon load	9000 kg	19,840 lb

Combat radius hi-lo-hi
- 2000 km E
- 1800 km — General Dynamics F-111F
- 1408 km — Su-24 'Fencer'
- Jaguar with external fuel
- 1390 km — Tornado GR.Mk 1 with max weapons
- 1000 km E — Mirage 2000
- 1000 km E — MiG-27 'Flogger-D'

Performance
Maximum Mach number at altitude, 'clean'		2.2
Maximum speed 'clean' 800 kts	1482 km/h	921 mph
Maximum speed with external stores 600 kts	1112 km/h	691 mph
Climb to 9144 m (30,000 ft) from brake release	under 2 minutes	
Combat radius, heavy weapon load, hi-lo-lo-hi	1390 km	864 miles
Ferry range	3890 km	2,417 miles
g limit	+7.5	

Weapons load

- General Dynamics F-111F 31,500 lb
- Tornado GR.Mk 1 20,000 lb
- Su-24 'Fencer' 17,635 lb
- Mirage 2000 13,225 lb
- SEPECAT Jaguar 10,500 lb
- MiG-27 'Flogger-D' 6,615 lb

Cockpit layout

Left: The pilot's cockpit of the Tornado IDS is dominated by the Marconi head-up display and, below it, the moving map. Flight instruments are largely conventional, although ergonomically well laid out, and the overall atmosphere is old-fashioned when compared with the latest American aircraft with their cathode ray tubes.

Right: The rear station in the Tornado IDS is clearly the heart of the navigation and weapons system. The RAF calls its occupant a 'navigator', although Weapons Systems Officer would, strictly speaking, be more accurate. The moving map display is flanked by two large TV screens which can display all the tactical information required. The joystick below is not a control column but a part of the weapons aiming system.

The SEPECAT JAGUAR

SEPECAT Jaguar: cat out of hell

The Jaguar has a wingspan shorter than that of a wartime Spitfire. But it can carry a heavy bombload over enormous distances, taking off from roads or semi-prepared strips, and can find its target in all weathers and deliver a devastating punch with unerring accuracy. Consistently underrated by its opponents, it is one of today's most effective attack aircraft.

One of the prime functions of an international collaborative programme in aviation is to combine the talents and resources of more than one country in the drive to develop new and more advanced technology. In the case of the SEPECAT Jaguar, however, it was international collaboration itself which was in the prototype stage, resulting in the service debut, in 1973, of the world's first multinationally-developed warplane. Product of an Anglo-French agreement signed at a time when the two partners were enthusiastically joining forces in numerous ventures, the Jaguar is a capable strike/attack aircraft which has performed well in the arms market. Now eclipsed in the RAF by Panavia's Tornado, it still performs a vital role with the French air force and is to continue rolling off the Indian licensed assembly lines until the end of the present decade.

Successful aircraft programmes all contain measures of luck and coincidence, but in the case of the Jaguar these factors had a higher profile than normal. France and the UK began the search for new advanced trainers early in the 1960s, and both gradually increased the emphasis to be placed on secondary attack capability until it became the primary consideration. The French specification was known as ECAT (Ecole de Combat et Appui Tactique), whilst that of the RAF was Air Staff Target 362, and the two countries individually chose the Breguet (later Dassault-Breguet) Br.121 and British Aircraft Corporation P.45 for development. A union of the two was arranged in May 1965, however, the British and French governments acting as marriage brokers. France was awarded design leadership and a joint firm known as the Société Européenne de Production de l'Avion d'Ecole de Combat et d'Appui Tactique (SEPECAT) was registered in that country to manage the programme.

After much discussion the SEPECAT partners agreed to several major changes of design required by the RAF, so completing transformation of the advanced trainer into the potent warplane seen on today's flightlines. A two-seat variant was nevertheless produced in comparatively small numbers, although its role is exclusively a conversion aircraft for the main model.

Role

Today's Jaguar exists primarily as a single-seat tactical aircraft optimized for close support of the army in the field, interdiction behind the battle zone, counter-air operations (against enemy airfields), reconnaissance and air defence. Whereas ground-attack aircraft had previously tended to be interceptor fighters which had passed their prime, the Jaguar ushered in a new phase in being designed from the outset for low-level missions at high speed. For that reason the wing loading and other aerodynamic features were chosen to provide a smooth ride and stable weapons platform in such a flight regime, although the aircraft still possesses good secondary air combat capability at mission altitude.

Compact, comparatively small and undoubtedly purposeful-looking, the Jaguar is a shoulder-wing aircraft of metal construction. The fuselage which is made in three sections, incorporates honeycomb panels for strength and lightness around the cockpit area, plus sandwich panels in other parts. Forward and centre components, up to and including the mainwheel bays, are French-built, with the UK supplying the rear fuselage and wings. The Dunlop twin main wheels to the Messier-Hispano-Bugatti landing gear are of low pressure ($5.91 kg/cm^2$; $84 lb/sq in$) for rough-field operation and have anti-skid units, optionally augmented by a 5.5-m (18-ft) diameter Irvin drag chute stowed in the extreme rear of the fuselage.

The wing is swept 40° at quarter chord and has 3° of anhedral. Built around a two-spar torsion box, its skin is machined or chemically etched from solid aluminium alloy and has integral stiffeners. Built as a single unit, the wing is attached to the fuselage at six points and has slats on the outer leading edges for enhanced manoeuvrability in flight phases that include air combat. The trailing edges are entirely occupied by double-slotted flaps which provide good low-speed characteristics, such as a landing speed of 115 kts (213 km/h; 132 mph). Interesting in the aerodynamic sense is the lack of ailerons, lateral control being via spoilers on the outer wing, just forward of the flaps. At low speeds these

◀ *This Jaguar International of the Nigerian air force was photographed over North Wales while on a test flight from the British Aerospace airfield at*

▲ *No. 2 Sqn is the last RAF Germany-based Jaguar squadron, and is tasked with all-weather tactical reconnaissance using a British Aerospace recce pod containing five*

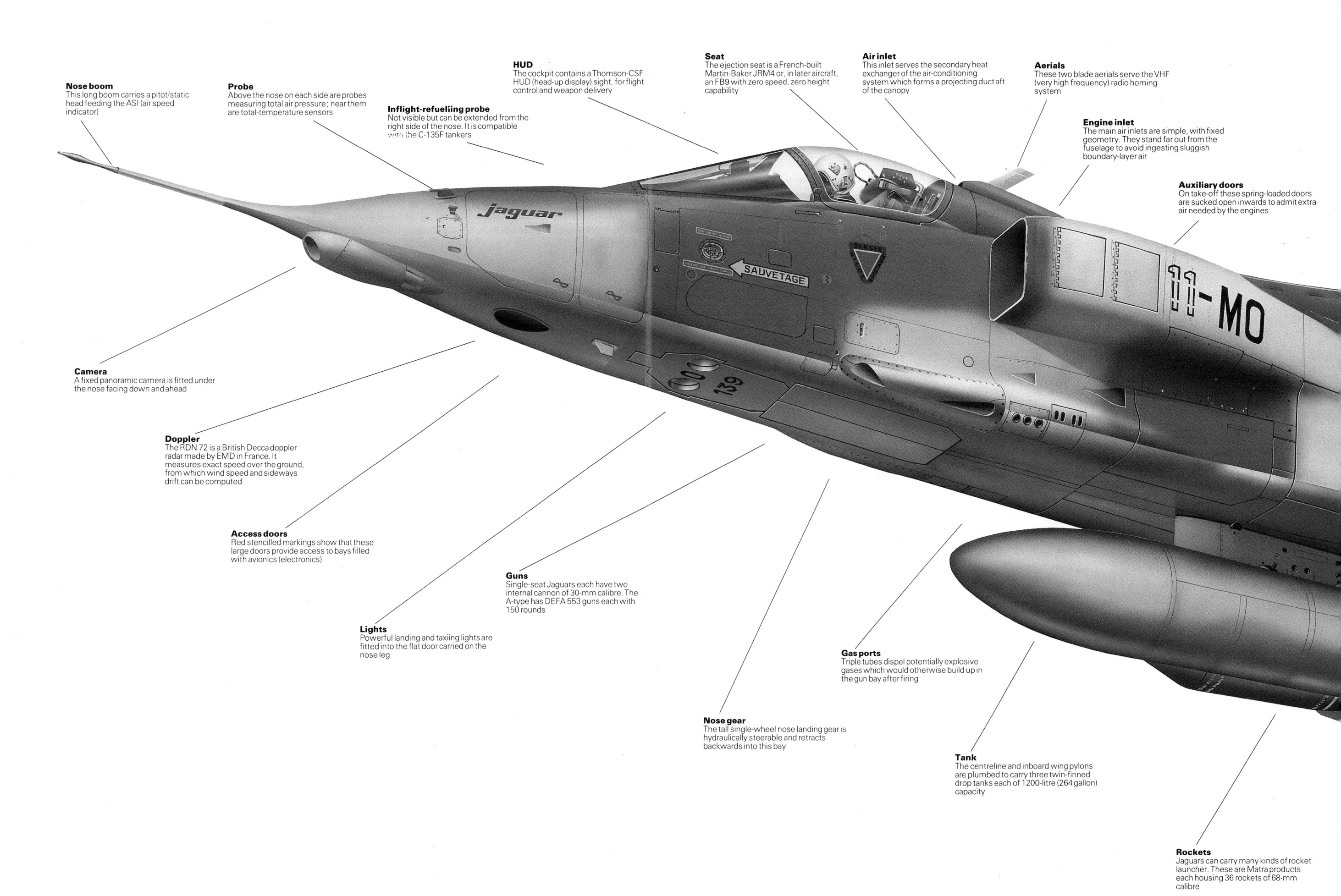

Nose boom
This long boom carries a pitot/static head feeding the ASI (air speed indicator)

Probe
Above the nose on each side are probes measuring total air pressure; near them are total-temperature sensors

Inflight-refuelling probe
Not visible but can be extended from the right side of the nose. It is compatible with the C-135F tankers

HUD
The cockpit contains a Thomson-CSF HUD (head-up display) sight, for flight control and weapon delivery

Seat
The ejection seat is a French-built Martin-Baker JRM4 or, in later aircraft, an FB9 with zero speed, zero height capability

Air inlet
This inlet serves the secondary heat exchanger of the air-conditioning system which forms a projecting duct aft of the canopy

Aerials
These two blade aerials serve the VHF (very high frequency) radio homing system

Engine inlet
The main air inlets are simple, with fixed geometry. They stand far out from the fuselage to avoid ingesting sluggish boundary-layer air

Auxiliary doors
On take-off these spring-loaded doors are sucked open inwards to admit extra air needed by the engines

Camera
A fixed panoramic camera is fitted under the nose facing down and ahead

Doppler
The RDN 72 is a British Decca doppler radar made by EMD in France. It measures exact speed over the ground, from which wind speed and sideways drift can be computed

Access doors
Red stencilled markings show that these large doors provide access to bays filled with avionics (electronics)

Guns
Single-seat Jaguars each have two internal cannon of 30-mm calibre. The A-type has DEFA 553 guns each with 150 rounds

Lights
Powerful landing and taxiing lights are fitted into the flat door carried on the nose leg

Gas ports
Triple tubes dispel potentially explosive gases which would otherwise build up in the gun bay after firing

Nose gear
The tall single-wheel nose landing gear is hydraulically steerable and retracts backwards into this bay

Tank
The centreline and inboard wing pylons are plumbed to carry three twin-finned drop tanks each of 1200-litre (264 gallon) capacity

Rockets
Jaguars can carry many kinds of rocket launcher. These are Matra products each housing 36 rockets of 68-mm calibre

are complemented by differential action of the all moving horizontal tailsurfaces.

Power is provided by a pair of Rolls-Royce Turboméca Adour afterburning turbofan engines, which resulted from an Anglo-French venture paralleling that of the airframe. Both RAF and Armée de l'Air Jaguars were delivered with the 3314-kg (7,305-lb) thrust Adour Mk 102, although those of the former began to be replaced by 3647-kg (8,040-lb) thrust Mk 104s in 1978. Export aircraft first had Mk 804s, which are equivalent to the Mk 104, yet have more recently progressed to the 4205-kg (9,702-lb) thrust Mk 811. Internal fuel of 4200 litres (924 Imp gal) in a total of four fuselage and two wing tanks may be augmented by up to three drop tanks, each of 1200-litres (264-Imp gal) capacity, on the centreline and two inboard wing hardpoints. Outer wing pylons are 'dry'.

Avionics

A resumé of Jaguar equipment and avionics must necessarily be prefixed by mention of one omission: radar. Though a version has been schemed with Thomson-CSF/ESD Agave nose radar for anti-shipping roles with Aérospatiale AM.39 Exocet missiles, all aircraft in service must employ other sensors for navigation and weapon delivery, thereby having only limited all-weather capability. For RAF Jaguars, which have the most comprehensive nav/attack system of early aircraft, the prime pilot aid is Marconi NAVWASS. This projects all information required for the two functions mentioned upon the Smiths HUD, it being necessary for the pilot only to enter in the Marconi-Elliott MCS 920 digital computer the co-ordinates of his waypoints and targets before starting a mission. Thereafter, his projected position during flight is presented on a moving map display mounted in the

centre of the instrument panel, and this can be manually corrected when overflying a distinctive ground feature in order to rectify any 'wandering' of the inertial system.

Beginning in early 1983, RAF Jaguar GR.Mk 1s and T.Mk 2s have been raised to Mks 1A and 2A standard by substitution of a Ferranti FIN 1064 for the original inertial nav system. Some 50 kg (110 lb) lighter, FIN 1064 occupies one-third of its predecessor's space and is similarly linked to the Smiths radio altimeter, Elliott air data computer, map display and other systems that includes a Ferranti LRMTS in the chisel-shaped nose.

A lower standard of avionics is fitted to French attack Jaguars, the main components being a SFIM 250-1 twin-gyro platform, Decca RDN 72 Doppler radar (Dassault-built), Creuzet 90 navigation computer, CSF 31 weapon-aiming computer, and Dassault fire-control computer for Martel ASMs. There are aerials for a CFTH radar warning receiver in fin and tailcone bullet fairings, in place of the RAF's Marconi ARI 18223 in its more obvious fin-top housing.

Eight Jaguar prototypes were ordered

and the first, a French Jaguar E two-seat trainer (E.01), made its maiden flight on 8 September 1968. In addition to five French-built aircraft, of which one was the unsuccessful Jaguar M naval version intended for the Aéronavale, there were also three British prototypes before series manufacture began. RAF models are the Jaguar B (T.Mk 2) two-seat trainer and Jaguar S (GR.Mk 1) single-seat attack aircraft, of which 35 and 165 respectively were delivered between 1973 and 1978, followed by three more trainers for the Empire Test Pilots' School (two) and Institute of Aviation Medicine (one). Delivered first to No. 226 OCU for pilot training,

▼ A Jaguar GR.Mk 1 of No. 54 Sqn carries four 454-kg (1,000-lb) bombs and two underwing drop tanks. No. 54 was the first of the RAF's Jaguar squadrons to form, and still forms a part of the three-squadron Jaguar wing at RAF Coltishall.

▲ No. 14 Sqn was the first Indian Jaguar unit to form, using aircraft borrowed from the RAF until new and licence-built aircraft were available. The Jaguar is known as 'Shamsher', a type of curved sword, in Indian service.

Jaguars were issued to Nos 6, 41 and 54 Squadrons at home, plus Nos 2, 14, 17, 20 and 31 Squadrons in West Germany, although the four last-mentioned (all based at Brüggen) and had been re-equipped with Panavia Tornados by October 1985 and their aircraft placed in storage.

Nos 2 and 41 Squadrons are partly committed to tactical reconnaissance, so carry a 500-kg (1,102-lb) centreline pod containing a fan of five F95 cameras plus one vertical IR linescane camera, with ordnance restricted to a pair of Hunting BL755 cluster bombs or two self-defence AIM-9 Sidewinder AAMs. Alternative loads for strike/attack aircraft include a single tactical nuclear weapon or conventional 454-kg (1,000-lb) bombs, often of the parachute-retarded type for low-level delivery.

France received 40 Jaguar E (Ecole) two-seat trainers and 160 Jaguar A (Appui) attack aircraft between 1972 and 1981, all from the Dassault-Breguet line at Toulouse. Internal armament is two 30-mm cannon, as with British models, except these are the DEFA 553 weapon and not the UK-produced Aden. The final 80 Jaguar A models have a Thomson-CSF TAV-38 laser rangefinder mounted beneath the forward fuselage (in the position formerly occupied by an OMERA 40 camera) and active ECM equipment. Aircraft of the Armée de l'Air are tasked with support in European or overseas theatres (deploying with the aid of their retractable inflight-refuelling probes), carrying an AN 52 tactical nuclear weapon or conventional armament.

Exports

Four export customers have been secured for the Jaguar, BAe handling all final assembly except in part of the Indian contract. Having announced the Jaguar winner of its Deep-penetration Strike Aircraft competition in 1978, the Indian air force took delivery in the following year of 18 loaned RAF aircraft (including two trainers) for service with No. 14 Squadron. Phase two of the programme began in 1981, when the first of 40 Warton-built aircraft was supplied from an order comprising 35 Jaguar International IS attack aircraft and five Jaguar International IB trainers. Finally, in Phase three, Hindustan Aeronautics Ltd at Bangalore is assembling 76 Jaguar kits, of which the first flew in March 1982. Locally the aircraft is named Shamsher, after a type of sword.

Phase two Jaguars have Adour Mk 804 engines and avionics similar to those of the RAF, but in Phase three there is a change to Adour Mk 811s and the Indian integrated DARIN system. More advanced, DARIN includes the Smiths HUDWAS, similar to that of the BAe Sea Harrier; a Ferranti COMED 2045 and a Sagem INS. The Ferranti LRMTS remains in the nose, and although India has denied reports that a few aircraft might be fitted for maritime attack with Agave radar in this position, the possibility remains of a podded Agave

installation combined with Exocet. Armament options are BL755 CBUs, Durandal, F1 pods, local bombs, plus R.550 Magic AAMs on overwing pylons and a centreline reconnaissance pod. India plans to form five Jaguar squadrons.

Oman has received two batches of Jaguars, each of 10 International OS attack aircraft and two OB trainers, beginning in 1977. The second contract features Mk 811 engines in place of Mk 804s and, reportedly, the ability to launch Exocet. All are equipped to fire Ford Aerospace AIM-9P Sidewinder AAMs from the outer underwing pylons, and the last two trainers are unusual in having fin RWR and a fixed refuelling probe in place of the nose pitot.

In South America, Ecuador took delivery of 10 single-seat Jaguar International ES models and two International EB trainers during 1977, arming them with R.550 Magics amongst other weapons. Ecuadorean Jaguars have Mk 804 engines. Most recently, in July 1983, Nigeria ordered 13 Jaguar International NS attack aircraft and five International NB trainers for delivery in 1984 and 1985, at the same

time reserving options for a further 18. All are fitted with Mk 811 versions of the Adour. The prospect of further Jaguar contracts now appears diminished, but by no means eliminated, and customers could still be found for some of the surplus RAF aircraft. Orders currently stand at a very respectable 573, yet it can be argued that this versatile and highly adaptable aircraft would have achieved even greater success had not its French parent been in the ambiguous position of selling a direct competitor.

▲ One ex-RAF Jaguar has been modified by British Aerospace as a trials aircraft for the Active Control Technology programme. Destabilized by ballast and leading-edge strakes, the aircraft is now a true control-configured vehicle, and has been flown to an instability of 10 per cent.

▼ Two Jaguar Internationals of the Omani air force are seen at low level over the desert. Oman has two Jaguar squadrons, both based at Masirah, and tasked with ground attack and air defence duties. AIM-9 Sidewinders are carried in the latter role.

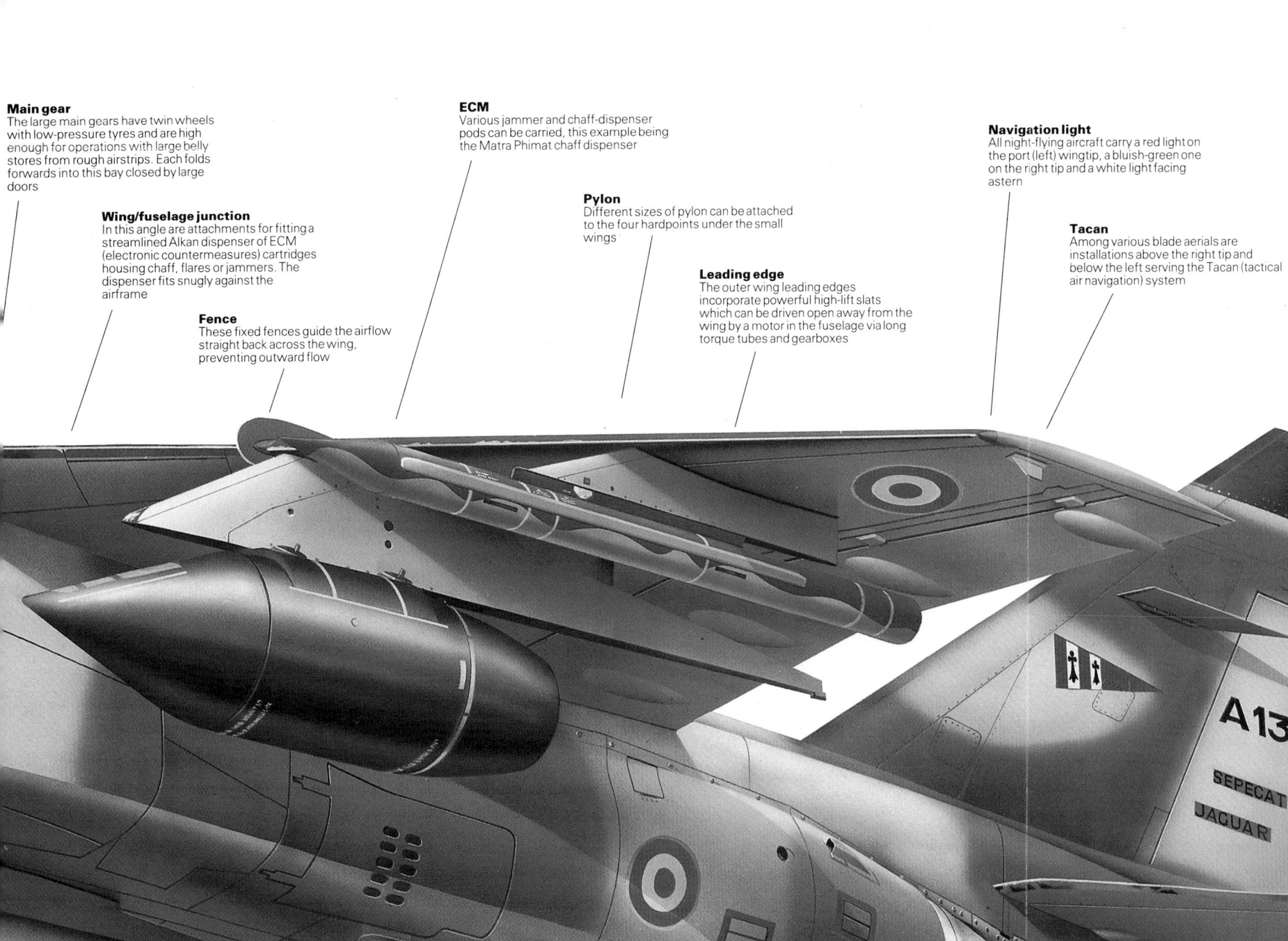

Main gear
The large main gears have twin wheels with low-pressure tyres and are high enough for operations with large belly stores from rough airstrips. Each folds forwards into this bay closed by large doors

Wing/fuselage junction
In this angle are attachments for fitting a streamlined Alkan dispenser of ECM (electronic countermeasures) cartridges housing chaff, flares or jammers. The dispenser fits snugly against the airframe

Fence
These fixed fences guide the airflow straight back across the wing, preventing outward flow

ECM
Various jammer and chaff-dispenser pods can be carried, this example being the Matra Phimat chaff dispenser

Pylon
Different sizes of pylon can be attached to the four hardpoints under the small wings

Leading edge
The outer wing leading edges incorporate powerful high-lift slats which can be driven open away from the wing by a motor in the fuselage via long torque tubes and gearboxes

Navigation light
All night-flying aircraft carry a red light on the port (left) wingtip, a bluish-green one on the right tip and a white light facing astern

Tacan
Among various blade aerials are installations above the right tip and below the left serving the Tacan (tactical air navigation) system

Aerial
The top of the fin is insulated to enclose aerials serving the VHF and UHF (ultra high frequency) communications systems

Navigation light
In addition to this white light most French A-type Jaguars have RWR (radar-warning receiver) aerials on the fin to warn of hostile radar emissions

VOR
The VHF omni-directional range is a basically civil navigation aid based on ground radio stations. It requires an aerial on each side of the fin

Tailcone
Inside the tailcone is a braking parachute, used on short or icy runways. Just above it (not visible) is the fuel jettison pipe

Airbrake
A perforated airbrake is fitted on each side of the rear fuselage, forced open (diagonally out and down) by a hydraulic jack

Drain
Various streamlined pipes enable fuel, oils and other fluids to drain out of the fuselage and engine bays

Ventral fins
The diagonal ventral fins are fixed and enhance stability at high speeds and high angles of attack

Fire doors
Should an engine catch fire on the ground a fire extinguisher can be thrust through these spring-loaded doors

Tailplane
Called a horizontal stabilizer in the USA, the tailplanes are single 'slabs' driven by a hydraulic power unit either in unison or, for roll control, in opposition

Hook
This arrester hook is lowered when an emergency landing has to be made without effective wheel brakes. It engages with a cable stretched across the runway

SEPECAT Jaguar in service

Royal Air Force

RAF Germany retains one Jaguar squadron, No. 2, which operates in the tactical reconnaissance roles. The four RAF Germany attack squadrons have now converted to the Tornado. The Coltishall Jaguar wing comprises three squadrons, the reconnaissance-dedicated No. 41 Squadron and two attack units, Nos 6 and 54 Squadrons, while Jaguar training is undertaken at No. 226 OCU, based at RAF Lossiemouth.

The MoD(PE) operates a small fleet of Jaguars on various test duties, from test-pilot training to research.

A Jaguar T.Mk 2 of No. 41 Sqn RAF of the Coltishall Jaguar wing.

Armée de l'Air

The Armée de l'Air fields two Jaguar wings, each with four squadrons, while one further wing (primarily Mirage-equipped) has one Jaguar squadron.
Escadre de Chasse 7 (comprising EC1/7 'Provence', EC2/7 'Argonne', EC3/7 'Languedoc' and EC4/7 'Limousin') operates in the strike and attack roles from St Dizier and Istres, with EC2/7 acting as the Jaguar training unit.
Escadre de Chasse 11 (comprising EC1/11 'Roussillon', EC2/11 'Vosges', EC3/11 'Corse' and EC4/11 'Jura') operates in the attack and defence-suppression roles from Toul-Rosières and Bordeaux-Mérignac. EC3/11 is tasked with supporting French units deployed overseas, while EC2/11 has operated in Chad.

The final French Jaguar unit is EC3/3 'Ardennes' which is tasked with anti-radar attack with Martel missiles, and with low-altitude air defence. The squadron is based at Nancy-Ochey.

A Jaguar E of EC 1/7 'Provence', based at St Dizier. The unit received Jaguars in 1973.

A Jaguar E of EC 4/11 'Jura', based at Bordeaux.

Fuerza Aerea Ecuatoriana

The 12 Jaguar Internationals delivered to Ecuador equip 2111° Escuadron 'Agulas' at BAM Taura, near Quito, and are used primarily in the attack role.

One of 12 Jaguar Internationals which equip 2111° Escuadron 'Agulas' near Quito.

A Jaguar International of Escuadron 'Agulas' over the Ecuadorean jungle.

Bharatiya Vay Sena (Indian Air Force)

India will eventually receive over 100 Jaguars, the majority to be built or assembled by HAL. The first Indian Jaguar squadron was No. 14, which formed at Ambala in July 1979. It was joined by No. 5 Squadron in August 1981, also at Ambala, and by No. 27 Squadron during 1984.

A Jaguar International of No. 5 Sqn, 'The Tuskers', based at Ambala since 1981.

Al Quwwat al Jawwiya al Sultan at Oman (Sultanate of Oman Air Force)

Oman operates the Jaguar primarily in the attack role, but with an important secondary air defence commitment. The first squadron, No. 8, formed at Masirah in 1978, and a second, No. 20, formed at the same base in 1983.

One of No. 20 Sqn's Masirah-based Jaguar Internationals.

Federal Nigerian Air Force

Nigeria's Jaguar squadron formed at Makurdi in 1984, operating in the attack role.

One of the Nigerian air force single-seat Jaguar Internationals wears the nation's green/white roundels, but no unit insignia.

Right: The Nigerian air force's Jaguar Internationals are perhaps the most attractive examples, in their three-tone camouflage scheme.

SEPECAT Jaguar variants

Prototypes: eight prototypes built, having the original short fin and variable intake ramps; two prototypes of each basic version, French and English single- and two-seaters; first to fly was the French two-seater

Jaguar A: French single-seater; final 30 have Martin/Thomson target TV acquisition and laser designatioon pod; 160 delivered; Adour Mk 102 engines

Jaguar B: British two-seater; designated **Jaguar T.Mk 2** by RAF; 38 delivered; Adour Mk 102 engines replaced by uprated Adour Mk 104s equivalent to Mk 804 in early Jaguar Internationals; known as **Jaguar T.Mk 2A** after installation of Ferranti FIN 1064 INS

Jaguar E: French two-seater; Adour Mk 102; 39 delivered, one lost before delivery

Jaguar S: British single-seater; designated **Jaguar GR.Mk 1** by RAF; basically similar to Jaguar A but with advanced inertial navigation and weapon-aiming system controlled by digital computer; all converted to have laser rangefinder and marked target-seeker in nose, and fin-mounted radar-warning receiver in prominent fairing; Adour Mk 102 engines replaced by uprated Adour Mk 104s; known as **Jaguar GR.Mk 1A** after installation of Ferranti FIN 1064 INS; some aircraft configured to carry a BAe reconnaissance pod under fuselage and/or AIM-9L Sidewinders on underwing pylons

Jaguar M: single prototype of carrier-capable maritime version for Aéronavale; underwent catapult trials at RAE Bedford and at sea, but abandoned in favour of all-French Super Etendard despite superior performance in virtually all respects

Jaguar International: export variant of Jaguar S with similar Ferranti NAVWASS; many equipment and armament options including overwing Matra R.550 Magic AAMs, Sea Eagle anti-shipping missiles etc; initial aircraft with Adour Mk 804 engines, later aircraft have more powerful Mk 811 Adour; Indian Jaguars assigned to anti-shipping duties may receive Agave nose radar; 164 ordered by end of 1984, some to be built under licence in India.

FBW Jaguar: single Jaguar S used as research aircraft for Active Control Technology programme funded by British MOD and using digital quadruplex fly-by-wire control system; no reversionary control

Jaguar ACT: the FBW Jaguar destabilized by the addition of rear fuselage ballast and fixed leading-edge strakes, thus becoming a control-configured vehicle; flown to instability of 10 per cent; used to gather data for EAP, not a planned production Jaguar variant

The Jaguar's cockpit is dominated by the display for its Marconi NAVWASS, and by the moving map display on the centre panel. Apart from these features the Jaguar's cockpit differs little from those of other fighters, having engine controls and instruments on the port console, communications equipment on the starboard, and flight and engine instruments on the main panel.

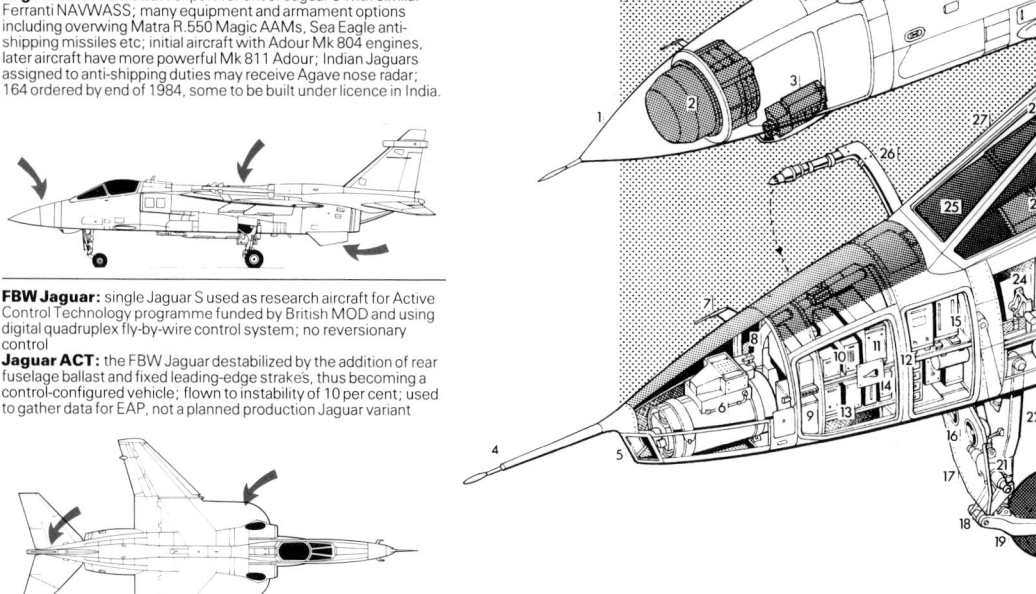

Jaguar International cutaway drawing key

1 Nose profile (Maritime Strike Variant)
2 Thomson-CSF Agave dual-role (air-air, air-ground) radar
3 Ferranti Type 105 Laser Ranger
4 Pitot tube
5 'Wedge-profile' optical sighting windows
6 Ferranti Laser Ranger and Marked Target Seeker
7 Total pressure probe (both sides)
8 Electronics cooling air duct
9 Air-data computer
10 Radio altimeter
11 Power amplifier
12 Avionics access doors
13 Waveform generator
14 Cooling air intake
15 Marconi Avionics nav/ attack system equipment
16 Landing/taxiing lamps
17 Nosewheel leg door
18 Towing lug
19 Nosewheel forks
20 Nosewheel
21 Steering jacks
22 Nose undercarriage leg strut
23 Artificial feel control units
24 Rudder pedals
25 Instrument panel shroud
26 Retractable inflight refuelling probe
27 Windscreen panels
28 Smiths Electronics head-up display
29 Instrument panel

30 Smiths FS6 head-down navigational display
31 Control column
32 Engine throttles
33 Pilot's side console panel
34 Martin-Baker Mk 9 'zero-zero' ejection seat
35 Seat and parachute combined safety harness
36 Honeycomb cockpit side panel
37 Plexiglas cockpit canopy cover (upward opening)
38 Ejection seat headrest
39 Canopy struts
40 Cockpit pressurization valve
41 Rear pressure bulkhead
42 Gun muzzle blast trough
43 Battery and electrical equipment bay
44 Port engine air intake
45 Gun gas vents
46 Spring-loaded secondary air intake doors
47 Boundary layer bleed duct
48 Forward fuselage fuel tank (total system capacity 924 Imp gal/1200 litres)
49 Air conditioning unit
50 Secondary heat exchanger
51 Starboard engine air intake
52 VHF homing aerials
53 Heat exchanger intake/ exhaust duct
54 Cables and hydraulic pipe ducting
55 Intake/fuselage attachment joint
56 Duct frames

57 Integrally-stiffened machined fuselage frames
58 Ammunition tank
59 30-mm Aden cannon
60 Ground power supply socket
61 Mainwheel stowed position
62 Main undercarriage hydraulic lock strut
63 Leading-edge-slat drive motors and gearboxes
64 Fuel system piping
65 Wing panel centreline joint
66 Anti-collision light
67 IFF aerial
68 Wing/fuselage forward attachment joint
69 Starboard wing integral fuel tank
70 Fuel piping provision for pylon mounted tank
71 Overwing missile pylon
72 Missile launch rail
73 Matra 550 Magic air-to-air missile
74 Starboard-leading-edge slat
75 Slat guide rails
76 Starboard navigation light
77 Tacan aerial
78 Flap guide rails and underwing fairings
79 Outboard double-slotted flap
80 Starboard spoilers
81 Inboard double-slotted flap
82 Flap honeycomb construction
83 Flap drive shaft and screwjacks
84 Spoiler control links
85 Wing/fuselage aft attachment joint
86 Heat exchanger air scoop
87 Control runs
88 Air conditioning supply ducting
89 Fuselage fuel tank access panels
90 Honeycomb intake duct construction

91 Engine intake frame
92 Hydraulic accumulator
93 Flap hydraulic motor and drive shaft
94 No. 2 system hydraulic reservoir
95 Primary heat exchanger
96 No. 1 system hydraulic reservoir
97 Heat exchanger exhaust ducts
98 Rear fuselage integral fuel tank
99 Inward/outward fuel vent valve
100 Dorsal spine fairing
101 Fin spar attachment joint
102 Tailfin construction
103 Starboard tailplane
104 Fin tip ECM fairing
105 VHF/UHF antenna fairing
106 Recognition light
107 Tail navigation light
108 VOR aerial
109 Rudder honeycomb construction
110 Fuel jettison pipe
111 Tailcone
112 Brake parachute housing
113 Rudder hydraulic jack
114 Tailplane trailing edge discontinuity
115 Honeycomb panel construction
116 Tailplane rib construction
117 Tailplane spar pivot joint
118 Differential all-moving tailplane hydraulic jack
119 Tailplane mounting frames
120 Fire extinguisher bottle
121 Arrester hook (extended)
122 Variable-area shrouded exhaust nozzle
123 Afterburner duct
124 Port ventral fin
125 Firewall

126 Engine rear suspension joint
127 Rolls-Royce Turboméca Adour 804 (-26) turbofan
128 Port inboard double-slotted flap
129 Engine accessories
130 Hydraulic systems ground servicing connectors
131 Airbrake hydraulic jack
132 Port airbrake (extended)
133 Wing fence (in place of missile pylon)
134 Spoiler hydraulic jack
135 Fixed portion of trailing edge
136 Port spoilers
137 Port outer double-slotted flap
138 Flap honeycomb construction
139 Wing tip fairing
140 Port navigation light
141 Matra Type 155 rocket launcher (18 SNEB rockets)
142 Outboard stores pylon
143 Port leading edge slat

144 Slat screw jacks
145 Port wing integral fuel tank
146 Machined wing skin/ stringer panel
147 Pylon fixing
148 Inboard stores pylon
149 Twin mainwheels
150 Pivoted axle beam
151 Shock absorber strut
152 Main undercarriage leg strut
153 Undercarriage pivot mounting
154 Fuselage sidewall construction
155 Main undercarriage leg door
156 Mainwheel doors
157 Fuselage centreline pylon
158 Reconnaissance pod
159 Infra-red linescan
160 Data converter
161 Air conditioning pack
162 Rear rotating camera drum (role interchangeable)
163 Twin Vinten F95 Mk 10 high oblique cameras

164 Drum rotating electric motor and gearbox
165 Forward rotating camera drum
166 Twin Vinten F95 Mk 10 low oblique cameras
167 Forward looking Vinten F95 Mk 7 reconnaissance camera
168 Matra Durandal, 430-lb (195-kg) penetration bomb
169 Pylon attachment shackles
170 264 Imp gal (1200 litres) auxiliary fuel tank

SEPECAT Jaguar warload

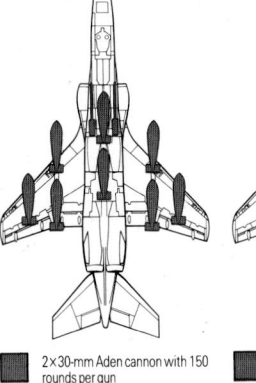

2×30-mm Aden cannon with 150 rounds per gun 8×1,000-lb (454-kg) bombs with Type 117 Mk 3 retarding tails	2×30-mm Aden cannon with 150 rounds per gun 2×1200-litre (264-Imp gal) tanks on inboard pylons 1×reconnaissance pod on centreline containing both cameras and linescan equipment 1×Philips-Matra Phimat chaff dispenser on port outer wing 1×Westinghouse ALQ-101-10 jamming pod on starboard outer pylon	2×30-mm DEFA 553 cannon with 150 rounds per gun 1×HSD/Matra AS.37 Martel anti-radar missile on centreline pylon 1×Matra R.550 Magic air-to-air missile on starboard outer pylon 2×RP36 1200-litre (264-Imp gal) drop tanks on inboard pylons 1×Philips Matra Phimat chaff dispenser on port outer pylon	2×30-mm DEFA cannon with 150 rounds per gun 1×AN52 nuclear weapon on centreline pylon 2×RP36 1200-litre (264-Imp gal) drop tanks on inboard pylons 2×Philips Matra Phimat chaff dispensers on outboard pylons	2×30-mm Aden cannon with 150 rounds per gun 6×Matra Durandal anti-runway weapons 2×Matra R.550 Magic air-to-air missiles on overwing pylons	2×30-mm Aden cannon with 150 rounds per gun 2×Ford Aerospace AIM-9P Sidewinder air-to-air missiles on outboard pylons 2×1200-litre (264-Imp gal) drop tanks on inboard pylons

RAF ground-attack

Although the RAF's Jaguars have now been withdrawn from Germany they remain very much an integral part of the front-line inventory. For longer-range missions 1200-litre (264-Imp gal) drop tanks can be carried on the inboard wing pylons.

RAF tactical reconnaissance

For reconnaissance duties in a high-threat environment the Jaguar can carry underwing jamming and chaff pods. Extra ECM capability can be installed at the cost of the brake parachute! In the armed reconnaissance role BL755 cluster bombs would replace the ECM and chaff pods.

French air force defence suppression

French Jaguars are frequently used in the defence-suppression role, with anti-radar missiles or with jamming and ESM pods, or with a mix of both.

French air force nuclear strike

French Jaguars retain a nuclear strike role, but also operate in conventional attack roles with rocket pods, and a variety of guided and unguided bombs and missiles.

Indian air force counter-air

Indian air force Jaguars operate in a number of attack roles, carrying a variety of weapons. Their most valuable task is counter-air, however, and the Jaguar/Durandal combination is a lethal one.

Omani air force air defence

The primary role of the Omani Jaguars is ground attack, but until the delivery of the recently ordered Tornado ADVs, they will have an important secondary air-defence role, using underwing-mounted Sidewinders.

Specification: Jaguar International

Wings
Span	8.69 m	(28 ft 6 in)
Area	24.18 m²	(260.28 sq ft)
Sweep at quarter chord	40°	

Fuselage and tail unit
Accommodation	pilot on Martin-Baker Mk 9 ejector seat	
Length overall	16.83 m	(55 ft 2.6 in)
Height overall	4.89 m	(16 ft 0.5 in)
Tailplane span	4.53 m	(14 ft 10.3 in)

Landing gear
Retractable tricycle landing gear with twin-wheel main and single wheel nose unit
Wheelbase	5.69 m	(18 ft 8 in)
Wheel track	2.41 m	(7 ft 10.9 in)

Weights
Empty	7000 kg	(15,432 lb)
Maximum take-off	15700 kg	(34,612 lb)
Maximum external load	4763 kg	(10,500 lb)
Internal fuel load	4200 litres	(924 Imp gal)

SEPECAT Jaguar recognition features

- Small wing fences immediately inboard of dogtooth
- Small, square-section, shoulder-mounted engine intakes, immediately behind the cockpit
- Slight anhedral on wing, more pronounced on tailplane
- Small, broad-chord, high-mounted wing, with leading-edge sawtooth and cranked trailing edge
- Small cockpit canopy fairing into fuselage spine; long, flat windscreen
- Distinctive hump on rear fuselage forward of tailfin
- Tall tapering fin, with RWR (radar warning receiver) on British and export aircraft
- Long nose, pointed on two-seaters and French aircraft but with chisel tip for LRMTS on British and export aircraft
- Perforated airbrakes aft of main landing gear
- Twin ventral fins under twin engine exhaust nozzles

Powerplant
Two Rolls-Royce Turboméca Adour Mk 804 afterburning turbofans		
Static thrust with afterburning, each	3647 kg	(8,040 lb)

Performance:

Maximum speed at 36,000 ft (10975 m)	Mach 1.6 (917 kts)	1699 km/h (1,056 mph)
Maximum speed at sea level	Mach 1.1 (729 kts)	1352 km/h (840 mph)
Combat radius on a lo-lo-lo mission with internal fuel	537 km	(334 miles)
Combat radius on a lo-lo-lo mission with external fuel	917 km	(670 miles)
Combat radius on a hi-lo-lo mission with external fuel	1408 km	(875 miles)
g limits	+8.6/+12 ultimate	
Take-off distance with tactical load to clear a 15-m (50-ft) obstacle	940 m	(3,085 ft)

Weapon load
Fairchild A-10A	7257 kg
Vought A-7D	6804 kg +
General Dynamics F-16	5443 kg
SEPECAT Jaguar	4763 kg
Harrier GR.Mk 3	3629 kg
Sukhoi Su-17	3000 kg E
MiG-27 'Flogger-D'	3000 kg E

Take-off run
Harrier	GR.Mk 3 max weight 1,000 ft
F-16	General Dynamics 1,200 ft E
SEPECAT Jaguar	'clean' 1,855 ft
Sukhoi Su-17	'clean' 2,000 ft E
MiG-27 'Flogger-D'	'clean' 2,200 ft E
Fairchild A-10A	max weight 4,000 ft
Vought A-7D	max weight 5,000 ft

Speed at low altitude
General Dynamics F-16	Mach 1.2 or 793 kts
SEPECAT Jaguar	Mach 1.1 or 729 kts
MiG-27 'Flogger-D'	Mach 1.1 or 727 kts E
Vought A-7D	Mach 1.06 or 701 kts
Sukhoi Su-17	Mach 1.05 or 694 kts E
Harrier GR.Mk 3	Mach 0.96 or 634 kts
Fairchild A-10A max	'clean' at sea level 381 kts

Radius hi-lo-hi
Vought A-7D	5670 kg external load 1762 km
SEPECAT Jaguar	max internal + external fuel 1408 km
Fairchild A-10A	with 20 min reserves 1000 km
MiG-27 'Flogger-D'	950 km E
General Dynamics F-16	1361 kg weapons 925 km +
Sukhoi Su-17	2,000 kg external load 630 km E
Harrier	GR.Mk 3 1995 kg weapons 333 km

Radius lo-lo-lo
SEPECAT Jaguar	internal and external fuel 917 km
Vought A-7D	1814 kg external load 885 km
General Dynamics F-16	1361 kg weapons 547 km
Fairchild A-10A	with 20 min reserves 463 km
MiG-27 'Flogger-D'	2900 kg weapon load 390 km E
Sukhoi Su-17	2,000 kg external load 360 km E
Harrier	GR.Mk 3 1995 kg weapons 185 km

The BRITISH AEROSPACE
BUCCANEER

Buccaneer: subsonic striker

Conceived as a low-level maritime strike aircraft, the Buccaneer spent most of its RAF career as an overland bomber, a role it performed with distinction. Unfortunately, overland operations caused severe fatigue problems and almost led to the type's retirement; instead, the fleet was refurbished and readopted a primarily maritime role.

Conceived as a carrier-borne low-level bomber and strike aircraft, the Buccaneer enjoyed a long but unspectacular life afloat. Then unwillingly accepted by the RAF, which wanted a faster, more sophisticated aircraft, the Buccaneer has earned an unequalled reputation as an ultra-low-level tactical bomber in both overland and maritime environments. The RAF's Buccaneers, procured originally as a stop-gap, remain a popular and effective strike tool, and a large number are being refitted to extend their lives into the 1990s.

The Buccaneer was originally developed as a counter to the threat posed by the Soviets' dramatic naval-building programme during the 1950s, and particularly the 'Sverdlov' class gun cruisers. From the start the Buccaneer was designed to be capable of operation from the Royal Navy's aircraft-carriers and to deliver a range of conventional or nuclear stores from a high-speed low-level attack. The ability to operate at very low level was felt to be of paramount importance, since it allowed tactical surprise to be achieved by flying under the enemy's radar. The Admiralty requirement (NA.39) which led to the Buccaneer was issued in June 1952 and called for a two-seat aircraft capable of carrying a nuclear weapon internally, with a radius exceeding 740 km (460 miles) and able to fly at Mach 0.85 at 200 ft (60 m).

The requirement posed several apparently irreconcilable problems, since many of the features necessary for successful operation from an aircraft-carrier were not consistent with the demands of low-level high-speed flight. Blackburn's design was bold and innovative, incorporating a comparatively small wing with excellent gust-response characteristics at low level. This type of wing would not normally be associated with the low-speed handling characteristics necessary for carrier operation, but Blackburn managed to provide these by incorporating full-span boundary-layer energization of the wings, ailerons and flaps using air bled from the engine compressor and ejected through leading-edge slots to prevent boundary-layer separation at low airspeeds and to generate extra lift (nearly double normal lift for landing with the flaps and ailerons drooped). A similar type of boundary-layer control was incorporated in the high-set tailplane, which would otherwise have had to be substantially larger, making it oversensitive at high speeds.

The Buccaneer's most noticeable aerodynamic feature is its wasp-waisted 'coke-bottle' fuselage, designed to reduce transonic drag in the cruise by adopting the 'area-rule' principle. This dictates that sudden changes in total cross-sectional area should be avoided, with no drastic increase resulting from the wing. In the Buccaneer's case the incorporation of the rule made a significant difference to drag, and also provided useful extra equipment and fuel space. For prolonged high-speed flight at very low altitudes the Buccaneer was made extremely strong, with a core structure of steel forgings and other structural components, including the wing panels, milled from solid panels.

The Blackburn submission, originally known as the B-103, was selected by the

▲ One of 'Shiny Twelve's' Buccaneers outside its hardened aircraft shelter. The RAF's Buccaneer force moved into hardened accommodation shortly after its move to Lossiemouth, dramatically reducing vulnerability on the ground.

▼ A No. 208 Squadron aircraft gets smartly airborne at Gibraltar during a major naval exercise. The pilot of this aircraft has cleaned up gear and flaps very rapidly as this rock-solid striker leaps mission-bound from the Rock.

Admiralty in July 1955, and an order for 20 development aircraft was placed. Seldom have so many pre-production aircraft been ordered for a British programme, but the policy was a sound way of speeding the process of getting the Buccaneer into service. Nine of the development batch were to be treated as prototypes (and as such were used for basic development work), five were used for Ministry of Aviation clearance trials and six were intended for flying trials by the Royal Navy. The large number of aircraft built allowed the simultaneous development of many components of the weapons system, and meant that aircraft losses would not unduly delay the programme. The Admiralty asked for a first flight date in April 1958, and remarkably Blackburn managed to achieve this, the prototype taking to the air on 30 April.

The Buccaneer entered Fleet Air Arm service in 1961, but the initial production version, the Buccaneer S. Mk 1 powered by two de Havilland Gyron Junior turbojets, proved to be rather underpowered. Take-off with full fuel was impractical and this

**British Aerospace Buccaneer S.Mk2B
No.12 Squadron 'Shiny Twelve'
Royal Air Force**

Rain/ice clearance
Rain and ice or sea spray is cleared by bleed air blown from a duct at the base of the windscreen

Windscreen
The windscreen is almost 6.35 cm (2.5 in) thick, and is laminated for extra strength; it has demonstrated spectacular birdstrike resistance over the years. It is demisted by hot air blown over the inside, and is electrically heated

Canopy
The large canopy can be jettisoned if a premeditated ejection is made, or is shattered by the MDC (miniature detonating cord) if a no-notice ejection is made. If the MDC fails, raised seat tops will break the canopy

Ejection seats
Pilot and navigator both sit on Martin-Baker Mk 6MSB ejection seats. These once had an underwater ejection capability, which has been removed, and can be used at zero speed and zero altitude. They are fitted with a simplified combined harness, which makes strapping in very swift, but have a total of 12 seat pins. The pilot's seat is offset to port, which allows the navigator an unobscured view of the emergency and warning panels in the front cockpit and improves seat separation during ejection

Blast screen
This protects the navigator from rocket blast from the pilot's ejection seat. In a no-notice ejection the pilot usually ejects first, after calling 'Eject, eject, eject' on the intercom, leaving the navigator in no doubt as to the gravity of the situation!

Anti-collision lights
RAF Buccaneers are gradually rece selectable red/white strobes in plac the old red anti-collision lights

Inflight-refuelling probe
The refuelling probe is offset to starboard by approximately 0.3 m to avoid obscuring forward view. It can be easily removed but is usually fitted as standard. Fuel can be received at up to 544 kg (1200 lb) per minute

Navigator's cockpit
The navigator's cockpit contains all navigation and radar equipment, all RWR, ECM and HF radio equipment and most weapons switchery. A small TV monitor is provided for TV Martel. The main navigation kit comprises a Doppler-fed GPI (Ground Position Indicator) and stopwatch. The current update programme will replace the GPI with an inertial platform

Starboard inner pylon
The starboard inner pylon can carry a streamlined data link pod for use in conjunction with TV Martel. Signals from the Marconi Vidicon camera are transmitted to the navigator's TV screen, and he locks on the TV seeker by manually driving a small graticule box over the image of the target. After the missile is fired it is steered by the navigator using a small control stick, sending signals via the data link pod.

Weapons-aiming marks
These painted marks on the refuelling probe serve as a check of the automatic weapons aiming system, and can be used for manually aiming the weapons if the automatics fail

Aerial
This aerial serves the main UHF radio

Radar
The Buccaneer is fitted with a Ferranti Blue Parrot radar. Although the equipment is now rather old, it has an excellent capability for discrimination of maritime targets. Its range is limited by the radar horizon even at high level

Radome
The radome is made from a non-radar reflective/absorptive material, but is not as birdstrike-resistant as the radomes on some more modern types. It can be completely removed for access to the antenna

Strike camera
This undernose fairing can contain a strike camera, but this is no longer routinely used

Pitot probe
This serves the standby flight instruments

Engine intakes
The engine intakes are large to provide a large mass of air flow for the high-bypass ratio turbofans and are elliptical in shape to minimize airflow distortion in the intake duct. The leading edges of the intakes are unpainted because they contain de-icing equipment.

Canopy strengthening
This metalwork reduces flexing of the canopy in flight

Fire extinguisher access
A frangible panel allows the insertion of a long-necked fire extinguisher if there is an engine fire during start-up

Engine access panel
These panels provide access to the Buccaneer's two Rolls-Royce RB168-1A Spey Mk 101 turbofans

BAe Dynamics AJ.168 TV Martel
The TV-guided variant of the Martel was developed by Hawker Siddeley Dynamics for carriage by the Buccaneer, although it could be carried by other aircraft types. The missile is powered by a solid fuel rocket motor, giving high subsonic performance and a range of between 30 and 60 miles, depending on launch height

Control fins
Martel's forward fins are fixed, but the rear fins move to respond to guidance commands

Rotary bomb door
The Buccaneer's bomb door can accommodate four 1,000-lb bombs, a photo-reconnaissance pack, luggage or equipment panniers, or 4,000 lb of fuel. An optional bulged door provides storage for an extra 1590 kg (3,500 lb) of fuel.

Inner pylon
Adapters may be fitted between the pylon and a desired store as required, allowing the carriage of radar or TV Martel, bombs or fuel tanks. Underwing fuel tanks fit almost conformally and generate little drag. Each carries 907 kg (2,000-lb) of fuel. In the tanker role the starboard tank can be replaced by a refuelling pod

Wing fold mechanism
The wings are folded hydraulically, and locked in the down position electro-mechanically. Panels covering the mechanism were subject to frequent removal and much wear and tear, and have thus been removed

Boundary layer control (BLC) slot
BLC reduces the aircraft's stalling speed by re-energizing the boundary layer at low speeds. The blow is always used in the landing configuration, except in certain emergencies, and reduces stalling speed by about 20 kts

AIM-9L Sidewinder
The 'nine-lima' has an all aspect homing seeker head, with AM-FN conical scan for increased seeker sensitivity and tracking stability. It has a new optical laser fuse and a 11.34-kg (25-lb) annular blast fragmentation warhead. Reconfigured control surfaces enhance manoeuvrability. A 1,000-lb retarded bomb can be used as an alternative form of defence. Such a weapon dropped in the path of a fighter in the six o'clock position would be very effective

Pitot probe
The pitot-static system feeds the main flight instruments and the air data computer (ADC) for the navigation and weapons systems

Vortex generators
Small metal vanes perpendicular to the wing surface and angled inwards by almost 30 degrees excite the boundary layer, and improve control effectiveness at low speeds.

imposed a serious range penalty. A production order for a new variant, powered by higher-thrust Rolls-Royce Spey turbofans, was placed in January 1962, before the Buccaneer had entered first-line service. The Spey gave up to 60 per cent more thrust than the Gyron Junior, and had a much lower fuel consumption. Fortunately the Spey could be installed without major structural alterations, although the larger engine inlets that were required meant that the aircraft needed new centre-section spectacle forgings. Two of the original development batch aircraft were converted to act as prototypes, and the first flew on 17 May 1963. Production switched to the Spey-engined Buccaneer S.Mk 2 after the 40th aircraft, and the S.Mk 2 entered squadron service in April 1965.

Exports

The second customer for the Buccaneer was the South African Air Force, which ordered 16 Spey-engined but largely denavalized aircraft during January 1963. This order was placed as a part of the Simonstown Agreement, whereby the UK undertook to supply maritime weaponry to South Africa in exchange for the use of Simonstown naval base. Buccaneers were procured by the SAAF as long-range anti-shipping strike aircraft but, being shore-based, had certain items of equipment deleted, and were designated Buccaneer S.Mk 50. The South African Buccaneers were also fitted with two retractable Bristol Siddeley BS605 single-chamber rocket engines in the rear fuselage for enhanced take-off performance in 'hot-and-high' conditions. No. 24 Squadron was re-formed at RNAS Lossiemouth in Scotland during May 1965 and South African crews began conversion training. The 16 aircraft initially ordered were delivered to South Africa in two batches of eight, the second batch going by sea after one of the first batch was lost in the South Atlantic. The UK's newly-elected Labour government had already imposed an arms embargo on South Africa and had threatened to ban delivery of the original aircraft, reportedly offering to sell them to India. The government would not allow South Africa to order a replacement aircraft, and cancelled an option held on a batch of 20 more Buccaneers. South Africa's Buccaneers are still in service, and are used in a variety of roles, including inflight-refuelling of both other Buccaneers and Dassault-Breguet Mirage F1 tactical fighters, but attrition has reduced their numbers to around half a dozen aircraft. For inflight-refuelling the Buccaneer can carry on a special starboard inner underwing hardpoint a hose-and-drogue unit with 636 litres (140 Imp gal) of fuel, other supplementary supply being provided by a 1955-litre (430 Imp gal) tank under the port wing and by the 2000-litre (440 Imp gal) ferry tank that can be accommodated in the weapons bay in place of bombs. With the Buccaneer's internal tankage of

7092 litres (1,560 Imp gal), this is a total of 11683 litres (2,570 Imp gal). As an alternative to the normal load of four 1,000 lb (454 kg) bombs in the weapons bay, the Buccaneer can carry four 500- or 540-lb (227- or 245-kg) bombs, or a camera and photoflash reconnaissance pack. The four underwing hardpoints can carry bombs, missiles, rocket-launcher pods and flares.

The RAF did not order the Buccaneer until July 1968, and then did so reluctantly as a stop-gap to fill the void left by the cancellation of the BAC TSR2 and the General Dynamics F-111K. Compared with the latter two aircraft the Buccaneer was felt to be antiquated, unsophisticated and slow, and suffered the additional disadvantage of being to all intents and purposes a Navy cast-off. In fact the Buccaneer was just what the RAF needed, since it was actually faster and longer-legged at low-level with four 1,000-lb bombs in the rotating-door bomb bay than an F-111 with a similar load, although it lacked the American aircraft's terrain-following radar. The superb TSR2 would have been better in every respect, but the Labour government had made sure that this aircraft could never be resurrected by ordering the destruction of the production jigs. (In any event, Mach 0.8 was probably the maximum attack speed with acceptable accuracy, using the technology then available.) The RAF originally ordered 26 S.Mk 2s, but it was simultaneously announced that the RAF would also receive 62 Buccaneers transferred from the Fleet Air Arm, whose carrier force was being run down rapidly. A further 19 Buccaneers were eventually built for the RAF, which also ultimately received all of the survivors of the Royal Navy's 84 Buccaneer S.Mk 2s.

The first RAF Buccaneer unit was No.12 'Shiny Twelve' Squadron, which formed at RAF Honington on 1 October 1969, primarily for maritime strike duties. Two further units, Nos 15 and 16 Squadrons, formed in 1970 and 1973 respectively, for overland strike duties at RAF Laarbruch, as part of NATO's 2nd Allied Tactical Air Force. The aircraft of the Laarbruch wing took over the nuclear role and QRA commitment from the RAF Germany English

▼ *This No. 208 Squadron Buccaneer is seen on the 'break' into Lossiemouth's circuit, its clamshell airbrakes slightly open. Full span boundary layer control is achieved by blowing bleed air through leading edge slots, considerably reducing landing speeds.*

▲ *Three of the SAAF No. 24 Squadron's Buccaneer S.Mk 50s seen at low level over the veldt. South African crews love the 'Easy Rider', as they call it, and have used the aircraft to devastating effect against terrorist bases outside South Africa's borders.*

Electric Canberra B(1).Mk 8 squadrons. No.237 Operational Conversion Unit formed at Honington during 1971 and took over from the Fleet Air Arm's 736 Squadron the responsibility for conversion, refresher and continuation training of all British Buccaneer aircrew. The UK's second Buccaneer squadron, No.208, was formed at Honington on 1 July 1974, but flew in the overland strike role. It was not until July 1979 that a second maritime Buccaneer squadron formed, when No.216 Squadron re-equipped with refurbished Fleet Air Arm aircraft after the retirement of HMS *Ark Royal*. The Buccaneer has enjoyed a successful career with the RAF, and the last new-build Buccaneer was not delivered until October 1977. The RAF Germany squadrons were regular participants in the Salmond Trophy bombing competition, and, despite lacking a modern nav/attack system, performed very well.

Training

The Buccaneer force has achieved its outstanding combat readiness and capability through constant training in conditions as realistic as possible during peacetime. Since 1977, the most realistic and demanding training has been by participation in the US Air Force 'Red Flag' exercises. The 'Red Flag' programme was set up as a result of USAF combat experience in the Vietnam War, when it was discovered that aircrew losses reduced markedly after about 10 missions had been flown. The aim of 'Red Flag' is to fly these initial missions synthetically, but realistically.

The basic concept is very simple: units based at Nellis AFB, Nevada form the 'enemy' or 'Red' force, whose task it is to defend a variety of targets spread over a range covering some 38850 km^2 (15,000 sq miles). Visiting units act as 'Blue' forces, attacking these targets with both live and simulated weapons. Massed tank formations, dummy airfields, industrial complexes and enemy SAMs are cleverly simulated, and protected by electronically-simulated ground-based threats, F-5E Tiger II aggressor aircraft and F-15 Eagles.

The RAF was first invited to participate in 'Red Flag' for the August 1977 exercise, and it sent a mixed force of Buccaneers and Avro Vulcans, which performed extremely well. The Buccaneers, in particular, impressed the USAF with their low-level flying. In 1978 Buccaneers were joined by RAF Jaguars, both types hitting their targets with pinpoint accuracy, evading defences successfully and even 'shooting down' 'Red' Force defending aircraft. The Buccaneer pilots welcomed the opportunity to attack targets at higher speeds and at much lower altitudes than was possible in UK training areas. In 1979 Buccaneers participated in the similar 'Maple Flag' exercise in Canada, where conditions more realistically simulate the West European environment.

In February 1980 the Buccaneers returned to 'Red Flag', but tragedy struck when one aircraft lost a wing and crashed, killing both crew. A fatigue crack in the front spar was responsible, and the accident resulted in the immediate grounding of the entire Buccaneer force while an in-depth structural survey was undertaken. Many aircraft were found to have similar cracks and some were scrapped, being felt to be beyond economic repair, while others underwent a long and costly rework. While they were without Buccaneers the squadrons received extra Hawker Hunters to allow a limited training programme to continue, and unaffected Buccaneers were allowed to resume flying during August. As a substantial number of aircraft could not be repaired, No.216 Squadron was disbanded. The first squadrons to resume operational flying were the two units of the Laarbruch strike wing, which continued to fly Buccaneers until they began to re-equip with Panavia Tornados in the summer of 1983. No.12 Squadron moved to RAF Lossiemouth in 1980, to be closer to its prime area of interest, the Norwegian Sea and the Faroes-Iceland gap. Controlled by No.18 Group, RAF Strike Command during peacetime, No. 12 Squadron is planned to pass to the command of SACLANT in war.

The large-scale introduction of the Tornado in the overland strike role allowed No.208 Squadron to be reassigned to maritime duties, and as such it moved to RAF Lossiemouth to join No.12 Squadron during July 1983, leaving only No.237 OCU at RAF Honington until October 1984, when it too moved to Lossiemouth. The Buccaneer will continue in the maritime strike role for many years, using TV-guided and anti-radar Martel missiles, 'Paveway' laser-guided bombs and the new British Aerospace Dynamics Sea Eagle anti-ship missile, which is just beginning to enter service. Curiously, during wartime the OCU would assume an overland role, and the two squadrons could do so if necessary. A rapid reversion to the overland role was in fact undertaken in September 1983, when six Buccaneers were deployed to RAF Akrotiri, Cyprus, in support of British troops serving with UN forces in Lebanon.

Surviving RAF Buccaneers are currently undergoing an update programme to extend aircraft life into the late 1990s. The first of about 60 modified aircraft will reach the squadrons in mid-1987, and the programme should be complete by the beginning of 1989. The update programme was originally to have included the provision of an extensively modified cockpit, with a head-up display, and various improvements to mission avionics. Financial constraints have dramatically reduced the scope of the programme, which will now cover only the fitting of a new Ferranti FIN 1063 inertial navigation system similar to that used by the Jaguar, new Plessey radios, an updated Ferranti 'Blue Parrot' radar, a Marconi Sky Guardian passive detection system and Tracor ALE-39 chaff and flare dispensers. The programme may be more modest than was at one time intended, but it will enable the RAF's low-flying Buccaneers to remain viable ship-killers for many years.

▲ *The Buccaneer has an impressive range, even at low level, but would routinely extend this by inflight-refuelling, either from Victor or VC10 tankers, as seen here, or from buddy-pack equipped Buccaneers. The Buccaneers could also act as a refuelling tanker for other types of fast-jet aircraft.*

▼ *This No. 237 OCU Buccaneer S.Mk 2B carries an AN/ALQ-131 ECM pod under its starboard wing, and a Pave Spike laser designating pod and AIM-9D Sidewinder AAM under its port wing.*

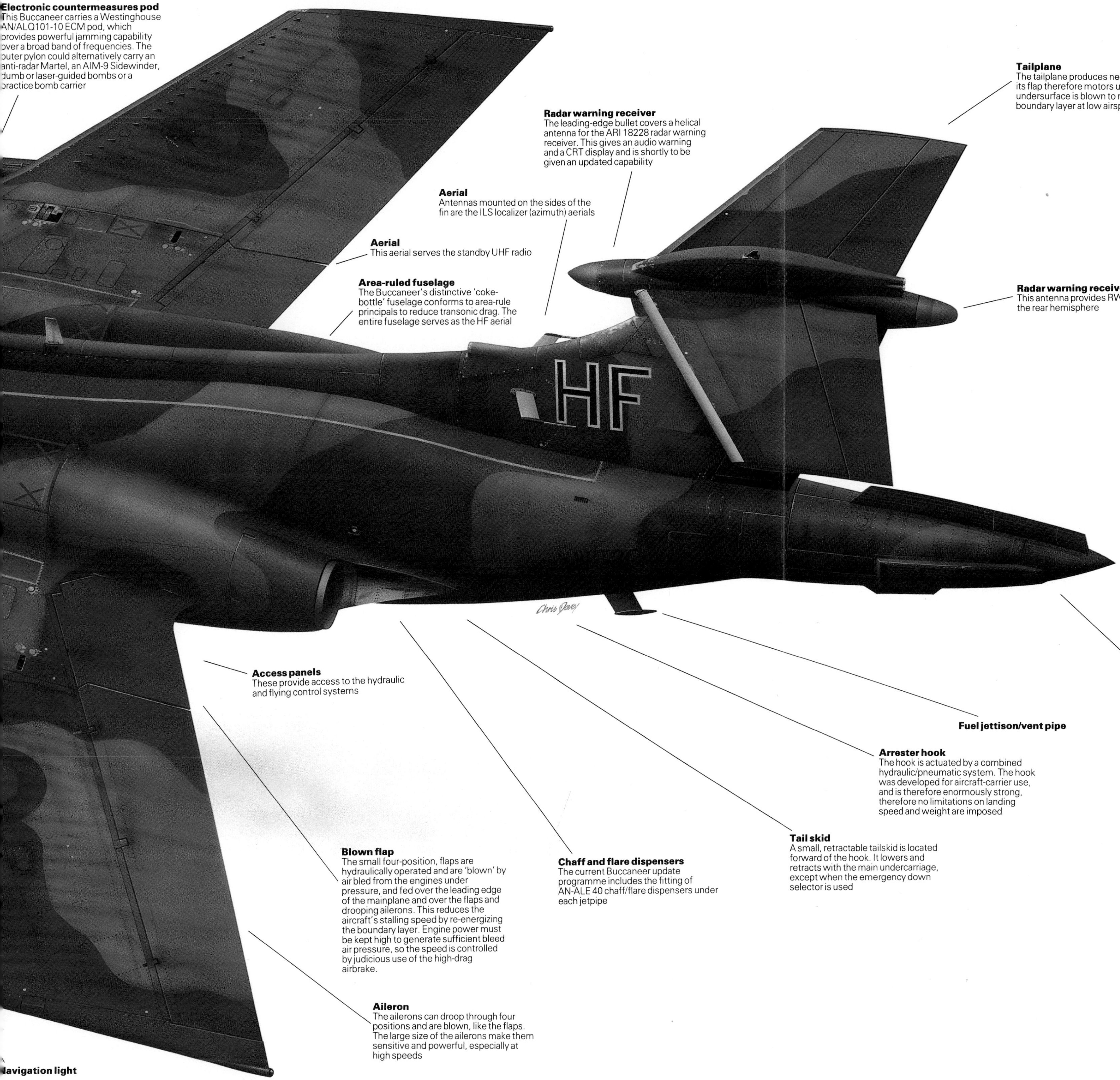

Electronic countermeasures pod
This Buccaneer carries a Westinghouse AN/ALQ101-10 ECM pod, which provides powerful jamming capability over a broad band of frequencies. The outer pylon could alternatively carry an anti-radar Martel, an AIM-9 Sidewinder, dumb or laser-guided bombs or a practice bomb carrier

Radar warning receiver
The leading-edge bullet covers a helical antenna for the ARI 18228 radar warning receiver. This gives an audio warning and a CRT display and is shortly to be given an updated capability

Aerial
Antennas mounted on the sides of the fin are the ILS localizer (azimuth) aerials

Aerial
This aerial serves the standby UHF radio

Area-ruled fuselage
The Buccaneer's distinctive 'coke-bottle' fuselage conforms to area-rule principals to reduce transonic drag. The entire fuselage serves as the HF aerial

Tailplane
The tailplane produces negative lift, and its flap therefore motors upwards. The undersurface is blown to re-energize the boundary layer at low airspeeds.

Radar warning receiver
This antenna provides RWR coverage in the rear hemisphere

Access panels
These provide access to the hydraulic and flying control systems

Airbrake
The large, hydraulically-operated, infinitely variable airbrakes are very effective and have no limiting speed. Emergency actuation is possible, and the Buccaneer usually lands with the brake fully extended to counter the high-power settings necessary on approach to maintain adequate blow pressures in the boundary layer control system

Fuel jettison/vent pipe

Arrester hook
The hook is actuated by a combined hydraulic/pneumatic system. The hook was developed for aircraft-carrier use, and is therefore enormously strong, therefore no limitations on landing speed and weight are imposed

Blown flap
The small four-position, flaps are hydraulically operated and are 'blown' by air bled from the engines under pressure, and fed over the leading edge of the mainplane and over the flaps and drooping ailerons. This reduces the aircraft's stalling speed by re-energizing the boundary layer. Engine power must be kept high to generate sufficient bleed air pressure, so the speed is controlled by judicious use of the high-drag airbrake.

Chaff and flare dispensers
The current Buccaneer update programme includes the fitting of AN-ALE 40 chaff/flare dispensers under each jetpipe

Tail skid
A small, retractable tailskid is located forward of the hook. It lowers and retracts with the main undercarriage, except when the emergency down selector is used

Aileron
The ailerons can droop through four positions and are blown, like the flaps. The large size of the ailerons make them sensitive and powerful, especially at high speeds

Navigation light

Buccaneer in service

Royal Air Force

The RAF retains two front-line Buccaneer squadrons, Nos 12 and 208, and an Operational Conversion Unit, No. 237 OCU. Together these units form RAF Lossiemouth's Maritime Strike Wing. New weapons, an extensive refit, viable tactics and superb training will enable the RAF's Buccaneer fleet to remain a useful asset for many years to come.

No. 12 Squadron
Base: RAF Lossiemouth
Formed: 1 October 1969
Equipment: Buccaneer S.Mk 2B, Hunter T.Mk 7, Hunter T.Mk 7A
Aircraft: XW527/GF; XW540/JF; XV864/KF; XN983/PF

No. 12 Squadron's famous fox's-head badge and 'F' code commemorates the squadron's inter-war association with the Fairey Fox.

No. 208 Squadron
Base: RAF Lossiemouth
Formed: 1 July 1974
Equipment: Buccaneer S.Mk 2B, Hunter T.Mk 7, Hunter T.Mk 7A
Aircraft: XV865/BS; XN981/FS; XX894/HS; XW542/KS

No. 208 Sqn's aircraft carry codes ending with the letter 'S' for Sphinx, marking a long association with the Middle East.

No. 237 Operational Conversion Unit
Base: RAF Lossiemouth
Formed: March 1971
Equipment: Buccaneer S.Mk 2A, Buccaneer S.Mk 2B, Hunter T.Mk 7, Hunter T.Mk 7A, Hunter T.Mk 8M
Aircraft: XV355/AC; XV863/CC; XX892/FC; XX899/JC

No. 237 OCU's Buccaneers and Hunters wear the unit's traditional crossed sabres and mortar board insignia on a red disc.

Ministry of Defence (Procurement Executive)

Buccaneers are used by the Royal Aircraft Establishment at Bedford, Farnborough and West Freugh, by the AAEE at Boscombe Down, and by British Aerospace at Warton, Hatfield, and Scampton. Their duties include weapons and radar trials. Various marks of Buccaneer are in use.

South African Air Force

South Africa's 16-strong Buccaneer fleet has been reduced by attrition to a force of about six aircraft, but their long range and impressive performance make them a valued tool in the SAAF inventory, and they have seen much action.

No. 24 Squadron 'The Pirates'
Base: Waterkloof
Formed: May 1965
Equipment: Buccaneer S.Mk 50
Aircraft: 413, 414, 426

South Africa's Buccaneer S.Mk 50s have been used extensively on 'externals', both in the strike role and as reconnaissance aircraft.

British Aerospace Buccaneer S.Mk 2B cutaway drawing key

The Buccaneer cockpit is an accurate indication of the age of the aircraft. Modification programmes have introduced some new controls and instruments, but the basic instrument and cockpit layout is of unmistakably 1950s origin. The rear cockpit is slightly more modern, and less cluttered in appearance, but both are a far cry from the cockpits of more modern types.

1 Inflight-refuelling probe
2 Radar scanner
3 Multi-mode search and fire control radar
4 Weapon recorder
5 Radome (folded)
6 Radome hinge
7 Weapon release computer
8 Windscreen rain dispersal duct
9 Windscreen wiper
10 Birdproof windscreen
11 Pilot's head-up display
12 Instrument panel shroud
13 Rudder pedals
14 Nosewheel leg hinge point
15 Landing and taxi lamp
16 Shock absorber strut
17 Nosewheel forks
18 Aft retracting nosewheel
19 Avionics equipment
20 Engine throttles
21 Canopy side rail
22 Pilot's ejector seat
23 Seat firing handle
24 Aft sliding canopy
25 Observer's blast shield
26 Observer's instrument display
27 Starboard engine air intake
28 Observer's ejector seat
29 Cockpit floor structure
30 Head-up display symbol generator
31 Port engine air inlet
32 Anti-icing air line
33 Air inlet duct
34 Cockpit aft pressure bulkhead
35 Forward main fuselage fuel tank
36 Canopy motor
37 Canopy top rail
38 Rolls-Royce RB.168-1A Spey Mk 101 turbofan
39 Bleed air ducting
40 Detachable bottom cowling
41 Engine front mounting
42 Firewall frame
43 Engine aft mounting
44 Forward fuselage structure
45 Bleed air cross-over duct
46 Canopy hand winding shuttle
47 Detachable engine top cowling
48 Starboard slipper tank
49 Data link acquisition pod
50 Data link inboard pylon
51 Martel air-to-surface missile
52 Wing fold hinge line
53 Leading edge blowing air duct
54 UHF antenna
55 Dorsal spine structure
56 Anti-collision light
57 Wing-fold actuator
58 Wing-fold operating link
59 Starboard outer pylon
60 ARI 18228 RWR aerial housing
61 Blown leading edge
62 Starboard navigation light
63 Formation light
64 Starboard blown aileron
65 Aileron actuator
66 Starboard wingtip (folded)
67 Aileron and flap blowing ducts
68 Starboard blown flap
69 Port wing tip (folded)
70 Centre fuselage fuel tank

Buccaneer variants

NA39 (prototype): first of a batch of 20 pre-production development aircraft; de Havilland Gyron Junior engines
Buccaneer DB (Development Batch): 19 pre-production aircraft used primarily for development and trials work; sometimes incorrectly referred to as Buccaneer S.Mk 1
Buccaneer S.Mk 1: production batch of 40 Gyron-engined aircraft for service with the Fleet Air Arm; retractable inflight-refuelling probe; small circular air intakes
Buccaneer S.Mk 2: two DB aircraft modified to serve as prototypes for Rolls-Royce Spey-engined variant, followed by 84 production aircraft; large elliptical air intakes and optional non-retractable inflight-refuelling probe above nose
Buccaneer S.Mk 2A: designation applied to non-Martel-equipped S.Mk 2s transferred from Royal Navy to RAF
Buccaneer S.Mk 2B: designation applied to new-build aircraft, all with provision for Martel, for RAF and MOD(PE); 49 production aircraft plus conversions from S.Mk 2A
Buccaneer S.Mk 2C: designation applied to non-Martel-equipped RN aircraft
Buccaneer S.Mk 2D: designation applied to Martel-equipped RN aircraft
Buccaneer S.Mk 50: export version of S.Mk 2 for South Africa; no power folding for wings, but otherwise fully navalized; two retractable Bristol Siddeley BS.605 rocket engines for 'hot and high' take-off thrust augmentation; 16 built for South African Air Force, one lost on delivery; second batch of 14 aircraft embargoed

TV Martel missile uses a Marconi Space and Defence Systems icon camera, and is steered by the Buccaneer navigator using a ll stick and display screen. Constant height is maintained using a ometric lock, and video signals from the missile are received by a amlined data link pod carried underwing.

The Buccaneer's unusual split-tailcone airbrakes provide enormous drag, but do not disrupt airflow over the airframe due to their rear-mounted position. They also, along with the Buccaneer's folding wings and nose radome, facilitate stowage on crowded aircraft-carrier hangar decks.

85 Forward ARI 18228
86 Blown tailplane leading edge
87 All moving tailplane structure
88 Tailplane flap
89 Tailplane flap actuator
90 Hinge attachment point
91 Top fairing
92 Rear navigation light
93 Formation light
94 Aft passive warning system antenna
95 Rudder structure
96 Rudder structure
97 Rudder operating link
98 Rudder actuator
99 Airbrake jack
100 Drag-link hinge attachment
101 Airbrake operating slide
102 Split tailcone airbrake
103 Top strake
104 Honeycomb reinforcing panel
105 Bottom strake
106 Airbrake (open)
107 Hinge arm
108 Aft fuselage structure
109 Vent pipe
110 Arresting hook
111 Jet efflux fairing
112 Engine jet pipe
113 Bomb door actuator
114 Bomb door aft hinge
115 Port blown flap structure
116 Flap actuator
117 Port blown aileron
118 Blowing air duct
119 Wing spar bolted attachment
120 Wing fold actuator
121 Top of main landing gear leg
122 Mainwheel well
123 Main landing gear jack
124 Inboard blown leading edge
125 Inboard pylon fitting
126 1955 litre (430 Imp gal) slipper tank
127 Wing fold main spar hinge
128 Rear spar hinge
129 Main landing gear levered suspension
130 Inboard retracting attachment
131 Mainwheel door
132 Outboard pylon fitting
133 Aileron operating rod
134 Port aileron actuator
135 Outer wing structure
136 Machined skin panels
137 Port wingtip
138 Formation light
139 Crash trip switches
140 Wing lifting lug
141 Port navigation light
142 Blown outboard leading edge
143 Pitot head
144 Port ARI 18228 aerial housing
145 Outboard pylon
146 Port Martel air-to-surface missile
147 Thirty-six tube rocket pod
148 Rotary bomb bay door
149 Bomb door locks
150 1,000-lb bomb (four internal)
151 Forward hinge point
152 1932 litre (425 Imp gal) bomb door auxiliary tank

BAe (HS/Blackburn) Buccaneer warloads

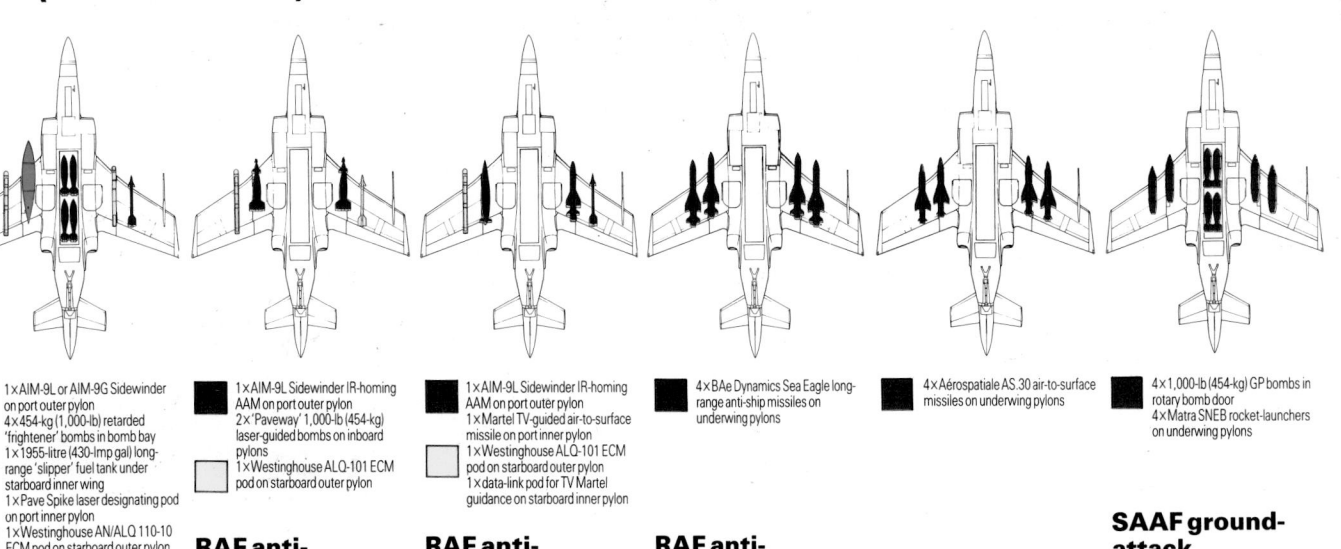

1×AIM-9L or AIM-9G Sidewinder on port outer pylon
4×454-kg (1,000-lb) retarded 'frightener' bombs in bomb bay
1×1955-litre (430-Imp gal) long-range 'slipper' fuel tank under starboard inner wing
1×Pave Spike laser designating pod on port inner pylon
1×Westinghouse AN/ALQ 110-10 ECM pod on starboard outer pylon

1×AIM-9L Sidewinder IR-homing AAM on port outer pylon
2×'Paveway' 1,000-lb (454-kg) laser-guided bombs on inboard pylons
1×Westinghouse ALQ-101 ECM pod on starboard outer pylon

1×AIM-9L Sidewinder IR-homing AAM on port outer pylon
1×Martel TV-guided air-to-surface missile on port inner pylon
1×Westinghouse ALQ-101 ECM pod on starboard outer pylon
1×data-link pod for TV Martel guidance on starboard inner pylon

4×BAe Dynamics Sea Eagle long-range anti-ship missiles on underwing pylons

4×Aérospatiale AS.30 air-to-surface missiles on underwing pylons

4×1,000-lb (454-kg) GP bombs in rotary bomb door
4×Matra SNEB rocket-launchers on underwing pylons

RAF airborne (LGB) designator

The Pave Spike/Paveway combination originally equipped No. 216 Squadron, which disbanded in 1980. The combination is now used by No. 208 Squadron in the anti-shipping role, while No. 237 OCU could assume an emergency war role designating for overland-strike Tornados.

RAF anti-shipping (LGB) bomber

LGB attacks are usually made by a six-ship formation, the two designating aircraft not usually acting as bombers. There is a clear division of responsibility between designating and attacking aircraft during LGB attacks. Paveway LGBs are too long to be carried internally.

RAF anti-shipping (TV Martel)

Only No. 12 Squadron uses the TV-guided Martel. Up to four can be carried per aircraft, but this load is exceptional. Against heavily defended targets the Buccaneer stands off, and in these circumstances a data-link pod and ECM equipment are essential.

RAF anti-shipping (Sea Eagle)

Both RAF Buccaneer squadrons will eventually receive the Sea Eagle. This missile does not require any designator or data-link pods, and up to four weapons may be carried on underwing pylons. Defences might be suppressed by other Buccaneers carrying BAe ALARM anti-radar missiles.

SAAF anti-shipping

South African Buccaneers have an important maritime commitment, and have been responsible for sinking a number of crippled oil tankers. Martel is not used by South Africa's Buccaneers, and there is no prospect of Sea Eagle being supplied.

SAAF ground-attack

The Buccaneer's rotating bomb door can be used to carry four 1,000-lb (454-kg) bombs, a multi-sensor reconnaissance pod, or a 440-Imp gal (2000-litre) fuel tank. South African Buccaneers have seen extensive service over Angola and Namibia, attacking SWAPO bases with rockets and bombs. A buddy refuelling pod can be carried on the starboard inner pylon on SAAF and RAF aircraft.

Specification: Buccaneer S.Mk 2B

Wings
Span	13.41 m	(44 ft 0 in)
Area	47.82 m²	(514.7 sq ft)

Fuselage and tail unit
Accommodation	two; pilot and navigator in tandem	
Length overall	19.33 m	(63 ft 5 in)
Height overall	4.95 m	(16 ft 3 in)
Tailplane span	4.34 m	(14 ft 3 in)

Landing gear
Dowty retractable tricycle landing gear
Wheelbase	6.30 m	(20 ft 8 in)
Wheel track	3.62 m	(11 ft 10.5 in)

Weights
Empty	13599 kg	(29,980 lb)
Maximum take-off	28123 kg	(62,000 lb)
Maximum external load	7257 kg	(16,000 lb)
Standard internal fuel load	7092 litres	(1,560 Imp gal)
or by weight	5661 kg	(12,480 lb)

Powerplant
Two Rolls-Royce Spey RB.168-1A Mk 101 non-afterburning turbofans
Thrust rating, each	5035 kg	(11,100 lb)

Buccaneer recognition features

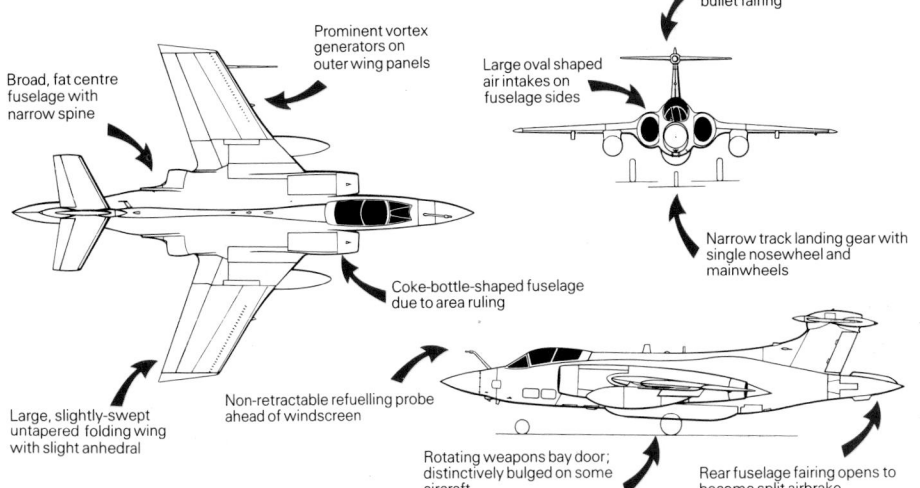

Prominent vortex generators on outer wing panels

T-tail with RWR radomes on fin bullet fairing

Large oval shaped air intakes on fuselage sides

Broad, fat centre fuselage with narrow spine

Narrow track landing gear with single nosewheel and mainwheels

Coke-bottle-shaped fuselage due to area ruling

Non-retractable refuelling probe ahead of windscreen

Large, slightly-swept untapered folding wing with slight anhedral

Rotating weapons bay door; distinctively bulged on some aircraft

Rear fuselage fairing opens to become split airbrake

Performance
Maximum speed at sea level	Mach 0.91 (600 kts)	1112 km/h (691 mph)
Attack speed at sea level	539 kts	1000 km/h (621 mph)
Maximum strike range with external fuel and normal weapons load	3701 km	(2,300 miles)
Combat radius with full warload, hi-lo-hi	966 km	(600 miles)
Take-off distance at maximum take-off weight	1036 m	(3,400 ft)
Landing run	960 m	(3,150 ft)

Weapon load

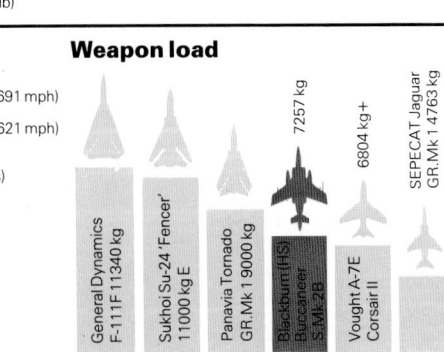

General Dynamics F-111F 11340 kg
Sukhoi Su-24 'Fencer' 11000 kg E
Panavia Tornado GR.Mk 1 9000 kg
Blackburn (HS) Buccaneer S.Mk 2B 7257 kg
Vought A-7E Corsair II 6804 kg +
SEPECAT Jaguar GR.Mk 1 4763 kg E
MiG-27 'Flogger-D' 4000 kg E

Take-off run
Sukhoi Su-24 'Fencer' not quoted
SEPECAT Jaguar GR.Mk 1 1,855 'clean'
MiG-27 'Flogger-D' 2,200 ft E
Panavia Tornado GR.Mk 1 2,900 ft E
General Dynamics F-111F 3,100 ft
Buccaneer S.Mk 2B 3,400 ft 'clean'
Vought A-7E Corsair II 6,000 ft

Maximum speed at optimum altitude
General Dynamics F-111F Mach 2.4
Panavia Tornado GR.Mk 1 Mach 2.2 'clean'
Sukhoi Su-24 'Fencer' Mach 2.18 E
MiG-27 'Flogger-D' Mach 1.7 E
SEPECAT Jaguar GR.Mk 1 Mach 1.6
Vought A-7E Corsair II Mach 1.04
Blackburn (HS) Buccaneer S.Mk 2B Mach 0.92

Maximum speed at sea level
General Dynamics F-111F Mach 1.2
Panavia Tornado GR.Mk 1 Mach 1.2
Sukhoi Su-24 'Fencer' Mach 1.2 E
SEPECAT Jaguar GR.Mk 1 Mach 1.1
Mikoyan-Gurevich MiG-27 'Flogger-D' Mach 1.1 E
Blackburn (HS) Buccaneer S.Mk 2B Mach 0.92
Vought A-7E Corsair II Mach 0.91 E

Combat radius hi-lo-hi
Panavia Tornado GR.Mk 1 1390 km
General Dynamics F-111F 1287 km
Blackburn (HS) Buccaneer S.Mk 2B 966 km (2500 kg weapons)
Sukhoi Su-24 'Fencer' 950 km
MiG-27 'Flogger-D' 950 km E
Vought A-7E Corsair II 885 km
SEPECAT Jaguar GR.Mk 1 852 km

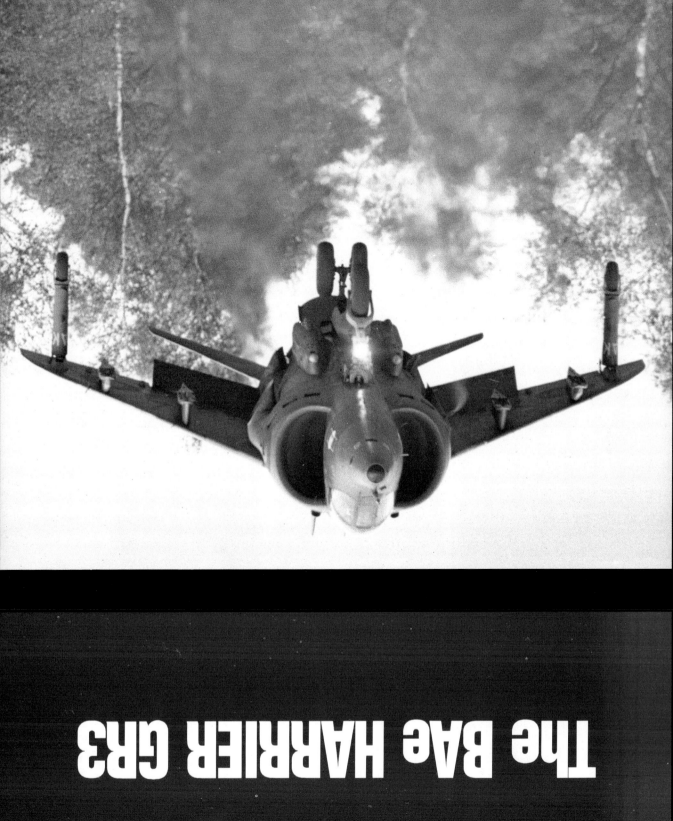

The BAE HARRIER GR3

Harrier: Hunter in Hiding

In war, concealment is survival. While theoretically more capable aircraft are sitting uselessly marooned on bombed-out airfields, Harriers would continue to operate out of numerous hidden dispersals up at the front, supporting land forces with highly effective ground attacks.

In the world of military equipment there have been comparatively few entirely novel weapon systems introduced to the battlefield since the dawn of recorded history. Rather, the advantage gained through the years by first one nation, then another, over their adversaries has been through refinement and improvement of a basic idea. Thus the medieval cannon has evolved into a radar- or laser-aimed weapon firing proximity-fused shells through a rifled barrel; or the frail aeroplane of World War I has become the potent combat machine flying in today's skies. The first great leap for military aviation was the jet engine with its ability to provide speeds formerly in the realms of science fiction. Then came the innovation which combined speed with the tractability of the helicopter – the Harrier.

In the mid-1950s, when there were being formulated the ideas which by painstaking development resulted in the Harrier, forward-thinking tacticians were looking with dismay at the fixed military installations

upon which the security of NATO depended. On the principle that a moving target is more difficult to hit, there was an obvious need for a high-performance aircraft capable of operating away from vulnerable airfields. The answer to this problem was the combination of a French concept, American funding and assistance, and British industry. On 21 October 1960, the first Hawker P.1127 cautiously raised itself a few inches from the ground, supported on the four columns of air from a Bristol-Siddeley Pegasus vectored-thrust turbofan engine.

Development

Much more work was required before what came to be known as the Harrier entered squadron service with the RAF. At first the P.1127 was seen merely as a concept-proving demonstrator for the supersonic and far more advanced P.1154, which would have also joined the Fleet Air Arm. To this end, nine militarized P.1127s, known as Kestrels, were flown by a unit of British, West German and US pilots based at West Raynham in Norfolk, but even as the Kestrel Evaluation Squadron was being formed, the P.1154 was cancelled on grounds of economy. As a partial replacement, the P.1127 was extensively redesigned, equipped with some P.1154 avionics, and called the Harrier GR.Mk 1. Introduction to service began on the first day of 1969 with the formation at Wittering of the Harrier Conversion Team, and

on 1 October of that year No. 1 Squadron was established with the world's first operational fixed-wing VTOL unit. Over a decade and a half later, only the Soviet Yakovlev Yak-36 'Forger', with its outdated fixed lifting-engine concept, has joined the unique club founded by the Harrier. Equally thin on the ground have been the nations which have bought Harriers, and allowing for the fact that those sold to the United States and Spain were for primarily seaborne deployment, the RAF's Harriers remain first in a field of one.

The comparatively modest total of four RAF squadrons has flown the Harrier, assisted by an operational conversion unit (OCU) and two flights formed to meet unforeseen demands far away from NATO, in Belize and the Falkland Islands. The signboard by the main gate of Wittering still proclaims it to be the 'Home of the Harrier', with No. 1 Squadron and No. 233 OCU in residence. The former is assigned to rapid intervention roles and has operated on behalf of the Allied Command Europe Mobile Force (ACEMF, otherwise known as 'NATO's fire brigade') and the similarly-tasked United Kingdom Mobile Force. The UKMF is under national control (but may, of course, be subordinated at any time to NATO's supreme commander), and as part of such, No. 1 Squadron was involved in the Falklands War.

Permanently in the potential front line are the Harriers of RAF Germany. Three units (Nos 3, 4 and 20 Squadrons) were

▼ *The Harrier operates at low level, where its agility is exploited to the full. The aircraft's lack of range is compensated for by being based close to the front and employing speedy turn-rounds between missions.*

◀ *In time of war, the Harrier's home would be a camouflage netting hide, usually cut into a tree-line. A maintenance team is attached to each hide, and most servicing and repair can be accomplished in the field.*

HUD
The aircraft has a Smiths Industries 6-50 Series combined head-up display and weapon aiming computer; the equipment processes weapon-aiming data and generates essential symbology for the pilot's display. Electronic and optical compensation is incorporated in the HUD to overcome any distortion in the bird-proof windscreen

Ejector seat
The pilot's Martin Baker Mk 9D zero/zero rocket ejection seat is augmented by an MDC (miniature detonating cord) incorporated in the manually-actuated rearward sliding canopy. This explodes the canopy immediately before the seat begins to operate

Yaw vane
This senses the aircraft's rotation about its vertical axis

UHF aerial
This serves the Plessey Avionics PTR 1721 UHF/VHF solid-state communications transmitter/receiver (transceiver)

IFF
This aerial serves the Cossor IFF (Identification friend or foe) transponder

Ram air intake
The intake serves the cockpit pressurization system; of British Aerospace design, the system has maximum pressure differential of 0.246 kg/cm² (3.5 lb/sq in)

Pitot tube
This extends into the airflow uninfluenced by any adjacent structures; the difference between the pitot tube pressure and standard atmospheric pressure (static) provides the basic air speed reading

Laser ranger
Retractable protective 'eyelids' protect the Ferranti Type 106 laser ranger and marked target seeker (LRMTS) against damage from debris thrown up during off-airfield operations

IFF aerial
The IFF aerial is mounted on the transponder housing. Transponders were installed in 1982 to allow safer operation from ships during the Falklands campaign

F.95 camera
An F.95 oblique camera is carried in the nose, mounted behind an optically flat panel

Forward pitch nozzle
Nozzles for the reaction control system are found in the nose, in the extended tailcone and at each wingtip

Engine intake
Enormous bell-mouthed low-drag intakes supply air to the Rolls-Royce Pegasus Mk 103 vectored-thrust turbofan engine, developing 9752 kg (21,500 lb) thrust

Matra SNEB rocket pod
Each of these launchers carries 19 68-mm (2.98-in) unguided rockets, normally fired in a salvo, although for training purposes rockets can be fired singly

Landing and taxi light

1,000-lb bomb
One 1,000-lb (454-kg) bomb can be carried on a pylon mounted under the centre fuselage between the gun pods. No. 4 Squadron aircraft carry a reconnaissance pod in this position

British Aerospace Harrier GR.Mk 3
No. 1 Squadron
Royal Air Force

Nosewheel
The nosewheel landing gear is a Dowty Rotol retractable unit

Aden gun pod
One 30-mm Aden gun pod with 150 rounds of ammunition is mounted on each side of the lower fuselage. During the Falklands war one of these was sometimes replaced by Blue Eric, a hastily improvised jammer in a modified gun pod

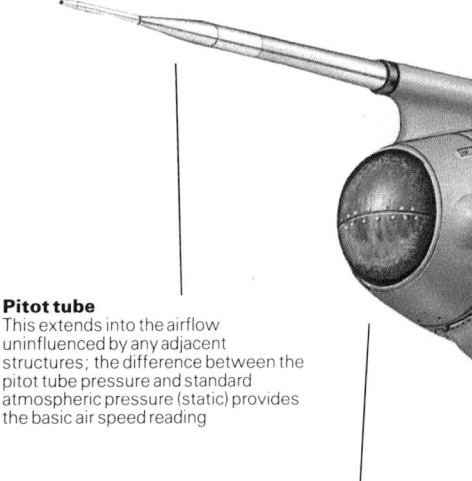

installed at Wildenrath, close to the Dutch border, in 1970-1. In February 1977, No. 20 Squadron disbanded and the remaining two units absorbed its aircraft and moved forward to Gütersloh, the only RAF airfield (apart from Berlin/Gatow) east of the Rhine.

The Harrier is a close-support aircraft, with the primary role of assisting I (British) Corps in the event of a conflict on NATO's Central Front. Off-airfield roles are taken seriously, with the result that about three times every year the Gütersloh wing takes to the German countryside to practise flying from dispersed sites. Squadrons usually divide into three flights for this purpose, hiding in the woods when not in the air.

In service
Operating from hides concealed with camouflage netting and fed with fuel hoses from large rubberized tanks some distance away, the Harriers would await their mission orders. Dispersal means operations from sites some 80 km (50 miles) behind the front line, so that each aircraft would be able to make rapid flights to the battle area, probably six or so per day, which is high for a combat jet. Pilots would fly perhaps three of these 20-minute missions without leaving the cockpit, receiving their instructions via a land line from the Forward Wing Operations Centre before taxiing out after rearming and refuelling. Assisting at this end would be an army officer attached to the squadron, while in the battle zone a forward air controller (probably an RAF officer working with the army) would direct the Harriers, flying in pairs, onto targets such as tank concentrations. In exercizes, Harriers have consistently demonstrated their ability to be overhead within about 15 minutes of a

request for air support being issued.

For the sake of simplicity, the aircraft has previously been described as having VTOL (Vertical Take-Off and Landing) capability. This is true, but even in its GR.Mk 3 configuration, with a 9752-kg (21,500-lb) thrust Pegasus Mk 103 giving 1134 kg (2,500 lb) more power than the engine first installed in the GR.Mk 1, the Harrier cannot lift a worthwhile warload without a short take-off run. Thus, training operations literally 'in the field' are flown from a 183-m (200-yard) strip of aluminium planking from which the aircraft leap into the air after gathering forward speed. In wartime, a stretch of road would suffice equally well. Landing can be accomplished vertically when weapons have been expended, except that in a dusty environment the aircraft generally maintains a slight forward motion to minimize debris ingestion by the engine.

Up to 2268 kg (5,000 lb) of weaponry may be attached to the Harrier's seven strongpoints, three of them beneath the fuselage. The two outboard belly positions usually carry a podded 30-mm Aden cannon each, conceivably with a 454-kg

(1,000-lb) bomb between them. The inboard wing pylons, each stressed to 544 kg (1,200 lb), can carry bombs, or on short missions a 455-litre (100-Imp. gal.) fuel tank, leaving the outer positions for ordnance weighing up to 295 kg (650 lb). Outboard loads can comprise a 272-kg (600-lb) Hunting BL755 CBU or a pod containing 18 68-mm (2.68-in) MATRA SNEB rockets.

During the Falklands War, Harriers also carried 'Paveway' laser-guided bombs and

▲ The Harrier can carry two Paveway laser-guided bombs. Two Paveways were dropped from Harriers in the Falklands, of which one hit its target. The other was not released with the correct trajectory.

▲ No. 4 Sqn makes up half the RAF Germany Harrier force, and is stationed along with No. 3 Sqn at

Gütersloh. The importance of the Harrier to NATO can be judged by its being stationed so close to the East German border.

▼ Norway is a vital area for NATO's defence, but is virtually devoid of airfields. Harrier would soon be moved into the warzone, operating out of woodland clearings and makeshift installations.

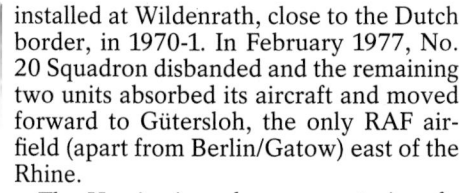

Royal Navy 50.8-mm (2-in) rocket pods, further being equipped for (but not carrying into battle) AIM-9 Sidewinder AAMs and AGM-45 Shrike anti-radiation missiles. Confusion of the enemy was assisted by a pair of Tracor AN/ALE-40 chaff/flare-dispensers hastily installed to the rear of the underfuselage airbrake and simplified Marconi Sky Shadow jamming equipment repackaged in a cannon pod.

Those avionics presently in the Harrier have been overtaken by the meteoric progress of miniaturization, yet remain adequate for their task. The principal navigation aid is the Ferranti FE541 inertial nav/attack system which incorporates a head-up display, moving map display and position computer. Ferranti also supplies the LRMTS installed in the nose (retrospectively in the case of early aircraft) for accurate weapon delivery, while for detection of threats, the aerials of a Marconi ARI 18223 RWR are mounted on the fin leading edge and the extreme rear fuselage.

Exports
Well before the advent of the Sea Harrier, or the operation of 10 No. 1 Squadron aircraft from HMS *Hermes* during the Falklands War, the US Marine Corps was regularly operating its 102 AV-8As and eight TAV-8A trainers from assault carriers. Delivered between 1971 and 1976, these aircraft were exactly what the USMC wanted for close support of amphibious landings. Therefore, the LRMTS was not installed and the FE541 retrospectively removed, although special fitments include Sidewinders on the outboard pylons, a twin-gyro attitude and heading reference system (AHRS) and a weapon-aiming computer (WAC).

After operating from their carriers to 'soften up' the opposition, US Marine Harriers come ashore with the troops and fly from sites made of AM-2 aluminium matting. These sites are located far closer to

the front line than those of RAF aircraft in order that the aircraft can keep up with the perimeter of the expanding beach-head. In the risky business of gaining a lodgement on a defended enemy shore, the US Marines have found that only the Harrier can respond with the speed demanded.

Over a five-year period, beginning in 1979, the USMC modified 47 AV-8As (Harrier Mk 50s as BAe designates them) to AV-8C standard with an American RWR, an AN/ALE-40 chaff/flare-dispenser, LIDs and other minor changes. The LIDs are a spin-off from the AV-8B Harrier II programme and comprise underfuselage strakes and a flap at their forward extremity. USMC Harriers will remain in service with four squadrons (one of them for training) until replaced by AV-8Bs.

Spain's naval air force, the Arma Aérea de la Armada, bought an initial six AV-8As and two TAV-8As through the US Navy in 1973, these having the local designation VA.1 and VAE.1 Matador respectively. Deliveries to the USA for working-up of the sole operating squadron took place in 1976 before Escuadrilla 008 was installed at Rota in December of that year for operations from the small carrier *Dedalo*. Five more single-seat aircraft, loosely known by the designation AV-8s, followed

directly from the UK during 1980, although Spain will acquire the AV-8B Harrier II as a replacement.

Representing a further major upgrading of the basic Harrier, the Harrier II is a subject for separate discussion, and its current availability means that few, if any more first-generation Harriers will be produced by BAe's works at Kingston-upon-Thames after current RAF attrition-replacement orders are satisfied. Now, in retrospect, it may be seen that the Harrier failed to achieve the large production runs which its advocates expected, but this surely is not evidence that they were wrong and that NATO's air marshals were right to have bought their current equipment elsewhere.

▼ A Harrier GR.Mk 3 from No. 1 Sqn RAF puts up a dashing display of firepower with its SNEB rockets. Though comparatively lightly armed, the essence of good ground attack is to be in the right place at the right time, and Harrier achieves that better than most.

▲ The US Marine Corps finds its AV-8Cs a unique and irreplaceable asset. Tasked to support beach-head landings, AV-8Cs would operate from assault carriers or makeshift landing strips near the action.

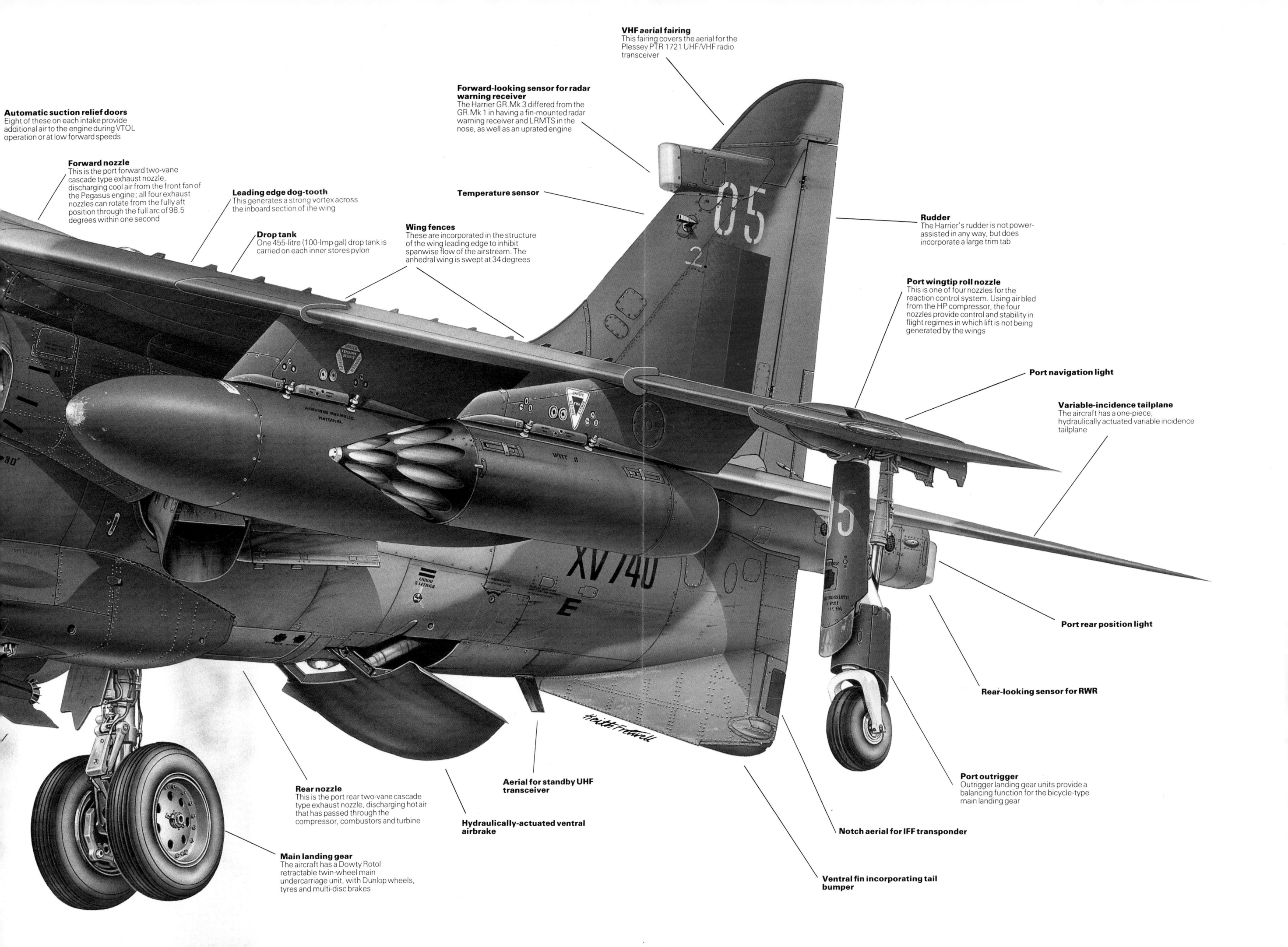

Automatic suction relief doors
Eight of these on each intake provide additional air to the engine during VTOL operation or at low forward speeds

Forward nozzle
This is the port forward two-vane cascade type exhaust nozzle, discharging cool air from the front fan of the Pegasus engine; all four exhaust nozzles can rotate from the fully aft position through the full arc of 98.5 degrees within one second

Leading edge dog-tooth
This generates a strong vortex across the inboard section of the wing

Drop tank
One 455-litre (100-Imp gal) drop tank is carried on each inner stores pylon

Wing fences
These are incorporated in the structure of the wing leading edge to inhibit spanwise flow of the airstream. The anhedral wing is swept at 34 degrees

Temperature sensor

Forward-looking sensor for radar warning receiver
The Harrier GR.Mk 3 differed from the GR.Mk 1 in having a fin-mounted radar warning receiver and LRMTS in the nose, as well as an uprated engine

VHF aerial fairing
This fairing covers the aerial for the Plessey PTR 1721 UHF/VHF radio transceiver

Rudder
The Harrier's rudder is not power-assisted in any way, but does incorporate a large trim tab

Port wingtip roll nozzle
This is one of four nozzles for the reaction control system. Using air bled from the HP compressor, the four nozzles provide control and stability in flight regimes in which lift is not being generated by the wings

Port navigation light

Variable-incidence tailplane
The aircraft has a one-piece, hydraulically actuated variable incidence tailplane

Port rear position light

Rear-looking sensor for RWR

Port outrigger
Outrigger landing gear units provide a balancing function for the bicycle-type main landing gear

Notch aerial for IFF transponder

Rear nozzle
This is the port rear two-vane cascade type exhaust nozzle, discharging hot air that has passed through the compressor, combustors and turbine

Aerial for standby UHF transceiver

Hydraulically-actuated ventral airbrake

Main landing gear
The aircraft has a Dowty Rotol retractable twin-wheel main undercarriage unit, with Dunlop wheels, tyres and multi-disc brakes

Ventral fin incorporating tail bumper

05
2
XV740
E
5

Harrier in service units and example aircraft

Royal Air Force

No. 1 Squadron
Base: RAF Wittering
Formed: 1 October 1969
Equipment: Harrier GR.Mk 3, T.Mk 4*
Aircraft: XV740 '05', XV790 '14', XW768 '08', XZ129 '06', XZ969 '01', ZW270 '12'*

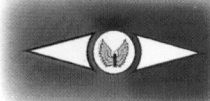
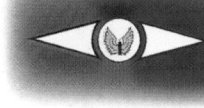

No. 3 Squadron
Base: RAF Gütersloh
Formed: 3 January 1972
Equipment: Harrier GR.Mk 3, T.Mk 4*
Aircraft: XV751 'AU', XW917 'AL', XZ965 'AM', XZ995 'AO', XZ145 'AT*', ZB603 'AZ'*

No. 4 Squadron
Base: RAF Gütersloh
Formed: 1 June 1970
Equipment: Harrier GR.Mk 3, T.Mk 4*
Aircraft: XV738 'B', XW630 'M', XW931 'V', XZ999 'I', XW927 'S'*, ZB600 'R'*

No. 233 Operational Conversion Unit
Base: RAF Wittering
Formed: 1 October 1970
Equipment: Harrier GR.Mk 3, T.Mk 4*
Aircraft: XV744 'D', XV783 'E', XZ964 'P', XZ971 'N', XW267 'T'*, XW925 'V'*

No. 1417 Flight
Base: Belize City Airport
Formed: 1975 (as Strike Command Detachment)
Equipment: Harrier GR.Mk 3
Aircraft: XZ966 'C', XZ996 'G', XZ998 'D'

US Marine Corps

VMA-231
Base: Cherry Point
Formed: October 1973
Equipment: AV-8A/C
Tail letters: 'CG'
Aircraft: 158385 '1', 158702 '02', 158950 '00', 159233 '03', 159249 '12', 159256 '21'

VMA-513
Base: Yuma
Formed: April 1971
Equipment: AV-8A/C
Tail letters: 'WF'
Aircraft: 158391 '00', 158701 '12', 158956 '03', 158975 '06', 159241 '13', 159257 '10'

VMA-542
Base: Cherry Point
Formed: December 1972
Equipment: AV-8A/C
Tail letters: 'WH'
Aircraft: 158700 '09', 158954 '00', 158964 '08', 159246 '17', 159258 '11', 159370 '07'

VMAT-203
Base: Cherry Point
Formed: 1975
Equipment: AV-8A/C, TAV-8A*
Tail letters: 'KD'
Aircraft: 159366 '17', 159371 '15', 159376 '10', 159378 '062'*, 159380 '02'*, 159383 '03'*

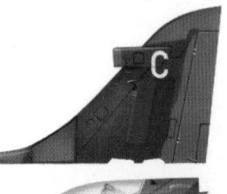
The standard RAF camouflage for the Harriers is wrap-round dark green and grey. All-green and all-grey schemes have been experimented with.

The three RAF Harrier squadrons have at least one two-seat 'T-bird' attached to the squadron. These are used for continuation training, photographic missions and for flying visiting VIPs. The Harrier T.Mk 4 retains full combat capability and would be used as such in times of war. This 'T-bird' belongs to No. 1 Sqn at Wittering.

Spanish Navy

Escuadrilla 008
Base: Rota
Formed: December 1976
Equipment: VA.1 Matador, VAE.1 Matador*

Aircraft: 159559/VA.1-2 '008-3', 159561/VA.1-4 '008-5', 161174 '008-9', 161178 '008-14', 159563/VAE.1-1 '008-7'*, 159564/VAE.1-2 '008-8'*

Escuadrilla 008 has two trainers, which have the local designation VAE.1 Matador. The gun packs can be clearly seen under the fuselage.

The AV-8s of the USMC are required to spend long periods at sea aboard amphibious warfare vessels. The Marines have taken to their aircraft, but, like the RAF, have suffered a high attrition rate.

Specification: BAe Harrier GR.Mk 3 (laser nose)

Wings
Span, standard	7.70 m	(25 ft 3 in)
with ferry extensions	9.04 m	(29 ft 8 in)
Chord at root	3.56 m	(11 ft 8 in)
Chord at tip	1.26 m	(4 ft 1.5 in)
Area, standard	18.68 m²	(201.10 sq ft)
with ferry extensions	20.07 m²	(216.0 sq ft)

Fuselage and tail unit
Length overall	14.27 m	(46 ft 10 in)
Height overall	3.63 m	(11 ft 11 in)
Tailplane span	4.24 m	(13 ft 11 in)

Landing gear
Wheelbase	3.45 m	(11 ft 4 in)
Wheel track (outriggers)	6.76 m	(22 ft 2 in)
Tyre pressures,		
main/nose	6.33 kg/cm²	(90 lb/sq in)
outriggers	6.68 kg/cm²	(95 lb/sq in)

Weights
Empty	6139 kg	(13,535 lb)
Maximum take-off	11431 kg	(25,200 lb)
Maximum internal fuel	2295 kg	(5,060 lb)
Ordnance, normal		
maximum	2268 kg	(5,000 lb)

Recognition features:

Outrigger wheels just inboard of wingtip

Small, moderately swept wings with dogtooth in leading edge; extreme anhedral

Low-set canopy and bulged upper fuselage give humped-back character

Laser ranger and marked target seeker in extended nose cone; pitot tube above

Relatively small fin with radar warning receiver on curved leading edge

Small wingtips may be replaced by Ferry tips of larger size

Large semicircular air intakes on fuselage sides, with square blow-in suction doors

Bicycle main undercarriage giving pronounced tail-down sit

Large, kinked tailplanes with sharp anhedral

British Aerospace Harrier GR.Mk 3 cutaway drawing

1 Pitot tube
2 Laser protective 'eyelids'
3 Ferranti Laser Ranger and Marked Target Seeker (LRMTS)
4 Cooling air duct
5 Oblique camera
6 Camera port
7 Windshield washer reservoir
8 Inertial platform
9 Nose pitch reaction control air duct
10 Pitch feel and trim actuator
11 IFF aerial
12 Cockpit ram air intake
13 Yaw vane
14 Cockpit air discharge valve
15 Front pressure bulkhead
16 Rudder pedals
17 Nav/attack 'head-down' display unit
18 Underfloor control linkages
19 Canopy external handle
20 Control column
21 Instrument panel shroud
22 Windscreen wiper
23 Birdproof windscreen panels
24 Head-up display
25 Starboard side console panel
26 Nozzle angle control lever
27 Engine throttle lever
28 Ejection seat rocket pack
29 Fuel cock
30 Cockpit pressurization relief valve
31 Canopy emergency release
32 Pilot's Martin-Baker Type 9D, zero-zero ejection seat
33 Sliding canopy rail
34 Miniature detonating cord (MDC) canopy breaker
35 Starboard air intake
36 Ejection seat headrest
37 Cockpit rear pressure bulkhead
38 Nose undercarriage wheel well
39 Boundary layer bleed air duct
40 Port air intake
41 Pre-closing nosewheel door
42 Landing/taxiing lamp
43 Nosewheel forks
44 Nosewheel
45 Supplementary air intake doors (fully floating)
46 Intake ducting
47 Hydraulic accumulator
48 Nosewheel retraction jack
49 Intake centre-body
50 Ram air discharge to engine intake
51 Cockpit air conditioning plant
52 Air conditioning system ram air intakes
53 Boundary layer bleed air discharge ducts
54 Starboard supplementary air intake doors
55 UHF aerial
56 Engine intake compressor face
57 Air refuelling probe connection
58 Forward fuselage integral fuel tank, port and starboard
59 Engine bay venting air scoop
60 Hydraulic ground connections
61 Engine monitoring and recording equipment
62 Forward nozzle fairing
63 Fan air (cold stream) swivelling nozzle
64 Nozzle bearing
65 Venting air intake
66 Alternator cooling air ducts
67 Twin alternators
68 Engine accessory gearbox
69 Alternator cooling air exhausts
70 Engine bay access doors
71 Gas turbine starter/ Auxiliary power unit, GTS/ APU
72 APU exhaust duct
73 Aileron control rods
74 Wing front spar carry-through
75 Nozzle bearing cooling air duct
76 Engine turbine section
77 Rolls-Royce Pegasus Mk 103 vectored thrust turbofan engine
78 Wing panel centreline joint rib
79 APU intake
80 Wing centre-section fairing panels
81 Starboard wing integral fuel tank, total internal fuel capacity 630 Imp gal (2864 litres)
82 Fuel system piping
83 Pylon attachment hardpoint
84 Aileron control rod
85 Reaction control air duct
86 Leading-edge dog-tooth
87 Starboard inner stores pylon
88 Jettisonable combat fuel tank, capacity 100 Imp gal (454 litres)
89 1,000-lb (454-kg) HE bomb
90 BL755 600-lb (272-kg) cluster bomb
91 Starboard outer stores pylon
92 Wing fences
93 Outer pylon hardpoint
94 Aileron hydraulic power control unit
95 Roll control reaction air valve
96 Starboard navigation light
97 Wing tip fairing
98 Profile of extended-span wing tip
99 Starboard outrigger fairing
100 Outrigger wheel retracted position
101 Starboard aileron
102 Fuel jettison pipe
103 Starboard plain flap
104 Trailing-edge root fairing
105 Water-methanol filler cap
106 Anti-collision light
107 Water-methanol injection system tank
108 Fire extinguisher bottle
109 Flap hydraulic jack
110 Fuel contents transmitters
111 Rear fuselage integral fuel tank
112 Ram air turbine housing
113 Turbine doors
114 Emergency ram air turbine (extended position)
115 Rear fuselage frames
116 Ram air turbine jack
117 Cooling air ram air intake
118 HF tuner
119 HF notch aerial
120 Rudder control rod linkages
121 Starboard all-moving tailplane
122 Temperature sensor
123 Tail fin construction
124 Forward radar warning receiver
125 VHF aerial
126 Fin tip aerial fairing
127 Rudder upper hinge
128 Honeycomb rudder construction
129 Rudder trim jack
130 Rudder tab
131 Tail reaction control air ducting
132 Yaw control port
133 Aft radar warning receiver
134 Rear position light
135 Pitch reaction control valve
136 Tailplane honeycomb trailing edge
137 Extended tailplane tip
138 Tailplane construction
139 Tail bumper
140 IFF notch aerial
141 Tailplane sealing plate
142 Fin spar attachment
143 Tailplane centre-section carry-through
144 All-moving tailplane control
145 Ram air exhaust duct
146 UHF standby aerial
147 Equipment air conditioning plant
148 Ground power supply socket
149 Twin batteries
150 Ventral equipment bay access door
151 Radio and electronics equipment racks
152 Electronics bay access door
153 Ventral airbrake
154 Airbrake hydraulic jack
155 Nitrogen pressurizing bottles for hydraulic system
156 Flap drive torque shaft
157 Rear spar/fuselage attachment joint

© Pilot Press Limited

ximum speed				
sea level	634 kts	1175 km/h	(730 mph)	
ximum Mach number in dive			1.3	
e to 40,000 ft (12190 m)		2 minutes 23 seconds		
m VTO				
vice ceiling		over 16764 m	(55,000 ft)	

Combat radius with
1361-kg (3,000 lb)
  external payload, hi-lo-hi   666 km   (414 miles)
  lo-lo-lo   370 km   (230 miles)
Ferry range   3426 km   (2,129 miles)
Time on station
  185 km (115 miles) from base   1 hour 30 minutes
Take-off run with
  maximum weapon load   305 m   (1,000 ft)
  g limits   +7.8 and −4.2

eed at sea level

- ssault Mirage 5   750kt
- G-27 'Flogger-D'   677kt E
- e Harrier   634kt
- 7 Corsair II   600kt
- '-8B Harrier II   590kt
- 10   381kt

ke off run

- 0ft   BAe Harrier at max weight
- 0ft   AV-8B Harrier II at max weight
- 25ft clean E   MiG-27 'Flogger-D'
- 0ft at max weight   A-10
- 50ft at max weight   Dassault Mirage 5
- 0ft at max weight   A-7 Corsair II

Combat radius Hi-lo-hi

- 1762km
- 1300km   A-7 Corsair II
- 1112km   Dassault Mirage 5 with 2000lb load
- 998km   AV-8B Harrier II
- 950km   A-10 Thunderbolt II with 20 min reserves
- 666km   MiG-27 'Flogger-D' with external fuel
- BAe Harrier

Combat radius lo-lo-lo

- 885km   A-7 Corsair II
- 650km with 2000-lb load   Dassault Mirage 5
- 463km   A-10 Thunderbolt II with 20 min reserves
- 390km   MiG-27 with 6400-lb load
- 370km   BAe Harrier with external payload
- 278km   AV-8B Harrier II

Time on station 185km from base

4 hour clock

AV-8B Harrier II	A-10 T' bolt II	BAe Harrier	A-7 Corsair II	MiG-27 'Flogger'	Dassault Mirage 5
180min	102min	90min	60minE	30min E	30min E

Weapon load

A-10 Thunderbolt II 16000-lb	A-7 Corsair II 15000-lb	AV-8B Harrier II 9200-lb	Dassault Mirage 5 8900-lb	BAe Harrier 8000-lb	MiG-27 'Flogger-D' 6615-lb

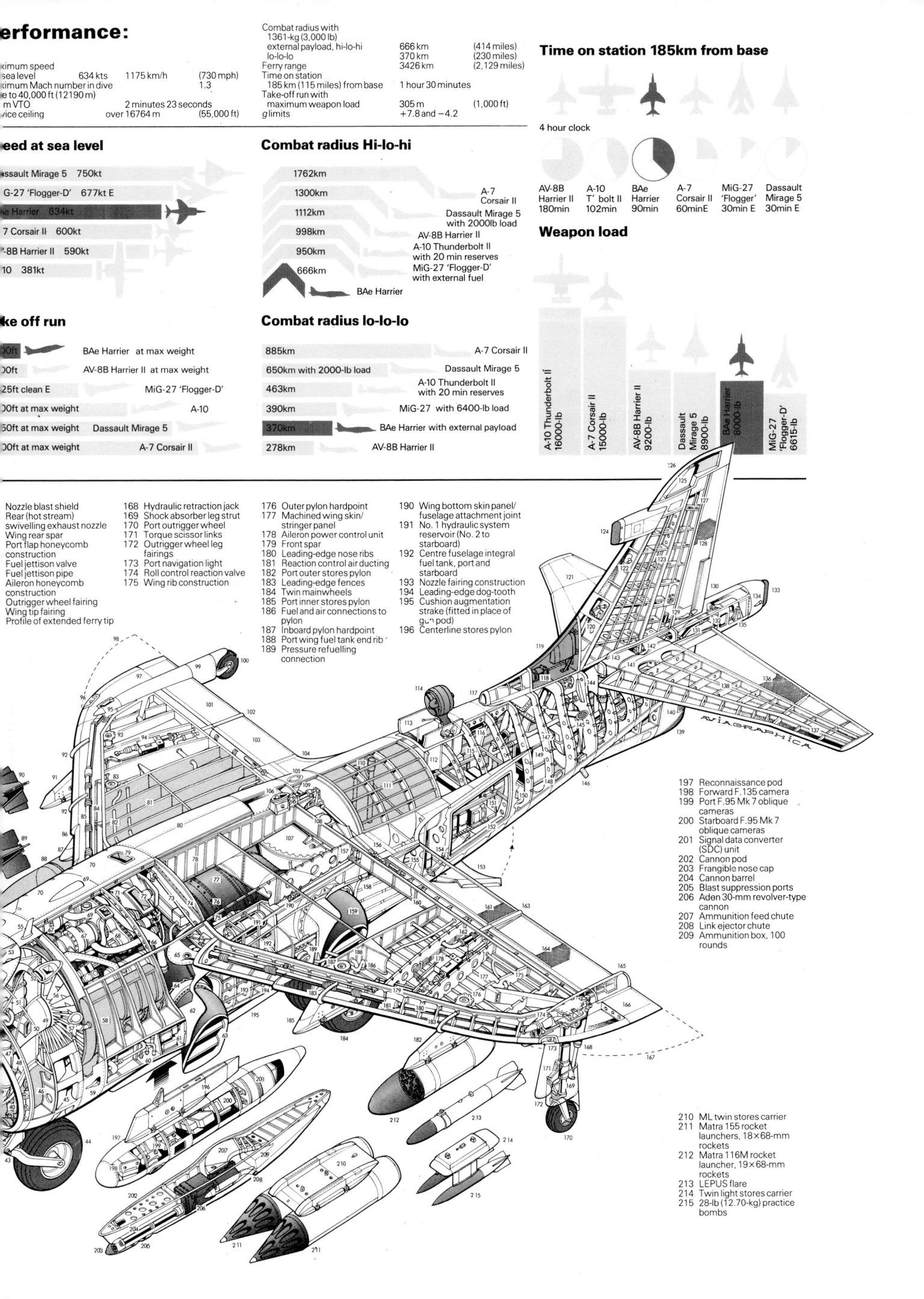

Nozzle blast shield
Rear (hot stream)
swivelling exhaust nozzle
Wing rear spar
Port flap honeycomb construction
Fuel jettison valve
Fuel jettison pipe
Aileron honeycomb construction
Outrigger wheel fairing
Wing tip fairing
Profile of extended ferry tip

168 Hydraulic retraction jack
169 Shock absorber leg strut
170 Port outrigger wheel
171 Torque scissor links
172 Outrigger wheel leg fairings
173 Port hydraulic reservoir
174 Roll control reaction valve
175 Wing rib construction

176 Outer pylon hardpoint
177 Machined wing skin/ stringer panel
178 Aileron power control unit
179 Front spar
180 Leading-edge nose ribs
181 Reaction control air ducting
182 Port outer stores pylon
183 Leading-edge fences
184 Twin mainwheels
185 Port inner stores pylon
186 Fuel and air connections to pylon
187 Inboard pylon hardpoint
188 Port wing fuel tank end rib
189 Pressure refuelling connection

190 Wing bottom skin panel/ fuselage attachment joint
191 No. 1 hydraulic system reservoir (No. 2 to starboard)
192 Centre fuselage integral fuel tank, port and starboard
193 Nozzle fairing construction
194 Leading-edge dog-tooth
195 Cushion augmentation strake (fitted in place of gun pod)
196 Centreline stores pylon

197 Reconnaissance pod
198 Forward F.135 camera
199 Port F.95 Mk 7 oblique cameras
200 Starboard F.95 Mk 7 oblique cameras
201 Signal data converter (SDC) unit
202 Cannon pod
203 Frangible nose cap
204 Cannon barrel
205 Blast suppression ports
206 Aden 30-mm revolver-type cannon
207 Ammunition feed chute
208 Link ejector chute
209 Ammunition box, 100 rounds

210 ML twin stores carrier
211 Matra 155 rocket launchers, 18×68-mm rockets
212 Matra 116M rocket launcher, 19×68-mm rockets
213 LEPUS flare
214 Twin light stores carrier
215 28-lb (12.70-kg) practice bombs

Harrier warload

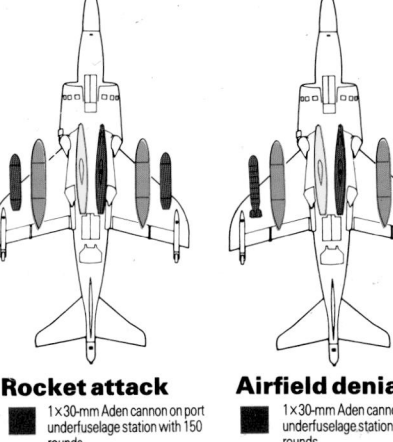

Rocket attack
- 1 × 30-mm Aden cannon on port underfuselage station with 150 rounds
- 2 × Royal Navy 36-round 2-in (50.8-mm) rocket pods on outer wing pylons
- 2 × 455-litre (100-Imp gal) drop tanks on inner wing pylons
- 1 × 'Blue Eric' ECM pod on starboard underfuselage station

During the Falklands war the hastily-improvised 'Blue Eric' jammer was carried instead of the starboard cannon. The 'Blue Eric' consisted of Tornado 'Sky Shadow' components in a Harrier gun pod, and augmented the aircraft's largely passive onboard ECM systems. Weapons like the RN 2-in rocket pod, intended for the Sea Harrier, were frequently used.

Airfield denial
- 1 × 30-mm Aden cannon on port underfuselage station with 150 rounds
- 2 × BL755 dispensers (each with 147 bomblets) on outer wing pylons
- 2 × 455-litre (100-Imp gal) drop tanks on inner wing pylons
- 1 × 'Blue Eric' ECM pod on starboard underfuselage station

During the Falklands war the attrition rate of the Sea Harrier force was lower than anticipated, and this allowed the Harrier GR.Mk 3s to operate solely in the strike role. Sidewinders were never carried operationally. Drop tanks were almost always carried to allow the RN aircraft-carriers to remain as far from the islands as possible.

Smart bombing
- 1 × 30-mm Aden cannon on port underfuselage station with 150 rounds
- 2 × 'Paveway' laser-guided 454-kg (1,000-lb) bombs on outer wing pylons
- 1 × 454-kg (1,000-lb) GP iron bomb on centre underfuselage station
- 2 × 455-litre (100-Imp gal) drop tanks on inner wing pylons
- 1 × 'Blue Eric' ECM pod on starboard underfuselage station

The laser-guided bomb is not standard equipment for the RAF's Harrier force in Europe, but was used in the Falklands campaign for attacks on precision targets, including a field gun in Port Stanley itself. These laser-guided weapons were used against targets designated by ground troops.

Ground attack
- 2 × 30-mm Aden cannon on underfuselage stations with 150 rounds per gun
- 2 × 19-round 68-mm (2.68-in) Matra SNEB rocket pods on outer wing pylons
- 2 × 455-litre (100-Imp gal) drop tanks on inner wing pylons

RAF Harriers in Europe operate with no known ECM equipment, although chaff can be loaded into the airbrake as a one-shot method of breaking the lock-on of enemy radars. Two or four SNEB rocket pods, cluster bombs or retarded bombs are among the weapons commonly used by Harriers, with or without external fuel.

Armed recon
- 2 × 30-mm Aden cannon on underfuselage stations with 150 rounds per gun
- 2 × BL755 dispensers (each with 147 bomblets) on outer wing pylons
- 2 × 455-litre (100-Imp gal) drop tanks on inner wing pylons
- 1 × reconnaissance pod on centreline underfuselage station

Although all RAF Harriers can carry the BAe reconnaissance pod, No. 4 is the only squadron with a permanent reconnaissance commitment. The pod contains four F95 Mk 7 and one F135 cameras, providing horizon-to-horizon stereoscopic coverage of the ground overflown. The latest version of the pod also contains BAe Type 401 infra-red linescan equipment.

USMC air support
- 2 × 30-mm Aden cannon on underfuselage stations with 150 rounds per gun
- 2 × AIM-9L Sidewinder air-to-air missiles on outer wing pylons
- 2 × 455-litre (100-Imp gal) drop tanks on inner wing pylons

The AV-8C is an important tool in the US Marine Corps' inventory, making possible close air support by aircraft based within a few minutes' flying time of the forward edge of the battle area, or on assault ships. Weapons favoured by the US Marine Corps include 'smart' and iron bombs, 2.75-in (69.9-mm) rockets and 5-in (127-mm) Zuni rockets. Sidewinders can be carried to make the AV-8C an excellent dogfighter.

Harrier cockpit

Left console
1 LP cock
2 Master On/Off switch
3 Emergency lighting switch
4 Pilot's hand controller
5 Autostabilizer pitch/roll test button
6 Throttle
7 Adjustable short take-off stop lever
8 Nozzle control lever
9 Landing gear selector
10 Landing gear warning lights
11 Emergency landing gear retract
12 Hydraulic pressure gauge

Left instrument panel
13 Standby compass
14 HUD control panel
15 HUD mode selector
16 Reconnaissance panel
17 UHF communications radio
18 Armament control panel
19 RPM/JPT gauge
20 Artificial horizon
21 Altimeter

Centre console
22 Gyro gunsight
23 Slip bubble
24 Inertial navigation and attack system
25 Moving map display
26 Direction indicator
27 Control column

Right instrument panel
28 Engine instruments
29 Fuel contents (port)
30 Fuel contents (starboard)
31 Fuel remaining
32 Fuel flow meter
33 Stopwatch

Right console
34 COAT gauge
35 Wing tank jettison
36 TACAN
37 Transponder
38 C-26 compass controls
39 Anti-g controls
40 Pilot's personal services

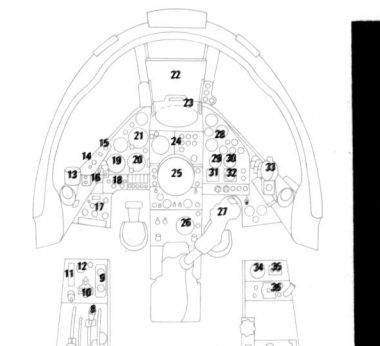

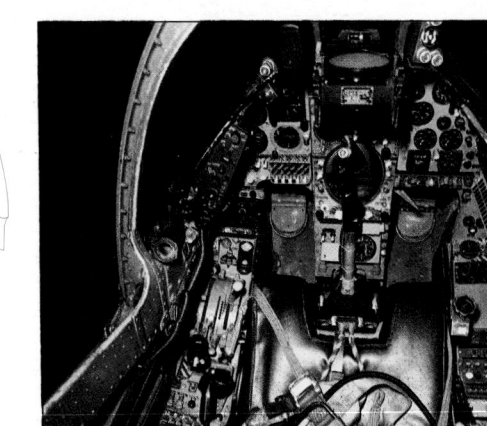

Harrier variants

P.1127: original prototypes; variations in wings, tailplanes, inlets and other features; usual powerplant 4990-kg (11,000-lb) thrust BS.53/3 Pegasus 2

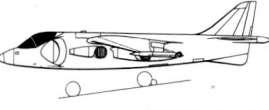

Kestrel: Tripartite Evaluation Squadron aircraft; extensive redesign with swept wings, different equipment and increased weight; usual engine 7031-kg (15,500-lb) thrust Pegasus 5

Harrier GR.Mk 1: first single-seat close-support/tactical reconnaissance version for RAF; some redesign and full operational equipment; powerplant 8618-kg (19,000-lb) thrust Pegasus 6 Mk 101; since uprated to GR.Mk 3

Harrier Mk 50: single-seat close-support/tactical reconnaissance version for US Marine Corps which designated it **AV-8A;** basic airframe similar to GR.Mk 3 but with equipment variations; 47 of these aircraft were

updated to **AV-8C** standard during 1979-83 under a CILOP (Conversion In Lieu Of Procurement) programme

Harrier Mk 53: version of the AV-8A for the Spanish navy; six procured through the USA under the designation **AV-8S;** in Arma Aérea de la Armada service is designated **VA.1 Matador**

Harrier Mk 55: identification of second batch of three aircraft as the AV-8A for the Spanish navy, which designates them VA.1 Matador

Harrier GR.Mk 1A: redesignation of GR.Mk 1s following retrofit with Pegasus 10 Mk 102 engines of 9299-kg (20,500-lb) thrust; since uprated to GR.Mk 3

Harrier Mk 52: BAe two-seat demonstrator with civil registration G-VTOL; generally similar to Harrier T.Mk 2 but now has Pegasus 103

Harrier T.Mk 2: tandem-seat dual trainer with combat capability; original powerplant as GR.Mk 1; now uprated to T.Mk 4

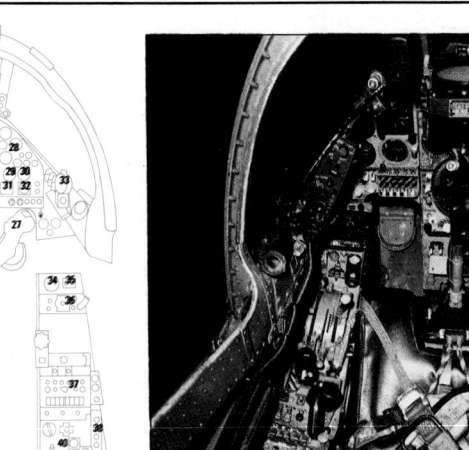

Harrier Mk 54: two-seat version for US Marine Corps which designated them **TAV-8A;** two were procured through the USA for the Spanish navy under the designation **TAV-8S;** in Spanish navy service they are designated **VAE.1 Matador**

Harrier T.Mk 2A: redesignation of T.Mk 2s following retrofit with Pegasus 10 Mk 102 engines; now uprated to T.Mk 4

Harrier GR.Mk 3: current in-service version for RAF; advanced avionics including inertial navigation and attack system, rear warning radar, and laser ranger and marked target seeker; 9752-kg (21,500-lb) thrust Pegasus 11 Mk 103; GR.Mk 1A survivors uprated to this standard

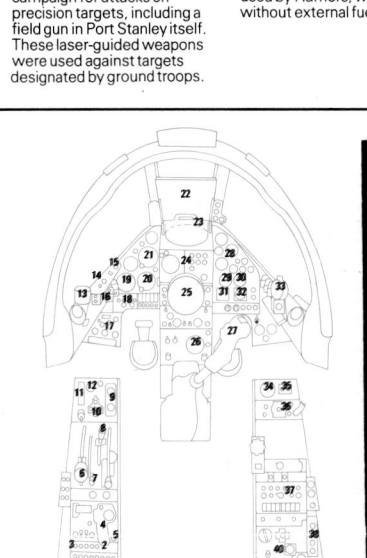

Harrier T.Mk 4: redesignation of T.Mk 2A following retrofit with Pegasus 11 Mk 103 powerplant

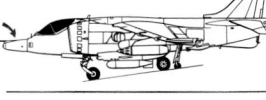

Harrier T.Mk 4A: current in-service two-seat version for the RAF

Sea Harrier FRS.Mk 1: multi-role variant of the Harrier for the Royal Navy; redesigned forward fuselage and different avionics systems; Pegasus 104 engine which differs from Pegasus 103 by improved corrosion

resistance and increased capacity gearbox

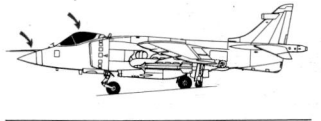

Harrier T.Mk 4N: designation of two-seat version for the Royal Navy

Sea Harrier FRS.Mk 51: designation of at least 10 aircraft similar to Royal Navy Sea Harriers in service with the Indian navy

Harrier T.Mk 60: two-seat trainer for Indian navy; these are of T.Mk 4N configuration with full Sea Harrier avionics except for the Blue Fox radar

Harrier Mk 80: proposed export version; would be similar to Sea Harrier but with laser ranger and marked target seeker in place of Blue Fox radar

Harrier GR.Mk 5: designation allocated originally to proposed 'big-wing' version of the Harrier that was not built; since allocated to the 60 McDonnell Douglas/BAe **AV-8B Harrier II** aircraft ordered for the RAF; initial deliveries scheduled for late 1986

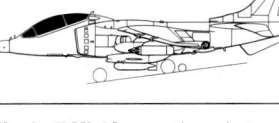

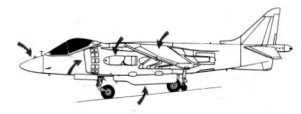

The BOEING B-52

Boeing B-52: the 'Buff' fights on

Boeing's monster bomber has carried the United States airborne nuclear deterrent for over 30 years, and spent eight of those embroiled in the heaviest bombing campaign in history. The enormous range and bombload of these leviathans is still in demand in today's low-level, stand-off environment.

First flown in prototype form during April 1952, Boeing's mighty B-52 Stratofortress entered service with Strategic Air Command at the end of June 1955, the first examples of this massive eight-engined bomber joining that command's 93rd Bomb Wing at Castle Air Force Base, California. Today, over 30 years down the road, the Stratofortress is still easily the most numerous bomber type to be found in SAC's operational inventory, more than 250 examples of the B-52G and B-52H variants remaining active in late 1985.

Even more remarkable, however, is the fact that most of these great veterans are likely to remain in service until well into the 1990s, if not to the end of the present century, there being no plans to retire the type in the short term. When the last 'Buff' (Big ugly fat fella) is finally retired, Boeing's 'big stick' will have established a service longevity record that is second to none.

Originally conceived purely as a strategic bomber and initially armed solely with nuclear weapons, the B-52 has in more recent years demonstrated a surprising degree of versatility for so old a design. Although nuclear deterrence is still viewed as the primary responsibility of the dozen or so bomb wings which are presently equipped with the Stratofortress, the type can also be employed in a purely conventional role with free-fall 'iron' bombs or 'smart' weapons such as the EO-guided GBU-15 cruciform-wing glide bomb and AGM-109H Tomahawk non-nuclear Medium-Range ASM. Other missions which can be undertaken with near-equal facility are show-of-force, defence suppression, minelaying and long-range ocean surveillance, while the type frequently provides support to NATO exercises.

In service

Although the B-52 is still quite clearly a most important part of the US arsenal, only two of the eight basic production variants remain in service, the tall-tailed B-52A to B-52F models having all been retired and, in most cases, scrapped. Both the models which continue to operate with SAC feature the short vertical tail surface introduced on the B-52G, and it is this derivative which is by far the more numerous, approximately 165 of the 193 aircraft built still being in service. In addition, about 95 examples of the final production model, the B-52H, are still active, these being the survivors of the original production total of 102 aircraft.

While essentially similar in external appearance, there are significant differences between the B-52G and the B-52H. For a start, the B-52G is powered by a battery of eight Pratt & Whitney J57-P-43WB turbojet engines, each of which generates some 6237-kg (13,750-lb) static thrust with water-methanol injection. Conversely, the B-52H (colloquially known throughout SAC as 'the Cadillac', an allusion to the fact that it is rather quieter and therefore somewhat less fatiguing to fly) features eight 7711-kg (17,000-lb) static thrust Pratt & Whitney TF33-P-3 turbofan engines.

▲ *The B-52 is a cumbersome beast, especially on the ground, where large tow-trucks are required to manoeuvre them. The two blisters under the nose house the LLLTV and FLIR sensors for the electro-optical viewing system.*

▼ *The development of surface-to-air missiles has meant that the 'Buff' has had to take to the trees to perform its mission. Handling an aircraft of this size at low level makes for interesting flying, and many low-level flying aids have been added.*

Boeing B-52G
2nd Bombardment Wing
Strategic Air Command
US Air Force

Spoilers
These are installed in the top of each wing, resembling a row of large hydraulically-driven lids. Normally flush with the upper surface, they can be opened together, to serve as brakes for a fast letdown, or on one side only to roll the aircraft or pick up a dropped wing

Chaff dispenser
At the inboard end of the spoilers above each wing is this large square compartment. It houses the Lundy ALE-24 bulk cutter and dispenser of metallized-glass chaff to blanket hostile radars

Emergency hatches
Roof hatches for emergency escape of the two upper-level backseaters: gunner (left) and EWO (electronic-warfare officer) on the right

Turbulators
Turbulators, or vortex generators, are aluminium blades about as large as a visiting card. They are arranged at zig-zag angles in straight rows, to churn up the boundary-layer air and keep it 'attached' to the skin

Inflight-refuelling receptacle
Should an air refuelling be necessary, the crew switch open these two doors to reveal underneath the receptacle into which a tanker boom operator can thrust the tip of the tanker's refuelling boom. The fuel pipe curves over to the left of the fuselage and thence runs to the wing tankage

Strakelets
This B-52 has not yet been converted as a CMC (cruise-missile carrier). After the conversion has been done, large fairings, called 'strakelets', are added here to make the aircraft visibly different to Soviet reconnaissance satellites

Astro bump
This covers the AFSATCOM (Air Force satellite communications) receive/transmit antenna, as well as astronavigation equipment

Noise jammer
Radome over ALT-28 aerial (antenna); this is the main forward-facing noise jammer to blot out hostile radars. It replaces five earlier ALT-series jammers used on earlier versions

6506

Radar
The main forward-looking multimode radar and the terrain-avoidance radar have caused considerable maintenance difficulties, and Norden Systems has torn it apart; the main radar now is a version of the APQ-156 with synthetic-aperture technology

Deception jammer
These nose side blisters cover the antennas for the forward-looking element in the ALQ-117 deception jamming system. Note the air cooling inlet ahead of it

ECM air inlet
This flush air inlet supplies cooling air to the main forward ECM and electronics bay. Items from seven systems, mainly part of the OAS (offensive avionics system), are located here

Landing gear
The B-52 has unique landing gear, with four two-wheel trucks arranged at front and rear of the fuselage. The two front trucks can be steered from the cockpit

Pylon attachment
These attachments under the inner wings can be used to carry long pylon beams which can carry two triplets of AGM-69 SRAMs or two triplets of AGM-86B ALCMs

Electro-optical viewing system
The most conspicuous 'add on' to the B-52G in recent years is the EVS (electro-optical viewing system). This provides the two pilots with high-quality pictures of the terrain ahead, especially at night or in bad weather. The system's sensors are in two pods, the left one housing a Westinghouse AVQ-22 LLTV (low-light TV) and the right blister a Hughes AAQ-6 FLIR (forward-looking infra-red)

Oil cooler
Additional ram air inlets under the centreline of each engine serve the coolers for the main engine oil systems

Generator
Early B-52s had electric generators and hydraulic pumps driven by 100,000-rpm turbines in the fuselage, driven by red-hot bleed air from the engines. The B-52G has generators driven direct from the engines, via hydraulic constant-speed drives. They result in these blisters, which incorporate the ram air cooling inlets for the hydraulic drives

Defensive armament also provides another distinguishing feature between the two versions: the older B-52G possesses a quartet of 0.5-in (12.7-mm) M3 machine-guns in its tail turret, while the B-52H is fitted with a single six-barrel 20-mm T171 Vulcan cannon, capable of spewing out shells at a rate of 6,000 rounds per minute.

The aircraft which now equip SAC's bomb wings are in fact very different from those which were delivered to the command between 13 February 1959, when the first B-52G joined the 5th Bomb Wing, and 26 October 1962, when the last B-52H was handed over to the 4136th Strategic Wing. In the intervening period, the aircraft have been subjected to numerous modification and updating programmes, all of which have been aimed at prolonging the Stratofortresses' operational careers. These objectives have been, and are still being, pursued along three broad fronts.

Specifically, these have involved extending fatigue life to a figure which is likely to approach three times the 5,000 hours originally projected; enhancing the type's chances of survival should it ever be required to penetrate Soviet airspace; and, finally, improving weapons capability in order that the type can inflict the maximum amount of damage in the event of being committed to combat. Updating the breed began as long ago as 1959 and has been an almost fabulously productive process, resulting in the B-52 being subjected to modifications which, cumulatively, have cost far more than the aircraft actually did in the first place.

Space limitations preclude detailed examination of the many modification programmes accomplished during the past 25 years or so, but there are some recently concluded and on-going initiatives which merit fairly close attention by virtue of the fact that they have had a significant impact on the type's current capability.

Modifications aimed at improving fuselage and wing life were concluded on the B-52G and B-52H during the early 1970s, and these should ensure that the basic structure remains sound until the end of the present century, always assuming of course that utilization remains at existing levels. However, SAC has been looking into the possibility of using a variant of an existing executive jet as a kind of B-52 sim-

ulator, and acquisition of such a type would be doubly beneficial in that not only would it permit B-52 flying hours to be cut but it would also enable realistic training to be accomplished at much reduced cost.

A rather more visible update resulted in the appearance of the now-familiar blister fairings on the fuselage undersides beneath the nose radar, these housing sensors for the ASQ-151 EVS. Additional equipment associated with EVS takes the form of display screens and controls at the pilot, co-pilot and navigator stations, provision of this piece of kit significantly improving capability at low level.

Avionics
Installed on all surviving B-52G and B-52H aircraft between 1971 and 1977 at a cost approaching $250 million, EVS basically comprises a Westinghouse AVQ-22 LLLTV camera on the port side and a Hughes AAQ-6 FLIR to starboard, each in a steerable turret, and these had an immediate impact in that the excellent quality of the resulting imagery raised crew confidence when operating in the potentially hazardous low-level flight regime. In addition, the EVS screens also feature alphanumeric symbols displaying such data as radar altitude, indicated airspeed, time be-

◄ The mighty B-52 still forms an important third of the United States' nuclear deterrent triad and, even after wide-scale introduction of the Rockwell B-1, will soldier on in a nuclear role, albeit as back-up to the new bomber.

▼ Full water-injection is needed to lift the giant off the runway, and this creates a dense smoke

screen. A stream take-off by 'Buffs' leaves the airfield completely shrouded in smoke.

▲ For many years, the B-52G force flew with three-tone upper surfaces and white undersides. Recently, aircraft have appeared with dark grey noses, whilst others now sport menacing two-tone dark grey and dark brown camouflage.

fore weapons release, aircraft attitude and artificial horizon, all of which makes the task of flying the aircraft a great deal easier.

Running more or less concurrently with EVS was the Phase VI avionics update, which was rather less visible although it did result in numerous appendages sprouting at various strategic points on the airframe. This, too, encompassed both the B-52G and B-52H variants and was mainly aimed at enhancing ECM capability, which in turn would result in greater likelihood of survival in the event of penetration of

enemy airspace. The Phase VI update was particularly complex in that it included installation of an ALQ-117 countermeasures set and an ALR-46 digital RWR, as well as provision of the ALQ-122 SNOE sensor/jammer package plus fitment of additional ALT-28 transmitters and ALE-20 flare launchers.

This, however, pales into insignificance when compared with the OAS which is now being installed on the B-52G and B-52H and which will eventually cost close to $2 billion by the time fleet-wide modification is completed in Fiscal Year 1989. First flown in prototype form in September 1980, the OAS update involves basically the replacement of existing navigation and weapons management systems by an entirely new digital-based solid-state system which includes TERCOM guidance. Elements of OAS are hardened against EMP effects and comprise new processors, controls and displays as well as a new radar altimeter, an attitude and heading reference system, dual inertial navigation equipment and missile interface units, none of which comes cheap.

Armament
Turning to weapons, the B-52's armoury has improved out of all recognition in comparison with that available when the type first entered service. Nevertheless, gravity weapons do still form a significant part of the US nuclear arsenal, but the North American AGM-28A/B Hound Dog missile which was deployed on both the B-52G and B-52H is gone, having disappeared from the SAC inventory in 1976.

Its place aboard the Stratofortress was taken by the Boeing AGM-69A SRAM which began to enter service with the 42nd Bomb Wing in March 1972, becoming operational on 4 August 1972. Each B-52 can carry up to 20 SRAMs, eight being housed internally on a rotary launcher plus six more on each of the two underwing hardpoints. Possessing a maximum range of the order of 160 km (100 miles), each SRAM has a single W-69 warhead with a yield of about 200 kilotons, and this weapon is still very much a part of SAC plans although it has been overshadowed

rather more recently by the Boeing AGM-86B ALCM.

Initially deployed only by B-52G units, ALCM has a range of about 2415 km (1,500 miles) and began to enter service with the 416th Bomb Wing in 1982, each ALCM aircraft being configured to carry 12 missiles underwing although the rotary launchers will eventually be modified to carry a further eight examples of this weapon. For the time being, though, B-52Gs operate with a mixture of ALCMs and SRAM missiles, or ALCMs and gravity bombs, being employed in a 'shoot and penetrate' mode, launching the AGM-86Bs from a position of relative safety before entering enemy airspace to deliver their remaining weapons. Although presently carried only by the B-52G, the ALCM is to be installed on the B-52H in a modification programme which was expected to begin in 1985 and which should more or less coincide with the entry into service of the Rockwell B-1B, this being the first entirely new bomber aircraft to join SAC since production of the B-52 and Convair B-58 Hustler terminated in 1962.

Despite the fact that all surviving examples of the Boeing B-52 Stratofortress are true veterans in that none are less than 23 years old, the trusty 'Buff' still

▲ Due to its exceptional range and large load-carrying capacity, the B-52 is ideal for maritime operations. Aerial sowing of mines is an important task for the B-52 fleet, as are long-range patrols. This G-model drops a mine in Korean waters.

▼ Seen prior to the EVS fit, these B-52Gs are accompanied to the runway by Boeing KC-135s. The tankers are an important part of the nuclear bomber force, enabling aircraft to remain airborne in time of crisis, away from the vulnerable airfields.

features prominently in SAC's SIOP and it would undoubtedly be committed to action in the event of nuclear war. Quite how well it would perform in such a conflict must remain a matter for conjecture, but there can be little doubt that the many and varied improvements incorporated in the basic design during the past two decades and more would provide the type with an excellent chance of performing its mission satisfactorily.

Paradoxically, if these features are ever put to the test in nuclear combat it will inevitably mean that both the B-52 and SAC have failed in their primary objective, for SAC still views its major function as being one of deterrence rather than of aggression.

Ailerons
There are no ailerons on the B-52; this part of the wing is fixed

Flaps
The huge slotted Fowler flaps are installed in two groups, separated by a small portion of fixed trailing edge in line with the inboard engine pod. Even so, sonic noise energy and wake buffet are so severe during a full-load take-off that the flaps soon crack

ECM cooling inlet
This ram air inlet supplies air through large ducts to cool several major ECM bays in the rear fuselage. The main pipes serve the lower group and the compartment in the tail

Datalink
This unusual antenna serves the new data-link system. Details are classified, but it certainly provides a secure digital link with the SAC command authorities which was not previously possible, probably with transmission (from low altitude) via satellite

Rear-warning radar
This blister covers one of the several antennas serving the Westinghouse ALQ-153. This new installation is a pulse-Doppler radar that gives warning of suspicious objects overtaking from astern, and precisely times deployment of chaff and jamming signals

Air exhaust and ECM antenna
This air exit discharges most of the heated air from the rear electronics compartments. It also covers one of the aft-facing ECM antennas themselves forming part of Phase VI avionics

Deception jammer
This retractable antenna serves the ALQ-117 deception jammer, supplied by ITT as part of the Rivet Ace programme that also added the EVS. ALQ-117 is itself now being upgraded to ALQ-172 standard. It does not merely obliterate hostile sensors but attempts to confuse them, in the 8 to 20 GHz waveband

Gun control radar
Fitted to the B-52G from the start, this radome covers the antenna of the ASG-15 fire control radar that directs the rear guns. The system is under the overall control of the gunner in the crew compartment

USAF 76506

ECM bay
Inside this area is one of the largest groups of ECM equipment, all of it added in the past five years. A major part of it is the large and costly Northrop ALQ-155 system, which is computer controlled and serves mainly a deception jamming function. Ten of the 'farms' of blade antennas here and under the forward fuselage form part of this system, and ALT-28 noise jammer is integrated with it

Tailplane control
The enormous tailplane is driven by an irreversible screwjack over a large angular range, as shown by these marks on the fuselage. It serves as the primary control for pitch and pitch trim

Brake parachute
The large braking parachute is located here, and is released through two doors in the top of the rear fuselage. Some of the 'window' shapes are classified ECM antennas

Rear warning receiver
This radome covers antennas for the ALQ-117 (172) deception jammer and the APR-25 crystal video rear warning receiver, which gives an initial coarse bearing of threats. Smaller antennas serve the Dalmo Victor/Itek ALR-46 digital threat warning receiver

Rear gun turret
The tail armament comprises four 0.50-in (12.7-mm) Browning machine-guns, with remote sighting and aiming over the entire rear hemisphere

Fuel tank
Early B-52s, now withdrawn, had gigantic external wing tanks; the B-52G has a 'wet wing' with much greater internal capacity but still has 700 US gal in each external tank

B-52 Stratofortress in service units and example aircraft

2nd Bomb Wing
Base: Barksdale AFB, Louisiana
Squadrons and aircraft:
62nd/596th BS (B-52G) 76506, 76512, 80219, 80251, 92586

5th Bomb Wing
Base: Minot AFB, North Dakota
Squadrons and aircraft:
23rd BS (B-52H) 00008, 00040, 10011, 10026, 10029

7th Bomb Wing
Base: Carswell AFB, Texas
Squadrons and aircraft:
9th/20th BS (B-52H) 00007, 00033, 00061, 10003, 10035

28th Bomb Wing
Base: Ellsworth AFB, South Dakota
Squadrons and aircraft:
77th BS (B-52H) 00026, 00030, 00054, 10004, 10017

42nd Bomb Wing
Base: Loring AFB, Maine
Squadrons and aircraft:
69th BS (B-52G) 76505, 76514, 80166, 80235, 92569

92nd Bomb Wing
Base: Fairchild AFB, Washington
Squadrons and aircraft:
325th BS (B-52G) 76475, 76499, 80168, 80227, 92593

93rd Bomb Wing
Base: Castle AFB, California
Squadrons and aircraft:
328th BS/4017th CCTS (B-52G) 76472, 76515, 80159, 80214, 92571

96th Bomb Wing
Base: Dyess AFB, Texas
Squadrons and aircraft:
337th BS (B-52H) recently relinquished its B-52s to become first B-1B unit

97th Bomb Wing
Base: Blytheville AFB, Arkansas
Squadrons and aircraft:
340th BS (B-52G) 76485, 76518, 80185, 80252, 92577

319th Bomb Wing
Base: Grand Forks AFB, North Dakota
Squadrons and aircraft:
46th BS (B-52G) no examples known

320th Bomb Wing
Base: Mather AFB, California
Squadrons and aircraft:
441st BS (B-52G) 76477, 76510, 80189, 80213, 92573

379th Bomb Wing
Base: Wurtsmith AFB, Michigan
Squadrons and aircraft:
524th BS (B-52G) 76474, 80165, 80217, 80244, 92589

410th Bomb Wing
Base: K.I. Sawyer AFB, Michigan
Squadrons and aircraft:
644th BS (B-52H) 00009, 00037, 00045, 10001, 10040

416th Bomb Wing
Base: Griffiss AFB, New York
Squadrons and aircraft:
668th BS (B-52G) 76487, 76501, 80160, 80231, 92602

Other Operators

43rd Strategic Wing
Base: Andersen AB, Guam
Squadrons and aircraft:
60th BS (B-52H) no examples known

NASA Dryden
Base: Edwards AFB, California
Aircraft: (NB-52B) 20008

Air Force Flight Test Center, 6512th Test Squadron
Base: Edwards AFB, California
Aircraft: (B-52G) 80245

Boeing B-52 recognition points
B-52 recognition points

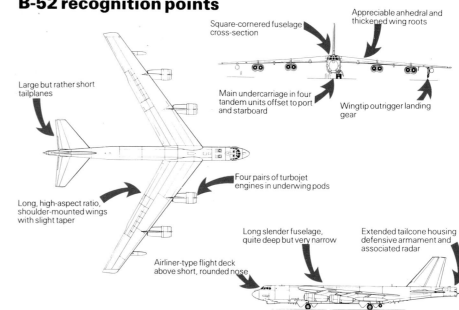

Square-cornered fuselage cross-section

Appreciable anhedral and thickened wing roots

Large but rather short tailplanes

Main undercarriage in four tandem units offset to port and starboard

Wingtip outrigger landing gear

Long, high-aspect ratio, shoulder-mounted wings with slight taper

Four pairs of turbojet engines in underwing pods

Airliner-type flight deck above short, rounded nose

Long slender fuselage, quite deep but very narrow

Extended tailcone housing defensive armament and associated radar

Specification:

Boeing B-52H Stratofortress

Wings
Span	56.39 m	(185 ft 0
Area	371.60 m²	(4,000.0

Fuselage and tail unit
Length overall	49.04 m	(160 ft 10
Height overall	12.40 m	(40 ft 8 ir
Tailplane span	16.95 m	(55 ft 7.5

Landing gear
Wheelbase	15.32 m	(50 ft 3 ir
Wheel track, over outer wheels	3.88 m	(12 ft 8.7

Weight
Maximum take-off exceeds	221353 kg	(488,000
Maximum internal fuel	135821 kg	(299,434
Maximum external fuel	4134 kg	(9,114 lb

The immense size of the B-52 makes it difficult to confuse with any other Western warplane. The size and swept-wi design show a similarity to the large Soviet bombers, the Myasishchev M-4 'Bison' and Tupolev Tu-142 'Bear'. The latter features turboprop engines mounted in slim nacelle whereas the 'Bison' has its engines buried in the wing ro Most B-52 confusion arises from the Boeing family of airliners (and, to some extent, the Douglas DC-8). The Boeing 707 and KC-135 are smaller but have a similar slim fuselage, whereas the much larger Boeing 747 features a wide fuselage. In plan view, the B-52 has much larger win and tailplane areas in relation to the fuselage than do the airliners.

Boeing B-52 variants

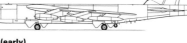

B-52A to B-52F
The early variants of the B-52 all featured tall vertical tail surfaces and a manned gun turret in the tail; J57 engines were standard throughout these versions. All have now been retired from USAF service, having seen much service throughout the Vietnam war. Illustrated is a B-52D, the most common early variant.

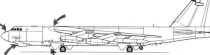

B-52G (early)
The B-52G introduced a number of improvements. The most notable of these were an integral tank, 'wet' wing housing an enormously increased fuel capacity, and a short vertical tail. The gunner was moved from his tail turret to sit in the cockpit alongside the electronic warfare officer, aiming the four 50-cal guns by radar. The version was used widely in Vietnam.

B-52G (contemporary)
The B-52 fleet has undergone many improvement programmes over the years. Current B-52Gs have a greatly increased ECM capability, which has resulted in the addition of more aerials and chaff dispensers. The change in role from high-level to low-level bombing resulted in the Electro-optical Visual Sensor (EVS) fit, with characteristic blisters for the Low-light Level TV (LLLTV) and Forward-looking Infra-red (FLIR) sensors under the chin. More ECM aerials are also housed on the side and front of the nose, and a further blister is now being incorporated on the side of the fin. Cruise-missile carrying B-52Gs have a distinctive wing root fairing for visual identification by the Soviets.

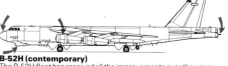

B-52H (early)
The B-52H introduced turbofans with far better fuel economy; both improvements resulted in a corresponding increase in range. The four rear guns are replaced by a six-barrel 20-mm Vulcan rotary cannon, with greater rate of fire. This is controlled from the cockpit.

B-52H (contemporary)
The B-52H fleet has received all the improvements over the years, including the EVS fit. Those due to be converted for cruise-missile carriage will have an internal rotary launcher as well as the G-model's wing pylon attachments.

Boeing B-52G Stratofortress cutaway drawing key

1 Nose radome
2 ALT-28 ECM antenna
3 Electronic countermeasures (ECM) equipment bay
4 Front pressure bulkhead
5 Electronic cooling air intake
6 Bombing radar
7 Low-light television scanner turret (EVS system), infra-red on starboard side
8 Television camera unit
9 ALQ-117 radar warning antenna
10 Underfloor control runs
11 Control column
12 Rudder pedals
13 Windscreen wipers
14 Instrument panel shroud
15 Windscreen panels
16 Cockpit eyebrow windows
17 Cockpit roof escape/ejection hatches
18 Co-pilot's ejection seat
19 Drogue chute container
20 Pilot's ejection seat
21 Flight deck floor level
22 Navigator's instrument console
23 Ventral escape/ejection hatch, port and starboard
24 Radar navigator's downward ejection seat, navigator to starboard
25 Access ladder and hatch to flight deck
26 EWO instructor's folding seat
27 Electronics equipment rack
28 In-flight refuelling receptacle, open
29 Refuelling delivery line
30 Electronic warfare officer's (EWO) ejection seat
31 Rear crew members escape/ejection hatches
32 EWO's instrument panel
33 Gunner's remote control panel
34 Gunner's ejection seat
35 Navigation instructor's folding seat
36 Radio and electronics r
37 Ventral entry hatch and ladder
38 Lower deck rear press bulkhead
39 ECM aerials
40 ECM equipment bay
41 Cooling air ducting
42 Upper deck rear press bulkhead
43 Water injection tank, capacity 1,200 US gal (4 litres)
44 Fuselage upper longer
45 Astro navigation anten
46 Tank access hatches
47 Leading edge 'strakele fitted to identify cruise missile carriers
48 Forward fuselage fuel
49 Air conditioning plant
50 Forward starboard mai undercarriage bogie
51 Landing lamp
52 Forward port main undercarriage bogie
53 Torque scissor links
54 Steering jacks
55 Main undercarriage do
56 Main undercarriage leg strut
57 Wing front spar/fuselag main undercarriage attachment frame

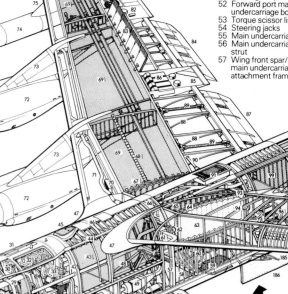

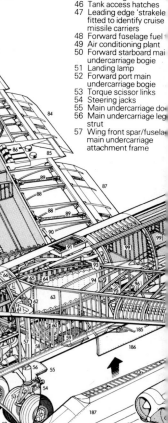

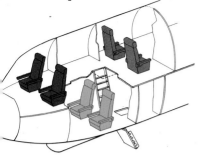

e: The B-52 crew is divided into three teams. In the rd cabin, the flight crew (blue) of pilot (port) and co-(starboard) handle the flying of the aircraft. Behind facing backwards, sit the defensive team (red), rising gunner (port) and electronic warfare officer board). On the lower deck, facing forward, sit the sive team (green), consisting of the navigator board) and the radar navigator/bombardier (port).

t: The 'office' of the B-52 is dominated by the eight ns of engine dials and the huge bunch of throttle les. On each side of the engine instruments are the two ns for the EV system (forward-looking infra-red and low level TV). Basic flight instruments are duplicated on the aircraft commander's (left) and co-pilot's (right) The co-pilot has most of the communications controls s side, whilst the secondary flight instruments are on the s side. On the left-hand side of the throttle bank is the elevator trim wheel.

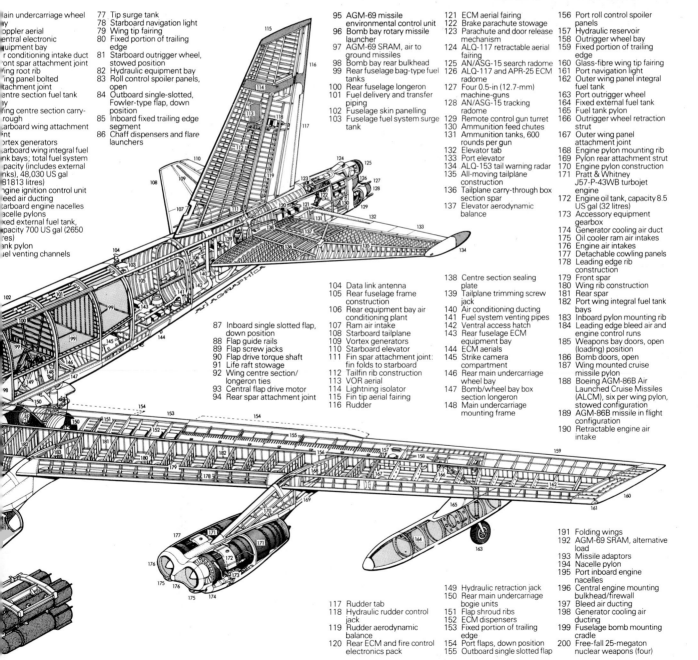

ain undercarriage wheel
y
oppler aerial
entral electronic
quipment bay
r conditioning intake duct
ront spar attachment joint
ing root rib
ing panel bolted
tachment joint
entre section fuel tank
ay
ing centre section carry-
rough
tarboard wing attachment
nt
ortex generators
tarboard wing integral fuel
nk bays; total fuel system
pacity (includes external
nks), 48,030 US gal
81813 litres)
ngine ignition control unit
eed air ducting
tarboard engine nacelles
acelle pylons
xed external fuel tank,
pacity 700 US gal (2650
res)
nk pylon
uel venting channels

77 Tip surge tank
78 Starboard navigation light
79 Wing tip fairing
80 Fixed portion of trailing edge
81 Starboard outrigger wheel, stowed position
82 Hydraulic equipment bay
83 Roll control spoiler panels, open
84 Outboard single-slotted, Fowler-type flap, down position
85 Inboard fixed trailing edge segment
86 Chaff dispensers and flare launchers

87 Inboard single slotted flap, down position
88 Flap guide rails
89 Flap screw jacks
90 Flap drive torque shaft
91 Life raft stowage
92 Wing centre section/longeron ties
93 Central flap drive motor
94 Rear spar attachment joint
95 AGM-69 missile environmental control unit
96 Bomb bay rotary missile launcher
97 AGM-69 SRAM, air to ground missiles
98 Bomb bay rear bulkhead
99 Rear fuselage bag-type fuel tanks
100 Rear fuselage longeron
101 Fuel delivery and transfer piping
102 Fuselage skin panelling
103 Fuselage fuel system surge tank
104 Data link antenna
105 Rear fuselage frame construction
106 Rear equipment bay air conditioning plant
107 Ram air intake
108 Starboard tailplane
109 Vortex generators
110 Starboard elevator
111 Fin spar attachment joint: fin folds to starboard
112 Tailfin rib construction
113 VOR aerial
114 Lightning isolator
115 Fin tip aerial fairing
116 Rudder
117 Rudder tab
118 Hydraulic rudder control jack
119 Rudder aerodynamic balance
120 Rear ECM and fire control electronics pack

121 ECM aerial fairing
122 Brake parachute stowage
123 Parachute and door release mechanism
124 ALQ-117 retractable aerial fairing
125 AN/ASG-15 search radome
126 ALQ-117 and APR-25 ECM radome
127 Four 0.5-in (12.7-mm) machine-guns
128 AN/ASG-15 tracking radome
129 Remote control gun turret
130 Ammunition feed chutes
131 Ammunition tanks, 600 rounds per gun
132 Elevator tab
133 Port elevator
134 ALQ-153 tail warning radar
135 All-moving tailplane construction
136 Tailplane carry-through box section spar
137 Elevator aerodynamic balance
138 Centre section sealing plate
139 Tailplane trimming screw jack
140 Air conditioning ducting
141 Fuel system venting pipes
142 Ventral access hatch
143 Rear fuselage ECM equipment bay
144 ECM aerials
145 Strike camera compartment
146 Rear main undercarriage wheel bay
147 Bomb/wheel bay box section longeron
148 Main undercarriage mounting frame
149 Hydraulic retraction jack
150 Rear main undercarriage bogie units
151 Flap shroud ribs
152 ECM dispensers
153 Fixed portion of trailing edge
154 Port flaps, down position
155 Outboard single slotted flap

156 Port roll control spoiler panels
157 Hydraulic reservoir
158 Outrigger wheel bay
159 Fixed portion of trailing edge
160 Glass-fibre wing tip fairing
161 Port navigation light
162 Outer wing panel integral fuel tank
163 Port outrigger wheel
164 Fixed external fuel tank
165 Fuel tank pylon
166 Outrigger wheel retraction strut
167 Outer wing panel attachment joint
168 Engine pylon mounting rib
169 Pylon rear attachment strut
170 Engine pylon construction
171 Pratt & Whitney J57-P-43WB turbojet engine
172 Engine oil tank, capacity 8.5 US gal (32 litres)
173 Accessory equipment gearbox
174 Generator cooling air duct
175 Oil cooler ram air intakes
176 Engine air intakes
177 Detachable cowling panels
178 Leading edge rib construction
179 Front spar
180 Wing rib construction
181 Rear spar
182 Port wing integral fuel tank bays
183 Inboard pylon mounting rib
184 Leading edge bleed air and engine control runs
185 Weapons bay doors, open (loading) position
186 Bomb doors, open
187 Wing mounted cruise missile pylon
188 Boeing AGM-86B Air Launched Cruise Missiles (ALCM), six per wing pylon, stowed configuration
189 AGM-86B missile in flight configuration
190 Retractable engine air intake
191 Folding wings
192 AGM-69 SRAM, alternative load
193 Missile adaptors
194 Nacelle pylon
195 Port inboard engine nacelles
196 Central engine mounting bulkhead/firewall
197 Bleed air ducting
198 Generator cooling air ducting
199 Fuselage bomb mounting cradle
200 Free-fall 25-megaton nuclear weapons (four)

Boeing B-52 warload

B-52Gs are configured to carry six AGM-86 air-launched cruise missiles on each pylon, with other weaponry, usually the SRAM, carried internally.

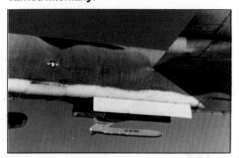

Cruise missiles will be carried on rotary launchers in the weapons bay of the B-52H. Eight rounds will be carried. This ALCM is seen falling from a test aircraft, just prior to the wings unfolding.

Maritime support
(B-52G)

■ 4×12.7-mm (0.5-in) remotely operated machine-guns with ASG-15 fire-control system
12×AGM-84 Harpoon anti-shipping missiles on underwing pylons

Those B-52Gs not modified to CMC configuration are being converted to replace the B-52D in the maritime support role, with the ability to carry out anti-shipping search and strike missions over a wide operational radius in the sea-control role. The sea control B-52G is supported by 'Outlaw Shark' Boeing E-3 AWACS platforms, which provide OTH (over the horizon) targeting. Maritime B-52s can also be used in the minelaying role.

Cruise missile carrier (B-52G and B-52H)

■ 4×12.7-mm (0.5-in) remotely operated machine-guns with ASG-15 fire-control system (B-52G) or
1×20-mm T171 cannon (B-52H)
8×Boeing AGM-69 SRAM short-range attack missiles on rotary launcher in the bomb bay
12×AGM-86 air-launched cruise missiles on inboard underwing pylons

Full-scale development of the B-52 as a cruise missile carrier began in 1978, and 99 B-52Gs plus 96 B-52Hs are being modified to carry 12 AGM-86s externally with SRAMs and other weapons internally. The B-52Hs will later be modified to carry 8×AGM-86s internally on a rotary launcher. Cruise missile carrying B-52Gs are fitted with distinctive wing root fairings in accordance with the SALT 2 agreement.

Defence suppression
(B-52G and B-52H)

■ 4×12.7-mm (0.5-in) remotely controlled machine-guns with ASG-15 fire-control system (B-52G), or
1×20-mm T171 cannon with Mod ASG-15 fire-control system (B-52H)
8×AGM-69 SRAM air-to-surface missiles on internally-carried rotary launcher
12×AGM-69 SRAM air-to-surface missiles on wing pylons

In this mission SRAM supersonic attack missiles, whose short-range designation belies their actual range (in excess of 161 km/100 miles), are individually targeted on known hostile defence complexes such as airfields, major radar sites and surface-to-air missile complexes.

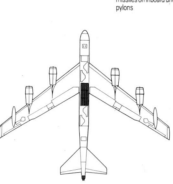

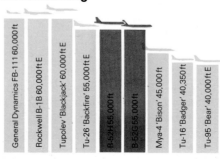

Freefall nuclear bombing
(B-52G and B-52H)

■ 4×12.7-mm (0.5-in) remotely operated machine-guns with ASG-15 fire-control system
8×B28 or B43, or
12×B61 or B83 bombs carried internally

This freefall nuclear payload can be combined with SRAM defence-suppression missiles on the wing pylons, and can be carried by the B-52G and B-52H models over the maximum mission radius of the two variants.

Freefall conventional bombing
(B-52H modified)

■ 1×20-mm T171 cannon with Mod ASG-15 fire-control system
84×Mk 82 500-lb (227-kg) GP iron bombs carried internally, and
24×Mk 82 500-lb (227-kg) GP iron bombs carried on underwing Multiple Ejector Racks (MERs)

The conventional limit for a B-52G in the same role is 12701 kg (28,000 lb), all carried internally.

Performance

Maximum speed above 36,090 ft (11000 m)
517 kts — Mach 0.90 or 958 km/h (595 mph)

Cruising speed above 36,090 ft (11000 m)
442 kts — Mach 0.77 819 km/h (509 mph)

Penetration speed at low altitude
between 352 kts 652 km/h (405 mph)
and 365 kts 676 km/h (420 mph)

Service ceiling — 55,000 ft (16764 m)

Range with maximum fuel but no inflight refuelling — 16093 km (10,000 miles)

Service ceiling

- General Dynamics FB-111 60,000 ft
- Rockwell B-1B 60,000 ft E
- Tupolev 'Blackjack' 60,000 ft E
- Tu-26 'Backfire' 55,000 ft E
- B-52H 55,000 ft
- B-52G 55,000 ft
- Mya-4 'Bison' 45,000 ft
- Tu-16 'Badger' 40,350 ft
- Tu-95 'Bear' 40,000 ft

Unfuelled range

- 16093 km B-52H
- 14600 km E Tupolev 'Blackjack'
- 12550 km Tu-95 'Bear'
- 12070 km B-52G
- 12000 km Rockwell B-1B
- 9650 km E Tu-26 'Backfire'
- 8000 km Mya-4 'Bison'
- 4800 km Tu-16 'Badger'
- 4707 km General Dynamics FB-111

Speed at high altitude

- Mach 2.5 General Dynamics FB-111
- Mach 2.1 E Tupolev 'Blackjack'
- Mach 1.92 Tu-26 'Backfire'
- Mach 1.25 Rockwell B-1B
- 538 kt Mya-4 'Bison'
- 535 kt Tu-16 'Badger'
- 516 kt B-52H
- 516 kt B-52G
- 500 kt Tu-95 'Bear'

Speed at sea level

- General Dynamics FB-111 Mach 1.2
- Tu-26 'Backfire' Mach 0.9
- Rockwell B-1B 521 kt
- Tu-95 'Bear' 450 kt E
- B-52H 365 kt
- B-52G 365 kt

Weapons load

- 50,000 lb E B-52H
- 50,000 lb E B-52G
- 48,000 lb Rockwell B-1B
- 45,000 lb E Tu-95 'Bear'
- 36,000 lb E Tupolev 'Blackjack'
- 30,000 lb Mya-4 'Bison'
- 30,000 lb FB-111
- 26,450 lb Tu-26 'Backfire'
- 19,800 lb Tu-16 'Badger'

The GRUMMAN
A-6 INTRUDER

Grumman Intruder: Mauling Mariner

While not an aircraft of true beauty, the effectiveness of the Grumman Intruder in operation cannot be doubted. Capable of carrying a vast array of weapons and delivering a knock-out punch, and with a dazzling variety of avionics, the A-6 is second to none in naval attack.

Conceived during the mid to late 1950s in response to a US Navy requirement for a new jet-powered medium attack aircraft capable of operating with equal facility by both day and night and with the ability to deliver nuclear weaponry, the Grumman A-6 Intruder made its maiden flight in prototype form as long ago as April 1960. The Intruder is still being built in modest numbers, and what the type lacks in aesthetic appeal it more than makes up in operational ability and, with yet another improved variant now in the pipeline, it seems certain that it will eventually set a record for production longevity.

Capable of carrying up to 8165 kg (18,000 lb) of ordnance on five external store stations beneath the wing and fuselage, the Intruder has a sophisticated package of radar and computer technology which permits the type to operate virtually 'blind' at low level and to deliver a variety of weapons with near-pinpoint accuracy in virtually all types of weather conditions.

Conventional 'iron' bombs obviously form part of the A-6E's armoury, but the latest examples are also fully capable of operating with the latest generation of 'smart' weapons, whilst the Harpoon air-to-surface anti-ship missile may also be carried and it is planned to add the HARM to the A-6E's already impressive weapons complement. A measure of self-defence capability is provided by the AIM-9 Sidewinder and, as already noted, the Intruder is equally capable of operating with nuclear weapons.

In the years which have passed since it first joined the fleet in February 1963, the basic airframe has changed little and, externally, today's Intruder looks much the same as those that were delivered to the Navy and Marine Corps during the 1960s. If one takes a look under the skin, however, the picture is very different, for the A-6 has demonstrated a remarkable ability to accommodate newer and more sophisticated items of electronic wizardry, and it is this flexibility which has been a primary factor in permitting the Intruder to remain a key element of the Navy's carrier borne sea-going forces.

In service

At the time the Intruder entered service it was without doubt one of the most sophisticated warplanes yet conceived, and its early years of service were not without problems since it took some considerable time for Navy technicians to become familiar with the complexities of Intruder subsystems and get 'fully up to speed' in the art of maintaining aircraft in peak operational condition. However, when everything was working as advertised, the initial A-6A model was infinitely superior to the

▲ Deck activity aboard a US Navy aircraft carrier as an A-6E is towed to its hold position among the other aircraft before flying begins. Normal complement aboard a carrier is 10 A-6Es alongside four KA-6D tankers within one squadron.

▼ Although a comparatively small strike force, the five US Marine Corps frontline A-6E units have a high degree of interoperation with their Navy counterparts, including carrier deployments for four of the squadrons.

Douglas A-1 Skyraider which it largely replaced, being able to operate independently in all but the most appalling weather conditions and with a most respectable weapons payload, as it demonstrated repeatedly during the course of the Vietnam War. Indeed, once the early trials and tribulations were overcome, ardent advocates of Grumman's attack aircraft seriously suggested that Navy aircraft carriers be loaded with nothing but Intruders,

Inflight-refuelling probe
All A-6 and EA-6B aircraft have a large fixed inflight-refuelling probe above the nose on the centreline. The usual tanker in carrier air wings is another A-6 version, the KA-6D

Radar
The main multimode radar is the Norden APQ-148, with separate main and tracking (and sometimes a synthetic-aperture) aerials

Wing root spoiler
This inboard section is a fixed sharp-edged flow spoiler to ensure that a stall starts here

ECM
This special section of leading edge incorporates main power transmitters for the ALQ-100 and 126B jammers

TRAM turret
The target recognition and attack multi-sensor is a power-driven turret incorporating a FLIR (forward-looking infra-red) sensor and a laser designator

Engine inlet
The plain engine inlets carry danger warnings and a small OAT (outside air temperature) probe

Crew access ladder
This section of inlet duct incorporates a fold-down crew boarding ladder

Wing leading edge
The entire outer leading edge is formed by powered slats, opened for high lift, and improving aircraft take-off performance

ECM
The wingtip spiral cavity aerials give warning of threats anywhere in the forward hemisphere

Navigation light
Each wingtip carries a steady, coloured navigation light; the left red and the right bluish-green

ECM
Various power amplifiers for the selected DECM (deception ECM) and radar jamming systems are housed in the wingtips

Formation lights
These lights assist formation flying at night or in poor visibility, in conjunction with the anti-collision lights

Speedbrakes
At each tip is a split surface, hydraulically opened up/down to form powerful airbrakes

TER weapons carriage
These are standard triple ejector racks; for some stores tandem TERs can be used

Seats
Pilot and navigator/WSO sit in Martin-Baker GRU5B or GRU7 ejection seats. The seats, which can recline for comfort on long missions, are not side-by-side: the nav/WSO is lower and further aft

Wing fences
Two large fences above each wing guide the airflow and keep it flowing axially back across the wing

Wing fold point
At this location the outer wings pivot upwards under hydraulic power, thus saving limited storage space aboard aircraft carriers

Spoilers
The entire wing inboard of the airbrakes is provided with hydraulically powered spoilers (called flaperons) used as the primary roll controls

Flaps
Except for the small outboard speedbrakes the entire trailing edge is occupied by slotted flaps depressed for high lift

CAPT E.W. WEISS

10

adding that these should be employed either singly or in small groups against targets in both North and South Vietnam when the weather conditions confined everybody to the ground. Clearly, when it came to putting bombs on target, the A-6 put up a first class performance.

Like most good wines and like many combat aircraft, the Grumman machine has also matured with the passing of the years. Operational experience and increasing familiarity with the special demands of all-weather attack have undoubtedly played a part in this but, as already noted, the type has been significantly updated in the intervening period, improvements in the avionics field playing a major role in helping Intruder to remain the Navy's sole carrierborne medium attack aircraft for the past 20 years. Like the Skyraider, the Intruder has also demonstrated the ability to take on new roles. It is probably fair to say that the Intruder is less versatile than the remarkable 'Spad', but this may well be a function of cost as much as anything else, since the A-6 has never come cheap.

Development

Thus far, production of new-build Intruders has been confined to just three basic models, namely the A-6A, the EA-6A and the A-6E, the combined total being only just over 660 aircraft. However, modification led to the appearance of three other variants, these being the A-6B, the A-6C and the KA-6D, only the last now being in service alongside the A-6E. In addition, of course, the basic Intruder airframe provided a good starting point for Grumman when the company began work on what appeared as the EA-6B Prowler electronic countermeasures platform.

Production of the original A-6A model eventually totalled 488 before Grumman turned to manufacturing the present A-6E version, but a derivative known as the EA-6A was acquired for operation by the US Marine Corps in the electronic countermeasures task and this too saw extensive combat action/ in Vietnam with VMCJ-1 from Da Nang. Some 27 EA-6As were produced between 1963 and 1969, 12 being obtained through modification of A-6As whilst the remainder were built as EA-6As. All are instantly identifiable by virtue of the bulbous fairing on the fin top which houses antennae, additional specialized electronic equipment (pod-mounted jammers and emitters) being carried beneath the fuselage and wing. Replaced in Marine Corps service by the rather more capable EA-6B during the latter half of the 1970s, the EA-6A is nevertheless still very active, most notably with electronic warfare squadrons of the Navy and Marine Corps Reserve, whilst about half-a-dozen operate with Navy squadron VAQ-33 in what might best be described as the ECM 'aggressor' role.

Modification of the A-6A for specialized roles did not cease with the EA-6A, however, for a further 19 aircraft were eventu-

ally brought to A-6B configuration in order to undertake the hazardous and demanding SAM-suppression role, there being three different variations on the A-6B theme, all employing anti-radiation missiles such as the Standard-ARM.

A dozen more A-6As metamorphosed to A-6C standard, being fitted with prominent ventral fairings containing FLIR and LLL-TV sensors as part of the TRIM package, and these also saw action in South East Asia, being employed to interdict the celebrated Ho Chi Minh Trail. Like the A-6A, these two sub-types no longer feature in the operational inventory.

Yet another model to arise from modification was the KA-6D tanker and this is still very active, each deployable Navy squadron usually going to sea with four KA-6Ds. Some 51 aircraft were initially converted to KA-6D configuration in 1970-1, attrition and the ageing process having resulted in further small batches of Intruder (a total of about 20) being fitted

▲ An A-6E TRAM Intruder closes towards the tanker aircraft, with fuel transferred via the prominent boom immediately ahead of the Intruder's windscreen. Underwing pylons can carry a wide variety of ordnance in addition to fuel tanks.

▼ An integral part of the modern Carrier Air Wing, the Intruder squadrons are assigned a variety of mission profiles including minelaying, close-support and precision attack. Here an A-6E TRAM awaits launch via the steam catapult.

with the hose-and-reel equipment required for the inflight-refuelling mission so as to 'top up' the number in fleet service.

The current production attack model is the A-6E, development of which began in the summer of 1967. This variant flew for the first time in prototype form during February 1970 and attained operational status with VA-85 aboard the USS *Forrestal* in September 1972. Introducing a dras-

tically revised avionics fit, the A-6E has been further enhanced since then, production switching to the so-called A-6E(TRAM) in the late 1970s, this incorporating a FLIR sensor and laser designator and spot seeker equipment in a prominent turret beneath the nose radome. The sensor package is, not surprisingly, wholly integrated with the Intruder to detect, identify and attack a variety of targets with much improved accuracy, employing either conventional or laser-guided weaponry, the latter being able to home on laser energy provided by the A-6E itself, by another aircraft fitted with a laser designator or by a ground-based operator. The Intruder can also illuminate targets for laser-guided ordnance carried and released by other aircraft.

Modification

In addition to having manufactured approximately 160 new-build examples of the A-6E to date, Grumman has also undertaken an extensive CILOP programme, no less than 240 A-6As, A-6Bs and A-6Cs being updated to A-6E standard during the course of the 1970s and many of these aircraft have since returned to Calverton for further retrospective modification to bring them up to the latest configuration. Such work looks set to continue in the immediate future since many of the Navy's sizeable fleet of Intruders will require re-winging as a result of fatigue-induced cracks. This last prompted the service briefly to ground the A-6 for inspection during the first half of 1985, Boeing subsequently being awarded a contract to supply new wings for the Intruder.

With regard to operational employment, the US Navy presently has a total of 13 deployable squadrons equipped with the Intruder, each of these normally going to sea with about 10 examples of the primary A-6E attack variant plus four KA-6D tankers. Normally, a Carrier Air Wing (CVW) includes one Intruder-equipped squadron in its line-up, although during 1983-4 CVW-3 embarked aboard the USS *John F. Kennedy* for a tour of duty in the Mediterranean and Indian Ocean with two A-6 squadrons, the second of these taking the place of the two Vought A-7E Corsair squadrons normally present.

In addition to the front-line deployable squadrons, the Navy also has two further units which do not operate at sea, these being assigned to the training role from the two major shore bases, one at Oceana, Virginia and the other at Whidbey Island, Washington.

Deployment

The Marine Corps also has a single training squadron (at Cherry Point, North Carolina) as well as five front-line all-weather attack squadrons, the latter being nominally based at El Toro, California or at Cherry Point, and equipped solely with the A-6E. In practice, however, it is usual for one Marine Intruder squadron to be for-

ward deployed to the 1st Marine Air Wing at Iwakuni in Japan, whilst it is not unknown for USMC A-6 units to join Navy CVWs on a temporary basis for tours of duty aboard aircraft-carriers, the most recent instance of this occurring in 1984 when VMA(AW)-533 operated as part of CVW-17 aboard the USS *Saratoga*. When embarked as part of a CVW, Marine units add the usual quartet of KA-6Ds to their complement, this being the only circumstance in which this service operates this model of the Intruder.

The only front-line squadron which now operates Intruders is VAQ-33 at Key West, Florida, this having a handful of EA-6As, a sub-type which also serves with three Reserve squadrons in the ECM role from the Naval Air Stations at Norfolk, Virginia and Whidbey Island, Washington.

Finally, small numbers of the A-6E also serve with a few test agencies. The most notable of these units is probably VX-5 at China Lake, California which serves as one element of the Navy's OTAEF, which is equipped with all front-line types engaged in the attack mission.

Looking to the future, the Navy and Marine Corps now seem set to acquire a

▲ Immediately recognizable by the large fairing atop the tail fin, the Grumman EA-6A tactical ECM derivative of the A-6 was designed to detect, classify and suppress enemy electronic activity in support of strike forces.

▼ An appropriate 'flexing of the muscles' post by a rugged workhorse of contemporary naval aviation. It is a fitting testimony to the excellence of design and mission effectiveness that there is no true successor in sight.

new version of the Intruder, the A-6F, at the start of the next decade. The go-ahead to proceed with development was given to Grumman in July 1984, and improvements earmarked for the new model included advanced high-resolution synthetic aperture radar, stand-off air-to-surface and beyond-visual-range air-to-air missile capability, new cockpit displays making extensive use of CRTs and digital avionics and, last but by no means least, new engines – a non-afterburning version of the General Electric F404 turbofan. First flight of the A-6F will take place in May 1987 and this, if successful, should lead to full production with effect from FY 1988, deliveries to fleet units following in 1990.

A-6 Intruder in service units and example aircraft

US Navy Atlantic Fleet

VA-34
Shore base: NAS Oceana, Virginia
Role: medium attack
Equipment: A-6E
Tail letters: 'AB'
Aircraft: 157002 '502', 161660 '503', 151548 '511'

VA-35
Shore base: NAS Oceana, Virginia
Role: medium attack
Equipment: A-6E and KA-6D
Tail letters: 'AJ'
Aircraft: (A-6E) 161668 '504', 159317 '511'; (KA-6D) 151789 '517'

VA-42
Shore base: NAS Oceana, Virginia
Role: Atlantic Fleet replacement training squadron
Equipment: A-6E
Tail letters: 'AD'
Aircraft: 149955 '500', 161086 '511', 155711 '522'

VA-55
Shore base: NAS Oceana, Virginia
Role: medium attack
Equipment: A-6E and KA-6D
Tail letters: 'AK'
Aircraft: (A-6E) 155718 '504', 161084 '512'; (KA-6D) 155583 '513'

VA-65
Shore base: NAS Oceana, Virginia
Role: medium attack
Equipment: A-6E and KA-6D
Tail letters: 'AG'
Aircraft: (A-6E) 151804 '500', 155589 '510'; (KA-6D) 149942 '514'

VA-75
Shore base: NAS Oceana, Virginia
Role: medium attack
Equipment: A-6E and KA-6D
Tail letters: 'AC'
Aircraft: (A-6E) 160431 '501', 158531 '504'; (KA-6D) 152934 '513'

VA-85
Shore base: NAS Oceana, Virginia
Role: medium attack
Equipment: A-6E
Tail letters: 'AC'
Aircraft: 159896 '540', 159900 '544', 161665 '552'

VA-176
Shore base: NAS Oceana, Virginia
Role: medium attack
Equipment: A-6E and KA-6D
Tail letters: 'AE'
Aircraft: (A-6E) 159178 '500', 157025 '511'; (KA-6D) 154133 '515'

The famous fin markings of VA-35 'Black Panthers' have seen many years of service on the Intruder, this aircraft displaying an interim low-visibility scheme with all markings appearing in black.

Pacific Fleet

VA-52
Shore base: NAS Whidbey Island, Washington
Role: medium attack
Equipment: A-6E and KA-6D
Tail letters: 'NL'
Aircraft: (A-6E) 161674 '502', 160423 '512'; (KA-6D) 151568 '513'

VA-95
Shore base: NAS Whidbey Island, Washington
Role: medium attack
Equipment: A-6E
Tail letters: 'NH'
Aircraft: 161090 '502', 161666 '504'

VA-115
Shore base: NAS Whidbey Island, Washington
Role: medium attack
Equipment: A-6E and KA-6D
Tail letters: 'NF'
Aircraft: (A-6E) 161109 '503', 159571 '510'; (KA-6D) 149485 '513'

VA-165
Shore base: NAS Whidbey Island, Washington
Role: medium attack
Equipment: A-6E and KA-6D
Tail letters: 'NG'
Aircraft: (A-6E) 159176 '50', 1604245 '510'; 151570 '516'

VA-128
Shore base: NAS Whidbey Island, Washington
Role: Pacific Fleet replacement training squadron
Equipment: A-6E
Tail letters: 'NJ'
Aircraft: 155673 '800', 159578 '808', 159310 '821'

VA-145
Shore base: NAS Whidbey Island, Washington
Role: medium attack
Equipment: A-6E and KA-6D
Tail letters: 'NE'
Aircraft: (A-6E) 154129 '501', 152954 '504'; (KA-6D) 152896 '515'

VA-196
Shore base: NAS Whidbey Island, Washington
Role: medium attack
Equipment: A-6E and KA-6D
Tail letters: 'NK'
Aircraft: (A-6E) 158528 '501', 152596 '506'; (KA-6D) 151787 '517'

Illustrating the role of the KA-6D tankers in each squadron are two aircraft from VA-165, a component of CVW-9 aboard USS Kitty Hawk.

US Marine Corps

VMA(AW)-121
Base: MCAS El Toro, California
Role: all-weather attack
Equipment: A-6E
Tail letters: 'VK'
Aircraft: 159902 '00', 155689 '07', 155669 '10'

VMA(AW)-224
Base: MCAS Cherry Point, North Carolina
Role: all-weather attack
Equipment: A-6E
Tail letters: 'WK'
Aircraft: 157010 '02', 159904 '07', 155681 '10'

VMA(AW)-242
Base: MCAS El Toro, California
Role: all-weather attack
Equipment: A-6E
Tail letters: 'DT'
Aircraft: 155716 '02', 155708 '05', 155621 '10'

VMA(AW)-332
Base: MCAS Cherry Point, North Carolina
Role: all-weather attack
Equipment: A-6E
Tail letters: 'EA'
Aircraft: 160429 '00', 152936 '11', 152923 '17'

VMA(AW)-533
Base: MCAS El Toro, California
Role: all-weather attack
Equipment: A-6E and KA-6D
Tail letters: 'AA'
Aircraft: (A-6E) 158051 '500', 159316 '505'; (KA-6D) 152913 '522'

VMAT(AW)-202
Base: MCAS Cherry Point, North Carolina
Role: Marine Corps A-6 training squadron
Equipment: A-6E
Tail letters: 'KC'
Aircraft: 155667 '00', 157013 '09', 155592 '14'

(Note: one USMC Intruder squadron is normally forward-deployed to Iwakuni, Japan on a rotational basis.)

Currently divided between California and North Carolina, the Marine Corps' A-6 force will remain in service probably into the 21st century.

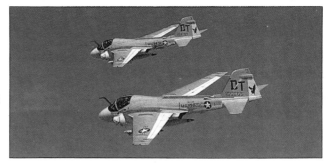

Other operators

VAQ-33
Base: NAS Key West, Florida
Role: naval ECM
Equipment: EA-6A
Tail letters: 'GD'
Aircraft: 147685 '109', 156990 '111'

VMAQ-4
Base: NAS Whidbey Island, Washington
Role: marine corps ECM
Equipment: EA-6A
Tail letters: 'RM'
Aircraft: 151600 '00', 149475 '02'

NWC
Base: NAS China Lake, California
Role: weapons development
Equipment: A-6E
Tail letters: none
Aircraft: 159569 '601', 151565 '603'

NATC/SATD
Base: NAS Patuxent River, Maryland
Role: evaluation and test
Equipment: A-6E
Tail letters: '7T'
Aircraft: 159567 '500', 154131 '502'

Below: Development and testing of new avionics, weaponry for the A-6 is an ongoing scheme. This Naval Weapons Centre aircraft is testing HARM (High-speed Anti-Radiation Missile).

VAQ-209
Base: NAS Norfolk, Virginia
Role: naval ECM
Equipment: EA-6A
Tail letters: 'AF'
Aircraft: 156987 '700', 151598 '704'

VX-5
Base: NAS China Lake, California
Role: evaluation and development
Equipment: A-6E
Tail letters: 'XE'
Aircraft: 155707 '20', 154124 '24'

VAQ-309
Base: NAS Whidbey Island, Washington
Role: naval ECM
Equipment: EA-6A
Tail letters: 'ND'
Aircraft: 156989 '612', 156991 '614'

PMTC
Base: NAS Point Mugu, California
Role: test and evaluation
Equipment: A-6E
Tail letters: none
Aircraft: 154162 '52', 159311 '54'

Grumman A-6 Intruder variants

A-6A: initial production model for service with USN/MC; total of 488 built but none remain in front-line service, the majority having been converted to KA-6D or A-6E configuration

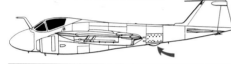

A-6B: specialized variant optimized for SAM-suppression duty, utilising Standard-ARM anti-radiation missile; total of 19 A-6As modified to A-6B configuration but no longer in service, survivors having been further updated to A-6E version

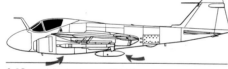

A-6C: specialized variant with TRIM (Trails, Roads Interdiction Multi-sensor) package comprising LLLTV and FLIR sensors in prominent ventral pod; total of 12 A-6As completed to this standard and employed to interdict Ho Chi Minh trail by night; survivors subsequently remanufactured to A-6E configuration

KA-6D: inflight-refuelling tanker version featuring hose and drogue assembly in space previously occupied by aft avionics 'bird-cage' on A-6A; about 70 KA-6Ds have been produced by conversion of A-6A model; presently in service with USN, each operational Intruder squadron normally deploying with four KA-6Ds as well as primary A-6E attack version

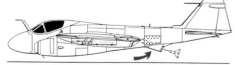

A-6E: current production and service version of Intruder, featuring updated avionics fit; entered operational inventory in 1971 and has been further updated since then, with latest configuration being the **A-6E(TRAM)** incorporating the Target Recognition Attack Multi-sensor package in nose-mounted steerable turret; has been produced in new-build and remanufactured form, older A-6As being brought to this standard as part of US Navy's CILOP (Conversion In Lieu Of Procurement) philosophy; presently equips 15 USN and six USMC medium attack squadrons
A-6F: variant for service with USN/MC from 1990 onwards; will be powered by non-afterburning version of General Electric F404 turbofan engine and will also feature new avionics and radar
EA-6A: specialized ECM variant to replace EF-10B Skyknight with USMC; produced in new-build and converted form, quantities completed being 15 and 12 respectively; replaced by EA-6B Prowler in front-line inventory but still equips one ECM 'Aggressor' unit as well as three second-line Reserve Force squadrons

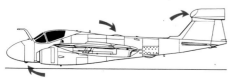

Grumman A-6E (Upgrade) Intruder cutaway drawing

1 Radome
2 Radome open position
3 Norden AN/APQ-148 multi-mode radar scanner
4 Scanner tracking mechanism
5 Intermediate frequency unit
6 ILS aerials
7 TRAM rotating turret mounting
8 Target Recognition and Attack Multisensor turret (TRAM)
9 Taxiing lamp
10 Deck approach lights
11 Nosewheel leg door
12 Hydraulic nosewheel steering unit
13 Catapult tow bar
14 Twin nosewheels, aft retracting
15 Retraction/breaker strut
16 Shock absorber leg strut
17 Torque scissor links
18 Radome latch
19 Hinged avionics equipment pallet, port and starboard
20 Radar scanner mounting
21 Radome hydraulic jack
22 Inflight-refuelling probe
23 ALQ-165 ECM system forward spiral antenna
24 Refuelling probe spotlight
25 Windscreen rain repellant air duct
26 Front pressure bulkhead
27 Nosewheel bay mounted pressure refuelling connection
28 Boundary layer splitter plate
29 Port engine air intake
30 Nosewheel bay electronic equipment racks
31 VHF aerial
32 UHF aerial
33 Intake duct framing
34 Temperature probe
35 Canopy emergency release handle
36 TACAN aerial
37 Folding boarding ladder
38 Integral boarding steps
39 Angle-of-attack transmitter
40 Boundary layer spill duct
41 Cockpit floor level
42 Rudder pedals
43 Engine throttle levers
44 Control column
45 Instrument panel shroud
46 Pilot's optical sighting unit/head-up display
47 Windscreen panels
48 Aft sliding cockpit canopy cover
49 Forward-Looking Infra-red (FLIR) viewing scope
50 Navigator/bombardier's Martin-Baker GRU-7 ejection seat
51 Ejection seat headrests
52 Seat reclining mechanism
53 Centre console
54 Pilot's GRU-7 ejection seat
55 Safety/parachute harness
56 Port side console panel
57 Electrical system equipment
58 Destruct initiator
59 Leading edge stall warning buffet strip
60 Engine intake compressor face
61 Engine bay venting air scoop
62 Accessory equipment gearbox
63 Pratt & Whitney J52-P-8B non-afterburning turbofan engine
64 Mainwheel door
65 Leading edge antenna fairing, port and starboard
66 ALQ-165 high, mid and low band ECM aerials
67 Mainwheel well
68 Hydraulic system reservoir
69 Cockpit rear pressure bulkhead
70 Cooling air spill louvres
71 Electrical equipment bay
72 Electronics and avionics equipment bay
73 Forward fuselage bag-type fuel tank
74 Weapons monitoring module
75 Sliding canopy rail
76 Canopy hydraulic jack
77 Canopy aft fairing
78 Starboard wing inboard integral fuel tank, total fuel capacity 8873-litres (1951 Imp gal/2344 US gal)
79 Fuel system piping
80 Inboard wing fence
81 Leading edge slat drive shaft
82 Slat guide rails
83 Slat screw jacks
84 AGM-65 Maverick air-to-surface missiles
85 Triple missile carrier/launcher
86 Starboard wing stores pylons
87 AIM-9P Sidewinder 'self defence' air-to-air missile

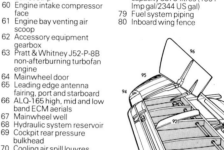

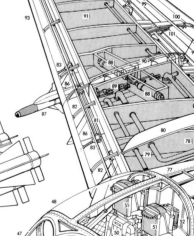

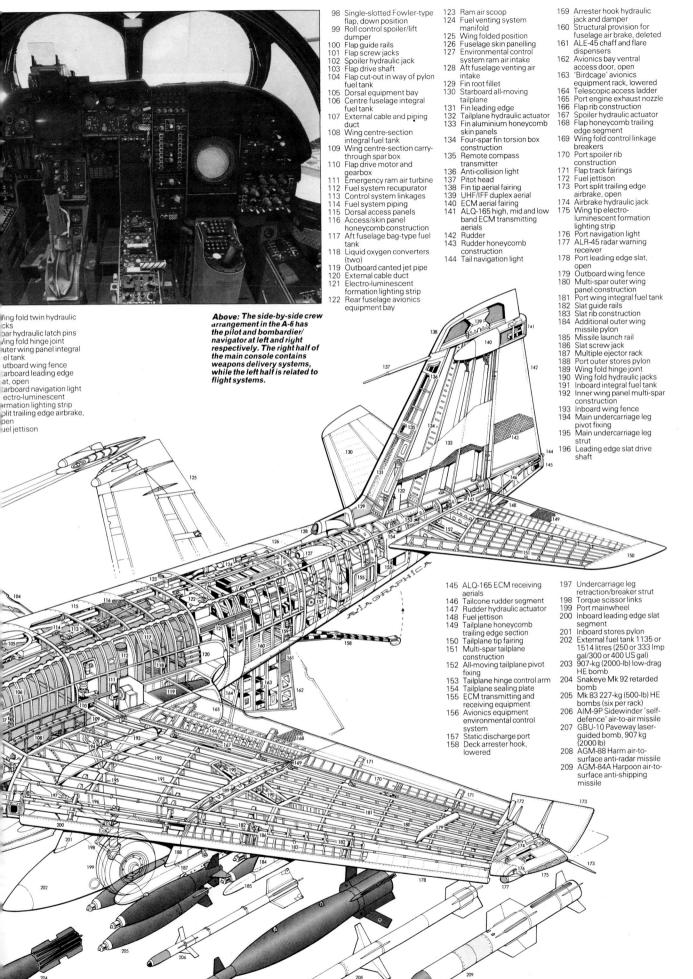

98 Single-slotted Fowler-type flap, down position
99 Roll control spoiler/lift dumper
100 Flap guide rails
101 Flap screw jacks
102 Spoiler hydraulic jack
103 Flap drive shaft
104 Flap cut-out in way of pylon fuel tank
105 Dorsal equipment bay
106 Centre fuselage integral fuel tank
107 External cable and piping duct
108 Wing centre-section integral fuel tank
109 Wing centre-section carry-through spar box
110 Flap drive motor and gearbox
111 Emergency ram air turbine
112 Fuel system recuperator
113 Control system linkages
114 Fuel system piping
115 Dorsal access panels
116 Access/skin panel honeycomb construction
117 Aft fuselage bag-type fuel tank
118 Liquid oxygen converters (two)
119 Outboard canted jet pipe
120 External cable duct
121 Electro-luminescent formation lighting strip
122 Rear fuselage avionics equipment bay

123 Ram air scoop
124 Fuel venting system manifold
125 Wing folded position
126 Fuselage skin panelling
127 Environmental control system ram air intake
128 Aft fuselage venting air intake
129 Fin root fillet
130 Starboard all-moving tailplane
131 Fin leading edge
132 Tailplane hydraulic actuator
133 Fin aluminium honeycomb skin panels
134 Four-spar fin torsion box construction
135 Remote compass transmitter
136 Anti-collision light
137 Pitot head
138 Fin tip aerial fairing
139 UHF/IFF duplex aerial
140 ECM aerial fairing
141 ALQ-165 high, mid and low band ECM transmitting aerials
142 Rudder
143 Rudder honeycomb construction
144 Tail navigation light

159 Arrester hook hydraulic jack and damper
160 Structural provision for fuselage air brake, deleted
161 ALE-45 chaff and flare dispensers
162 Avionics bay ventral access door, open
163 'Birdcage' avionics equipment rack, lowered
164 Telescopic access ladder
165 Port engine exhaust nozzle
166 Flap rib construction
167 Spoiler hydraulic actuator
168 Flap honeycomb trailing edge segment
169 Wing fold control linkage breakers
170 Port spoiler rib construction
171 Flap track fairings
172 Fuel jettison
173 Port split trailing edge airbrake, open
174 Airbrake hydraulic jack
175 Wing tip electro-luminescent formation lighting strip
176 Port navigation light
177 ALR-45 radar warning receiver
178 Port leading edge slat, open
179 Outboard wing fence
180 Multi-spar outer wing panel construction
181 Port wing integral fuel tank
182 Slat guide rails
183 Slat rib construction
184 Additional outer wing missile pylon
185 Missile launch rail
186 Slat screw jack
187 Multiple ejector rack
188 Port outer stores pylon
189 Wing fold hinge joint
190 Wing fold hydraulic jacks
191 Inboard integral fuel tank
192 Inner wing panel multi-spar construction
193 Inboard wing fence
194 Main undercarriage leg pivot fixing
195 Main undercarriage leg strut
196 Leading edge slat drive shaft

Above: The side-by-side crew arrangement in the A-6 has the pilot and bombardier/navigator at left and right respectively. The right half of the main console contains weapons delivery systems, while the left half is related to flight systems.

Wing fold twin hydraulic cks
ar hydraulic latch pins
ing fold hinge joint
uter wing panel integral el tank
utboard wing fence
arboard leading edge
at, open
arboard navigation light
ectro-luminescent
rmation lighting strip
plit trailing edge airbrake, pen
uel jettison

145 ALQ-165 ECM receiving aerials
146 Tailcone rudder segment
147 Rudder hydraulic actuator
148 Fuel jettison
149 Tailplane honeycomb trailing edge section
150 Tailplane tip fairing
151 Multi-spar tailplane construction
152 All-moving tailplane pivot fixing
153 Tailplane hinge control arm
154 Tailplane sealing plate
155 ECM transmitting and receiving equipment
156 Avionics equipment environmental control system
157 Static discharge port
158 Deck arrester hook, lowered

197 Undercarriage leg retraction/breaker strut
198 Torque scissor links
199 Port mainwheel
200 Inboard leading edge slat segment
201 Inboard stores pylon
202 External fuel tank 1135 or 1514 litres (250 or 333 Imp gal/300 or 400 US gal)
203 907-kg (2000-lb) low-drag HE bomb
204 Snakeye Mk 92 retarded bomb
205 Mk 83 227-kg (500-lb) HE bombs (six per rack)
206 AIM-9P Sidewinder 'self-defence' air-to-air missile
207 GBU-10 Paveway laser-guided bomb, 907 kg (2000 lb)
208 AGM-88 Harm air-to-surface anti-radar missile
209 AGM-84A Harpoon air-to-surface anti-shipping missile

Grumman A-6 Intruder warload

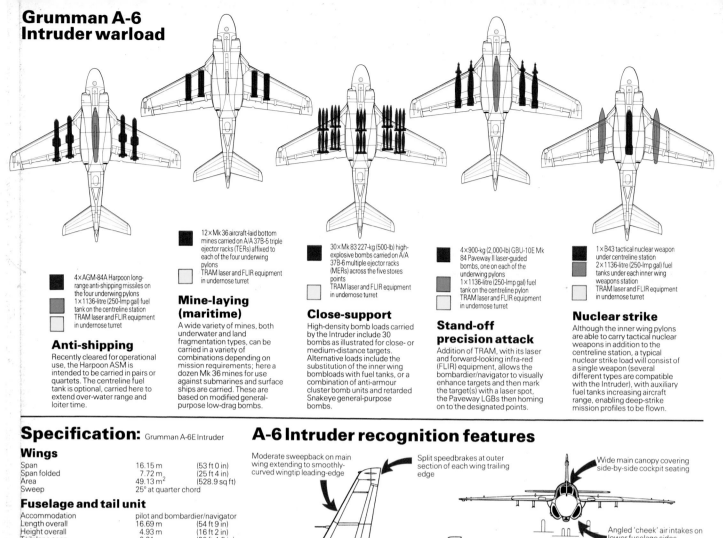

4 × AGM-84A Harpoon long-range anti-shipping missiles on the four underwing pylons
1 × 1136-litre (250-Imp gal) fuel tank on the centreline station
TRAM laser and FLIR equipment in undernose turret

Anti-shipping

Recently cleared for operational use, the Harpoon ASM is intended to be carried in pairs or quartets. The centreline fuel tank is optional, carried here to extend over-water range and loiter time.

12 × Mk 36 aircraft-laid bottom mines carried on A/A 37B-5 triple ejector racks (TERs) affixed to each of the four underwing pylons
TRAM laser and FLIR equipment in undernose turret

Mine-laying (maritime)

A wide variety of mines, both underwater and land fragmentation types, can be carried in a variety of combinations depending on mission requirements; here a dozen Mk 36 mines for use against submarines and surface ships are carried. These are based on modified general-purpose low-drag bombs.

30 × Mk 83 227-kg (500-lb) high-explosive bombs carried on A/A 37B-6 multiple ejector racks (MERs) across the five stores points
TRAM laser and FLIR equipment in undernose turret

Close-support

High-density bomb loads carried by the Intruder include 30 bombs as illustrated for close- or medium-distance targets. Alternative loads include the substitution of the inner wing bombloads with fuel tanks, or a combination of anti-armour cluster bomb units and retarded Snakeye general-purpose bombs.

4 × 900-kg (2,000-lb) GBU-10E Mk 84 Paveway II laser-guided bombs, one on each of the underwing pylons
1 × 1136-litre (250-Imp gal) fuel tank on the centreline pylon
TRAM laser and FLIR equipment in undernose turret

Stand-off precision attack

Addition of TRAM, with its laser and forward-looking infra-red (FLIR) equipment, allows the bombardier/navigator to visually enhance targets and then mark the target(s) with a laser spot, the Paveway LGBs then homing on to the designated points.

1 × B43 tactical nuclear weapon under centreline station
2 × 1136-litre (250-Imp gal) fuel tanks under each inner wing weapons station
TRAM laser and FLIR equipment in undernose turret

Nuclear strike

Although the inner wing pylons are able to carry tactical nuclear weapons in addition to the centreline station, a typical nuclear strike load will consist of a single weapon (several different types are compatible with the Intruder), with auxiliary fuel tanks increasing aircraft range, enabling deep-strike mission profiles to be flown.

Specification: Grumman A-6E Intruder

Wings

Span	16.15 m	(53 ft 0 in)
Span folded	7.72 m²	(25 ft 4 in)
Area	49.13 m²	(528.9 sq ft)
Sweep	25° at quarter chord	

Fuselage and tail unit

Accommodation	pilot and bombardier/navigator	
Length overall	16.69 m	(54 ft 9 in)
Height overall	4.93 m	(16 ft 2 in)
Tailplane span	6.21 m	(20 ft 4.5 in)

Landing gear

Retractable tricycle landing gear with single-wheel main units and twin-wheel nose unit

Wheel track	3.31 m	(10 ft 10.5 in)

Weights

Empty	12132 kg	(26,746 lb)
Maximum take-off for catapult launch	26580 kg	(58,600 lb)
Maximum take-off for field launch	27397 kg	(60,400 lb)
Maximum external load	8165 kg	(18,000 lb)
Maximum internal fuel	7230 kg	(15,939 lb)
Maximum external fuel	3638 kg	(8,020 lb)

Powerplant

Two Pratt & Whitney J52-P-8B turbojets

Static thrust, each	4218 kg	(9,300 lb)

A-6 Intruder recognition features

Moderate sweepback on main wing extending to smoothly-curved wingtip leading-edge

Split speedbrakes at outer section of each wing trailing edge

Wide main canopy covering side-by-side cockpit seating

Angled 'cheek' air intakes on lower fuselage sides

All-moving tailplane without separate elevators

Large surface area tailfin including electronic antenna in fairing immediately above rudder

Inflight-refuelling probe immediately ahead of windscreen

Large, almost bulbous nose radome

Undernose turret housing sensor equipment

Deep forward fuselage housing engines in lower portion

Performance:

Maximum speed at sea level	560 kts	1037 km/h (644 mph)
Service ceiling	42,400 ft	(12925 m)
Initial climb rate	7,620 ft	(2323 m) per minute
Maximum range with maximum military load	1627 km	(1,011 miles)
Take-off distance to clear 50-ft (15-m) obstacle	1390 m	(4,560 ft)

Weapons load

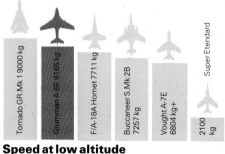

Tornado GR.Mk 1 9000 kg
Grumman A-6E 8165 kg
F/A-18A Hornet 7711 kg
Buccaneer S.Mk 2B 7257 kg
Vought A-7E 6804 kg+
Super Etendard 2100 kg

Service ceiling

Tornado 50,000ft+
F/A-18A Hornet 50,000ft+
Super Etendard 45,000ft
Grumman A-6E 42,000ft+
Vought A-7E 42,000ft E
Buccaneer S.Mk 2B 40,000ft+ E

Speed at high altitude

Tornado GR.Mk 1 Mach 2.2 'clean'
F/A-18A Hornet Mach 1.8+
Super Etendard Mach 1
Buccaneer S.Mk 2B Mach 0.92
Vought A-7E Mach 0.9
Grumman A-6E Mach 0.8

Speed at low altitude

Tornado GR.Mk 1 Mach 1.2
F/A-18A Hornet Mach 1
Super Etendard Mach 0.95
Vought A-7E Mach 0.9
Buccaneer S.Mk 2B Mach 0.85
Grumman A-6E Mach 0.85

Operational range (internal fuel)

Buccaneer S.Mk 2B 3700 km
Vought A-7E 2300 km
F/A-18A Hornet 2130 km
Grumman A-6E 1627 km
Super Etendard 1500 km
Tornado GR.Mk 1 1390 km

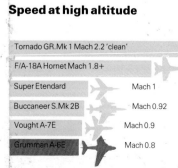

The VOUGHT A-7
CORSAIR II

A-7 Corsair II: Super SLUF

The Vought A-7 Corsair II may not win many aircraft beauty contests against the sleeker designs, but its most common nickname, 'Short Little Ugly Fella' (the polite version), hides the truth; it is short, fat – and deadly. Time and time again the A-7 has demonstrated its truly awesome accuracy in weapons delivery, answering its detractors with successful action against diverse targets around the world.

When a Vought design team under J. Russell Clark designed the A-7 Corsair II in 1964-5, its intent was to use existing technology to produce a strike aircraft with superb navigation and weapons-delivery potential. It did not have to be supersonic, and it did not have to be pretty. Men were dying in Vietnam and the A-7, the only warplane to be introduced to that conflict as a result of lessons learned in it, would be able to carry a heavy load, loiter in the target area, and cope effectively with MiGs, missiles and anti-aircraft fire. Clark's team produced the aircraft and John W. Konrad made the first flight of the A-7A Corsair II (152580) at Dallas on 27 September 1965. Initial carrier qualification tests were carried out aboard USS *America* (CVA-66) on 9 November 1966 by Commander Fred Treber in the seventh A-7A airframe.

The A-7 did not seem particularly impressive at first, and no one could have predicted that the aircraft would remain a principal weapon in the American arsenal two full decades later. In 1986 the A-7 remains the principal light attack aircraft aboard 10 of the US Navy's 13 carriers, and is operated by 14 Air National Guard

squadrons. No one could have predicted, either, that the A-7 would become well-loved, yet the aeroplane has won respect and affection from all who fly it. Its advocates, without denying that the Corsair II got off to a poor start, argue that plans to replace it are premature.

In regular Air Force service, the A-7D was far better liked by pilots and maintenance people than is generally acknowledged. Men who had flown the mighty 'Thud' (Republic F-105) or supersonic 'Hun' (North American F-100) were at first appalled to transfer into a stubby, blunt-nosed, subsonic warplane which even Vought's programme director, Sol Love, admitted was ugly. Their feelings changed dramatically when they discovered that they could fly a strike mission knowing something no strike pilots had ever known before: their exact latitude and longitude on Earth, precisely to the foot. Pinpoint navigation and ordnance delivery is accepted as 'state of the art' today, the Panavia Tornado being one aircraft with this capability, but the A-7D and its Navy counterpart, the A-7E, were first to have it. The A-7D's superb NWDS (Navigation

and Weapons Delivery System) put its 9072-kg (20,000-lb) bombload squarely on target. The A-7D also had the right gun in the General Electric M61A1 Vulcan cannon with 1,032 rounds, and the right engine in the 6464-kg (14,250-lb) thrust Allison TF41-A-1 turbofan, a development of the Rolls-Royce Spey. Virtually the same features were introduced on the naval A-7E.

By the time Air Force A-7Ds reached South East Asia with the 354th TFW at Korat in October 1972, the aircraft was

▲ *Doing what the Corsair II does best, a US Navy TA-7C two-seat trainer drops a pair of general-purpose bombs. The current computerized navigation and weapons delivery system is the AN/ASN-91(V), which has maintained the aircraft's excellent record of accuracy in the delivery of a wide range of ordnance.*

▼ *Capable of worldwide deployment to bolster US forces, the 14 Air National Guard A-7 squadrons are equipped with the A-7D single-seater. This highly potent attack force is set to receive a further boost to its combat capabilities as two squadrons convert to FLIR-equipped aircraft for night-time missions.*

widely understood to be capable of carrying out a precision attack, carrying a formidable load and delivering that load squarely on target. The A-7D was surprisingly trouble-free, designed for walk-around maintenance without ladders or stanchions, and could be quickly 'turned around' to fly one mission after another.

Air force A-7Ds of the 354th TFW took over the 'Sandy' mission, replacing the Douglas A-1E Skyraider as the strike escort for the Sikorsky HH-53C helicopter in behind-the-lines SAR missions. At the same time a second A-7D unit, the 3rd TFS under Lieutenant Colonel Edward R. ('Moose') Skowron, also flew SAR missions in South East Asia. Navy A-7Es and Air Force A-7Ds served in their more traditional role as bombers during the 'Eleven-Day War' of 18/29 December 1972, called 'Linebacker II', when a massive air campaign finally forced North Vietnam to agree to a settlement. In May 1975, when Cambodian forces seized the American merchant vessel SS *Mayaguez*, Air Force A-7Ds flew missions in support of the crew's rescue.

Development

Other active-duty A-7D units were the 355th TFW at Davis-Monthan AFB, Arizona and the 23rd TFW at England AFB, Louisiana. In October 1977 the latter wing crossed the Atlantic to snap up all the awards available to it at the Royal Air Force Tactical Bombing Competition at Lossiemouth, Scotland, outperforming new RAF SEPECAT Jaguars. Also in 1977, the USAF began retrofitting its A-7D fleet with Automated Maneuvering Flaps to improve the aircraft's performance at high angles of attack and to counter its tendency to 'depart' when nose-high. At about the same time, the TISL or 'Pave Penny' system was added to a chin protuberance

and slaved to the A-7D's HUD, improving target acquisition and bombing accuracy. Attempts to sell an A-7G variant to Switzerland foundered, and President Carter's qualms on arms transfer killed a later plan to make 100 A-7s available to Pakistan. Portugal purchased two batches of A-7P aircraft, which were rebuilds of existing A-7A/B airframes retaining the early engine and gun, while Greece purchased 60 A-7H single-seaters and five TA-7H two-seat aircraft.

It is no exaggeration to say that almost everyone with first-hand knowledge feels that the USAF's decision to replace the A-7D with the Fairchild A-10A Thunderbolt II was ill-conceived and premature. Today, the A-7D has virtually left regular Air Force service to serve only in the Air National Guard (ANG, or the Guard) but it retains a vital place.

The A-7D was initially delivered to the Air National Guard in October 1975 when the 188th TFS at Kirtland AFB, New Mexico began flying the type. Among 14 ANG squadrons which now fly the tough, stubby attack craft, only Kirtland's and the Sandston, Virginia-based 149th TFS do not

▲ *The folded outer wing panels betray the Navy origins of this, one of 50 refurbished A-7A Corsair IIs supplied to Portugal as the A-7P. The aircraft have A-7E-standard avionics and are powered by the TF30-P-408 turbofan. Visible below the cockpit is the prominent inflight-refuelling probe, suitable for probe/drogue connections.*

▼ *Though it is now giving way to the F/A-18 Hornet, the Corsair II force of the US Navy is still a considerable one, with the type due to see active duty through the early 1990s. Recent events over Libya have seen the A-7E proving itself once again to be an excellent weapons platform, with successful attacks on enemy radar sites.*

employ the two-letter tailcodes, called tactical unit identifiers, found on most USAF tactical aircraft. For the Guard's A-7D fleet, a superb safety record with the type has kept the scattered Air National Guard squadrons at a low attrition rate, more than able to meet their contingency commitments to NATO, Korea and the Central Command.

The US Navy's A-7E variant (again, sharing with the A-7D improved gun, navigation/delivery system and engine) en-

tered combat on 26 May 1970 when LTJG Dave Lichtermann of the 'Blue Diamonds' of VA-146 flew a strike from USS *America* (CVA-66) against a Viet Cong gun emplacement. The A-7A, A-7B and A-7E fought through the end of the South East Asia war, the A-7B remaining in Reserve service into the mid-1980s. Current A-7Es are being improved with retrofit of FLIR, giving them significantly improved night- and bad-weather attack capability. Current plans are that of the two squadrons of A-7Es aboard each carrier which operates them, one will have FLIR. The A-7E has also seen combat recently, in Grenada and Lebanon.

Combat

In 1983, while US Marines were on the ground in Beirut and the USA hoped that their presence would bolster the government of President Amin Gemayel, A-7Es from USS *Eisenhower* (CVN-69) came under fire on several occasions and a decision was made to permit the A-7E aviators to make their logbook entries in green ink, signifying combat. The squadrons were the 'Waldomen' of VA-66 and the 'Clinchers' of VA-12.

More action in Lebanon was to come. In fact, aboard USS *Independence* (CV-62), the 'Valions' of VA-15 under Commander Mike Korda and the 'Golden Warriors' of VA-86 under Commander Michael O'Brien were in the unique position of seeing action in two wars on a single carrier cruise. 'Indy' had set forth for a trans-Atlantic crossing when a change in orders diverted the carrier southward for Operation 'Urgent Fury', the October 1983 American invasion of the tiny nation of Grenada. Joining the other US forces committed to the seizure of the Caribbean nation, the A-7E squadrons flew round-the-clock strikes in a permissive environment of the kind rarely encountered any longer in modern warfare, with no elec-

tronic or missile threat. To quote Commander 2nd Fleet, US Navy, 'the A-7 provided the turning point, enabling [our] force to quickly gain the upper hand.'

Vietnam, Grenada, Lebanon: these may not mark the end of the A-7 Corsair II's combat role, for the aircraft will be with the US Navy until 1991 and with the ANG into the next century. The Navy's two-seat variant, the TA-7C (briefly known at one point as the YA-7H) performs a critical training role and is the subject of an ambitious programme begun in 1985 to convert the 49 surviving airframes from TF30 to TF41 turbofan engines. Six of these naval two-seaters were converted into EA-7L EW aircraft to serve with squadron VAQ-34 at NAS Miramar, California. A proposal for a supersonic version of the A-7, known as the Strikefighter or Corsair III and to be made by converting existing airframes, is now being actively promoted, but other types are likely to have a better chance of competing for budget dollars.

Training

The final variant of the SLUF, the two-seat A-7K, is the only variant which never served with the USAF but went directly to the Air National Guard. The first A-7K (73-1008) was a conversion of an existing A-7D, while a further 30 airframes in the A-7K series have been built. The 1,545th and last airframe in the A-7 series, an A-7K (81-77), was quietly delivered in September 1984, ending the production run of this important type. It is understood that two A-7K two-seaters are being provided to each Air Guard squadron which operates the A-7D, primarily for training although the A-7K is fully combat-capable.

▼ *Over 200 US Navy A-7Es have been upgraded to A-7E FLIR configuration to greatly improve night attack capabilities. The large underwing pod houses a FLIR gimballed sensor linked to a master-HUD in the cockpit. It is intended that Navy Carrier Air Wings will have one of the two Corsair II squadrons equipped with the A-7E FLIR model.*

▲ *An Air National Guard A-7K trainer displays one of the many weapons configurations the Corsair II can carry into battle. The Paveway II laser-guided bombs typify the 'smart' weapons which can be used accurately in conjunction with the Pave Penny seeker carried under the chin.*

A-7 Corsair II in service

United States Air Force

Following a distinguished front-line service career, the A-7 has all but disappeared, giving way to the Fairchild A-10A during the early 1980s. The remaining units which fly the A-7 are engaged in a variety of testing and training programmes, while various extant airframes can be found in use in the ground instruction role (designated GA-7D) at the Chanute, Lowry and Sheppard Technical Training Centers.

Tactical Air Command

Unit: 4450th Tactical Training Group
Base: Nellis AFB, Nevada
Tailcode letters: 'LV'
Example aircraft: (A-7D) 00941, 96202, 96225; (A-7K) 90469

Air Force Systems Command

Unit: 6512th Test Squadron/Air Force Flight Test Center
Base: Edwards AFB, California
Tailcode letters: 'ED'
Example aircraft: (A-7D) 14583, 96195, 96217

Air National Guard

Equipping a total of 14 ANG squadrons, the A-7 forms an important element within the Guard structure. Many of the aircraft were passed on from deactivated front-line units and serve alongside aircraft built specifically for the Guard. A variety of operational roles are assigned to the A-7 force, these including close air support for Army units defending the Panama Canal Zone. In the event of mobilization, the ANG A-7 force would be 'gained' by Tactical Air Command with around 300 aircraft available for action.

Note: TFS = Tactical Fighter Squadron; TFW = Tactical Fighter Wing; TFG = Tactical Fighter Group; TFTS = Tactical Fighter Training Squadron; TFTG = Tactical Fighter Training Group

107th TFS/127th TFW
Base: Selfridge ANGB, Mich.
Tailcode letters: 'MI'
Example aircraft: (A-7D) 00991, 10352, 41738

107th TFS/127th TFW

112th TFS/180th TFG
Base: Toledo Airport, Ohio
Tailcode letters: 'OH'
Example aircraft: (A-7D) 00992, 41747; (A-7K) 10672

120th TFS/140th TFW
Base: Buckley ANGB, Co.
Tailcode letters: 'CO'
Example aircraft: (A-7D) 00986, 01001, 20231

120th TFS/140th TFW

124th TFS/132nd TFW
Base: Des Moines A/P, Iowa
Tailcode letters: 'IA'
Example aircraft: (A-7D) 50402, 96203; (A-7K) 10077

124th RFS/132nd TFW

125th TFS/138th TFG
Base: Tulsa Airport, Ok.
Tailcode letters: 'OK'
Example aircraft: (A-7D) 31014, 41751; (A-7K) 00295

146th TFS/112th TFG
Base: Pittsburgh A/P, Penn.
Tailcode letters: 'PT'
Example aircraft: (A-7D) 01017, 41739; (A-7K) 10074

149th TFS/192nd TFG
Base: Richmond Airport, Va.
Tailcode letters: none carried
Example aircraft: (A-7D) 00979, 31015; (A-7K) 00288

152nd TFTS/162nd TFTG
Base: Tucson Airport, Az.
Tailcode letters: 'AZ'
Example aircraft: (A-7D) 41741, 50408; (A-7K) 90462

162nd TFS/178th TFG
Base: Springfield A/P, Oh.
Tailcode letters: 'OH'
Example aircraft: (A-7D) 10298, 31012, 96233

166th TFS/121st TFW
Base: Rickenbacker ANGB, Ohio
Tailcode letters: 'OH'
Example aircraft: (A-7D) 10294, 10303, 10314

174th TFS/185th TFG
Base: Sioux City A/P, Ia.
Tailcode letters: 'HA'
Example aircraft: (A-7D) 20173, 96210; (A-7K) 10073

175th TFS/114th TFG
Base: Sioux Falls A/P, SD.
Tailcode letters: 'SD'
Example aircraft: (A-7D) 01030, 20176; (A-7K) 00292

188th TFS/150th TFG
Base: Kirtland AFB, NM
Tailcode letters: none
Example aircraft: (A-7D) 10379, 20237, 20238

198th TFS/156th TFG
Base: Minoz Airport, PR
Tailcode letters: 'PR'
Example aircraft: (A-7D) 20224, 20245, 96226

United States Navy

For many years the standard equipment of the US Navy's light attack squadrons, the A-7 Corsair II has had its operational capabilities greatly enhanced through several updated models. Today, the Light Attack Wings have a force of A-7Es and A-7E FLIR (Forward-Looking Infra-Red) aircraft, with two squadrons being deployed within each carrier Air Wing. As with the majority of US Navy aircraft types, the A-7s are grouped together in two communities: Light Attack Wing Pacific at NAS Lemoore, California, for Pacific Fleet units, and Light Attack Wing One based at NAS Cecil Field, Florida, for the Atlantic Fleet units. Today the Corsair II is gradually giving way to the McDonnell Douglas F/A-18A Hornet in front-line service, though the venerable 'SLUF' is set to continue in use well into the 1990s.

VA-12, NAS Cecil Field, Florida
Carrier Air Wing: CVW-7
Carrier: USS Dwight D. Eisenhower (CVN-69)
Example aircraft: (A-7E) 157480/AG-402, 159264/AG-406, 158835/AG-414

VA-15, NAS Cecil Field, Florida
Carrier Air Wing: CVW-6
Carrier: USS Independence (CV-62)
Example aircraft: (A-7E) 159638/AE-300, 160879/AE-306, 158819/AE-312

VA-22, NAS Lemoore, California
Carrier Air Wing: CVW-11
Carrier: USS Enterprise (CVN-65)
Example aircraft: (A-7E) 158017/NH-301, 160726/NH-303, 156856/NH-320

VA-27, NAS Lemoore, California
Carrier Air Wing: CVW-15
Carrier: USS Carl Vinson (CVN-70)
Example aircraft: (A-7E) 159300/NL-400, 160858/NL-403, 156838/NL-414

VA-37, NAS Cecil Field, Florida
Carrier Air Wing: CVW-6
Carrier: USS Independence (CV-62)
Example aircraft: (A-7E) 159661/AE-305, 156829/AE-306, 156824/AE-307

VA-42, NAS Oceana, Virginia
Atlantic Fleet replacement training squadron
Example aircraft: (A-7E) 157479/AD-425

VA-46, NAS Cecil Field, Florida
Carrier Air Wing: CVW-1
Carrier: USS America (CV-66)
Example aircraft: (A-7E) 159974/AB-300, 160613/AB-302, 158004/AB-310

VA-56, NAF Atsugi, Japan
Carrier Air Wing: CVW-5
Carrier: USS Midway (CV-41)
Example aircraft: (A-7E) 160737/NF-402, 159658/NF-411, 158657/NF-413

VA-66, NAS Cecil Field, Florida
Carrier Air Wing: CVW-7
Carrier: USS Dwight D. Eisenhower (CVN-69)
Example aircraft: (A-7E) 157581/AG-300, 160736/AG-302, 158827/AG-311

VA-72, NAS Cecil Field, Florida
Carrier Air Wing: CVW-1
Carrier: USS America (CV-66)
Example aircraft: (A-7E) 160549/AB-401, 159996/AB-404, 157478/AB-413

VA-81, NAS Cecil Field, Florida
Carrier Air Wing: CVW-17
Carrier: USS Saratoga (CV-60)
Example aircraft: (A-7E) 157538/AA-402, 157510/AA-407, 156890/AA-417

VA-82, NAS Cecil Field, Florida
Carrier Air Wing: CVW-8
Carrier: USS Nimitz (CVN-68)
Example aircraft: (A-7E) 159986/AJ-301, 157472/AJ-303

VA-83, NAS Cecil Field, Florida
Carrier Air Wing: CVW-17
Carrier: USS Saratoga (CV-60)
Example aircraft: (A-7E) 160867/AA-304, 159269/AA-307, 160717/AA-310

VA-86, NAS Cecil Field, Florida
Carrier Air Wing: CVW-8
Carrier: USS Nimitz (CVN-68)
Example aircraft: (A-7E) 159289/AJ-404, 159652/AJ-406

VA-87, NAS Cecil Field, Florida
Carrier Air Wing: CVW-6
Carrier: USS Independence (CV-62)
Example aircraft: (A-7E) 160560/AE-400, 157570/AE-407, 159988/AE-412

VA-93, NAF Atsugi, Japan
Carrier Air Wing: CVW-5
Carrier: USS Midway (CV-41)
Example aircraft: (A-7E) 160544/NF-303, 159999/NF-306, 160542/NF-310

VA-94, NAS Lemoore, California
Carrier Air Wing: CVW-11
Carrier: USS Enterprise (CVN-65)
Example aircraft: (A-7E) 160870/NH-403, 159302/NH-412, 157501/NH-416

VA-97, NAS Lemoore, California
Carrier Air Wing: CVW-15
Carrier: USS Carl Vinson (CVN-70)
Example aircraft: (A-7E) 160733/NL-304, 158828/NL-311, 157508/NL-317

VA-105, MCAS Iwakuni, Japan
Example aircraft: (A-7E) 160877/AE-401

VA-122, NAS Lemoore, California
Pacific Fleet replacement training squadron
Example aircraft: (A-7E) 156836/NJ-233; (TA-7C) 156788/NJ-207, 156753/NJ-225

VA-146, NAS Lemoore, California
Carrier Air Wing: CVW-9
Carrier: USS Ranger (CV-61)
Example aircraft: (A-7E) 158674/NG-304, 160862/NG-306, 159676/NG-311

VA-147, NAS Lemoore, California
Carrier Air Wing: CVW-9
Carrier: USS Ranger (CV-61)
Example aircraft: (A-7E) 158012/NG-402, 158665/NG-405, 157435/NG-411

VA-174, NAS Cecil Field, Florida
Atlantic Fleet replacement training squadron
Example aircraft: (A-7E) 156869/AD-402, 156812/AD-407, 158836/AD-446

VA-192, NAS Lemoore, California
Carrier Air Wing: CVW-19
Carrier: ?
Example aircraft: (A-7E) 158011/NM-307, 159642/NM-310, 159293/NM-313

VA-195, NAS Lemoore, California
Carrier Air Wing: CVW-19
Carrier: ?
Example aircraft: (A-7E) 158003/NM-401, 156835/NM-406, 156889/NM-407

VAQ-34, NAS Miramar, California
Example aircraft: (EA-7L) 156741/GD-201, 156743/GD-202, 156757/GD-204

VA-72, NAS Cecil Field, Florida

VA-97, NAS Lemoore, California

VA-174, NAS Cecil Field, Florida

VA-195, NAS Lemoore, California

United States Naval Air Reserve Force

Forming an important strike element within the two Reserve Carrier Air Wings, the five Corsair II-equipped squadrons follow the standard Navy East and West Coast basing policy, though the units are not grouped together. The majority of operational flying is conducted from each squadron's land base though deployments aboard aircraft-carriers are conducted for carrier qualifications (CARQUALS). As with many Reserve units, the aircraft in service have been relegated from front-line duties, and consequently they are often early-model Corsair IIs. The standard model for several years has been the A-7B, but this is now being gradually replaced by the A-7E as examples become available from front-line squadrons re-equipping with the McDonnell Douglas F/A-18A Hornet.

VA-203, NAS Cecil Field, Florida
Carrier Air Wing: CVWR-20
Example aircraft: (A-7B) 154463/AF-314

VA-204, NAS New Orleans, Louisiana
Carrier Air Wing: CVWR-20
Example aircraft: (A-7B) 154406/AF-406, 154520/AF-410, 154433/AF-413

VA-205, NAS Atlanta, Georgia
Carrier Air Wing: CVWR-20
Example aircraft: (A-7E) 157491/AF-500, 156829/AF-501

VA-304, NAS Alameda, California
Carrier Air Wing: CVWR-30
Example aircraft: (A-7B) 154485/ND-401, 154456/ND-405, 154545/ND-415

VA-305, NAS Point Mugu, California
Carrier Air Wing: CVWR-30
Example aircraft: (A-7B) 154554/ND-500, 154416/ND-510, 154382/ND-514

United States Navy Miscellaneous Research, Test and Evaluation agencies

As a front-line US Navy aircraft, the Corsair II is naturally involved in a variety of programmes aiming to improve and enhance existing performance and associated equipment. The majority of the agencies listed are field centres assisting in the various aims encompassed by Naval Air Systems Command – the continued research and development, testing and evaluation of aircraft and systems. Examples include the Naval Air Development Center which is tasked with the advancement of technology to enhance current weapons systems capabilities, and the Naval Weapons Evaluation Facility which conducts research into weapons delivery methods for both conventional and nuclear ordnance.

VX-5, NAF China Lake, California
Example aircraft: (A-7E) 160616/XE-04, 160722/XE-05

Naval Air Development Center, NAF Warminster, Pennsylvania
Example aircraft: (NA-7E) 156802

Naval Air Engineering Center, NAS Lakehurst, New Jersey
Example aircraft: (A-7B) 154373

Naval Weapons Center, NAF China Lake, California
Example aircraft: (A-7E) 160857/708, 160710/710; (TA-7C) 156768/701

Naval Weapons Evaluation Facility, Kirtland AFB, New Mexico
Example aircraft: (A-7E) 156752/752

Pacific Missile Test Center, NAS Point Mugu, California
Example aircraft: (TA-7C) 154464/81, 156777/85

Strike Aircraft Test Directorate/Naval Air Test Center, NAS Patuxent River, Maryland
Example aircraft: (A-7E) 159296/7T-401, 156874/7T-405

Greece

The first export customer for the A-7 was the Helliniki Aeroporia (Hellenic Air Force), with an order for 60 single-seaters designated A-7H (H for Hellenic). The first aircraft was delivered in 1977, this order being followed by six TA-7H trainers delivered in 1980. From the original batches, 52 A-7Hs and five TA-7Hs remain in service, the aircraft serials being their original US Bureau of Aeronautics (BuNo.) numbers.

340 Mira/115 Ptérix
Base: Soudha Bay
Example aircraft: (A-7H) 159664, 159933; (TA-7H) 161219, 161221

345 Mira/115 Ptérix
Base: Soudha Bay
Example aircraft: (A-7H) 159663, 159917; (TA-7H) 161222

347 Mira/110 Ptérix
Base: Lárissa
Example aircraft: (A-7H) 159958, 159955

Hellenic Air Force

159929

Portugal

Acquisition of the A-7 Corsair II for use by the Força Aérea Portuguesa has been split into two main orders. The first was for 20 A-7P (P for Portugal) single-seaters, these being delivered in 1981-82. The follow-on order in 1983 covered a total of 24 A-7Ps and six TA-7P two-seat trainers. This second order is providing the aircraft for Esquadra 304, and deliveries are almost complete. A sole TA-7C was on loan for a time, this bearing the US Navy serial 154404. The A-7s are serialled 5501 to 5544, while the TA-7Ps are 5545 to 5550.

Escuadra 302
Base: Monte Real
Example aircraft: (A-7P) 5508, 5514; (TA-7P) 5545

Escuadra 304
Base: Monte Real
Example aircraft: (A-7P) 5527, 5539, 5544

Portuguese Air Force

5504

A-7 variants

A-7A: initial USN variant; TF30-P-6 engine; 199 built; conversions to A-7P, TA-7P and NA-7A; all US Navy variants have a refuelling probe on forward right fuselage which swings out and up to accommodate drogue from tanker aircraft; A-7A and A-7B models have external stirrup-type ladder steps for pilot; two 20-mm M nose cannon

A-7B: USN production variant; 196 built; TF30-P-6 engine; conversions to TA-7C and A-7P; navy-style refuelling probe; ladder steps; A-7A and A-7B retrofitted with fillet at rear of upper vertical tail housing ECM gear, also found on later models; two 20-mm Mk 12 nose cannon

A-7C: USN equivalent to A-7E but delivered with TF30 engine rather than TF41 intended for A-7E; one 20-mm M61A1 nose cannon with gun ports on port side of aircraft

TA-7C: USN two-seat trainer/combat aircraft; two-seat variant are distinguished by lengthened fuselage and accommodation second crew member; canopy hinges sideways instead of sliding back; 96 converted, of which 49 scheduled to receive TF41 engine

Vought A-7K Corsair II cutaway drawing key

1 Radome
2 Radar scanner dish
3 Radar tracking mechanism
4 Pitot tubes
5 Rain dispersal air ducts
6 AN/APQ-126(V) forward looking radar transmitter/receiver
7 Cooling air louvres
8 Engine air intake
9 ILS aerial
10 Forward radar warning antenna
11 'Pave Penny' detector unit
12 Intake duct framing
13 Boron carbide (HCF) cockpit armour panelling
14 Armoured front pressure bulkhead
15 Rudder pedals
16 Control column
17 Instrument panel shroud
18 AN/AVQ-7(V) head-up-display (HUD)
19 Windscreen panels
20 Cockpit canopy cover, hinged to starboard
21 Ejection seat canopy breakers
22 Face blind firing handle
23 Seat safety lever
24 Starboard side console panel
25 Pilot's Douglas Escapac 1-C2 ejection seat
26 Port side console panel
27 Engine throttle control
28 Boarding steps
29 Cannon muzzle blast trough
30 Retractable boarding ladder
31 Taxiing lamp
32 Nosing undercarriage shock absorber leg strut
33 Levered suspension axle beam
34 Twin nosewheels
35 Nosewheel doors
36 Cannon barrels
37 Rear seat boarding steps
38 Canopy emergency release
39 Angle of attack sensor
40 Rear seat control linkages
41 Rear instrument panel shroud
42 2nd pilot/instructor's ejection seat
43 Cockpit coaming
44 Rear throttle lever
45 Ammunition feed and link return chutes
46 M61A-1 Vulcan, 20-mm rotary cannon
47 Gun gas spill duct
48 Liquid oxygen container
49 Emergency hydraulic accumulator
50 Electronics system built-in test panel
51 Ventral doppler aerial
52 Rear radio and electronics equipment bay
53 Cooling air extractor fan
54 Forward fuselage fuel cells, total internal fuel capacity 5394 litres (1425 US gal)
55 Fuselage stores pylon, 227-kg (500-lb) capacity

Vought A-7 Corsair II

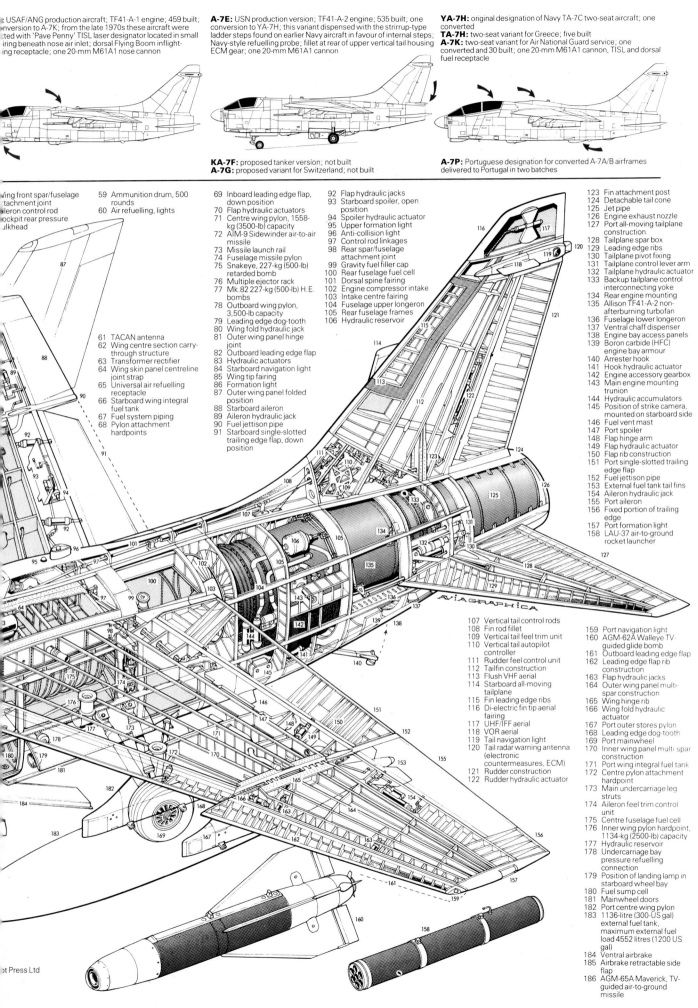

: USAF/ANG production aircraft; TF41-A-1 engine; 459 built; inversion to A-7K; from the late 1970s these aircraft were ted with 'Pave Penny' TISL laser designator located in small ring beneath nose air inlet; dorsal Flying Boom inflight-ing receptacle; one 20-mm M61A1 nose cannon

A-7E: USN production version; TF41-A-2 engine; 535 built; one conversion to YA-7H; this variant dispensed with the stirrup-type ladder steps found on earlier Navy aircraft in favour of the Navy-style refuelling probe; fillet at rear of upper vertical tail housing ECM gear; one 20-mm M61A1 cannon

YA-7H: original designation of Navy TA-7C two-seat aircraft; one converted
TA-7H: two-seat variant for Greece; five built
A-7K: two-seat variant for Air National Guard service; one converted and 30 built; one 20-mm M61A1 cannon, TISL and dorsal fuel receptacle

KA-7F: proposed tanker version; not built
A-7G: proposed variant for Switzerland; not built

A-7P: Portuguese designation for converted A-7A/B airframes delivered to Portugal in two batches

---

Wing front spar/fuselage attachment joint
ileron control rod
ockpit rear pressure ulkhead

59 Ammunition drum, 500 rounds
60 Air refuelling, lights

61 TACAN antenna
62 Wing centre section carry-through structure
63 Transformer rectifier
64 Wing skin panel centreline joint strap
65 Universal air refuelling receptacle
66 Starboard wing integral fuel tank
67 Fuel system piping
68 Pylon attachment hardpoints

69 Inboard leading edge flap, down position
70 Flap hydraulic actuators
71 Centre wing pylon, 1558-kg (3500-lb) capacity
72 AIM-9 Sidewinder air-to-air missile
73 Missile launch rail
74 Fuselage missile pylon
75 Snakeye, 227-kg (500-lb) retarded bomb
76 Multiple ejector rack
77 Mk.82 227-kg (500-lb) H.E. bombs
78 Outboard wing pylon, 3,500-lb capacity
79 Leading edge dog-tooth
80 Wing fold hydraulic jack
81 Outer wing panel hinge joint
82 Outboard leading edge flap
83 Hydraulic actuators
84 Starboard navigation light
85 Wing tip fairing
86 Formation light
87 Outer wing panel folded position
88 Starboard aileron
89 Aileron hydraulic jack
90 Fuel jettison pipe
91 Starboard single-slotted trailing edge flap, down position

92 Flap hydraulic jacks
93 Starboard spoiler, open position
94 Spoiler hydraulic actuator
95 Upper formation light
96 Anti-collision light
97 Control rod linkages
98 Rear spar/fuselage attachment joint
99 Gravity fuel filler cap
100 Rear fuselage fuel cell
101 Dorsal spine fairing
102 Engine compressor intake
103 Intake centre fairing
104 Fuselage upper longeron
105 Rear fuselage frames
106 Hydraulic reservoir

107 Vertical tail control rods
108 Fin rod fillet
109 Vertical tail feel trim unit
110 Vertical tail autopilot controller
111 Rudder feel control unit
112 Tailfin construction
113 Flush VHF aerial
114 Starboard all-moving tailplane
115 Fin leading edge ribs
116 Di-electric fin tip aerial fairing
117 UHF/IFF aerial
118 VOR aerial
119 Tail navigation light
120 Tail radar warning antenna (electronic countermeasures, ECM)
121 Rudder construction
122 Rudder hydraulic actuator

123 Fin attachment post
124 Detachable tail cone
125 Jet pipe
126 Engine exhaust nozzle
127 Port all-moving tailplane construction
128 Tailplane spar box
129 Leading edge ribs
130 Tailplane pivot fixing
131 Tailplane control lever arm
132 Tailplane hydraulic actuator
133 Backup tailplane control interconnecting yoke
134 Rear engine mounting
135 Allison TF41-A-2 non-afterburning turbofan
136 Fuselage lower longeron
137 Ventral chaff dispenser
138 Engine bay access panels
139 Boron carbide (HFC) engine bay armour
140 Arrester hook
141 Hook hydraulic actuator
142 Engine accessory gearbox
143 Main engine mounting trunion
144 Hydraulic accumulators
145 Position of strike camera, mounted on starboard side
146 Fuel vent mast
147 Port spoiler
148 Flap hinge arm
149 Flap hydraulic actuator
150 Flap rib construction
151 Port single-slotted trailing edge flap
152 Fuel jettison pipe
153 External fuel tank tail fins
154 Aileron hydraulic jack
155 Port aileron
156 Fixed portion of trailing edge
157 Port formation light
158 LAU-37 air-to-ground rocket launcher
159 Port navigation light
160 AGM-62A Walleye TV-guided glide bomb
161 Outboard leading edge flap
162 Leading edge flap rib construction
163 Flap hydraulic jacks
164 Outer wing panel multi-spar construction
165 Wing hinge rib
166 Wing fold hydraulic actuator
167 Port outer stores pylon
168 Leading edge dog-tooth
169 Port mainwheel
170 Inner wing panel multi-spar construction
171 Port wing integral fuel tank
172 Centre pylon attachment hardpoint
173 Main undercarriage leg struts
174 Aileron feel trim control unit
175 Centre fuselage fuel cell
176 Inner wing pylon hardpoint, 1134-kg (2500-lb) capacity
177 Hydraulic reservoir
178 Undercarriage bay pressure refuelling connection
179 Position of landing lamp in starboard wheel bay
180 Fuel sump cell
181 Mainwheel doors
182 Port centre wing pylon
183 1136-litre (300-US gal) external fuel tank, maximum external fuel load 4552 litres (1200 US gal)
184 Ventral airbrake
185 Airbrake retractable side flap
186 AGM-65A Maverick, TV-guided air-to-ground missile

ot Press Ltd

AVIAGRAPHICA

A-7 warload

A-7E USN adverse-weather flak-suppression

1×M61A1 Vulcan 20-mm cannon with 1,000 rounds in the port side of the nose
2×AIM-9L Sidewinder all-aspect IR-homing AAMs on the fuselage sides (stations 4 and 5)
12×Mk 20 Rockeye cluster bomb units on the wings (stations 1, 3, 6 and 8)
1×FLIR pod on the starboard pylon
1×Goodyear ALE-39 jammer on station 6

The A-7E can carry a great clutter of external payload, and the typical flak-suppression load illustrated here is but one example, in this instance optimized for squadrons flying FLIR-equipped aircraft and operating against relatively close-range targets with high-density defences. The ALE-39 jammer is mounted flush on the side of the bomb station.

A-7D ANG RESCAP

1×M61A1 20-mm cannon with 1,000 rounds in the port side of the nose
2×AIM-9L Sidewinder all-aspect IR-homing AAMs on the fuselage sides (stations 4 and 5)
6×Mk 20 Rockeye cluster bomb units on the wings (stations 6 and 8)
1×BLU-38 (Bomb Large Unit, carrying riot-nonpressant chemical under the port wing (station 1)
1×ALQ-1-19 ECM pod under the port wing (station 3)

The A-7D proved itself an able RESCAP (REScue Combat Air Patrol, or 'Sandy') aircraft in the Vietnam War, and such a mission could still be undertaken by ANG A-7Ds in support of Sikorsky HH-53 and HH-60 helicopters today. The modern battlefield poses severe problems for RESCAP missions, but the A-7D has long loiter time at useful radius.

A-7E USN SAM-suppression

1×M61A1 Vulcan 20-mm cannon with 1,000 rounds in the port side of the nose
2×AIM-9L Sidewinder all-aspect IR-homing AAMs on the fuselage sides (stations 4 and 5)
2×AGM-88A HARM anti-radiaiton missiles under the wings (stations 2 and 7)
2×Aero-D 300-US gal (1136-litre) drop tanks under the wings (stations 3 and 6)

Having proved itself against SA-2 'Fan Song' radars in South East Asia with loads of two or four AGM-45 Shrike or AGM-78A Standard ARM missiles, the A-7E is still a capable SAM-suppression platform for medium/long-range operations against moderately dense anti-air defences. Aircraft from non-FLIR squadrons use the latest HARM missile which continues to home on radars even after they have shut down.

A-7E USN BARCAP

1×M61A1 Vulcan 20-mm cannon with 1,000 rounds in the port side of the nose
2×AIM-9L Sidewinder all-aspect IR-homing AAMs on the fuselage sides (stations 4 and 5)
2×Aero-D 300-US gal (1136-litre) drop tanks under the wings (stations 3 and 6)

The BARCAP mission (BARCAP, protecting the parent carrier from air threat) is normally assigned to the Grumman F-14A Tomcat, but non-FLIR A-7Es can substitute for Tomcats if the carrier's catapults are 'down', the Corsair II being able to launch without such aid whereas the Tomcat cannot. The A-7E generally uses no external tanks, but the BARCAP mission is usually flown with two, and rarely four, external tanks. Such substitutions are possible only in good weather.

A-7D ANG 'smart' bombing

1×M61A1 Vulcan 20-mm cannon with 1,000 rounds in the port side of the nose
2×AIM-9P Sidewinder all-aspect IR-homing AAMs on the fuselage sides (stations 4 and 5)
2×Mk 84 'Paveway' 1,000-lb (454-kg) laser-guided or electro-optical 'smart' bombs on the inner underwing hardpoints (stations 4 and 6)

It is believed that many examples of the 'Paveway' family of 'smart' bombs are stockpiled at key locations for the use of Air National Guard A-7D aircraft deployable to Europe, the Middle East, South Korea and Panama in times of crisis. Used against targets designated by a forward air controller or ground troops, in conjunction with the 'Pave Penny' TISL, these weapons are effective against heavy targets such as bridges and buildings.

A-7D Heavy bombing mission

1×M61A-1 20-mm Vulcan cannon with 1,000 rounds of ammunition in the port forward fuselage
2×AIM-9L Sidewinder infra-red AAMs, one per fuselage side pylon
18×Snakeye retarded bombs on the outer two pylons per wing. The very outer pylons carry three Snakeyes each on TERs, while the middle pylons carry six Snakeyes each on MERs
2×Aero-D 1135-litre (300-US gal) external fuel tanks, one each on the very inner wing pylons
Chaff/flare dispenser in rear underfuselage
Strike camera in mid underfuselage

The A-7 is famed for its ability to carry a wide range of weaponry in large quantities. This configuration is typical for intensive attacks, the aircraft coming in over the targets at low level and at relatively slow speed, the use of retarded bombs thus allowing for a safe departure.

Specification: Vought A-7D Corsair II

Wings
Span, unfolded	11.81 m	(38 ft 9 in)
folded	7.24 m	(23 ft 9 in)
Area	34.84 m²	(375 sq ft)
Sweep at quarter-chord	35°	

Fuselage and tail unit
Accommodation	pilot only on a Douglas Escapac rocket-powered ejector seat	
Length overall	14.06 m	(46 ft 1.5 in)
Height overall	4.90 m	(16 ft 0.9 in)
Tailplane span	5.52 m	(18 ft 1.5 in)

Landing gear
Hydraulically retractable tricycle landing gear with single-wheel main units and twin-wheel nose unit
Wheel track	2.90 m	(9 ft 6 in)
Wheel base	4.83 m	(15 ft 10 in)

Weights
Empty	8988 kg	(19,915 lb)
Maximum take-off	19051 kg	(42,000 lb)
Maximum external load, nominal	9072 kg	(20,000 lb)
Maximum practical with maximum internal fuel	4309 kg	(9,500 lb)
Maximum practical with reduced internal fuel	6804+ kg	(15,000+ lb)
Internal fuel load	4202 kg	(9,263 lb)

A-7E FLIR Corsair II recognition features

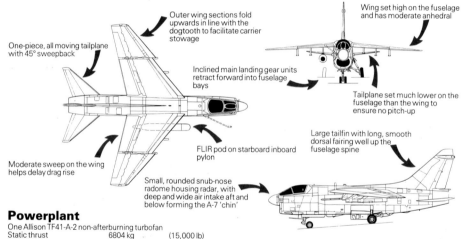

Outer wing sections fold upwards in line with the dogtooth to facilitate carrier stowage

One-piece, all moving tailplane with 45° sweepback

Inclined main landing gear units retract forward into fuselage bays

FLIR pod on starboard inboard pylon

Moderate sweep on the wing helps delay drag rise

Small, rounded snub-nose radome housing radar, with deep and wide air intake aft and below forming the A-7 'chin'

Wing set high on the fuselage and has moderate anhedral

Tailplane set much lower on the fuselage than the wing to ensure no pitch-up

Large tailfin with long, smooth dorsal fairing well up the fuselage spine

Powerplant
One Allison TF41-A-2 non-afterburning turbofan
Static thrust	6804 kg	(15,000 lb)

Performance:

Maximum speed at sea level	606 kts	1123 km/h	(698 mph)
Service ceiling		51,000 ft	(15545 m)
Combat radius at unspecified altitude with unspecified load		1432 km	(890 miles)
Ferry range with internal fuel		3671 km	(2,281 miles)
with internal/external fuel		4604 km	(2,861 miles)
Take-off run at maximum take-off weight		1524 m	(5,000 ft)

Weapon load

- Grumman A-6E 8165 kg
- F/A-18A Hornet 7711 kg
- Buccaneer S.Mk 2B 7257 kg
- Vought A-7E 6804 kg+
- 4500 kg A-4M Skyhawk
- 3629 kg Sea Harrier
- 3600 kg Yak-38 'Forger-A'
- 'Flogger-B' 2000 kg MiG-23

Service ceiling
- MiG-23 'Flogger-B' 61,000 ft
- Sea Harrier 50,000 ft+
- F/A-18A Hornet 50,000 ft
- A-4M Skyhawk 42,250 ft
- Grumman A-6E 42,000 ft+
- Vought A-7E 42,000 ft
- Buccaneer S.Mk 2B 40,000 ft+ E
- Yak-38 'Forger-A' 40,000 ft E

Speed at high altitude
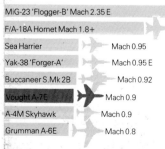
- MiG-23 'Flogger-B' Mach 2.35 E
- F/A-18A Hornet Mach 1.8+
- Sea Harrier Mach 0.95
- Yak-38 'Forger-A' Mach 0.95 E
- Buccaneer S.Mk 2B Mach 0.92
- Vought A-7E Mach 0.9
- A-4M Skyhawk Mach 0.9
- Grumman A-6E Mach 0.8

Speed at low altitude
- MiG-23 'Flogger-B' Mach 1.2 E
- F/A-18A Hornet Mach 1
- Vought A-7E Mach 0.9
- A-4M Skyhawk Mach 0.9
- Buccaneer S.Mk 2B Mach 0.85
- Grumman A-6E Mach 0.85
- Sea Harrier Mach 0.85
- Yak-38 'Forger-A' Mach 0.8 E

Operational range (internal fuel)
- Buccaneer S.Mk 2B 3700 km
- Vought A-7E 2300 km
- F/A-18A Hornet 2130 km
- Grumman A-6E 1627 km
- Sea Harrier 1500 km
- MiG-23 'Flogger-B' 1300 km
- Yak-38 'Forger-A' 1000 km E
- A-4M Skyhawk 547 km

The GENERAL DYNAMICS
F-111

F-111: Tripoli Troubleshooter

The history of the F-111 has been chequered to say the least, but through it all the 'Aardvark' has emerged as an extremely potent weapons platform with commendable mission versatility. Specializing in bad-weather operations, the F-111 has earned the respect it deserves.

Colloquially known as the 'Aardvark', the General Dynamics F-111 is assured of a place in aviation history by virtue of the fact that it was the first variable-geometry or 'swing-wing' aircraft to attain quantity production for any air arm in the world. Today, of course, VG is a commonplace feature of modern combat aircraft, types such as the Panavia Tornado, Grumman F-14 Tomcat and Mikoyan-Gurevich MiG-23/27 'Flogger' all using such wings to achieve satisfactory low-speed handling qualities, good range/payload characteristics and superior field performance without compromising capability at the other end of the speed scale.

The design and manufacturing teams for these later aircraft seem to have encountered few serious developments problems. But the same was most certainly not true of the F-111, General Dynamics running into great difficulty during the course of development. Even after the type attained operational service it continued to fall victim to a succession of problems, being grounded on several occasions as a result of accidents, whilst the fact that it was something of a political 'hot potato' added fuel to the fires of controversy which raged around the F-111 for several years. Like most innovative types, it took time to develop fixes, but once these had been incorporated the F-111 began to show definite signs of living up to its early promise. Indeed, it has now matured into a most effec-tive warplane and one which occupies a unique slot in the USAF inventory, for it is the only tactical fighter with that service possessing the ability to operate at low level by day or night in all conditions.

Development

Development of what eventually evolved into the F-111 can be traced back to July 1960, when Specific Operational Requirement No. 183 was issued by the USAF: in essence this called for a new fighter capable of fulfilling such disparate missions as air superiority, conventional and nuclear strike, and reconnaissance. One of the key aspects of SOR183 concerned the VG wing, the USAF being of the opinion that this represented the most suitable line of approach whilst also expressing the view that a turbofan engine would be worthy of consideration. Had the Air Force been allowed to proceed independently the F-111's subsequent history might have been less chequered, but the fact that the US Navy was also engaged in the preliminary stages of the search for a new fighter to replace the McDonnell Douglas F-4 Phantom prompted Secretary of Defense Robert McNamara to recommend that the two requirements be combined into a single programme known by the acronym TFX. Not surprisingly, this recommendation met considerable opposition within the two armed forces, but McNamara stuck to his guns, a new request for proposals

▲ Lurking in its lair, an F-111F sits in silence, awaiting its next demanding mission. A pioneer in getting down low in the worst of weather, locating the target and blasting it with a deadly array of weapons, the F-111 is a valuable warrior.

▼ This view shows an F-111E roaring off after a commendably short take-off run, clearly illustrating the full-span trailing edge, double-slotted flaps which help provide excellent low-speed handling as well as the all-moving slab-like stabilators.

being issued at the end of September 1961. In the event, nine responses were received during December of that year, the same month in which the designation F-111 was allocated.

Study of these submissions revealed that none was acceptable in its original form, but Boeing and General Dynamics were invited to refine their concepts further and the next few months witnessed considerable in-fighting as the services sought to reconcile their requirements in the face of McNamara's continuing intransigence. Eventually, after extensive redesign and despite Air Force recommendation of the Boeing contender, the General Dynamics submission emerged victorious, initial procurement of 23 development aircraft (18

USAF F-111As and five USN F-111Bs) being authorized. Manufacture of the USAF examples was entrusted to General Dynamics' Fort Worth factory, whilst the Navy aircraft was the responsibility primarily of Grumman at Bethpage. The two variants made their first flights on 21 December 1964 and 18 May 1965 from Carswell AFB and Calverton respectively.

Flight testing soon began to reveal problems, but the F-111A model did eventually attain operational status almost three years later when the first production examples began to join the 474th Tactical Fighter Wing at Cannon AFB, New Mexico in mid-October 1967, this unit moving to Nellis AFB, Nevada early in 1968.

In service
Like most types then in or about to enter USAF service, the F-111 was introduced to combat at the earliest possible date, 'Combat Lancer' being the code name assigned to the deployment of six F-111As from Nellis to Takhli, Thailand in March 1968. This initial exposure to the hazards of combat proved to be most inauspicious, two F111As being lost during the course of the first 55 missions against targets in North Vietnam. Replacements were despatched from Nellis, but before they arrived another F-111A was reported missing on 22 April, this effectively marking the end of the Aardvark's combat debut, although it was not until November that the surviving aircraft returned to the USA.

Several years elapsed before the F-111 returned to the rigours of war during the final stages of the Vietnam conflict. This time, two entire squadrons with a combined strength of about 50 aircraft were committed to action at the end of September 1972, and despite several losses the aircraft performed well, logging more than 3,000 missions before 'Linebacker II' prompted the North Vietnamese to return to the negotiating table in earnest.

Often operating alone or in small 'packages', the Aardvark repeatedly flew when

other types were grounded by poor weather, this period effectively signalling that the F-111 was at last maturing into a most effective warplane. Nevertheless, there were still many problems.

Although the Air Force eventually succeeded in getting the aircraft it had originally wanted, the same claim could not be made for the Navy which had never been particularly enthusiastic about the F-111B. Eventually, unacceptable weight growth coupled with a serious performance shortfall resulted in a production hold order being placed on the type during July 1986. By that time, the five development F111Bs has been joined in the flight test programme by the first two production examples, which eventually proved to be the last F-111Bs completed, funding for 30 more of the latter being blocked by the Senate and the House Armed Services Committee. This effectively killed the F-111B, but it was not until August 1968 that the F-111B programme was officially cancelled, a further blow to General Dynamics which was still recovering from the British decision to abandon plans to acquire 50 examples of a variant designated F-111K.

As far as the initial model was concerned, only 17 RDT&E F-111As were completed, the 18th and last example being employed as the FB-111A prototype. These initial aircraft were followed by 141 production machines, the last of which was delivered to the USAF at the end of August 1969. By then, the first example of the second production version (rather confus-

▲ Piercing the sky on a low-level, high-speed run, an F-111F illustrates the maximum wing sweepback of 72.5° – giving the aircraft an almost delta-wing appearance. The twin TF30 afterburning turbofans give the aircraft very impressive high speeds.

▼ One of the contemporary weapons configurations of the F-111F includes laser-guided bombs, air defence missiles, laser designating equipment and an ECM pod – a lethal combination which no enemy would want to receive, night or day.

ingly designated F-111E) had flown, this being the forerunner of 94 aircraft and it initially entered service with the 27th TFW at Cannon AFB, New Mexico in the autumn of the same year although most of these aircraft were subsequently deployed overseas with the 20th TFW at RAF Upper Heyford, England. There followed some 96 examples of the considerably more capable F-111D, which featured much revised avionics, this variant also making its debut with the 27th TFW. Production of tactical fighter models for the USAF terminated with 106 copies of the F-111F. Introducing a considerably more powerful version of the TF30 turbofan engine, the F-111F was first assigned to the 347th TFW at Mountain Home AFB, Idaho but, following a complex realignment exercise involving the F-111A, F111D and F-111F versions, this too is now also in Europe, equipping four squadrons at RAF Lakenheath.

The remaining major version developed for service with the USAF was the FB-111A, which presently equips two Stra-

tegic Air Command bomb wings in the north-eastern corner of the USA. Optimized for strategic rather than tactical missions, the FB-111A prototype (originally laid down as the 18th RDT&E F-111A) flew for the first time at the end of July 1967 and was followed into the air by the first production example just under a year later. Even then, it was not until mid-October 1969 that deliveries to SAC began, this command eventually receiving 75 of the 76 production specimens built, one being written off in a pre-delivery accident. Very much a hybrid, the FB-111A is essentially a marriage of the F-111D fuselage and inlets to the larger wing of the F-111B/C. It also features stronger landing gear and has a different variant of the TF30 engine.

Exports

On the export front, the F-111 also achieved modest success, Australia purchasing some two dozen examples of a version known as the F-111C in 1963. Intended to replace the veteran English Electric Canberra light bomber with Nos 1 and 6 Squadrons at RAAF Amberley, the Australians had to wait for no less than 10 years before deliveries began, the need for extensive modification playing no small part in bringing about a huge increase in unit cost to the embarrassment of all parties. So serious was the delay that, pending availability of the F-111C, the RAAF was eventually provided with 24 F-4E Phantoms on a loan basis, these operating until 1972-3 when the 23 survivors returned to the USA. Almost inevitably, attrition has claimed a few victims during the decade or so that the F-111Cs have been in service, but the RAAF's small fleet was topped up recently when a handful of surplus USAF F-111As were delivered.

Most of the surviving F-111Cs have been subjected to extensive rework, permitting them to remain in the operational inventory for the foreseeable future.

Another overseas customer was the Royal Air Force, which ordered 46 F-111Ks and four TF-111K proficiency trainers during 1966, these being intended to fill the gap left by the cancellation of BAC TSR-2. In the event, as noted elsewhere, they fared no better than their predecessor, being cancelled at the beginning of 1968 in one of the frequent bouts of defence spending reductions undertaken by the UK in the 1960s. However, two of these aircraft were virtually complete by that time and they were eventually turned over to the USAF which employed them for test purposes, reputedly in non-flying status. Subassemblies and components intended for later aircraft were also put to good use, being absorbed by the FB111A.

As far as the other models of the F-111 are concerned, these too look like being around for some considerable time to come. Although vast amounts of money have been invested in the acquistion of

▼ UK-based F-111Fs carry the Pave Tack pod, semi-recessed in the former weapons bay; this contains laser-designator and forward-looking infra-red. This turret was used to self-designate laser-guided bombs during the raid on Tripoli. Note the ALQ-131 ECM pod.

▲ Extensions to the fuselage length and wing span, strengthened landing gear, more powerful engines and increased fuel capacity distinguish the FB-111A bomber from the F-111. Two Bomb Wings use this model with nuclear weapons.

large numbers of new tactical aircraft in recent years, the USAF still has nothing in the inventory to match the F-111's all-weather capability, whilst its impressive payload and range characteristics will almost certainly mean that replacing the Aardvark will be no easy matter.

Several years after it last saw action in South East Asia, the F-111 was called upon for one of the more daring raids of recent years; F-111Fs of the 46th TFW spearheaded the US attack on Libya in April 1986, striking targets in Tripoli with laser-guided and retarded bombs.

F-111/FB-111 in service

United States Air Force, Tactical Air Command

The largest USAF Command in terms of numbers of aircraft operated has two Tactical Fighter Wings equipped with different models of the F-111, both forming part of the 12th Air Force. The 366th TFW gave up its F-model aircraft some 10 years ago to the 48th TFW within USAFE, while the 27th TFW remains the sole operator of the F-111D. The wings are each equipped with a training squadron for type conversion, while the 57th FWW is engaged in ongoing test programmes and training in operational tactics. Aircraft from this unit are detached to the two TFW bases for training with the front-line crews and their aircraft.

524th TFTS
523rd TFS
522nd TFS

27th Tactical Fighter Wing
Base: Cannon AFB, New Mexico
Squadrons and fin-tip colours: 522nd TFS (red), 523rd TFS (blue), 524th TFTS (yellow)
Tailcode letters: 'CC'
Equipment: F-111D
Example aircraft: 80131, 80142; 80114, 80128; 80148, 80172

366th Tactical Fighter Wing
Base: Mountain Home AFB, Idaho
Squadrons and fin-tip colours: 389th TFTS (yellow); 391st TFS (blue)
Tailcode letters: 'MO'
Equipment: F-111A
Example aircraft: 70046, 70067; 70095, 70108

391st TFS
389th TFTS

57th Fighter Weapons Wing
Base: McClellan AFB, California (detached from Nellis AFB, Nevada)
Squadrons and fin-tip colours: 431st TES (yellow/black checks)
Tailcode letters: 'WA'
Equipment: F-111F
Example aircraft: 02400, 40186

57th FWW

United States Air Forces in Europe

Examples of the F-111 have been based in the United Kingdom since late 1970 when the first F-111E arrived for the 20th TFW at RAF Upper Heyford. Today, this Wing along with the F-111F-equipped 48th TFW at RAF Lakenheath have some 160 F-111s, these providing the long-range attack contribution by the United States to NATO and the defence of Europe. Both Wings come under the command of the 3rd Air Force and form the core of NATO's air-launched nuclear deterrent in addition to the use of conventional weapons.

20th Tactical Fighter Wing
Base: RAF Upper Heyford, Oxfordshire
Squadrons and fin-tip colours: 55th TFS (blue/white checks); 77th TFS (red); 79th TFS (tiger stripes)
Tailcode letters: 'UH'
Equipment: F-111E
Example aircraft: 80006, 80036; 80017, 80077; 70123, 80050

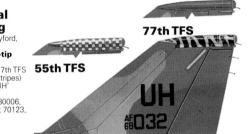

77th TFS
55th TFS
79th TFS

48th Tactical Fighter Wing
Base: RAF Lakenheath, Suffolk
Squadrons and fin-tip colours: 492nd TFS (blue); 493rd TFS (yellow); 494th TFS (red); 495th TFTS (green)
Tailcode letters: 'LN'
Equipment: F-111F
Example aircraft: 02370, 10886; 02383, 21452; 21443, 30707; 02392, 21446

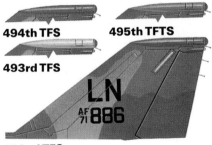

494th TFS
495th TFTS
493rd TFS
492nd TFS

United States Air Force, Strategic Air Command

The two Bomb Wings which operate the FB-111A are both part of the 8th Air Force, and are part of the SAC nuclear deterrent force. Some 60 examples of this strategic bomber are currently in service, though plans for any future development of the type seem highly unlikely now that the Rockwell B-1B is in service. Aircraft are hardly ever seen outside the continental USA, though obviously their operations in times of real tension would mean their use against overseas targets. The force is likely to receive a new colour scheme in the near future as part of the application of dark grey/dark green camouflage to the SAC bomber force.

380th Bomb Wing
Base: Plattsburgh AFB, New York
Squadrons: 528th BS, 529th BS and 4007th Combat Crew Training Squadron
Equipment: FB-111A
Example aircraft: 80240, 80246, 80255, 80257, 80284, 96507

509th Bomb Wing
Base: Pease AFB, New Hampshire
Squadrons: 393rd BS, 715th BS
Equipment: FB-111A
Example aircraft: 80246, 80255, 80269, 80273, 80276, 96503

Royal Australian Air Force

Following the protracted delays in getting the 24 F-111Cs into operational service, the two squadrons which are equipped with the aircraft have now been flying their machines for some 13 years, the aircraft proving highly effective and versatile over a number of mission profiles. The original F-111C force has suffered some attrition, but a handful of ex-USAF F-111As have been acquired to make good the losses. At least two, possibly four, aircraft have undergone conversion to RF-111C standard, with a special sensor pallet being fitted in the weapons bay to enable reconnaissance duties to be performed. Additionally, the F-111C serving with the ARDU is testing compatibility with the Harpoon air-to-surface missile, thus hopefully giving the F-111 force an anti-shipping capability.

No. 1 Squadron/No. 82 Strike Wing
Base: RAAF Amberley, Queensland
Equipment: F-111C
Example aircraft: A8-125, A8-132, A8-148

No. 6 Squadron/No. 82 Strike Wing
Base: RAAF Amberley, Queensland
Equipment: F-111A/C, RF-111C
Example aircraft: A8-109, A8-112, A8-128, A8-146, A8-126, A8-143

Aircraft Research & Development Unit
Base: RAAF Edinburgh, New South Wales
Equipment: F-111C
Example aircraft: A8-132

United States Air Force, Air Force Systems Command

The F-111 continues to serve with test and evaluation agencies as part of ongoing programmes to continue and enhance the aircraft and its associated systems and also to act as a test vehicle for technology which may be incorporated in future aircraft designs. Prominent among these programmes is the use of an F-111A fitted with a Mission Adaptive Wing (MAW). This joint USAF/NASA programme uses the F-111 as part of the broader Advanced Fighter Technology Integration project, with operations conducted from Edwards AFB. The ADTC in Florida uses the F-111 in its development and testing of non-nuclear weapons for tactical and strategic forces.

Control of F-111 overhaul and modernization is assigned to the Sacramento Air Logistics Center at McClellan AFB, California, this being part of Air Force Logistics Command. Aircraft from the various F-111 units pass through this Center on a regular basis, though much of the work for USAFE F-111s is carried out in the United Kingdom.

In addition to front-line operational service, the F-111 is engaged on various research projects. This machine is fitted with a mission-adaptive wing incorporating variable camber.

Air Force Flight Test Center
Base: Edwards AFB, California
Squadron and fin-tip colours: 6512nd TS (blue/white)
Tailcode letters: 'ED'
Equipment: F-111A/D/E
Example aircraft: 60053, 80085, 70115

Armament Development & Test Center
Base: Eglin AFB, Florida
Squadron and fin-tip colours: 3246th TW (red/white)
Tailcode letters: 'AD'
Equipment: F-111E
Example aircraft: 70118, 80058

This view of the F-111D forward instrument panel clearly shows the prominent terrain-following radar scope panel at top. At bottom right is the attack radar scope panel, its range being indicated.

44 UHF recovery
45 ECM antennas (port and starboard)
46 Forward fuselage fuel bay
47 Ground refuelling receptacle
48 Weapons bay
49 Module pitch flaps (port and starboard)
50 Aft flotation bag stowage
51 Aerial refuelling receptacle
52 Primary heat-exchanger (air-to-water)
53 Ram air inlet

54 Rate gyros
55 Rotating glove
56 Inlet variable spike
57 Port intake
58 Air brake/landing gear door
59 Auxiliary inlet blow-in doors
60 Rotating glove pivot point
61 Inlet vortex generators
62 Wing sweep pivot
63 Wing centre-box assembly
64 Wing sweep actuator
65 Wing sweep feedback
66 Control runs
67 Rotating glove drive set
68 Inboard pivot pylons (2)
69 Auxiliary drop tanks (600 US gal/2271 litres)
70 Outboard fixed pylon(s) subsonic/jettisonable
71 Slat drive set
72 Wing fuel tank (389.2 US gal/1473 litres)
73 Leading-edge slat
74 Starboard navigation light
75 Flap drive set
76 Outboard spoiler actuator
77 Starboard spoilers
78 Inboard spoiler actuator
79 Flaps
80 Wing swept position
81 Auxiliary flap
82 Auxiliary flap actuator
83 Nuclear weapons and weapon control equipment package

F-111 variants

F-111A: initial production model for service with US Air Force; development batch of 17 RD&E aircraft followed by 141 production examples; production aircraft powered by 8392-kg (18,500-lb) thrust TF30-P-3s, armament comprising one M61 Vulcan 20-mm cannon and one 750-lb (340-kg) nuclear free-fall B43 bomb or two 750-lb bombs housed internally plus up to 13608 kg (30,000 lb) of external stores on six underwing hardpoints; flown for first time on 21 December 1964

F-111B: navalized derivative intended for service with US Navy in fleet fighter role; five RDT&E aircraft and two production specimens completed before project cancelled in July 1968; would have used six AIM-54A Phoenix air-to-air missiles as primary armament; unacceptable weight growth principal factor in cancellation; first flight on 18 May 1965 by TF30-P-3 powered aircraft, but production model would have used TF30-P-12 engines

F-111C: export model for Royal Australian Air Force, which ordered 24 aircraft to replace Canberra light bomber; basically similar to F-111A but features eight underwing pylons; eventually entered service with RAAF in 1973 and still operational

F-111D: vastly improved variant with Mk II avionics and more powerful TF30-P-9 engines; first flown on 15 May 1970, and total of 96 built for service with TAC

F-111E: improved F-111A with modified air inlets and detail changes; powered by TF30-P-3 engine and first flown on 20 August 1969; total of 94 built, initially for service with TAC but deployed to UK from 1970 onwards, equipping USAFE's 20th TFW at RAF Upper Heyford

F-111F: simplified version of F-111D, employing considerably more powerful TF30-P-100 engines and less complex avionics fit; has since been retrofitted with 'Pave Tack' sensor package to improve night/all-weather capability; joined TAC inventory in 1971 but later transferred to USAFE, joining 48th TFW at RAF Lakenheath; F-111 production ceased with delivery of 106th example

FB-111B: proposed improved strategic bomber model with General Electric F101 or similar engines and SRAM armament; original study advocated conversion of existing FB-111As and F-111Ds, but not proceeded with

FB-111H: proposed advanced strategic bomber version with General Electric F101 engines, advanced avionics and with an enlarged internal weapons bay; did not progress beyond study phase

The rear end of the F-111 is dominated by the huge variable-area exhaust nozzles. The large side fairings contain ECM equipment.

General Dynamics F-111D cutaway drawing key

1 Hinged nose cone
2 Attack radar
3 Terrain-following radar
4 Nose hinges (2)
5 Radar mounting
6 Nose lock
7 Angle-of-sideslip probe
8 Homing antenna (high)
9 Forward warning antenna
10 Homing antenna (low and mid)
11 ALR-41 antenna
12 Flight control computers
13 Feel and trim assembly
14 Forward avionics bay (Advanced Mk II digital computer)
15 Angle-of-attack probe
16 UHF Comm/Tacan No. 2
17 Module forward bulkhead and stabilization flaps (2)
18 Twin nosewheels

19 Shock strut
20 Underfloor impact attenuation bag stowage (4)
21 Nosewheel well
22 LOX converter
23 Rudder pedals
24 Control column
25 LOX heat exchanger
26 Auxiliary flotation bag pressure bottle
27 Weapons sight
28 Forward parachute bridle line
29 De-fog nozzle
30 Windscreen
31 Starboard console
32 Emergency oxygen bottles
33 Crew seats
34 Bulkhead console
35 Wing sweep control handle

36 Recovery chute catapult
37 Provision/survival pack
38 Attenuation bags pressure bottle
39 Recovery chute
40 Aft parachute bridle line
41 UHF data link/AG IFF No. 1 (see 123)
42 Stabilization-brake chute
43 Self-righting bag

84 Wing sweep/Hi Lift control box
85 Flap, slat and glove drive mechanism
86 Starboard engine bay
87 Yaw feel spring
88 Roll feel spring
89 Yaw trim actutor
90 Yaw damper servo
91 Roll stick position transducer
92 Pitch trim actuator (manual)

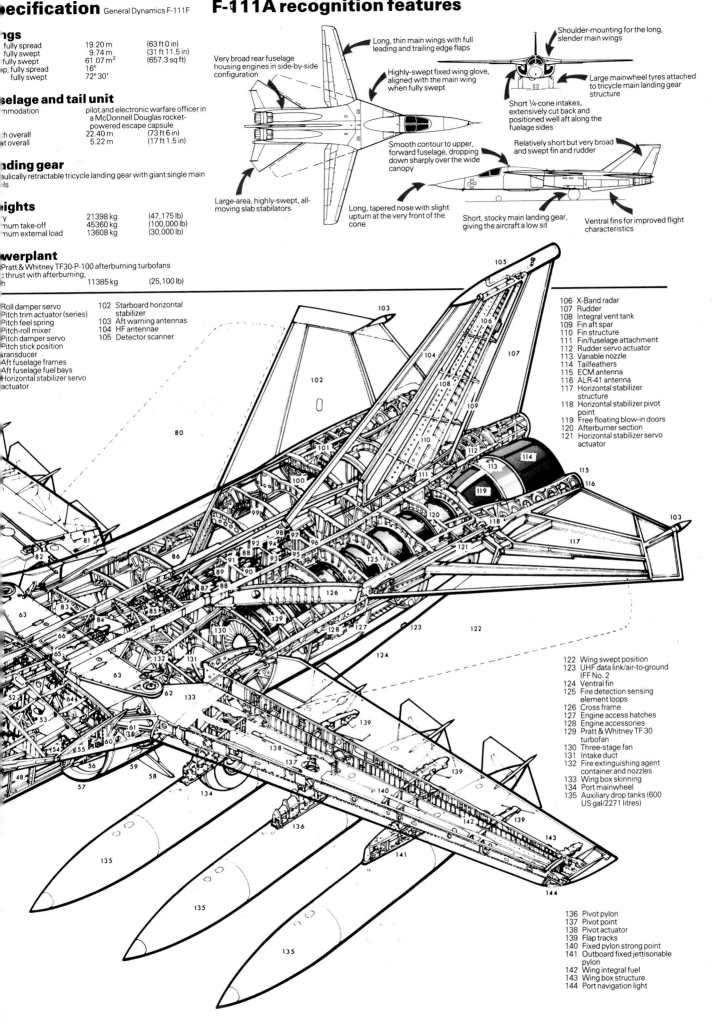

Roll damper servo
Pitch trim actuator (series)
Pitch feel spring
Pitch-roll mixer
Pitch damper servo
Pitch stick position transducer
Aft fuselage frames
Aft fuselage fuel bays
Horizontal stabilizer servo actuator

102 Starboard horizontal stabilizer
103 Aft warning antennas
104 HF antennae
105 Detector scanner

106 X-Band radar
107 Rudder
108 Integral vent tank
109 Fin aft spar
110 Fin structure
111 Fin/fuselage attachment
112 Rudder servo actuator
113 Variable nozzle
114 Tailfeathers
115 ECM antenna
116 ALR-41 antenna
117 Horizontal stabilizer structure
118 Horizontal stabilizer pivot point
119 Free floating blow-in doors
120 Afterburner section
121 Horizontal stabilizer servo actuator

122 Wing swept position
123 UHF data link/air-to-ground IFF No. 2
124 Ventral fin
125 Fire detection sensing element loops
126 Cross frame
127 Engine access hatches
128 Engine accessories
129 Pratt & Whitney TF 30 turbofan
130 Three-stage fan
131 Intake duct
132 Fire extinguishing agent container and nozzles
133 Wing box skinning
134 Port mainwheel
135 Auxiliary drop tanks (600 US gal/2271 litres)

136 Pivot pylon
137 Pivot point
138 Pivot actuator
139 Flap tracks
140 Fixed pylon strong point
141 Outboard fixed jettisonable pylon
142 Wing integral fuel
143 Wing box structure
144 Port navigation light

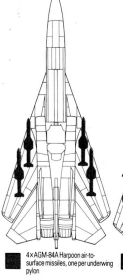
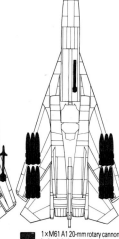
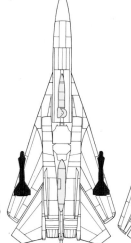
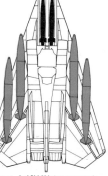

■ 4×AGM-84A Harpoon air-to-surface missiles, one per underwing pylon

■ 2×AIM-9P Sidewinder heat-seeking air-to-air missiles, one shoulder-mounted on each of the outer section of the pylons carrying the fuel tanks

▨ 2×2273-litre (500-Imp gal) auxiliary fuel tanks, one per outer underwing pylon

■ 1×M61 A1 20-mm rotary cannon in the right-hand section of the internal weapons bay with 2,084 rounds of ammunition
12×Mk 82 227-kg (500-lb) Snakeye low-drag retarded 'iron' bombs, carried in tandem triplets on two multiple ejector racks (MERs), one per outer underwing pylon

■ 4×B61 thermonuclear tactical free-fall bombs, two side-by-side in the internal weapons bay and one on each of the inner underwing pylons
2×AIM-9P heat-seeking air-to-air missiles, one shoulder-mounted on each of the outer section of the pylons carrying the fuel tanks
▨ 2×2273-litre (500-Imp gal) auxiliary fuel tanks, one per outer underwing pylon

■ 2×GBU-15 Cruciform Wing Weapon (CWW) electro-optical 'smart' bombs, one per outer wing pylon
▢ 1×AN/AVQ-26 Pave Tack laser designator pod semi-recessed in the internal weapons bay
1×AN/AXQ-14 two-way data-link weapon control and guidance pod under the rear fuselage

■ 2×AGM-69A short-range attack missiles (SRAMs), side-by-side in the internal weapons bay
▨ 4×2273-litre (500-Imp gal) auxiliary fuel tanks on underwing pylons

F-111C anti-shipping strike

Current munitions available to the RAAF F-111C force include items such as the Snakeye 'smart' bomb and the Pave Tack laser designator pod, but the warload above will represent a major boost to the F-111 strike capability. The configuration is currently undergoing evaluation, tactics including the saturation of a seaborne target with all four missiles being fired consecutively on a single approach. For longer-range missions and/or increased target area loiter, two missiles could be replaced by auxiliary fuel tanks. Current plans call for the Harpoon to enter RAAF front-line service by 1988/89.

RF-111C reconnaissance

Various combinations of low/medium-altitude panoramic cameras and electronic sensors can be fitted in the reconnaissance package now occupying the internal weapons bay. Cameras include vertical and oblique format for general and post-strike reconnaissance. The sensor equipment includes infra-red linescan.

The sole operational version of the F-111 configured for dedicated reconnaisance duties, the small force of RAAF RF-111Cs has the entire internal weapons bay fitted with photographic and electronic sensor equipment, though the underwing panels can still be used for both auxiliary fuel and a variety of weapons. Exact details of the reconnaissance equipment are unavailable, though the standard form of such pallets is related above, no doubt including a configuration allowing for overwater reconnaissance around the vast coastline of Australia.

F-111D low-level bombing

Use of the M61 A1 cannon has never been made by F-111 models other than the F-111D. The bomb load illustrated is by no means the maximum weapons load that can be carried, rather a realistic configuration if aircraft performance is not to be seriously degraded, particularly as this mission will take the aircraft down as low as 100 ft (30 m) over the battlefield. Full use will be made of the excellent terrain-following radar, the aircraft hugging the contours of the land with minimum clearance in an attempt to avoid detection by enemy radar.

F-111E tactical nuclear strike

On the tactical models of the F-111, the internal weapons bay is used exclusively for carriage of nuclear bombs and not conventional free-fall munitions. The bombs carried can have their explosive yield varied depending on mission requirements, the number of weapons carried also varying from two to six. The two air-to-air missiles provide a degree of self-defence, the attack radar supplying range information to the pilot's lead-computing optical sight (LCOS).

F-111F tactical precision attack

An important element in the overall updating of F-111 weapons and the associated delivery systems, the GBU-15 units can be fitted to the standard 907-kg (2,000-lb) bomb and the CBU-75 cluster munitions dispenser. The nose area includes an electro-optical unit, this relaying images to the cockpit visual display via the data-link pod carried under the rear fuselage. This latter item also guides the GBU-15 by emitting signals from its phased-array aerial system. Pave Tack acts as a laser designator pod, providing range information on a tracked target to the aircrew via a cockpit display, thus allowing for precision delivery of the weapons. The pod can then swivel aft to scan for target damage information, this being taped if necessary.

FB-111A stand-off attack

An important element within Strategic Air Command, the FB-111A force can carry a variety of nuclear bombs and air-launched cruise missiles, as well as its primary warload of SRAMs. A maximum of two can be carried internally, though the external underwing pylons could each carry the weapon. The fuel tanks are almost mandatory if the FB-111A is to perform anything like a long-range mission, six tanks (an additional pair on outside, unswivelling pylons) providing an intercontinental mission capability, though these would have to be jettisoned if the wings were to be swept further than 26°.

Performance

Sustained speed at
35,000 ft (10670 m) Mach 2.2; 1267 kts; 2348 km/h (1,459 mph)
Speed at low level   Mach 1.2; 793 kts; 1469 km/h (913 mph)
Service ceiling in clean condition   60,000 ft (18290 m)
Maximum range with internal/external
fuel more than   4707 km (2,925 miles)
Take-off run to clear 15-m (50-ft)
obstacle   950 m (3,120 ft)

Maximum weapon load

General Dynamics F-111F 13340 kg
Sukhoi Su-24 'Fencer' 11000 kg E
McDonnell Douglas F-15E Eagle 10705 kg
Panavia Tornado GR.Mk 1 9000 kg
Grumman A-6E Intruder 8165 kg
Jaguar 4763 kg SEPECAT
Mikoyan-Gurevich MiG-27 'Flogger-D' 4000 kg E
Nanchang Q-5 'Fantan' 2000 kg

Service ceiling

General Dynamics F-111F 60,000 ft+
McDonnell Douglas F-15E Eagle 60,000 ft+
Sukhoi Su-24 'Fencer' 54,100 ft E
Mikoyan-Gurevich MiG-27 'Flogger-D' 52,500 ft E
Nanchang Q-5 'Fantan' 52,500 ft
Panavia Tornado GR.Mk 1 50,000 ft+
SEPECAT Jaguar 50,000 ft E
Grumman A-6E Intruder 42,400 ft

Maximum speed at high altitude

McDonnell Douglas F-15E Eagle Mach 2.5+
General Dynamics F-111F Mach 2.4
Panavia Tornado GR.Mk 1 Mach 2.2 'clean'
Sukhoi Su-24 'Fencer' Mach 2.18 E
Mikoyan-Gurevich MiG-27 'Flogger-D' Mach 1.7 E
SEPECAT Jaguar Mach 1.6
Nanchang Q-5 'Fantan' Mach 1.12
Grumman A-6E Intruder Mach 0.8

Maximum speed at sea level

McDonnell Douglas F-15E Eagle Mach 1.23
General Dynamics F-111F Mach 1.2
Sukhoi Su-24 'Fencer' Mach 1.2 E
Panavia Tornado GR.Mk 1 Mach 1.2
SEPECAT Jaguar Mach 1.1
Mikoyan-Gurevich MiG-27 'Flogger-D' Mach 1.1 E
Nanchang Q-5 'Fantan' Mach 0.99
Grumman A-6E Intruder Mach 0.85

Combat radius hi-lo-hi (external fuel)

Grumman A-6E Intruder 1627 km
General Dynamics F-111F 1480 km
Panavia Tornado GR.Mk 1 1390 km
McDonnell Douglas F-15E Eagle 1200 km+
Mikoyan-Gurevich MiG-27 'Flogger-D' 950 km E
Sukhoi Su-24 'Fencer' 950 km E
SEPECAT Jaguar 852 km
Nanchang Q-5 'Fantan' 690 km E

The McDONNELL DOUGLAS F-4G PHANTOM

Phantom II: The St Louis Slugger

Aircraft may come and go, but the truly great designs, live forever. So it is with the mighty F-4 Phantom II, a design which continues to meet a wide range of operational requirements around the world. In the vanguard of users are the US armed forces, for whom this big, bold beast has helped win many a battle in a variety of operational scenarios over nearly three decades.

The slat-wing F-4S Phantoms aboard USS *Midway* (CV-41) in the Western Pacific are soon to be replaced by McDonnell Douglas F/A-18A Hornets, leaving no Phantoms on carrier decks anywhere in the world. By 1988, the US Navy's Phantom inventory will have been whittled down to a mere two reserve squadrons. But the Phantom was exclusively Navy property when the story began in the early 1950s (at the McDonnell Aircraft Company's St Louis facility) with Herman Barkey's design team conceiving a brute-sized, twin-engine fighter originally seen for the strike role and designated AH-1. When it first flew on 27 May 1958 with test pilot Robert C. Little at the controls, the F4H-1 Phantom had been through extensive design changes and was now a fleet interceptor, designed to protect US Navy carrier battle groups using APQ-50 radar and missiles such as the radar-guided AAM-N-6 (later AIM-7) Sparrow and IR-homing AAM-N-7 (later AIM-9) Sidewinder. Much of the effectiveness of the Phantom was credited to its powerplant, two 7326-kg (16,150-lb) thrust General Electric J79-GE-2A afterburning turbojets in the first aircraft with improved variants in later Phantoms. In its

era the J79 was a breakthrough, solving the need for a high-ratio compressor by using a single high-pressure rotor with upstream rows of intermediate stator blades able to be pivoted to exactly the right angular setting for the airflow. The engines gave the aircraft enormous power and double insurance against battle damage. They also were renowned for leaving black smoke trails to entice enemy AAA gunners and, while the US Navy's F-4B variant is 'smokeless', most still do.

Development

Forty-seven F-4A developmental airframes were followed by the US Navy/Marine Corps F-4B Phantom, which scored the first and last MiG kills of the South East Asia war. In service with the fleet by 1962, the Navy aircraft quickly lost their purely interceptor status and became dogfighters and mud movers. A family of reconnaissance Phantoms and another of Phantoms for foreign users, outside the scope of this narrative, followed. The F-4B had J79-GE-8A/B engines, APQ-72 radar with an 81-cm (32-in) dish, and the Lear AJB-3 bombing system; 651 came off the production line. Some 228 were rebuilt to

▲ *For any enemy ground forces unlucky enough to see the broad profile of the F-4 hurtling down towards them, admiration for its versatility and sheer power would attest to the aircraft's excellent fighting qualities. Here an F-4G rolls in to attack a radar.*

▼ *Only two squadrons of Phantoms remain in front-line US Navy service, although there are several reserve units. A number of aircraft are used for armament and equipment test purposes, such as this VX-4 F-4J, seen in the company of Lockheed's test SR-71A.*

F-4N standard under a SLEP which introduced the helmet-sight VTAS, SEAM and improved avionics.

The F-4J, first flown 27 May 1966, was equipped with 8119-kg (17,900-lb) thrust J79-GE-19 engines and added to the Phantom's capability an improved TACAN, the upgraded AJB-7 bombing system, and drooped ailerons intended to reduce carrier approach speed from 137 to 125 kts (254 to 232 km/h; 158 to 144 mph). On 10 May 1972 in an F-4J Phantom (BuNo 155800) of VF-96 'Fighting Falcons', Lieutenant Randall Cunningham became the Vietnam war's first pilot ace by scoring his third, fourth and fifth MiG kills. Of 522

F-4Js delivered to the Navy, 248 were retrofitted with various improvements, including leading-edge manoeuvre slats, to receive the designation F-4S.

When Brigadier General Michael P. Sullivan recently became the first man to attain 5,000 flight hours in the Phantom, he illustrated the longevity and importance of the F-4 type for the US Marine Corps. In 1962 the Marines were just a step behind the Navy in acquiring the F-4B model. In April 1965 they introduced the F-4B to South Vietnam when VMFA-531 'Gray Ghosts' arrived at Da Nang. The Marines also operated the F-4J and F-4N before transitioning to today's F-4s. They are expected on occasion to fill in for their Navy brethren on carrier decks. On 11 September 1972, Major Thomas 'Bear' Lasseter and Captain John D. Cummings flying an F-4J Phantom (BuNo 155526) of VMFA-333 'Shamrocks' went into North Vietnam from USS *America* (CV-66) and shot down a MiG-21, the only Marine air-to-air kill of the South East Asia conflict.

The Marines regard their air arm as an adjunct to their elite ground fighting force and are more interested in the Phantom as a warplane that can loiter for extended periods in a target area than as a fighter possessing long range. Close air support being so essential to the Marines, it must be said that the Phantom is a generation behind present-day strike aircraft for precision delivery of ordnance.

In service

The Phantom remains the most numerous fighter in the Marine Corps, three squadrons at MCAS Beaufort, South Carolina not converting to the F/A-18A Hornet until 1988. Three more Marine F-4S squadrons which bask in the sun at MCAS Kaneohe Bay, Hawaii will not see the Hornet until 1993, and no plans have been made to replace the F-4S in reserve units.

In a typical real-world situation, the 3rd Marine Division at Camp Pendleton, California might be rushed to the Persian Gulf to block a Soviet invasion. F-4S Phantoms might deploy with the aid of inflight-refuelling to a friendly country granting 'user rights', like Oman or Somalia. While newer fighters clear the air of enemy opposition, the big, powerful F-4S Phantom would support the Marines on the ground, carrying the diversity of ordnance loads for which the Phantom is famous. Against a hard target, the load might be six 750-lb (340-kg) iron bombs, while fluid troop concentrations might be attacked with CBU-58 Rockeye II cluster bombs.

In January 1962, Colonels Gordon Graham and George Laven delivered to the US Air Force two examples of the F-110A Phantom, redesignated F-4C later in that year, which was almost a carbon copy of the machine designed to fly from carrier decks. The Air Force fighter needed a self-contained cartridge pneumatic starter not found on the Navy variant, but the F-4C remained essentially a land-based version of a nautical craft. Production amounted to 583 aircraft, many of them participating in heavy fighting in South

East Asia. As noted, a few remain on duty with ANG squadrons today, but the F-4C was in certain respects a transition for the Air Force: having eaten humble pie to acquire a Navy aircraft, the Air Force wanted better ordnance delivery. It also wanted something the Navy never had, namely a gun.

The F-4D Phantom, first flown 9 December 1965, was the first step towards translating carrier-based potency into Air Force needs. The D model introduced the partly solid-state APQ-109 fire-control radar (highly advanced in its day, but a handicap now), a lead-computing gunsight, and an ASQ-91 weapon release com-

▼ *Once a significant part of USAFE, the Phantom numbers are rapidly dwindling; these 86th TFW aircraft are being replaced by F-16C/Ds. When current replacement plans are complete, only the 26th TRW RF-4Cs and the 52nd TFW F-4G 'Wild Weasels' will remain in Europe.*

▲ *A sight soon to disappear into the annals of history – the launch of US Navy F-4s from an aircraft-carrier somewhere on the world's oceans. For many years the backbone of US Navy Fleet defence and strike forces, the Phantom II will soon end its days at sea.*

puter making it able to deliver 'smart' bombs or PGMs. The F-4D was also supposed to introduce the IR-homing AIM-4D Falcon missile, but these were received so poorly in South East Asia that Robin Olds ordered the Falcons trashed and rewired his F-4Ds to continue using Sidewinders. The senior US airman in the UK today, Major General Thomas McInerney, helped introduce the F-4D to combat in 1967 and was impressed that its new systems permitted bomb release from higher altitude, while other strike aircraft had to get closer to targets like the Thanh Hoa Bridge, so creating greater exposure to ground fire. McInerney and his companions still wanted a gun, and the centreline SUU-16/A pod carrying a 20-mm cannon was not sufficient. The SUU-23/A pod introduced in the late 1960s is an improvement, but is still weighty and creates drag.

Armament

The gun, an internally mounted M61A1 Vulcan 20-mm 'Gatling' style cannon with 640 rounds, finally appeared aboard the F-4E Phantom, first flown on 30 June 1967. The cannon-armed Phantom had been demanded by pilots, including Olds who missed his fifth air-to-air kill and ace status when (in an F-4D) he was too close to a MiG to use a missile and possessed no gun.

In the end, it was ACM training rather than an internal gun which enabled US airmen to prevail over the North Vietnamese MiG, but the F-4E became the most numerous of Phantoms and the principal export model, no fewer than 949 being built. As pointed out by Colonel Edward Hillding, whose 469th TFS introduced the E model to combat at Korat in November 1968 (with McInerney again in attendance), 'The F-4E was a wholly different Phantom – longer, heavier, different fuel [capacity], different radar.' The F-4E had

8119-kg thrust J79-GE-17 engines, smaller APQ-120 nose radar, and an extra (seventh) fuel cell in the rear fuselage to counterbalance the weight of the gun. Until 1969, all Air Force Phantoms were flown by two pilots, and the F-4E was first to introduce the present-day crew of pilot and navigator, the latter officially termed a WSO. From 1972, F-4Es still in production were built with a slatted leading edge

After testing other types including the F-4D variant and the Grumman EA-6B Prowler, the Air Force adopted the F-4G as its standard 'Advanced Wild Weasel' platform, replacing the Republic F-105F and F-105G (and a small handful of special F-4Cs) which pioneered 'Wild Weasel' missions in Vietnam. The term embraces EW and SAM suppression missions by dedicated electronic warplanes hunting down hostile SAM installations (using radar for lock-on, tracking or missile guidance) and destroying them before or during an attack by other friendly aircraft on nearby targets.

Some 116 F-4E airframes were converted to F-4G standard, having the 20-mm gun deleted and being equipped with the APR-38 system which provides comprehensive radar homing and warning and employs no fewer than 52 special aerials, including those in the former gun pod and others in a new fairing at the top of

the vertical tail. Ordnance carried by the 'Wild Weasel' includes electro-optical AGM-65 Maverick missiles on each inboard pylon, two AGM-88A HARMs outboard, and AIM-9L Sidewinder all-aspect missiles for air-to-air engagements.

While the 'pure fighter' F-4E begins its ANG service by joining the 131st TFW, Missouri ANG at Lambert-St Louis Airport (where three airframes are evaluating a new, single-piece, bird-resistant windscreen likely to be retrofitted to all Phantoms) reports persist that a further number of F-4E airframes, perhaps a large number, will be converted to F-4G 'Wild Weasels'. It has taken three decades to get from Phantom to 'Wild Weasel', but the F-4G is only beginning its contribution to the solid record of achievement.

▼ The latest and most capable of the F-4 models operated by the US Air Force is the F-4G 'Wild Weasel V', the widely-dispersed force enabling anti-radiation operations to be conducted in support of other F-4 attack operations, e.g. eliminating enemy SAM radar sites.

▲ Though showing its age somewhat against the modern service aircraft, the F-4S still plays a significant role within US Marine Corps aviation operations. Its ruggedness and heavy payload capabilities make it an excellent close air support/strike aircraft.

F-4 in service

United States Air Force, Tactical Air Command

Tasked with organizing, training, equipping and maintaining combat forces which can deploy rapidly, and to ensure that the USAF strategic air defence forces can meet both peacetime and wartime air defence requirements, Tactical Air Command employs the F-4 at the forefront of its operations. As with other Commands the F-4 is gradually giving way to the F-15 and F-16, but it still plays an important role as a tactical fighter and electronic combat suppression aircraft. What was Air Defense Tactical Air Command (ADTAC) is now the 1st Air Force, this being responsible for the command and control of the interceptor forces, while the tactical F-4 elements come under the command of the 9th and 12th Air Forces. In times of war these forces would be considerably bolstered by tactical and interceptor squadrons from the Air National Guard and Air Force Reserve.

This McDonnell Douglas F-4E, with the prominent undernose cannon fairing, is in the markings of the 69th TFS/347th TFW.

9th Air Force
4th Tactical Fighter Wing
Base: Seymour-Johnson AFB, North Carolina
Tailcode letters: 'SJ'
Squadrons: 334th, 335th, 336th & 337th TFS

Aircraft model: F-4E
Example aircraft: (334th TFS) 20162, 31176, 31182, 41627; (335th TFS) 21478, 70379, 31183; (336th TFS) 20161, 31171, 40665, 41639; (337th TFS) 60379, 70272, 60361

31st Tactical Fighter Wing
Base: Homestead AFB, Florida
Tailcode letters: 'ZF'
Squadrons: 307th, 308th & 309th TFS
Aircraft models: F-4D/E
Example aircraft: (307th TFS) 67698; (308th TFS) 50729, 67635; (309th TFS) 67463

347th Tactical Fighter Wing
Base: Moody AFB, Georgia
Tailcode letters: 'MY'
Squadrons: 68th, 69th & 70th TFS
Aircraft model: F-4E
Example aircraft: (68th TFS) 70360, 80320, 80357, 80495; (69th TFS) 70396, 80389, 80427, 80494; (70th TFS) 80318, 80366, 80423, 80449

12th Air Force

35th Tactical Training Wing
Base: George AFB, California
Tailcode letters: 'GA'
Squadrons: 20th & 21st TFTS
Aircraft model: F-4E
Example aircraft: (20th TFTS) 70235, 70288, 70311; (21st TFTS) 60338, 70241, 80351

37th Tactical Fighter Wing
Base: George AFB, California
Tailcode letters: 'WW'

Squadrons: 561st, 562nd & 563rd TFS
Aircraft models: F-4E/G
Example aircraft: 561st TFS (F-4G) 97209, 97303, 97561, 97574; 562nd TFS (F-4E) 70233, 90270, (F-4G) 97288, 90284; 563rd TFS (F-4G) 90279, 97204, 97550

Tactical Air Warfare Center
Base: Eglin AFB, Florida
Tailcode letters: 'OT'
Example aircraft: (F-4E) 20168, 60306, 97589

United States Pacific Air Forces

As the air component of the unified Pacific Command, PACAF's mission is to plan and execute offensive and defensive air operations assigned to it, defending US interests stretching over a vast area which covers more than half the Earth's surface, including more than 35 countries. Active airfields are dotted round the region, principally in Japan, South Korea, the Philippines and Hawaii. The 5th and 13th Air Force administer PACAF operations, the F-4 units (still the most numerically important in the region) coming under their control.

5th Air Force
51st Tactical Fighter Wing
Bases: Osan AB, South Korea (36th TFS); Taegu AB, South Korea (497th TFS)
Tailcode letters: 'OS' (36th TFS); 'GU' (497th TFS)

Aircraft model: F-4E
Example aircraft: (36th TFS) 70351, 80407, 80329, 80376; (497th TFS) 80305, 80323, 80453, 97294

13th Air Force
3rd Tactical Fighter Wing
Base: Clark AFB, Philippines
Tailcode letters: 'PN'
Squadrons: 3rd TFS & 90th TFS
Aircraft models: F-4E/G

Example aircraft: 3rd TFS (F-4E) 80355, 10237, 11073, 31198; 90th TFS (F-4E) 80310, 90290, 11391; (F-4G) 90267, 97208, 97583

The sand and two-tone green 'Vietnam' tactical camouflage is worn less and less by today's USAF F-4s, most having adopted the 'European One' colours. This 3rd TFW F-4E illustrates the older scheme, along with flamboyant shark's-mouth on the lower nose.

United States Air Forces in Europe

For so long a major element within the USAFE aircraft force, the F-4 is now rapidly disappearing, giving way to the General Dynamics F-16 Fighting Falcon. The 86th TFW is well advanced with its re-equipment plans, its F-4Es being returned to the USA and distributed amongst Air National Guard units in the main. The mix of F-4Es and F-4Gs which equip the three squadrons of the 52nd TFW will start to replace their E models with F-16Cs during 1987 on a one-for-one basis, a programme that is intended to be finished by the end of 1987. Preceding this, a dozen F-4Gs will return to the USA in mid-1986, their place in West Germany being taken by a dozen F-4Gs. These units come under the control of the 17th Air Force, the units making a valuable contribution to NATO and the defence of Western Europe.

17th Air Force
52nd Tactical Fighter Wing
Base: Spangdahlem AB, West Germany
Tailcode letters: 'SP'
Squadrons: 23rd TFS, 81st TFS & 480th TFS
Aircraft models: F-4E/G
Example aircraft: 23rd TFS (F-4E) 21482, 40666, 41059; (F-4G) 90255, 97228, 97566; 81st TFS (F-4E) 40657, 41038, 41645; (F-4G) 90286, 97293,

97587; 480th TFS (F-4E) 20167, 21485, 40653; (F-4G) 90269, 97270, 97579

86th Tactical Fighter Wing
Base: Ramstein AB, West Germany
Tailcode letters: 'RS'
Squadron: 526th TFS
Aircraft model: F-4E
Example aircraft: 80381, 80408, 90244

This F-4E Phantom II's yellow and black fin-stripe and 'SP' tailcode letters identify it as an 81st TFS/52nd TFW machine, based at Spangdahlem AB in West Germany.

United States Air Force, Air National Guard

By far the largest user of the F-4 in the US armed forces, the Air National Guard force is based around the F-4C/D/E with the Cs being progressively replaced by the later models, the F-4E becoming more prevalent as it is retired from USAFE and home-based units in favour of types such as the F-15 Eagle and F-16 Fighting Falcon. The Phantom II is the ANGs primary tactical fighter, its importance underlined by the fact that there are current programmes which will modify F-4D and -E airframes to allow carriage of the AIM-9L and -M models of the Sidewinder AAM, and the fitting of low-smoke engines.

Current duties for the ANG Phantom II force include interception, close air support, air superiority and battlefield interdiction. In times of war the majority of ANG F-4 units would be 'gained' by Tactical Air Command, eight of the units being assigned to the 1st Air Force for fighter interception duties (the seven FISs and the 114th TFTS). Out on its own is the 199th TFS which would join PACAF. In peacetime flying, the importance of the ANG F-4 units can be appreciated by the fact that it provides 26 per cent of the Air Force's tactical fighters and some 73 per cent of the interceptor force – the F-4 playing its part to the full.

Amongst the most colourful ANG F-4s are the aircraft of the 171st FIS/191st FIG, Michigan ANG. Illustrated is an F-4C.

110th TFS/131st TFW Missouri ANG
Base: St. Louis IAP, Missouri
Tailcode letters: 'SL'
Aircraft model: F-4E
Example aircraft: 80338, 80410, 90305, 90307

111th FIS/147th FIG Texas ANG
Base: Ellington AFB, Texas
Aircraft model: F-4C
Example aircraft: 40712, 40828, 40908

113th TFS/181st TFG Indiana ANG
Base: Hullman Regional AP, Indiana

Tailcode letters: 'HF'
Aircraft model: F-4C
Example aircraft: 37657, 40675, 40724

114th TFTS/142nd FIG Oregon ANG
Base: Kingsley Field, Oregon
Aircraft model: F-4C
Example aircraft: 37549, 40673, 40888

121st TFS/113th TFW District of Columbia ANG
Base: Andrews AFB, Maryland
Tailcode letters: 'DC'

Aircraft model: F-4D
Example aircraft: 67556, 67677, 67693

123rd FIS/142nd FIG Oregon ANG
Base: Portland IAP, Oregon
Aircraft model: F-4C
Example aircraft: 37670, 40707, 40893

127th TFTS/184th TFG Kansas ANG
Base: McConnell AFB, Kansas
Aircraft model: F-4D
Example aircraft: 50705, 60274, 68693

128th TFS/116th TFW Georgia ANG
Base: Dobbins AFB, Georgia
Aircraft model: F-4D
Example aircraft: 67614, 67735, 68689

134th TFS/158th TFG Vermont ANG
Base: Burlington IAP, Vermont

Tailcode letters: 'VT'
Aircraft model: F-4D
Example aircraft: 50790, 60243, 60266

136th FIS/107th FIG New York ANG
Base: Niagara Falls IAP, New York
Aircraft model: F-4C
Example aircraft: 37581, 40660, 40822

141st TFS/108th TFW New Jersey ANG
Base: McGuire AFB, New Jersey
Tailcode letters: 'NJ'
Aircraft model: F-4E
Example aircraft: 80375, 80526, 80534

160th TFS/187th TFG Alabama ANG
Base: Dannelly Field, Alabama
Tailcode letters: 'AL'
Aircraft model: F-4D
Example aircraft: 67644, 67708, 67754

163rd TFS/122nd TFW Indiana ANG
Base: Fort Wayne MAP, Indiana
Tailcode letters: 'FW'
Aircraft model: F-4E
Example aircraft: 80512

171st FIS/191st FIG Michigan ANG
Base: Selfridge ANGB, Michigan
Aircraft models: F-4C/D
Example aircraft: (F-4C) 37514, 37626; (F-4D) 50737

177th TFTS/184th TFG Kansas ANG
Base: McConnell AFB, Kansas
Aircraft model: F-4D
Example aircraft: 67520, 67633, 67759

178th FIS/119th FIG North Dakota ANG
Base: Hector Field, North Dakota
Aircraft model: F-4D
Example aircraft: 40977, 50647, 67498

184th TFS/188th TFG Arkansas ANG
Base: Fort Smith MAP, Arkansas
Aircraft model: F-4C
Example aircraft: 37411, 37646, 40912

194th FIS/144th FIW California ANG
Base: Fresno Air Terminal, California
Aircraft model: F-4D
Example aircraft: 50740, 60279, 67741

196th TFS/163rd TFG California ANG
Base: March AFB, California
Aircraft models: F-4C/D
Example aircraft: (F-4C) 37686, 37693, 40665, 40923

199th TFS/154th CG Hawaii ANG
Base: Hickam AFB, Hawaii
Aircraft model: F-4C
Example aircraft: 37647, 40851, 40913

United States Air Force Reserve

Given the mainly transport-orientated nature of AFRes operations and aircraft-equipped units, it is not surprising that the Phantom II is serving with only a handful of Tactical Fighter Squadrons (TFSs). This small but effective force is now exclusively equipped with the F-4D, though no doubt the F-4E will start filtering down from front-line units in due course. The squadrons are organized along the standard Squadron/Wing structure, with squadrons based away from the Wing HQ receiving support from the Group HQ. Squadrons based at Wing HQ report directly to that Wing HQ. All the squadrons will be 'gained' by Tactical Air Command in times of war, part of a total of 12 AFRes squadrons which would report to this Command within the front-line Air Force.

6th Air Force

89th TFS/906th TFG
Base: Wright-Patterson AFB, Ohio
Tailcode letters: 'DO'
Aircraft model: F-4D
Example aircraft: 67699, 67706, 67749, 67755

93rd TFS/482nd TFW
Base: Homestead AFB, Florida
Tailcode letters: 'FM'
Aircraft model: F-4D
Example aircraft: 67552, 67563, 68715, 68824

457th TFS/301st TFW
Base: Carswell AFB, Texas

Tailcode letters: 'TH'
Aircraft model: F-4D
Example aircraft: 68737, 68786, 68794, 68825

465th TFS/507th TFG
Base: Tinker AFB, Oklahoma
Tailcode letters: 'SH'
Aircraft model: F-4D
Example aircraft: 67618, 67750, 68701, 68709

704th TFS/924th TFG
Base: Bergstrom AFB, Texas
Tailcode letters: 'TX'
Aircraft model: F-4D
Example aircraft: 68739, 68788, 68802, 68819

United States Air Force Test and Evaluation units

The F-4 continues to serve with various agencies for a wide range of purposes, much of this revolving around weapons and their operational use, this also being covered by test and evaluation units within Tactical Air Command. Air Force Systems Command is concerned with advances in aerospace technology and their applications in an operational environment. This is particularly applied to the design, construction and testing of various projects, the 3246th Test Wing (ADTC) using its F-4s for work relating to all non-nuclear weapons for tactical forces. The 6512th Test Squadron (AFFTC) evaluates aircraft following their delivery by the manufacturers, usually retaining some examples for further research work, close co-operation being maintained by both the units with their counterparts in TAC.
The Ogden Air Logistics Center is responsible for the major overhauls and modification/upgrading programmes associated with the USAF F-4 forces, in addition to the standard planned inspections and service life overhauls, the unit retaining a small number of aircraft for its own use. This unit is controlled by Air Force Logistics Command.

Air Force Systems Command

Air Force Flight Test Center
Base: Edwards AFB, California
Tailcode letters: 'ED'
Squadron: 6512th TS
Example aircraft: (F-4C) 37408; (F-4D) 67483; (F-4E) 60289, 60294

Armament Development & Test Center
Base: Edwards AFB, California
Tailcode letters: 'AD'
Wing: 3246th TW
Example aircraft: (F-4C) 40869; (F-4D) 68699; (F-4E) 11072, 20126

Air Force Logistics Command Ogden Air Logistics Center
Base: Hill AFB, Utah
Example aircraft: (F-4D) 67455, 67688; (F-4E) 60301, 80450

United States Navy

After a long and highly distinguished service career as the US Navy's primary front-line fighter, the venerable F-4 Phantom II had all but given way to the Grumman F-14A Tomcat and McDonnell Douglas F/A-18A Hornet. Today, only two squadrons remain active, both flying as part of the Pacific Fleet aircraft carrier forces, but their days with the F-4S are numbered. Shortly they will begin transitioning to the Hornet.

VF-151 'Vigilantes'
Carrier: USS *Midway* (CV-41)
Air Wing: CVW-5
Tailcode letters: 'NF'
Aircraft model: F-4S
Example aircraft: 153868-203, 153910-206, 155565-212

VF-161 'Chargers'
Carrier: USS *Midway* (CV-41)
Air Wing: CVW-5
Tailcode letters: 'NF'
Aircraft model: F-4S
Example aircraft: 157261-100, 155746-105, 155897-113

A VF-161 F-4S wears one of several low-visibility tactical colour schemes.

United States Naval Air Reserve

As with the front-line US Navy forces the Reserve forces are in the process of retiring their remaining active Phantom IIs in favour of more modern types. The two remaining squadrons currently fly the F-4S, newer models having been handed down over the years from the front-line units as they re-equipped. From August 1986 the F-4S will start to be retired from the two units as the first Grumman F-14A Tomcats arrive at NAS Dallas for ground instruction and maintenance training.

VF-201 'Red Raiders'
Air Wing: CVWR-20
Home base: NAS Dallas, Texas
Tailcode letters: 'AF'
Aircraft model: F-4S
Example aircraft: 153828-102, 153887-103, 155572-110

VF-202
Air Wing: CVWR-20
Home base: NAS Dallas, Texas

Tailcode letters: 'AF'
Aircraft model: F-4S
Example aircraft: 155893-207, 153904-211, 153824-213

The Texas home-base of VF-201 is represented on the fin of this F-4S by a state map.

Youngest of the AFRes F-4D units is the 89th TFS/906th TFG based at Wright-Patterson AFB, Ohio. Note the stylized black trim around the cockpits and on the canopy framing.

McDonnell Douglas F-4E Phantom II cutaway drawing key

1. Starboard tailplane
2. Static discharger
3. Honeycomb trailing edge panels
4. Tailplane mass balance weight
5. Tailplane spar construction
6. Drag chute housing
7. Tailcone/drag chute hinged door
8. Fuselage fuel tanks vent pipe
9. Honeycomb rudder construction
10. Rudder balance
11. Tail warning radar fairing
12. Tail navigation light
13. Fin tip antenna fairing
14. Communications antenna
15. Fin rear spar
16. Variable intensity formation lighting strip

17. Rudder control jack
18. Tailplane pivot mounting
19. Tailplane pivot seal
20. Fixed leading edge slat
21. Tailplane hydraulic jack
22. Fin front spar
23. Stabilator feel system pressure probe
24. Anti-collision light
25. Stabilator feel system balance mechanism
26. Tailcone cooling air duct
27. Heat resistant tailcone skinning
28. Arrester hook housing
29. Arrester hook, lowered
30. Starboard fully variable exhaust nozzle

31. Rudder artificial feel system bellows
32. Fin leading edge
33. Ram air intake
34. Fuselage No 7 fuel cell, capacity 318 litres (84 US gal)
35. Engine bay cooling air outlet louvres
36. Arrester hook actuator and damper
37. Fuel vent piping
38. Fuselage No 6 fuel cell, capacity 806 litres (213 US gal)
39. Jet pipe shroud construction

40. Engine bay hinged access doors
41. Rear AIM-7E-2 Sparrow air-to-air missile
42. Semi-recessed missile housing
43. Jet pipe nozzle actuators
44. Afterburner jet pipe
45. Fuselage No 5 fuel cell, capacity 681 litres (180 US gal)
46. Fuel tank access panels
47. Fuel system piping
48. Tailplane control cable drum
49. Fuselage No 4 fuel cell, capacity 761 litres (201 US gal)

AViAGRAPHiCA

ited States Navy Test and Evaluation units

-4 in its navalized forms continues to serve with several
US Navy's test and evaluation units, most of these
ting under the control of Naval Air Systems Command,
avy agency responsible for the development,
rement and service support of aircraft and their
iated systems. A mixture of Navy F-4 models are in use,
h in general their numbers are decreasing. Duties
le support of Strike Aircraft Test Directorate evaluation
rierborne aircraft and their equipment, use by the Naval
ons Center in support of weapons development and
orms of delivery within the context of modern air
re – the testing of new missiles on behalf of the Pacific
e Test Center.

VX-4 'Evaluators'
Base: NAS Point Mugu,
California
Tailcode letters: 'XF'
Example aircraft: (F-4S)
155539/XF-1, 158360/XF-7

Lakehurst Naval Air Test Center
Base: NAS Lakehurst, New Jersey
Example aircraft: (F-4N)
150485/MG-10

Naval Weapons Center
Base: NAF China Lake, California
Example aircraft: (QF-4N)
150993/407, 152303/408

Pacific Missile Test Center
Base: NAS Point Mugu, California
Example aircraft: (F-4J)
155563/92, 151504/94

Strike Aircraft Test Directorate/Naval Air Test Center
Base: NAS Patuxent River, Maryland
Tailcode letters: '7T'
Example aircraft: (F-4J)
153077/101, 157286/120

tarboard engine bay
onstruction
ACAN antenna
uselage No 3 fuel cell,
apacity 556 litres (147 US
al)
ngine oil tank
eneral Electric J79-GE-
7A turbojet engine
ngine accessories
Ving rear spar attachment
Mainwheel door
um undercarriage wheel
vell
ateral control servo
ctuator
Hydraulic accumulator
ower surface airbrake
ack
lap hydraulic jack
tarboard flap
Honeycomb control
urface construction
tarboard aileron
ileron power control unit
lutter damper

68 Spoiler housing
69 Wing tank fuel vent
70 Dihedral outer wing panel
71 Rear identification light
72 Wing tip formation lighting
73 Starboard navigation light
74 Radar warning antenna
75 Outer wing panel
construction
76 Outboard leading edge slat
77 Slat control linkage
78 Slat hydraulic jack
79 Outer wing panel
attachment
80 Starboard wing fence
81 Fuel vent system shut-off
valves
82 Top of main undercarriage
leg

83 Outboard pylon
attachment housing
84 Inboard slat hydraulic jack
85 Starboard outer pylon
86 Mainwheel leg door
87 Mainwheel brake discs
88 Starboard mainwheel
89 Starboard external fuel
tank, capacity 1400 litres
(370 US gal)
90 Inboard leading edge slat,
open
91 Slat hinge linkages
92 Main undercarriage
retraction jack
93 Undercarriage uplock
94 Starboard wing fuel tank,
capacity 1192 litres (315
US gal)
95 Integral fuel tank
construction

96 Inboard pylon fixing
97 Leading edge ranging
antenna
98 Starboard inboard pylon
99 Twin missile launcher
100 AIM-9 Sidewinder
101 Hinged leading edge
access panel
102 Wing front spar
103 Hydraulic reservoir
104 Centre fuselage formation
lighting
105 Fuselage main frame
106 Engine intake compressor
face
107 Intake duct construction
108 Fuselage No 2 fuel cell,
capacity 700 litres (185 US
gal)
109 Air-to-air refuelling
receptacle, open
110 Port main undercarriage
leg
111 Aileron power control unit
112 Port aileron
113 Aileron flutter damper
114 Port spoiler
115 Spoiler hydraulic jack
116 Wing fuel tank vent pipe
117 Port outer wing panel
118 Rearward identification
light
119 Wing tip formation lighting
120 Port navigation light
121 Radar warning antenna
122 Port outboard leading edge
slat
123 Slat hydraulic jack
124 Wing fence
125 Leading edge dog tooth
126 Inboard leading edge slat,
open
127 Port external fuel tank,
capacity 1400 litres (370
US gal)

128 Inboard slat hydraulic jack
129 Port wing fuel tank,
capacity 1192 litres (315
US gal)
130 Upper fuselage light
131 IFF antenna
132 Avionics equipment bay
133 Gyro platform
134 Fuselage No 1 fuel cell,
capacity 814 litres (215 US
gal)
135 Intake duct
136 Hydraulic connections
137 Starter cartridge container
138 Pneumatic system air
bottle
139 Engine bleed air supply
pipe
140 Forward AIM-7 missile
housing
141 Ventral fuel tank, capacity
2271 litres (600 US gal)
142 Bleed air louvre assembly,
lower
143 Avionics equipment bay
144 Variable intake ramp jack
145 Bleed air louvre assembly,
upper
146 Radar operator's Martin-
Baker ejection seat
147 Safety harness
148 Face blind seat firing
handle
149 Rear cockpit canopy cover
150 Front canopy hinges
151 Inter-canopy bridge
section glazing
152 Radar operator's
instrument console
153 Canopy jack
154 Port intake
155 Pilot's Martin-Baker
ejection seat
156 Intake front ramp
157 Starboard intake
158 Bleed air holes
159 Boundary layer splitter
plate
160 ALQ-119 electronic
countermeasures pod
(replaces forward Sparrow
missile)

161 HOBOS 907-kg (2000-lb)
guided bomb
162 Nosewheel door
163 AIM-7E-2 Sparrow missile
semi-recessed housing
164 Forward formation lighting
165 Air conditioning plant
166 Battery
167 Pilot's starboard side
console
168 Ejection seat safety
harness
169 Engine throttles
170 Port intake front ramp
171 Forward cockpit canopy
cover
172 Port inboard wing pylon
173 Pylon attachments
174 Triple ejector release unit
175 Mk 82 low profile 227-kg
(500-lb) bombs
176 Extended bomb fuses
177 Windscreen panels
178 Pilot's lead computing
sight
179 Instrument panel shroud
180 Control column
181 Rudder pedals
182 Cockpit front pressure
bulkhead
183 Refrigeration plant
184 Communications antenna
185 Nosewheel jack
186 Nose undercarriage leg
strut
187 Twin nosewheels
188 Nosewheel torque links
189 Landing and taxiing lamps
190 Air conditioning ram air
intake
191 Angle of attack probe
192 Ammunition drum 640
rounds
193 Rain dispersal duct nozzle
194 ADF antenna
195 Gun bay frame
construction
196 M61A-1 20-mm rotary
barrel cannon
197 Cannon fairing
198 AN/APQ-120 fire control
radar
199 Radar antenna mounting
200 Gun muzzle fairing
201 Radar scanner
202 Radome
203 Pitot tube

F-4 Phantom II warload

1×SUU-23/A Vulcan six-barrel 20-mm cannon pod with 1,200 rounds mounted on the underfuselage centreline station
4×AIM-9L Sidewinder IR-homing AAMs, one pair shoulder-mounted on each inner pylon triple ejector rack
4×AIM-7D Sparrow semi-active radar-homing AAMs, each semi-recessed in one of the four underfuselage stations
2×370-US gal (1401-litre) drop tanks, one on each outer underwing station

Enhanced air-to-air interception
One feature lacking from the early models of the F-4 was an internally-mounted cannon, such a weapon being omitted in the belief that guided missiles would be all-conquering. Reality proved this to be wrong and the Vulcan cannon pod has become a regular sight on the F-4C and F-4D as well as the Navy/Marine Corps models.

12×Mk 82 Snakeye high-drag 500-lb (227-kg) bombs, three on each inner underwing pylon triple ejector rack and six mounted in two triple clusters on the underfuselage centreline multiple ejector rack
1×ALQ-119 dual-mode ECM jammer pod, mounted in the forward port semi-recessed station
2×370-US gal (1401-litre) drop tanks, one on each outer underwing pylon

Ground attack
A wide variety of bombs can be carried depending on specific mission requirements, this configuration representing the usual quantities of bombs carried per pylon. Taking off with maximum thrust, the aircraft climbs to its optimum cruise altitude, later dropping down to sea level and searching out the target(s). A search time of 5 minutes is available at military thrust, plus a reserve of 20 minutes loiter at sea level.

4×AIM-9L Sidewinder IR-homing AAMs one pair shoulder-mounted on each inner pylon triple ejector rack
4×AIM-7D Sparrow semi-active radar-homing AAMs, each semi-recessed in one of the four underfuselage stations
2×370-US gal (1401-litre) drop tanks, one on each outer underwing station

Standard air-to-air interception
Common on US Navy F-4s for many years, this configuration is still used by Air National Guard and Air Force Reserve units tasked with intercepting enemy intruders over the USA. The patrol often involves flying at maximum endurance altitudes, full use being made of the powerful engines to give high closing speeds on the target. The AIM-9s provide a short-range attack capability, while the AIM-7s allow for a degree of stand-off target destruction.

1×M61A1 Vulcan 20-mm cannon with 640 rounds mounted internally in the forward fuselage
6×AGM-65 Maverick air-to-surface missiles, mounted in groups of three on the inner underwing pylon triple ejector racks
1×ALQ-131 advanced ECM jamming pod mounted in the forward port semi-recessed station
2×370-US gal (1401-litre) drop tanks, one on each outer underwing station

F-4E precision attack/close-air support
This is one of the modern weapons configurations available to the large F-4E force, both in Europe and North America, various models of the Maverick being compatible with the F-4E fire-control system. If there is a stabilized ground laser designator or other aircraft flying with laser designating equipment, the AGM-65C/E can be used, while the AGM-65D IR Maverick can be launched day or night in adverse weather conditions.

1×AGM-45A Shrike anti-radiation air-to-surface missile mounted on the port inner underwing pylon
1×AGM-65 Maverick air-to-surface missile mounted on the starboard inner underwing pylon
1×ALQ-119 dual-mode ECM jammer pod mounted in the forward port underfuselage semi-recessed station
2×370-US gal (1401-litre) drop tanks, one on each outer underwing station
1×600-US gal (2271-litre) drop tank mounted on the underfuselage centreline station

F-4G anti-radar attack
Designed specifically to go in, root out and destroy enemy air-defence systems, the F-4G 'Advanced Wild Weasel' offers formidable detection and attack capabilities through a wide range of weapons and its highly effective APR-38 system, the latter providing threat information and data for automatic weapons release and a blind-bombing capability. In this configuration the emphasis is on attack.

2×AIM-9M Sidewinder IR-homing AAMs, one on each inner underwing pylon
2×AGM-88A HARM anti-radiation air-to-surface missiles, one on each outer underwing pylon
2×AIM-7F Sparrow semi-active radar-homing AAMs, one semi-recessed in each of the two rear underfuselage stations
1×ALQ-131 advanced ECM jamming pod mounted in the forward port underfuselage semi-recessed station
1×600-US gal (2271-litre) drop tank mounted on the underfuselage centreline station

F-4G advanced anti-radar attack
This is the latest radar-suppression configuration now being used by F-4G 'Advanced Wild Weasel' units with the HARM (High-speed Anti-Radiation Missile) replacing the Shrike as the primary attack weapon and allowing for a greater range of potential targets to be attacked other than those associated with surface-to-air systems.

Specification: F-4E Phantom II

Wings
Span	11.71 m	(38 ft 5 in)
Width wings folded	8.39 m²	(27 ft 6.5 in)
Area	29.24 m²	(530.0 sq ft)

Fuselage and tail unit
Accommodation pilot and radar intercept officer on ejector seats
Length overall	19.20 m	(63 ft 0 in)
Height overall	5.03 m	(16 ft 6 in)
Tailplane span	5.47 m	(17 ft 11.5 in)

Landing gear
Retractable tricycle landing gear with single-wheel main and twin wheel nose units
Wheelbase	7.12 m	(23 ft 4.5 in)
Wheel track	5.45 m	(17 ft 10.5 in)

Weights
Empty	13757 kg	(30,328 lb)
Combat take-off	18818 kg	(41,487 lb)
Maximum take-off	28030 kg	(61,795 lb)
Maximum external load	7257 kg	(16,000 lb)
Internal fuel load	5575 kg	(12,290 lb)
Maximum external fuel	4005 kg	(8,830 lb)

F-4E Phantom II recognition features

The fuselage sides are bulged but with smooth contours to house the side-by-side engine arrangement

Pronounced anhedral on the one-piece, all-moving stabilator

Outer main wing sections have 12° dihedral

Very wide-track, single-wheel main landing gear

Very noticeable downward angle of the fuselage when viewed head-on

Very deep but relatively narrow engine air intakes, the boundary-layer splitter plate extending well forward

Very broad, swept vertical tail surfaces

The fuselage tapers very sharply aft of the engine exhaust nozzles

Long, narrow and smoothly-contoured main canopies and windshield blending into the aircraft spine at the rear

A long, slimmer nose characterizes the F-4E, the whole section having very evident downward slant

The M61 A1 cannon has a long and prominent undernose fairing with the muzzle at the front

Sharply-inclined tailcone fairing separates the engine exhaust nozzles. An arrester hook is carried below

Performance:

Maximum speed, at 40,000 ft (12190 m) Mach 2.25 or 1290 kts (2390 km/h; 1,485 mph)
Maximum speed at sea level	Mach 1.18 or 780 kts	(1445 km/h; 898 mph)
Cruising speed at optimum altitude	508 kts	(941 km/h; 585 mph)
Initial rate of climb	61,400 ft	(18715 m) per minute
Combat ceiling	57,200 ft	(17435 m)
Service ceiling	62,250 ft	(18975 m)
Combat radius Hi-Lo-Hi with two 1400 litre (370 US gal) tanks	680 km	(423 miles)
Ferry range	3034 km	(1,885 miles)
Take-off distance to clear 50 ft (15 m) obstacle	1792 m	(5,880 ft)

Service ceiling

- McDonnell Douglas F-4E 62,250 ft
- Mikoyan-Gurevich MiG-23MF ('Flogger-B') 61,000 ft E
- BAC Lightning F.Mk 6 60,000 ft +
- McDonnell Douglas F-4K/M (Spey) 60,000 ft
- McDonnell Douglas F-15E 60,000 ft +
- Mikoyan-Gurevich MiG-21 MF ('Fishbed-J') 50,000 ft
- Panavia Tornado F. Mk 2 50,000 ft +
- General Dynamics F-16A 50,000 ft +

Initial rate of climb per minute

- McDonnell Douglas F-4E 61,400 ft
- BAC Lightning F.Mk 6 50,000 ft
- McDonnell Douglas F-15E 50,000 ft
- General Dynamics F-16A 40,000 ft + E
- MiG-21MF ('Fishbed-J') 36,090 ft E
- MiG-23MF ('Flogger-B') 36,090 ft E
- McDonnell Douglas F-4K/M (Spey) 32,000 ft E
- Panavia Tornado F.Mk 2 30,000 ft E

Maximum speed at high altitude

- McDonnell Douglas F-15E Mach 2.5 +
- Mikoyan-Gurevich MiG-23MF ('Flogger-B') Mach 2.35 E
- BAC Lightning F.Mk 6 Mach 2.27
- McDonnell Douglas F-4E (J79) Mach 2.25
- Panavia Tornado F.Mk 2 Mach 2.16
- McDonnell Douglas F-4K/M (Spey) Mach 2.1
- Mikoyan-Gurevich MiG-21MF ('Fishbed-J') Mach 2.1
- General Dynamics F-16A Mach 2.0 +

Maximum speed at sea level

- McDonnell Douglas F-15E Mach 1.23
- McDonnell Douglas F-4K/M (Spey) Mach 1.2
- Mikoyan-Gurevich MiG-23MF ('Flogger-B') Mach 1.2 E
- McDonnell Douglas F-4E (J79) Mach 1.18
- Panavia Tornado F.Mk 2 Mach 1.1
- Mikoyan-Gurevich MiG-21MF ('Fishbed-J') Mach 1.06
- BAC Lightning F.Mk 6 Mach 1.06
- General Dynamics F-16A Mach 1.0

Combat radius Hi-Lo-Hi

- McDonnell Douglas F-15E 1200 km +
- Mikoyan-Gurevich MiG-23MF ('Flogger-B') 1000 km E
- General Dynamics F-16A 925 km +
- McDonnell Douglas F-4K/M (Spey) 805 km
- Mikoyan-Gurevich MiG-21MF ('Fishbed-J') 740 km
- Panavia Tornado F.Mk 2 725 km E
- McDonnell Douglas F-4E (J79) 680 km
- BAC Lightning F.Mk 6 600 km

The A10 THUNDERBOLT II

Thunderbolt II: rough, tough, slow and low

Looking more like an escapee from a wartime German drawing board than a modern combat aircraft, the Fairchild Republic A-10A has earned the respect of both its pilots and adversaries. Questions abound over its survivability in the battlezone, yet the strength and firepower of the Warthog will play an enormous part in any future land battle.

Judged solely on aesthetic grounds, the Fairchild Republic A-10A Thunderbolt II has to be one of the least attractive aircraft to have appeared in recent years. Standing high above the ground on its gawky landing gear, with engines which look as if they have been added almost as an afterthought, the A-10A gives a first impression that is almost invariably unflattering, and the type's generally angular appearance undoubtedly played a major part in it being dubbed 'Wart Hog' by pilots of the US Air Force.

On the ground it may appear grotesque. In the air, although the type still looks decidedly odd, it soon became clear that in the hands of a skilled pilot the A-10A is a remarkable performer and one that is well suited for its primary mission of battlefield interdiction. Possessing almost unparalleled agility and manoeuvrability at low level, the Thunderbolt II also has the ability to carry a most impressive array of ordnance, and these two factors conspire to make it a weapon to be at once feared and respected, although there are many who hold the opinion that its low speed would render it vulnerable to enemy defences when operating over a hotly contested battlefield.

While not quite as versatile as the Douglas A-1 Skyraider, the A-10A might with some justification lay claim to the mantle of 'Skyraider of the 1970s' and, indeed, it is in many ways similar to the classic 'Spad', being exceedingly tough yet simple to maintain, fairly easy to fly and, perhaps most important of all, able to loiter within the vicinity of the battlefield with a quite respectable weapons load for prolonged periods. 'Handsome is as handsome does' they often say, and on this basis the Thunderbolt II can be described only as a beautiful aircraft. Nevertheless, the quantity produced for service with the USAF is relatively modest when compared with the products of other contemporary programmes such as the McDonnell Douglas F-15 and General Dynamics F-16 for, with the two prototypes and six pre-production examples taken into account, the total number of A-10s built was just 721, the last example of which was handed over to the USAF on 20 March 1984.

The low-cost philosophy which was an inherent aspect of the entire project means that although the A-10A is an unusual design, it possesses few innovative features. Construction is largely conventional, the fuselage consisting of three major sub-assemblies, namely front, centre and rear with four continuous longerons and multiple frames providing the basic structure. Aluminium alloy is predominant, although extensive use is made of titanium armour plating in and around the cockpit where it protects the pilot and vulnerable items such as control column linkages. The wing is a triple-spar structure made up of a one-piece centre section with integrally strengthened skinning and two outer panels based on conventional rib, stringer and skin methods of construction, as are the vertical and horizontal tail surfaces. The offset nosewheel and main landing gear units all retract forwards, the mainwheels being housed in fairings located on the extreme leading edge of the wing centre section. This rather unusual arrangement permits a greater amount of wing area to be set aside for the carriage of

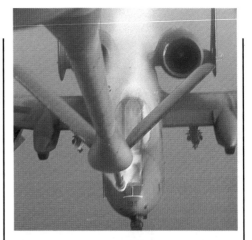

▲ Inflight-refuelling is not an important part of the A-10's combat operations, but does enable it to deploy quickly to global hotspots as part of America's rapid reaction forces. This 81st TFW 'Boar' receives a faceful as the KC-135's boom is retracted.

◄ The harsh, snowy wastes of Alaska would be ideal for the tough Soviet troops and equipment, and would provide a good hold on the American mainland. The USAF has consequently stationed A-10s here to counter any attempted armoured drive across the territory.

weaponry.

Motive power is furnished by two General Electric TF34-GE-100 high-bypass-ratio turbofan engines. Each is rated at 4112-kg (9,065-lb) static thrust, and the engines are positioned high up on the aft fuselage side, where the hot gases are partially masked by the wing, thus reducing the type's infra-red signature from below and making it less vulnerable to heat-seeking missiles.

Total integral fuel capacity is of the order of 4853 kg (10,700 lb), this being contained in four self-sealing cells, two surmounting the wing box directly aft of the cockpit and two more located in the wing centre section. Additional fuel may be carried in auxiliary drop tanks, the Thunderbolt II having no less than 11 stores stations which permit it to carry a maximum external payload of 7257 kg (16,000 lb). However, with a full weapons payload internal fuel capacity is limited. As far as weaponry is concerned, the A-10A is able to operate with most of the items of conventional ordnance now found in the US arsenal, these including AGM-65 Maverick air-to-surface missiles, Rockeye cluster bomb units, 'Paveway' laser-guided bombs, 'Hobos' electro-optically guided bombs, Mk 84 2,000-lb (907-kg) bombs, Mk 82 500-lb (227-kg) bombs and napalm.

In addition there is the quite fearsome integral General Electric GAU-8/A Avenger seven-barrelled 30-mm Gatling-type rotary cannon around which the A-10A was more or less built. A truly massive weapon, this is some 6.71m (22 ft) long, tips the scales at an impressive 1856 kg (4,091 lb) and fires shells which weigh slightly more than 0.91 kg (2 lb), the associated ammunition drum being able to accommodate a total of 1,174 rounds of either high explosive or armour-piercing incendiary shells. High explosive rounds are intended mainly for use against what are euphemistically described as 'soft' targets such as vehicles or supply dumps, while armour-piercing ammunition is more normally employed against 'hard' targets such as tanks and armoured personnel carriers. Ammunition is fed to the firing chambers by a double-ended linkless system driven by dual hydraulic motors operating off the Thunderbolt II's hydraulic systems. Two rates of fire (2,100 rpm or 4,200 rpm) are available, only a single motor being used when the lower rate is selected. Almost inevitably, the remarkable rate of fire has led to some restrictions being imposed to avoid the possibility of overheating, and the design firing duration is 10 2-second bursts with a 60-second period between each burst.

Although the A-10 is compatible with a variety of hardware, the most commonly used mix employed in the tank-busting role would be four to six maverick air-to-surface missiles backed up by the GAU-8/A gun, this enabling targets to be engaged at short range as well as in a sort of 'stand-off' mode in instances where the threat from enemy anti-aircraft weapons (such as the ZSU-23-4 Shilka multi-barrelled mobile 23-mm cannon system, the SA-8 'Gecko' mobile surface-to-air missile system and the SA-13 SAM) are considered to be high. Operating tactics will, of course, play an important part in any battle, and these are continually being refined in the light of developing Soviet capability. Basically, though, it appears that the A-10's remarkable manoeuvrability will be a key factor in ensuring its survival for, when flying at normal cruise speed at ultra low level, it can take full advantage of all available cover while looking for targets, only emerging into the high-threat area for sufficient time to permit a target to be engaged, thereafter getting back down 'amongst the weeds' as soon as possible. In this way, the time available for enemy anti-aircraft systems visually to acquire and lock-on to the A-10 is kept to the barest minimum. Detailed studies of West Germany's Fulda Gap (long viewed as a likely area for combat) have resulted in the finding that the hilly terrain would significantly impair the capability of the ZSU-23-4 if the target kept below an altitude of 90m (300ft). One additional benefit of such low-level operations is that it limits the risk of destruction by enemy fighter aircraft for, although Soviet forces do have some 'look-down/shoot-down' capability, this is unlikely to be able to deal effectively with a slow-moving machine like the Thunderbolt II.

Performance

With regard to performance, sheer speed was never a key factor in its design, with the result that the A-10's maximum speed with weapons is rather on the low side, being just 368 kts (682 km/h/424 mph) in level flight while it can cruise at about 336 kts (623 km/h/387 mph) with maximum payload at an altitude of 1525 m (5,000 ft). However, since the A-10 is expected to spend much of its time at altitudes of the order of 15-30 m (50-100 ft) over the battlefield, manoeuvrability was clearly of paramount importance and there can be few who would question the A-10's ability in this area, the aircraft possessing a quite remarkable turn radius. In addition, the A-10 is no slouch when it comes to field performance, being able to lift a respectable payload even when flying from forward strips of just 305-m (1,000-ft) length, while at maximum gross weight it unsticks in 1220 m (4,000 ft).

The first full production A-10A made its maiden flight on 21 October 1975, delive-

The A-10 concept stemmed from the need for a counter-insurgency aircraft for use in the jungles of South East Asia. Like its Central Front heliborne partner, the Bell AH-1 Cobra, the role quickly changed to dedicated anti-armour following the end of the war in Vietnam.

ries to Tactical Air Command beginning just a few months later (in February 1976) when the 355th Tactical Fighter Training Wing at Davis-Monthan AFB, Arizona received its first example. As its designation implies, the 355th TFTW was selected to serve as the principal training unit, the honour of being the first fully combat-capable A-10 wing falling to the 354th Tactical Fighter Wing at Myrtle beach AFB, South Carolina which began to convert from the

---

▲ *The incredible GAU-8/A Avenger cannon forms the heart of the A-10; the aircraft was more or less designed round it. Armament is housed in a titanium box for protection. Both armour-piercing (for tanks) and high-explosive (for trucks and buildings) rounds are carried, each weighing about 0.91 kg (2 lb).*

◄ *The gun is restricted to short bursts as the weight*

of fire can cause the aircraft to slow down dramatically.

▼ *The AGM-65 Maverick TV-guided missile provides the A-10 with stand-off ability, enabling it to destroy tanks without getting too close to areas of intense ground-fire. In the future, infra-red and laser-guided versions should be available, allowing the A-10 to make fire-and-forget attacks.*

Vought A-7D Corsair in July 1977 and which has since been joined by the 23rd TFW at England AFB, Louisiana. One other TAC component which also operates the 'Warthog' is the 57th Fighter Weapons Wing at Nellis AFB, Nevada, this important unit being principally concerned with formulating operational doctrine, conceiving and evaluating tactics, and assessing new weapons: consequently, it operates some examples of most of the types presently found in the TAC inventory.

Deployment

In addition to these US-based units, the Thunderbolt II has been deployed overseas in fairly substantial numbers, examples of the type now equipping one European-based wing as well as elements of the Alaskan Air Command and the pacific Air Forces. Second-line squadrons of the Air Nation Guard and the Air Force Reserve have also taken delivery of the A-10A, this marking a welcome continuation of the trend towards giving reserve forces equipment comparable with that of their front-line counterparts, and there is no doubt that the advent of the Thunderbolt II has significantly enhanced the capa-

bility of these elements.

One of the key aspects of operational doctrine (and one which was largely proven by the UK-based 81st TFW) entails the use of the so-called FOL (Forward Operating Location). Essentially, this means that the parent wing routinely detaches a portion of its overall complement to other bases where this portion operates on a semi-autonomous basis, dispersal of the force in this way increasing the chances of a substantial part of the unit's strength surviving in the event of a surprise counter-airfield attack. In the case of the 81st TFW, six such FOLs apparently exist (the only four that have been publicly identified being Ahlhorn, Leipheim, Norvenich and Sembach) in West Germany, which is perceived as being the most likely battlefield in the event of a major conventional conflict. Each FOL normally serves as home for about eight to 10 Thunderbolt IIs, the support infrastructure concentrating on meeting operational and tactical requirements in the event of war rather than routine peacetime considerations. Thus, the FOLs are relatively austere, possessing little in the way of sophisticated support equipment, aircraft being rotated regularly from the wing's main bases at Bentwaters and Woodbridge where 'deep' maintenance is performed.

A company proposal to produce a two-seat night/adverse-weather version of the Thunderbolt II resulted in the first of the six pre-production machines being modified to serve as a prototype, this making a successful maiden flight on 4 May 1979. In the event USAF plans to acquire a limited number of a variant known as the A-10B were not implemented and the project was eventually abandoned. Nevertheless, despite the fact that production for the USAF ceased in 1984, Fairchild Republic continues to promote single- and two-seat variants of the Thunderbolt II on the export market, and it is not beyond the realms of possibility that the type could one day be reinstated in production for an overseas customer.

A-10A Thunderbolt II in service units and example aircraft

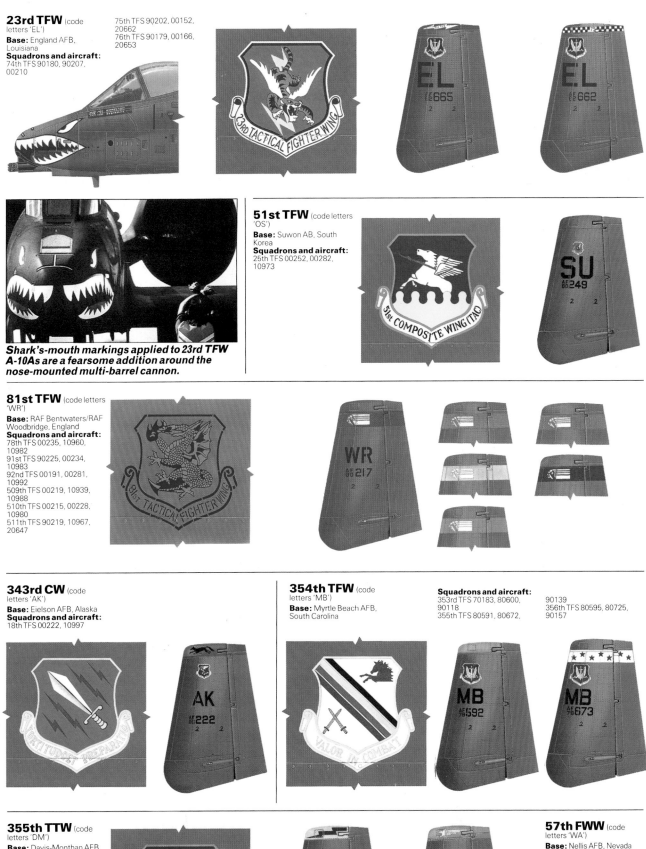

23rd TFW (code letters 'EL')
Base: England AFB, Louisiana
Squadrons and aircraft:
74th TFS 90180, 90207, 00210
75th TFS 90202, 00152, 20662
76th TFS 90179, 00166, 20653

Shark's-mouth markings applied to 23rd TFW A-10As are a fearsome addition around the nose-mounted multi-barrel cannon.

51st TFW (code letters 'OS')
Base: Suwon AB, South Korea
Squadrons and aircraft:
25th TFS 00252, 00282, 10973

81st TFW (code letters 'WR')
Base: RAF Bentwaters/RAF Woodbridge, England
Squadrons and aircraft:
78th TFS 00235, 10960, 10982
91st TFS 90225, 00234, 10983
92nd TFS 00191, 00281, 10992
509th TFS 00219, 10939, 10988
510th TFS 00215, 00228, 10980
511th TFS 90219, 10967, 20647

343rd CW (code letters 'AK')
Base: Eielson AFB, Alaska
Squadrons and aircraft:
18th TFS 00222, 10997

354th TFW (code letters 'MB')
Base: Myrtle Beach AFB, South Carolina
Squadrons and aircraft:
353rd TFS 70183, 80600, 90118
355th TFS 80591, 80672, 90139
356th TFS 80595, 80725, 90157

355th TTW (code letters 'DM')
Base: Davis-Monthan AFB, Arizona
Squadrons and aircraft:
333rd TFTS 50264, 50289, 70187
357th TFTS 50267, 60549, 70201
358th TFTS 50279, 60516, 70222

57th FWW (code letters 'WA')
Base: Nellis AFB, Nevada
Squadrons and aircraft:
A-10 FWS 90169, 00225, 10958

Air National Guard Units

The A-10 has provided a major step forward in the equipment operated by ANG and AFRes units in recent years, with responsibilities including the reinforcement of front-line units.

176th TFS/128th TFW (code letters 'WI')
Base: Truax Field, Wisconsin
Aircraft: 70250, 70263

138th TFS/174th TFW (code letters 'NY')
Base: Syracuse, New York
Aircraft: 80653, 80711

138th TFS/174th TFG

138th TFS/174th TF

118th TFS/103rd TFG (code letters 'CT')
Base: Bradley Field, Connecticut
Aircraft: 80586, 90103

131st TFS/104th TFG (code letters 'MA')
Base: Barnes Airport, Westfield, Maine
Aircraft: 80611, 80644

104th TFS/175th TFG (code letters 'MD')
Base: Martin Airport, Baltimore, Maryland
Aircraft: 80627, 90088

118th TFS/103rd TFG

131st TFS/104th TFG

131st TFS/104th TFG

104th TFS/175th T

Air Force Reserve Units

434th TFW (code letters 'IN')
Base: Grissom AFB, Indiana
Squadrons and aircraft:
45th TFS 70192, 70234

442nd TFG (code letters 'KC')
Base: Richards-Gebaur AFB, Missouri
Squadrons and aircraft:
303rd TFS 80605, 90114

917th TFG (code letters 'BD')
Base: Barksdale AFB, Louisiana
Squadrons and aircraft:
46th TFTS 80696, 90106
47th TFS 90094, 90156

926th TFG (code letters 'NO')
Base: New Orleans NAS, Louisiana
Squadrons and aircraft
706th TFS 60540, 70273

45th TFS

47th TFTS

46th TFS

Fairchild A-10A Thunderbolt II cutaway drawing key

1 Cannon muzzles
2 Nose cap
3 ILS aerial
4 Air-to-air refuelling receptacle (open)
5 Nosewheel bay (offset to starboard)
6 Cannon barrels
7 Rotary cannon barrel bearing
8 Gun compartment ventilating intake
9 L-band radar warning aerial
10 Electrical system relay switches
11 Windscreen rain dispersal air duct
12 Pave Penny laser receiver and tracking pod
13 Windscreen panel
14 Head-up display symbol generator
15 Pilot's head-up display screen
16 Instrument panel shroud
17 Air-to-air refuelling pipe
18 Titanium armour cockpit enclosure
19 Rudder pedals
20 Battery
21 General Electric GAU-8/A 30-mm seven-barrelled rotary cannon
22 Ammunition feed ducts
23 Steering cylinder
24 Nose undercarriage leg strut
25 Nosewheel
26 Nosewheel scissor links
27 Retractable boarding ladder
28 Ventilating air outlets
29 Ladder stowage box
30 Pilot's side console panel

31 Engine throttles
32 Control column
33 McDonnell Douglas ACES 2 ejection seat
34 Headrest canopy breakers
35 Cockpit canopy cover
36 Canopy hinge mechanism
37 Space provision for additional avionics
38 Angle-of-attack probe
39 Emergency canopy release handle
40 Ventral access panels to gun compartment
41 Ammunition drum (1,174 rounds)
42 Ammunition drum armour plating
43 Electrical system servicing panel
44 Ventral fin
45 Spent cartridge-case return chute
46 Control cable runs
47 Avionics compartments
48 Forward/centre fuselage joint bulkhead
49 Aerial selector switches
50 IFF aerial
51 Anti-collision light
52 UHF/TACAN aerial
53 Starboard wing integral fuel tank
54 Wing skin plating
55 Outer wing panel attachment joint strap
56 Starboard fixed wing pylons
57 ALE-37A chaff dispenser pod
58 ALQ-119 electronic countermeasures pod
59 Pitot tube

60 Starboard drooped wing tip fairing
61 Split aileron/deceleron mass balance
62 Deceleron open position
63 Starboard aileron/deceleron
64 Deceleron hydraulic jack
65 Aileron hydraulic jack
66 Control linkages
67 Aileron tab
68 Tab balance weight
69 Slotted trailing edge flaps
70 Outboard flap jack
71 Flap synchronizing shafts
72 Fuselage self-sealing fuel cells (maximum internal fuel capacity 10,700 lb/4853 kg)
73 Fuselage main longeron
74 Longitudinal control and services duct
75 Air conditioning supply duct
76 Wing attachment fuselage main frames
77 Gravity fuel filler caps
78 Engine pylon fairing
79 Pylon attachment joint
80 Starboard intake
81 Intake centre cone
82 Engine fan blades
83 Night/adverse weather two-seater variant
84 Radar pod (forward looking infra-red in starboard pod)
85 Engine mounting struts
86 Nacelle construction
87 Oil tank
88 General Electric TF34-GE-100 turbofan
89 Rear engine mounting
90 Pylon trailing edge fillet
91 Engine exhaust duct

92 Fan air duct
93 Rudder hydraulic jack
94 Starboard tail fin
95 X-band aerial
96 Rudder mass balance weight
97 Starboard rudder
98 Elevator tab
99 Tab control rod
100 Starboard elevator
101 Starboard tailplane
102 Tailplane attachment frames
103 Elevator hydraulic jacks
104 Tailcone
105 Tail navigation light
106 Rear radar warning receiver aerial
107 Honeycomb elevator construction
108 Port vertical tailfin construction
109 Honeycomb rudder panel
110 Rudder hydraulic jack
111 Formation light
112 Vertical fin ventral fairing
113 Tailplane construction
114 Tailplane control links
115 Port engine exhaust duct
116 Tailboom frame construction
117 VHF/AM aerial
118 Fuel jettison
119 VHF/FM aerial
120 Fuel jettison duct
121 Hydraulic reservoir
122 Port engine nacelle attachment joint
123 Cooling system intake and exhaust duct
124 Engine bleed air ducting
125 Auxiliary power unit
126 APU exhaust
127 Engine nacelle access door

128 Air conditioning plant
129 Port engine intake
130 Trailing edge wing root fillet
131 Fuselage bomb rack
132 Inboard slotted flap
133 Flap guide rails
134 Rear spar
135 Flap shroud structure
136 Honeycomb trailing edge panel
137 Outboard slotted flap
138 Port deceleron open position
139 Aileron tab
140 Aileron hinges
141 Port split aileron/deceleron
142 Drooped wing tip fairing construction
143 Port navigation light
144 Honeycomb leading edge panels
145 Wing rib construction
146 Centre spar
147 Leading edge spar
148 Two outer fixed pylons (1,000-lb/453.6-kg capacity)
149 ALQ-119 electronic countermeasures pod
150 ALE-37A chaff dispenser
151 Port mainwheel
152 2,500-lb (1134-kg) capacity stores pylon
153 Main undercarriage leg strut
154 Undercarriage leg doors
155 Main undercarriage leg pivot fixing
156 Port mainwheel semi-recessed housing
157 Pressure refuelling point
158 Undercarriage pod fairing

irchild A-10A warload

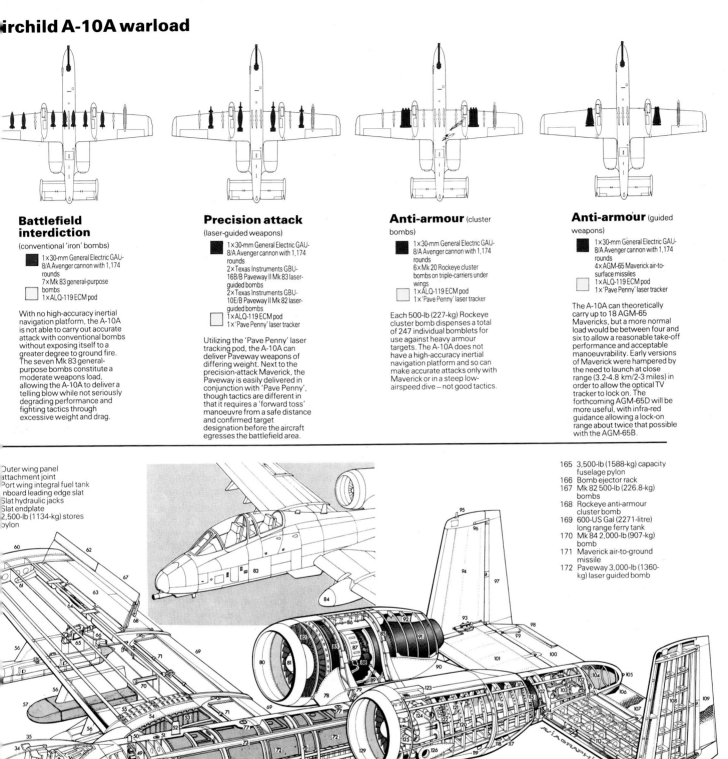

Battlefield interdiction
(conventional 'iron' bombs)

- 1 × 30-mm General Electric GAU-8/A Avenger cannon with 1,174 rounds
- 7 × Mk 83 general-purpose bombs
- 1 × ALQ-119 ECM pod

With no high-accuracy inertial navigation platform, the A-10A is not able to carry out accurate attack with conventional bombs without exposing itself to a greater degree to ground fire. The seven Mk 83 general-purpose bombs constitute a moderate weapons load, allowing the A-10A to deliver a telling blow while not seriously degrading performance and fighting tactics through excessive weight and drag.

Precision attack
(laser-guided weapons)

- 1 × 30-mm General Electric GAU-8/A Avenger cannon with 1,174 rounds
- 2 × Texas Instruments GBU-16B/B Paveway II Mk 83 laser-guided bombs
- 2 × Texas Instruments GBU-10E/B Paveway II Mk 82 laser-guided bombs
- 1 × ALQ-119 ECM pod
- 1 × 'Pave Penny' laser tracker

Utilizing the 'Pave Penny' laser tracking pod, the A-10A can deliver Paveway weapons of differing weight. Next to the precision-attack Maverick, the Paveway is easily delivered in conjunction with 'Pave Penny', though tactics are different in that it requires a 'forward toss' manoeuvre from a safe distance and confirmed target designation before the aircraft egresses the battlefield area.

Anti-armour (cluster bombs)

- 1 × 30-mm General Electric GAU-8/A Avenger cannon with 1,174 rounds
- 6 × Mk 20 Rockeye cluster bombs on triple-carriers under wings
- 1 × ALQ-119 ECM pod
- 1 × 'Pave Penny' laser tracker

Each 500-lb (227-kg) Rockeye cluster bomb dispenses a total of 247 individual bomblets for use against heavy armour targets. The A-10A does not have a high-accuracy inertial navigation platform and so can make accurate attacks only with Maverick or in a steep low-airspeed dive – not good tactics.

Anti-armour (guided weapons)

- 1 × 30-mm General Electric GAU-8/A Avenger cannon with 1,174 rounds
- 4 × AGM-65 Maverick air-to-surface missiles
- 1 × ALQ-119 ECM pod
- 1 × 'Pave Penny' laser tracker

The A-10A can theoretically carry up to 18 AGM-65 Mavericks, but a more normal load would be between four and six to allow a reasonable take-off performance and acceptable manoeuvrability. Early versions of Maverick were hampered by the need to launch at close range (3.2-4.8 km/2-3 miles) in order to allow the optical TV tracker to lock on. The forthcoming AGM-65D will be more useful, with infra-red guidance allowing a lock-on range about twice that possible with the AGM-65B.

Outer wing panel
attachment joint
Port wing integral fuel tank
nboard leading edge slat
Slat hydraulic jacks
Slat endplate
2,500-lb (1134-kg) stores
pylon

165 3,500-lb (1588-kg) capacity fuselage pylon
166 Bomb ejector rack
167 Mk 82 500-lb (226.8-kg) bombs
168 Rockeye anti-armour cluster bomb
169 600-US Gal (2271-litre) long range ferry tank
170 Mk 84 2,000-lb (907-kg) bomb
171 Maverick air-to-ground missile
172 Paveway 3,000-lb (1360-kg) laser guided bomb

© Pilot Press Limited

Specification:

Fairchild A-10A Thunderbolt II

Wings

Span	17.53 m	(57 ft 6 in)
Chord, at root	3.04 m	(9 ft 11.5 in)
at tip	1.99 m	(6 ft 6.4 in)
Area	47.01 m²	(506.0 sq ft)

Fuselage and tail unit

Length overall	16.26 m	(53 ft 4 in)
Height overall	4.47 m	(14 ft 8 in)

Landing gear

Wheelbase	5.40 m	(17 ft 8.75 in)
Wheel track	5.25 m	(17 ft 2.5 in)

Weights

Empty	11321 kg	(24,959 lb)
Take-off, operating from forward airstrip with four Mk 82 bombs, 750 rounds of ammunition and 2041 kg (4,500 lb) of fuel	14865 kg	(32,771 lb)
Maximum take-off	22680 kg	(50,000 lb)
Maximum internal fuel	4853 kg	(10,700 lb)
Maximum auxiliary fuel in drop tanks	2410 kg	(5,314 lb)
Maximum weapon load	7257 kg	(16,000 lb)
Maximum weapon load with full internal fuel	6505 kg	(14,341 lb)

Fairchild Republic A-10A Thunderbolt II recognition points

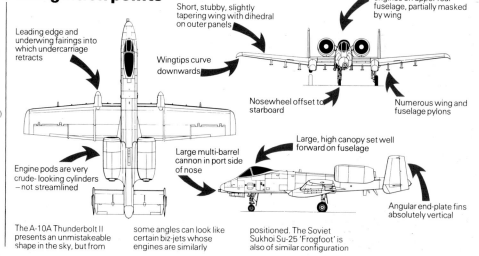

Leading edge and underwing fairings into which undercarriage retracts

Short, stubby, slightly tapering wing with dihedral on outer panels

Twin, pod-mounted engines on upper rear fuselage, partially masked by wing

Wingtips curve downwards

Nosewheel offset to starboard

Numerous wing and fuselage pylons

Large, high canopy set well forward on fuselage

Engine pods are very crude-looking cylinders – not streamlined

Large multi-barrel cannon in port side of nose

Angular end-plate fins absolutely vertical

The A-10A Thunderbolt II presents an unmistakeable shape in the sky, but from some angles can look like certain biz-jets whose engines are similarly positioned. The Soviet Sukhoi Su-25 'Frogfoot' is also of similar configuration

Performance:

Maximum speed, 'clean' at sea level	381 kts	707 km/h	(439 mph)
Cruising speed at sea level	300 kts	555 km/h	(345 mph)
Combat speed, with six Mk 82 bombs at 5,000 ft (1524 m)	380 kts	705 km/h	(438 mph)
Cruising speed at 5,000 ft (1524 m)	336 kts	623 km/h	(387 mph)
Initial rate of climb per minute	1829 m	(6,000 ft)	
Combat radius with 20-minute fuel reserves:			
close air support, 1.7 hours loiter	463 km	(288 miles)	
deep strike	998 km	(620 miles)	
Ferry range	3949 km	(2,454 miles)	

Weapon load

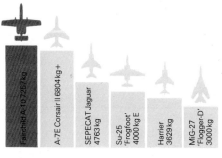

Fairchild A-10 7257 kg
A-7E Corsair II 6804 kg+
SEPECAT Jaguar 4763 kg
Su-25 'Frogfoot' 4000 kg E
Harrier 3629 kg
MiG-27 'Flogger-D' 3000 kg

Time on station 185 km from base

SEPECAT Jaguar	Fairchild A-10	Su-25 'Frogfoot'	BAe Harrier	A-7D Corsair II	MiG-27 'Flogger-D'
110 min E	102 min	100 min	90 min	60 min	30 min E

Speed at sea level

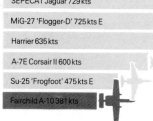

SEPECAT Jaguar 729 kts
MiG-27 'Flogger-D' 725 kts E
Harrier 635 kts
A-7E Corsair II 600 kts
Su-25 'Frogfoot' 475 kts E
Fairchild A-10 381 kts

Take-off run

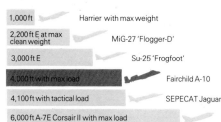

1,000 ft — Harrier with max weight
2,200 ft E at max clean weight — MiG-27 'Flogger-D'
3,000 ft E — Su-25 'Frogfoot'
4,000 ft with max load — Fairchild A-10
4,100 ft with tactical load — SEPECAT Jaguar
6,000 ft A-7E Corsair II with max load

Combat radius lo-lo-lo

SEPECAT Jaguar 917 km with external fuel
A-7D Corsair II 885 km
Fairchild A-10 463 km with 20 min reserve
MiG-27 'Flogger-D' 390 km E with 2900-kg load
Harrier 370 km
Su-25 'Frogfoot' 300 km E

Fairchild A-10 Thunderbolt II variants

YA-10A: designation of two prototypes (71-1369/1370) for evaluation against the competing Northrop YA-9A

A-10A: sole production version of which 739 were planned, but funding was terminated in 1984 after 713 had been completed (including the six D, T & E pre-production aircraft)

N/AW A-10: company-funded night/all-weather derivative of the A-10A, produced as a conversion of the first of the six D, T & E aircraft (73-1664) leased from the USAF; basic dimensions unchanged but height of vertical tail surfaces increased by 0.51 m (1 ft 8 in) and empty weight increased by 948 kg (2,091 lb); role equipment included General Electric LLTV (low-light TV) sensors, Texas Instruments AAR-42 FLIR (forward-looking infra-red) and Westinghouse WX-50 terrain-avoidance radar; no production

A-10B: planned two-seat trainer version using structure of N/AW A-10 and retaining full operational capability; procurement of 30 was intended for Air National Guard and US Air Force Reserve but was ultimately not funded

Right: Avionics in the A-10A have been kept to a minimum. The instrument panel has fuel gauges at extreme right and a panel of 12 dials covering engine and APU operation. Immediately above these are the altimeter and variometer, with the large video display screen for use in Maverick missile launches to their right. The centre panel is occupied by the artificial horizon and direction indicator. The left-hand area has weapons select and release panels, with the dials above including airspeed indicator, angle of attack and stand-by artificial horizon. On top of the instrument panel is the head-up display (HUD) unit, which displays information such as vertical speed and flight angle, distance and time to pre-programmed waypoints and navigation details, linked to the inertial navigation system.

Below: The A-10B night/adverse weather development has a two-seat enlarged cockpit, increased fin height and two avionic subsystem pods on underfuselage pylons. These avionics were to be incorporated in the wing leading-edge and landing gear fairings for the intended production A-10B.

The NORTH AMERICAN ROCKWELL B.1.B.

Rockwell B-1B: cruise on, B-1

Although the B-1B is indisputedly an extremely advanced warplane, packed with sophisticated navigation and attack systems, there are still nagging doubts about its ability to penetrate enemy airspace.

During the first 21 years following its establishment on 18 September 1947, the United States Air Force placed into service nine types of bombers: three were tactical bombers (the North American B-45, Martin B-57 and Douglas B-66) and six were strategic bombers (the Boeing B-50, Convair B-36, Boeing B-47, Boeing B-52, Convair B-58 and General Dynamics FB-111). However, the FB-111A, which was first accepted on 8 October 1968, almost became the last US manned bomber as changing operational environment and political bickering long frustrated SAC endeavours to obtain new aircraft. At last, after a 17-year drought, the first Rockwell International B-1B was turned over to SAC on 29 June 1985. Unfortunately, the politically-unloved B-1B soon found itself embroiled in a controversy.

Development
According to a March 1987 report issued by the House Armed Services Committee: 'The biggest problem confronting the B-1B is not its weight growth, its fuel leaks or its uncertain electronic countermeasures. The greatest problem is the Air Force itself, which exerts more effort to obscure the B-1's problems than to correct them. In the bluntest of terms, the United States Air Force has been a greater threat to the success of the B-1 bomber than the Soviet Union.' Conversely, at about the same time, the commander of the first operational wing, the 96th Bombardment Wing

at Dyess AFB, Texas, quietly stated: 'I don't have any show-stoppers. Nothing's keeping me out of the air. The problems we've seen are teething problems except for the fuel leaks, and that's behind us.' He also added: 'We're having no problems here, but we are maturing the airplane in a cautious manner just because we don't see any need to increase any risk.'

Without access to classified data, but faced on one hand with some obvious congressional grandstanding and on the other with a concerted effort within the Air Force to downplay problems, it is difficult to pass an unbiased judgement. However, one should remember that for one year after it entered service in June 1955 the mighty B-52 Stratofortress also experienced some serious fuel leaks and that its first production model, the B-52B of which 50 were built, had only an abbreviated service life lasting barely one year. In the end, these teething troubles did not prevent later models of the B-52 from having a long, and as yet far from finished, military career. Clearly, before having their mentors voice ill-advised criticisms, young congressional staffers would benefit from studying past programmes and from seeking to understand the Air Force 20-year quest (from the SLAB study of 1961 to the B-1B) for a survivable manned bomber as the third leg of the 'Triad' nuclear deterrence concept.

In December 1957, two and a half years after the first B-52B had been delivered to

SAC, the Air Force initiated the development of a new heavy bomber by awarding to North American Aviation Inc. a contract to design and build two XB-70 prototypes. No one could then have predicted that more than 27 years were to go by before a partial successor for the B-52 could be placed into service. The surprisingly quick end of the B-70 as a bomber came in May 1960, four years before the roll-out of its first prototype: by bringing down Francis Gary Powers' Lockheed U-2B, early Soviet surface-to-air missiles had proved that the days of high-flying subsonic bombers were numbered. The Air Force immediately recognized the need to develop aircraft capable of penetrating the new Soviet defences.

The results were a series of 'alphabet soup' studies, including the Subsonic Low Altitude Bomber (SLAB) in 1961, the Extended Range Strike Aircraft (ERSA) in 1963, the Advanced Manned Precision Strike System (AMPSS) in 1964, and the

▲ The four B-1A prototypes were originally delivered in an overall anti-flash white colour scheme reminiscent of that used by Britain's V-bombers during the late 1950s. This scheme was felt to be too conspicuous in the low-level penetration role.

▼ The third and fourth B-1 prototypes received an unusual desert camouflage scheme. The fourth aircraft was aerodynamically much closer to the production B-1B, and is seen here en route to the 1982 Farnborough Air Show for the type's European debut.

Advanced Manned Strategic Aircraft (AMSA) in the 1965-9 period, with the last finally leading to the development of the Rockwell B-1A ordered in June 1970. President Carter's cancellation of the B-1A production in June 1977 brought about more acronyms such as SAL (Strategic ALCM Launcher), CMCA (Cruise Missile Carrier Aircraft), LRCA (Long-Range Cruise Aircraft), MRB (Multi-Role Bomber), NTP (Near-Term Penetrator) and SWL (Strategic Weapons Launcher), as political wishful thinking was no substitute for manned bombers. At last, the B-1B was ordered on 29 January 1982 as it best met the requirements.

When the first B-1A production contracts were placed in December 1976, the aircraft had been scheduled to enter service in mid-1979 as a nuclear-armed (SRAMs and free-fall bombs) strategic bomber capable of penetrating enemy defences either at low altitude and high subsonic speeds or at high altitude and high Mach. This role, however, was considered too limited by Carter, who in June 1977 cancelled the B-1A production contracts in favour of a development programme for ALCMs. Nevertheless, the president directed that B-1 testing and development be continued, thus keeping the Rockwell programme alive until Carter's successor, President Reagan, announced in October 1981 the intent of his administration to order 100 B-1Bs.

Performance

Notwithstanding their almost identical external appearances, the B-1A and B-1B turned out to be quite different, the latter being developed into a more flexible and capable aircraft. Optimized for 'nap of the earth' nuclear penetration at near supersonic speeds, the B-1B has had its design revised to gain the added capability of undertaking a variety of secondary missions (e.g. cruise missile carriage, conventional bombing, and long-range sea surveillance and interdiction), and has thus been ensured of remaining a viable

weapons system well into the next century. The principal design changes to endow the B-1B with increased operational flexibility and greater survivability against improved Soviet defences included: strengthening of the airframe to increase maximum take-off weight from 179172 kg (395,000 lb) to 216365 kg (477,000 lb); use of strengthened landing gear; modification of the forward weapons bay to carry eight ALCMs; increase in maximum weapon load from 34020 kg (75,000 lb) to 56700 kg (125,000 lb); a 11340-kg (25,000 lb) increase in fuel load when carrying the maximum weapon load; substitution of upward-ejecting seats for the ejection capsule as used on the first three B-1As; and reduction of the radar cross section.

To achieve a significant reduction in the aircraft's radar cross section, the variable engine inlets of the B-1A were replaced with fixed inlets, thus also reducing maximum speed at 50,000 ft (15240 m) from Mach 2.0 to Mach 1.25 but increasing speed 'on the deck' from Mach 0.85 to Mach 0.92. Furthermore, the internal design of the inlets was modified to incorporate radar reflective baffles shielding the fan face, the overwing fairings were streamlined, and the use of radar absorption materials was greatly increased. In addition, the aircraft's ECM systems were substantially upgraded: the B-1A's 88 black boxes weighing more than 2268 kg (5,000 lb) were replaced in the B-1B by 118

▲ The B-1B is optimized for ultra-low level penetration missions at high subsonic speed. Cruise missiles are carried internally on rotary launchers, and on external pylons under the wing roots. Conventional free-fall bombs can also be carried.

▼ The B-1B is only slightly smaller than the Boeing B-52 which it is replacing, but it is dwarfed by the McDonnell Douglas KC-10A Extender seen here. A standard USAF refuelling receptacle is located in the nose of the B-1B.

more compact boxes weighing less than 5,000 lb.

When the first B-1B (82-0001) made its maiden flight on 18 October 1984, five months ahead of schedule and within budget, a rare occurence in military aircraft projects, it benefited from much flight experience gained with the four B-1A prototypes. Before the resumption of flight trials in March 1983, this experience had totalled 1,895.2 hours in 347 flights between 23 December 1974 (when 74-0158 was first airborne) and 29 April 1981 (when 76-0174 made the last programmed B-1A flight test) and proved invaluable. Furthermore, it enabled the Air Force to take delivery of the first B-1B only eight months after the maiden flight of the first production aircraft, in spite of the loss of the second B-1A on 29 August 1984. This haste, which was in part due to a Congressional mandate that the B-1B be operational in 1986 and which resulted in the aircraft reaching IOC when less than 60 per

cent of scheduled testing activities had been completed, now appears to have been excessive. Insufficient time was allotted to test and evaluate not only the relatively minor and easy to incorporate airframe changes distinguishing the B-1B from the B-1A, but also the far more advanced ECM systems.

Critics of the B-1B notably contend that the aircraft is too heavy and consequently cannot fly as high as the old B-52s, has deficient flight controls, is experiencing repeated leakages of its integral fuel tanks and hydraulic systems, and was placed in service without adequate spare parts being made available to support continued testing and service operations. Moreover, in their more serious allegations, they assert that its terrain-following radar is not reliable for the aircraft to be operated safely at low altitudes, that its defensive avionics system is not performing as planned and cannot be operated simultaneously with its offensive avionics system, and that its Central Integrated Test System gives excessively frequent false alarms. Understandably, in view of the $20.5-billion B-1B programme cost for a fleet of only 100 bombers, many influential members of Congress and the media are increasingly concerned that the failure to correct these alleged deficiencies will result in a serious gap in the USA's defences and an unparalleled waste of taxpayers' money.

The first of these criticisms, excessive weight and resultant degradation of cruise altitude, is undoubtedly the least deserved of all and reflects the critics' lack of understanding of the B-1B's mission as, since high-flying aircraft are too vulnerable, it was purposely optimized for low-altitude penetration below enemy radar.

More valid but overstated, the claim that the flight controls are deficient will hopefully be unfounded as soon as the effectiveness of a recently developed stall inhibitor

▼ *A production B-1B taxis out at Palmdale, showing off its sinister dark green and grey colour scheme. The paint almost certainly incorporates some degree of 'stealth' technology, giving it a low infra-red and radar signature.*

▲ *The second B-1A prototype was used for trials of the B-1B flight control system, and for weapons release trials. It was eventually lost in September 1984, killing Rockwell's chief test pilot and seriously injuring two of the crew.*

system can be demonstrated. Similarly, leaks in the fuel and hydraulic systems are, almost, problems of the past as improved manufacturing methods and better maintenance have reduced these leaks to levels equivalent to those experienced with other aircraft types. On the other hand, inadequate spare parts provisioning (a problem not specific to the B-1B as the Department of Defense is frequently forced to save on spare parts procurement in order to remain within budget) will take longer to solve and continues to force the Air Force to cannibalize parts, using a few B-1Bs as 'spare part warehouses'.

Avionics

The haste with which the B-1B was placed in service meant that its OAS, albeit developed from that already used by B-52G/Hs and thus expected to require shorter than normal flight evaluation, could not be fully validated during abbreviated flight trials. Consequently, when the 96th BW achieved IOC, its crews were not authorized to make automatic terrain-following flights below 1,000 ft (305 m) above ground level and at speeds in excess of Mach 0.85, whereas the aircraft had been designed for flights down to 200 ft (60 m) at Mach 0.92. Progressively, these limits have been brought down to 500 ft (150 m) and Mach 0.90 and will soon reach design values, wiping out this criticism.

Problems with interferences between the offensive and defensive avionics systems and with the unreliability of the CITS are so far proving the most serious difficulties faced by the B-1B. Although CITS false alarms dropped from some 115 per flight at the end of 1986 to 75 per flight in the spring of 1987, the unreliability of this self-diagnostic test equipment remains alarmingly poor and far exceeds the contractually required level of three false alarms per flight. True, this deficiency does

not impact on flight safety but it does lead to excessive 'down time' due to the need to check whether CITS-reported failures are genuine or false.

Developed by the AIL Division of Eaton Corporation from its ALQ-161 originally planned for the B-1A and first tested in the model's fourth prototype (76-0174), the B-1B's defensive avionics system consists of four primary sub-systems: the radio frequency surveillance/electronics countermeasures system (RFS/ECMS); the tail-warning function (TWF); the defensive management system (DMS); and the expendable countermeasures system (EXCM). In service both the passive detection subsystem and the EXCM system, eight dispensers each containing either 120 chaff cartridges or 12 IRCM flares, have proved to be effective and reliable.

Currently, the active function of the ALQ-161A continues to be the source of major developmental problems, as the B-1B defensive avionics system is not capable of coping with all known electronic threats and its use may result in interferences with the aircraft's terrain-following system. Consequently, much of the activities of the Combined Test Force at Edwards AFB is now devoted to getting the active jammers to work as advertised, and in the spring of 1987 the Air Force was forced to admit that this may not be achieved for another 1.5 to 2 years.

Only time will tell if the B-1B can mature into a worthy B-52 successor and will have as long an operational career as the Stratofortress. In the meantime, while answering ever more pointed criticisms from Congress and the media, Rockwell International and SAC can take some comfort in the knowledge that Tupolev and the Aviatsiya Dal'nevo Deistviya appear to have even greater difficulties with their 'Blackjack', the Soviet equivalent of the B-1B.

Rockwell B-1B in service

Born out of the US Air Force's Advanced Manned Strategic Aircraft (AMSA) programme of the mid-1960s, the Rockwell B-1B has suffered a bumpy ride on its way to front-line operational service with Strategic Air Command. Initial contracts in 1970 covered five flying prototypes, two static test airframes and 240 production standard B-1s, the last of which was to be delivered during 1981. The first prototype took to the air in December 1974 and the fourth (the number having been cut back by one) in August 1975 as part of the extensive flight test programme. Cancellation by the Carter Administration during 1977 was a severe blow, but two prototypes continued limited flying, and the emergence of a strategic air-launched missile carrier requirement brought the aircraft back into the running. The Reagan Administration's hardline defence led to the programme being reactivated on 2 October 1981 with an order for 100 B-1Bs (this figure including two for permanent testing). The Fiscal Year allocations allow for the following construction programme:

Deliveries to Strategic Air Command began on 7 July 1986 with the second production B-1B going to the 4018th Combat Crew Training Squadron (since redesignated 338th Strategic Bombardment Training Squadron), 96th Bomb Wing at Dyess AFB for work-up. The last aircraft is scheduled to enter service during 1988. The aircraft allocation per wing is as follows:

28th Bombardment Wing
Squadrons: 37th and 77th BS
Base: Ellsworth AFB, South Dakota
Example aircraft: 50071

96th Bombardment Wing
Squadrons: 337th BS and 338th SBTS
Base: Dyess AFB, Texas
Example aircraft: 30069, 40052, 50064, 50075

319th Bombardment Wing
Squadron: 46th BS
Base: Grand Forks AFB, North Dakota
Example: none yet assigned

384th Bombardment Wing
Squadron(s): not yet confirmed
Base: McConnell AFB, Kansas
Example aircraft: none yet assigned

Air Force Systems Command
The first and ninth B-1Bs are permanently assigned to the 6512nd TS as part of a continuing research, test and development programme. The aircraft fly as part of a combined test force.

6512nd Test Squadron/ Air Force Flight Test Center
Base: Edwards AFB, California
Example aircraft: 20001, 40049

The first production B-1B was rolled out at Palmdale on 4 September 1984, and was eventually delivered to the 96th Bomb Wing at Dyess AFB during June 1985.

The main fault experienced by the B-1B in USAF service has been the vulnerability of the terrain-following radar to interference from the active ECM jamming system.

This B-1B is seen plugging into a Boeing KC-135 Stratotanker during its journey to Dyess AFB from Le Bourget, where it had been visiting the Paris Air Show.

Performance

Maximum level speed at 50,000 ft (15240 m) Mach 1.25 or 716 kts; 1328 km/h (825 mph)
Combat cruising speed at 500 ft (150 m) Mach 0.92 or 607 kts; 1125 km/h (699 mph)
Service ceiling at reduced weights over 60,000 ft (18290 m)
Maximum unrefuelled range 11990 km (7,450 miles)

Weapon load

- Rockwell International B-1B 29030 kg typical
- General Dynamics FB-111A 17000 kg
- Tupolev Tu-26 'Backfire' 12000 kg E
- Sukhoi Su-24 'Fencer' 11000 kg E
- Panavia Tornado GR.Mk1 9000 kg
- British Aerospace (HS) S.Mk 2 Buccaneer 7257 kg
- Dassault-Breguet Mirage IVA 4000 kg

Service ceiling

- Dassault-Breguet Mirage IVA 65,600 ft
- General Dynamics FB-111A 60,000 ft +
- Tupolev Tu-26 'Backfire' 55,000 ft E
- Sukhoi Su-24 'Fencer' 54,135 ft E
- Rockwell International B-1B 50,000 ft E
- Panavia Tornado GR.Mk1 50,000 ft+
- British Aerospace Buccaneer (HS) S.Mk 2 40,000 ft + E

Maximum speed at high altitude

- Dassault-Breguet Mirage IVA Mach 2.2
- General Dynamics FB-111A Mach 2.2
- Panavia Tornado GR.Mk1 Mach 2.2 'clean'
- Sukhoi Su-24 'Fencer' Mach 2.18 E
- Tupolev Tu-26 'Backfire' Mach 1.92 E
- Rockwell International B-1B Mach 1.25 E
- British Aerospace S.Mk 2 Buccaneer Mach 0.85

Maximum speed at low altitude

- Sukhoi Su-24 'Fencer' Mach 1.2 E
- General Dynamics FB-111A Mach 1.1
- Dassault-Breguet Mirage IVA Mach 1.1 E
- British Aerospace (HS) S.Mk 2 Buccaneer Mach 0.92
- Tupolev Tu-26 'Backfire' Mach 0.9 E
- Rockwell International B-1B Mach 0.8 E

Range

- Rockwell International B-1B 12000 km E
- Tupolev Tu-26 'Backfire' 11000 km E
- General Dynamics FB-111A 5000 km E
- Sukhoi Su-24 'Fencer' 3900 km E
- Buccaneer British Aerospace (HS) S.Mk 2 3700 km E
- Dassault-Breguet Mirage IVA 3200 km E
- Panavia Tornado GR.Mk1 3000 km E

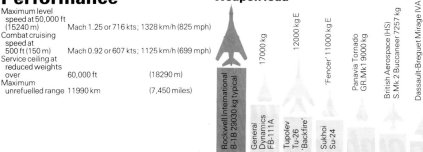

B-1 recognition features

Specification: Rockwell B-1B

Wings

Span, unswept	41.67 m	(136 ft 8.5 in)
swept	23.84 m	(78 ft 2.5 in)
Area	181.16 m²	(1,950 sq ft)

Fuselage and tail unit

Accommodation	pilot, co-pilot, offensive and defensive systems officers	
Length overall	44.81 m	(147 ft 0 in)
Height overall	10.24 m	(33 ft 7.25 in)
Tailplane span	13.67 m	(44 ft 10 in)

Landing gear

Retractable tricycle landing gear with four-wheeled main bogies and twin nosewheels

Wheel track	4.42 m	(14 ft 6 in)
Wheelbase	17.53 m	(57 ft 6 in)

Weights

Empty	87090 kg	(192,000 lb)
Maximum take-off	216364 kg	(477,000 lb)

Powerplant

Four General Electric F101-GE-102 afterburning turbofans

Thrust rating, each with reheat	13948 kg	(30,750 lb)
Available fuel	740237 litres	(195,550 US gal)
Available fuel (with bomb bay tanks)	845528 litres	(223,365 US gal)

Variable-geometry outer wing sections

Thick wing section blends into fuselage

Engines mounted in tv nacelles under inboard section

Smooth contours to fuselage

Small canard foreplanes

Mid-set tai

Long dorsal strake

Exhaust nozzles project beyond trailing edge

Smooth contours to fuselage

Long, ogival ta

Long, heavy landing gear units

B-1B warload

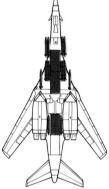

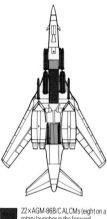

38 × AGM-69A Short Range Attack Missiles (24 on three rotary launchers in the internal weapons bay and 14 on the eight external hardpoints)

32 × B-83 free-fall nuclear bombs (24 on three rotary launchers in the internal weapons bays and eight on the eight external hardpoints)

22 × AGM-86B/C ALCMs (eight on a rotary launcher in the forward weapons bay and 14 on the eight external hardpoints)

1 × 18170-litre (4,800-US gal) auxiliary fuel tank ahead of the ALCMs in the forward weapons bay
1 × 32080-litre (8,475-US gal) auxiliary fuel tank in the rear weapons bay

128 × 500-lb (227 kg) Mk 82 free-fall 'iron' bombs in the internal weapons bays and 44 on the eight external hardpoints

© Pilot Press Lt

Nuclear penetration (SRAM)

The SRAMs have warheads in the 170-200 kiloton range and can be launched at distances up to 220 km (137 miles). Three types of rotary launcher are used for the delivery of nuclear weapons

Nuclear penetration (free-fall)

The B-83 is the primary free-fall nuclear bomb for use by the B-1B force, though the smaller, less powerful B-61 can also be carried. Earlier models such as the B-28 and B-43 are being retired.

Cruise missile platform

The dimensions of the ALCM mean that the bulkhead dividing the two forward weapons bays has to be repositioned to provide a larger aft section.

Conventional bombing

An awesome capability is provided by this warload, which would devastate a large area in a similar manner to the B-52 saturation bombing missions during the Vietnam war.

B-1 variants

B-1 no. 1 (74-0158): first of the four flying prototypes for B-1 RDT&E programme; first flown on 23 December 1974 and used specifically for flight qualification tests; total of 79 flights completed; features include a long nose test boom, short forward fuselage, crew escape module, two-dimensional engine inlets, pre-production long engine nozzles and pointed tailcone; powered by four General Electric YF101-GE-100 turbofan engines; retroactively designated B-1A when the B-1B production order was announced (as were the second, third and fourth B-1 prototypes); now withdrawn from use

B-1 no. 2 (74-0159): used for evaluation of structural load parameters in ground and air tests; first flown on 14 June '74; 60 flights completed; distinguishing features as per B-1 no. 1; received interim modifications to act as test aircraft for B-1B programme; duties include weaponry release and separation, engine and systems evaluation; also received B-1B flight control system configuration; aircraft crashed and written off on 29 August '84

B-1 no. 3 (74-0160): assigned to offensive/defensive weapons systems trials; first flew on 1 April '76, completing 138 flights; distinguishing features as per B-1 no. 1, but spine fairing added during ECM tests; navigation lights removed during test programme and 'Crosseye' ECM equipment fitted (though later partially removed); aircraft now withdrawn from use

B-1 no. 4 (76-0174): tasked with ECM/ESM/ECCM systems evaluation but with more comprehensive systems integration; 70 flights completed as part of the original programme; first flown 14 February '79; aerodynamically more similar to the production standard B-1B, features including a blunt tailcone and rear sensor cut-outs, shorter, more ogival nose radome, longer forward fuselage and ejection seats; brought up to B-1B standard and first

flown as such on 30 July '84 with full offensive/defensive avionics systems; two-dimensional engine inlets and longer nozzles retained; fuselage spine fitted but later removed

B-1B: full production standard model for service with US Air Force; powered by four General Electric F101-GE-102 turbofan engines each rated at 13608 kg (30,000 lb st); externally very similar to the B-1As, but changes include the replacement of variable geometry engine inlets by fixed inlets, shorter engine nacelles, blunt tailcone replacing sharper example on B-1As, a new, shorter ogival radome, forward fuselage has been lengthened in similar manner to B-1A no. 4; internal changes include the replacement of the crew escape capsule by four Weber ACES II ejector seats, structural strengthening and increase in overall gross weights, strengthened landing gear and up to eight external hardpoints for ordnance or fuel; a movable bulkhead dividing the two forward weapons bays has been incorporated from the ninth production B-1B and will be retrofitted to the first eight examples; small sweptback vanes with 30° anhedral each side of the nose

ockwell International B-1B cutaway drawing key

Rockwell International B-1B cutaway drawing

(left column, partially cut off)
- adome
- ulti-mode phased array
- dar scanner
- w-observable shrouded
- anner tracking
- echanism
- dar mounting bulkhead
- dome hinge joint
- flight-refuelling
- ceptacle, open
- ose avionics equipment
- ys
- PQ-164 offensive radar
- stem
- ual pitot heads
- replane hydraulic
- tuator
- ructural mode control
- stem (SMCS) ride
- ntrol foreplane
- replane pivot fixing
- ont pressure bulkhead
- ose landing gear wheel
- y
- osewheel doors
- ntrol cable runs
- ckpit floor level
- dder pedals
- ntrol column,
- adruplex automatic
- ght control system
- strument panel shroud
- ndscreen panels
- etachable nuclear flash
- reen, all window
- sitions
- -pilot's ejector seat
- -pilot's emergency
- cape hatch
- erhead switch panel
- ot's emergency escape
- tch
- ckpit eyebrow window
- ector seat launch/
- ounting rails
- ot's Weber ACES 'zero-
- ro' ejector seat
- ing sweep control lever
- ckpit section framing
- ilet
- ose landing gear drag
- ace
- xin landing lamps
- xiing lamp
- ock absorber strut

46 Radar hand controller
47 Crew cabin side window panel
48 Offensive Systems Operators' ejector seat (OSO)
49 Cabin roof escape hatches
50 Defensive Systems Operators' ejector seat (DSO)
51 Rear pressure bulkhead
52 External emergency release handle
53 Underfloor air conditioning ducting
54 Air system ground connection
55 External access panels
56 Avionics equipment racks, port and starboard
57 Cooling air exhaust duct
58 Astro navigation antenna
59 Forward fuselage joint frame
60 Air system valves and ducting
61 Dorsal systems and equipment duct
62 Weapons bay extended range fuel tank
63 Electric cable multiplexes
64 Forward fuselage integral fuel tank
65 Electronics equipment bay
66 Ground cooling air connection
67 Defensive avionics system transmitting antennas
68 Weapons bay door hinge mechanism
69 Forward weapons bay
70 Weapons bay doors, open
71 Retractable spoiler
72 Movable (non-structural) weapons bay bulkhead to suit varying load sizes
73 Rotary dispenser hydraulic drive motor
74 Fuel system piping
75 Communications antennas, port and starboard

76 Starboard lateral radome
77 ALQ-161 defensive avionics system equipment
78 Forward fuselage fuel tanks
79 Control cable runs
80 Rotary weapons dispenser
81 AGM-69 SRAM short-range air-to-surface missiles
82 Weapons bay door and hinge seals
83 Port defensive avionics system equipment

84 Fuselage flank fuel tanks
85 Defensive avionics system transmitting antennas
86 Port lateral radome
87 Port navigation light
88 Wing sweep control screw jack
89 Wing pivot hinge fitting
90 Lateral longeron attachment joints
91 Wing pivot box carry-through
92 Wing sweep control jack hydraulic motor
93 Carry-through structure integral fuel tank
94 Upper longeron/carry-through joints
95 Starboard wing sweep control hydraulic motor
96 Wing sweep control screw jack
97 Starboard navigation light
98 Wing sweep pivot fixing
99 Wing root flexible seals
100 Aperture closing horn fairing
101 Flap/slat interconnecting drive shaft
102 Fuel pump
103 Fuel system piping
104 Starboard wing integral fuel tanks
105 Leading edge slat drive shaft
106 Slat guide rails
107 Slat screw jacks
108 Leading edge slat segments (seven), open
109 Wing tip strobe light
110 Fuel system vent tank
111 Wing tip fairing
112 Static dischargers
113 Fuel jettison
114 Fixed portion of trailing edge
115 Starboard spoilers, open
116 Spoiler hydraulic jacks
117 Single-slotted Fowler-type flap, down position
118 Flap screw jacks
119 Flap guide rails
120 Wing root housing fairings
121 Dorsal spine fairing
122 Wheel bay dorsal fuel tank
123 Main landing gear leg strut
124 Port main landing gear stowed position
125 Wheel bay avionics equipment racks
126 Fuselage lateral longeron
127 Wing root housing
128 Engine bleed air ducting
129 Ventral retractable air scoop
130 Fuel cooling heat exchanger

131 Heat exchanger spill air louvres
132 Rear rotary weapons dispenser
133 Control ducting
134 Tailplane longeron
135 Wing glove section tail fairing
136 Starboard wing fully swept position

137 Starboard engine exhaust nozzles
138 Longeron joint
139 Automatic stability and control system equipment (SCAS)
140 Tailplane control linkages
141 Fin root support structure
142 Fin/tailplane fairing
143 Fin spar attachment joint
144 Tailplane tandem hydraulic control jacks
145 All-moving tailplane pivot fixing
146 Fin multi-spar construction
147 Fin leading edge ribs
148 Starboard all-moving tailplane
149 Static dischargers
150 Fin tip antenna fairing
151 Defensive avionics system receiving antennas
152 Rudder honeycomb construction
153 Rudder powered hinges
154 Two-segment upper rudder
155 Rudder automatic stability and control system equipment (SCAS)
156 Tail warning radar equipment
157 Tailcone radome fairing
158 Lower rudder segment
159 Tail radome
160 Defensive avionics system transmitting antennas
161 Tailplane trailing edge rib construction
162 Static dischargers
163 Tailplane tip fairing
164 Multi-spar tailplane construction
165 Port all-moving tailplane
166 Tailplane skin panelling

167 ALQ-161 defensive avionics system equipment racks
168 Vortex generators
169 Ventral communications antennas
170 Fin attachment fuselage main frames
171 Rear fuselage integral fuel tank
172 Tank pressurization nitrogen bottle
173 Rear fuselage lower longeron
174 Rear weapons bay bulkhead
175 Weapons bay doors
176 Engine nacelle mounting beam
177 Radar absorbent material (RAM) coated skin panelling
178 Trailing edge wing root fairing
179 Aft external cruise missile carriage
180 Port engine afterburner nozzles
181 Wing glove section tail fairing
182 Afterburner ducting
183 Variable area afterburner nozzle control jacks
184 General Electric F101-GE-102 afterburning turbofan engines

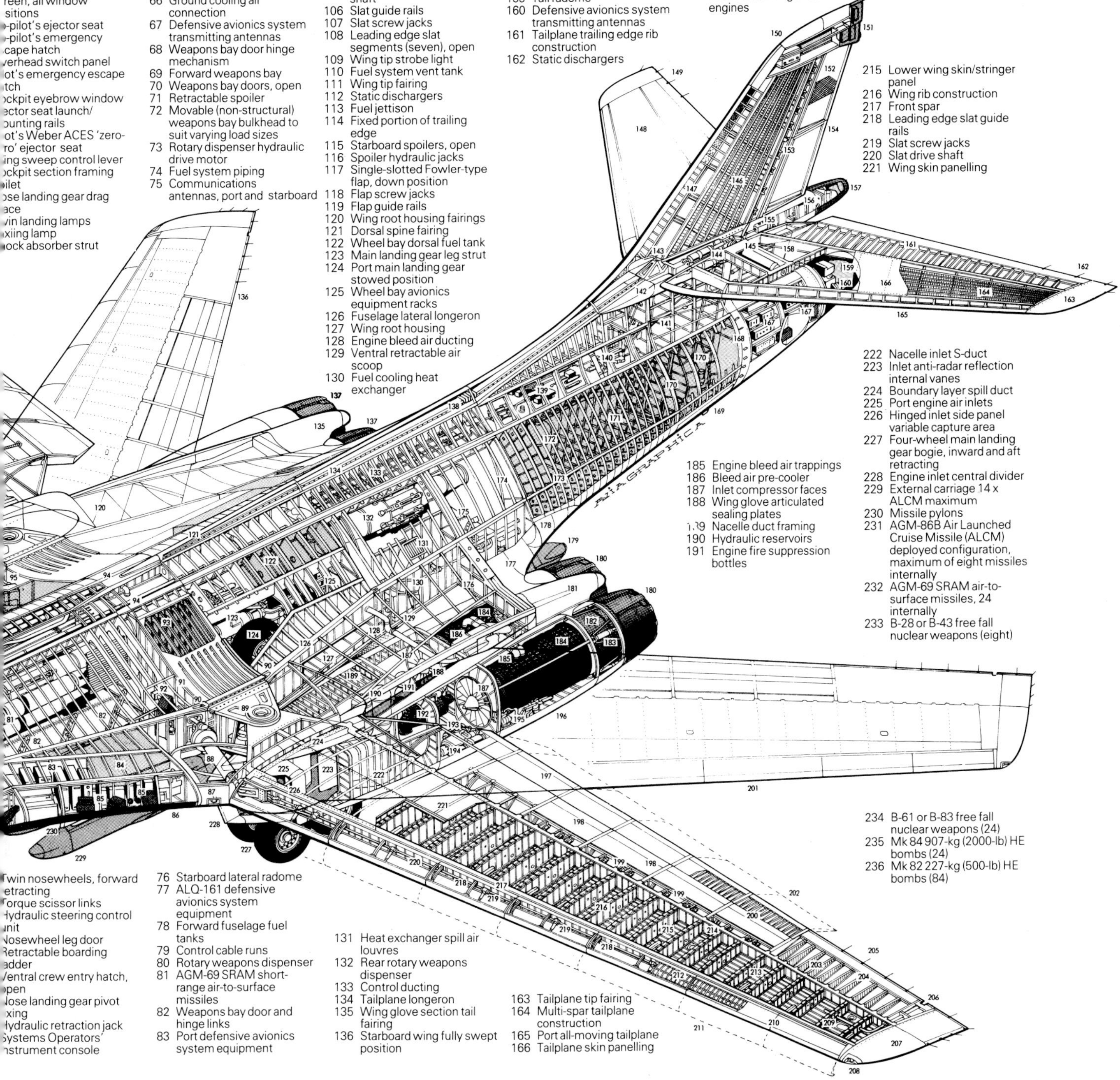

185 Engine bleed air trappings
186 Bleed air pre-cooler
187 Inlet compressor faces
188 Wing glove articulated sealing plates
189 Nacelle duct framing
190 Hydraulic reservoirs
191 Engine fire suppression bottles

192 Garrett Auxiliary Power Unit (APU), port and starboard
193 Airframe mounted engine accessory equipment gearbox
194 Electrical system generator
195 Engine fuel system equipment, fully automatic digital engine control
196 Engine cowling panels
197 Port single-slotted Fowler-type flaps
198 Port spoiler panels (four)
199 Spoiler hydraulic jacks
200 Flap rib construction
201 Port wing fully swept position
202 Flap down position
203 Trailing edge ribs
204 Fixed portion of trailing edge
205 Static dischargers
206 Fuel jettison
207 Port wing tip fairing
208 Wing tip strobe light
209 Fuel vent tank
210 Port leading edge slat segments
211 Slat open position
212 Slat rib construction
213 Port wing integral fuel tank
214 Rear spar

215 Lower wing skin/stringer panel
216 Wing rib construction
217 Front spar
218 Leading edge slat guide rails
219 Slat screw jacks
220 Slat drive shaft
221 Wing skin panelling

222 Nacelle inlet S-duct
223 Inlet anti-radar reflection internal vanes
224 Boundary layer spill duct
225 Port engine air inlets
226 Hinged inlet side panel variable capture area
227 Four-wheel main landing gear bogie, inward and aft retracting
228 Engine inlet central divider
229 External carriage 14 x ALCM maximum
230 Missile pylons
231 AGM-86B Air Launched Cruise Missile (ALCM) deployed configuration, maximum of eight missiles internally
232 AGM-69 SRAM air-to-surface missiles, 24 internally
233 B-28 or B-43 free fall nuclear weapons (eight)

234 B-61 or B-83 free fall nuclear weapons (24)
235 Mk 84 907-kg (2000-lb) HE bombs (24)
236 Mk 82 227-kg (500-lb) HE bombs (84)

The McDONNELL DOUGLAS A4 SKYHAWK

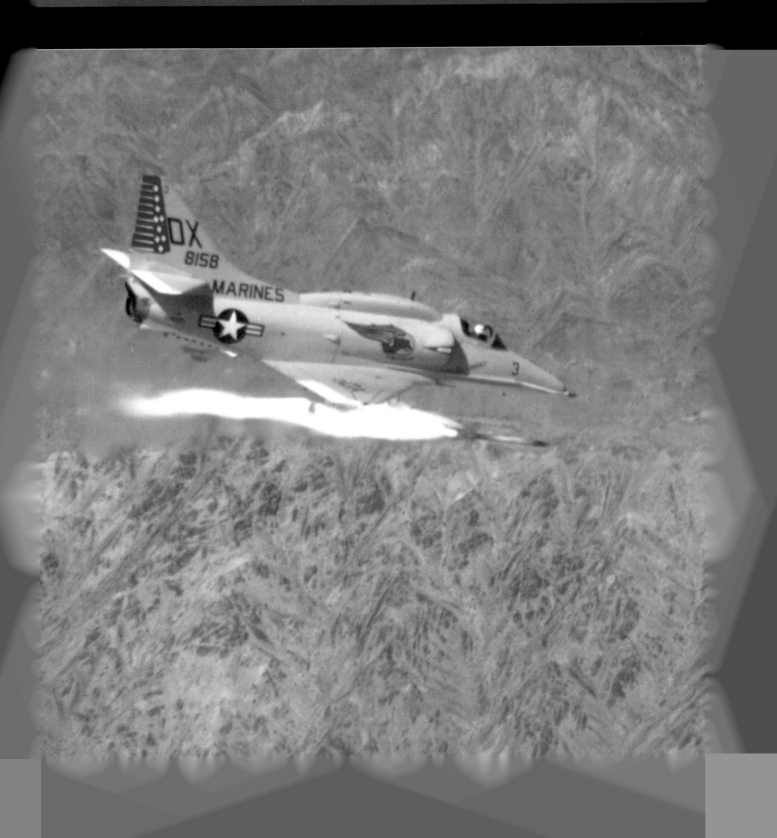

A-4 Skyhawk: bantam bomber

Never has an aircraft proved its critics to be so totally wrong as the Skyhawk, a lightweight and compact design that has turned the logic that 'big is always better' on its head in a career lasting over 30 years.

▲ Agile performance, a high rate of turn and a relatively small overall size are factors which have made the Skyhawk a tough opponent for aspiring fighter pilots as part of the advanced flying training programme.

▼ The Skyhawk has proved the versatility of its design by appearing in many forms over the years, this being a late-model A-4M. Of note are the nose ECM recording and suppression aerial and fin tip ECM antenna housing.

Entirely without warning the small formation of aircraft appeared at low level, making straight for the two almost defenceless landing ships as they unloaded troops and stores near Fitzroy. Two aircraft made for the *Sir Tristram* and the remaining three for *Sir Galahad*, their bombs scoring direct hits and inflicting heavy casualties.

The events of 8 June 1982 summarize the current status of the versatile little fighter-bomber whose prototypes were ordered by the US Navy almost 30 years to the day before the Fitzroy debacle. Respected by its pilots for fine handling qualities and a very useful load-carrying capability, the Skyhawk is no longer a match for today's advanced weapon systems. However, constant updating of the basic design has delayed the ageing process and permitted the A-4 to remain in the front line of several air arms as a versatile and economic warplane. Second-hand Skyhawks are even now receiving comprehensive updates to maintain them in combat condition, perhaps until the turn of the century.

As in so many other cases, the key to the Skyhawk's longevity has not been sophistication, but simplicity. The US Navy requirement had called for a lightweight, single-engined and carrier-based high-performance daylight attack aircraft capable of close support, dive-bombing and inter-

diction roles, using conventional or nuclear weaponry. The design team led by Ed Heinemann of Douglas (long before the merger with McDonnell) adopted a near-fanatical obsession with weight during the Skyhawk's drawing board period, this being the sole 'secret' embodied in the entire aircraft. Rigid discipline ensured that not one ounce was added to the structure unless absolutely necessary. This allowed the design to rely upon conventional methods of construction and established technology in its internal systems, thereby reducing cost.

Designated A4D until the tri-service system was introduced in 1962, the prototype Skyhawk flew at El Segundo for the first time on 22 June 1954. It had also been designed to operate without fighter escort, and a convincing demonstration of its abilities was provided in the following year when it became the first attack aircraft to hold the world airspeed record for the 500-km (310.7-mile) closed circuit, at 603.4 kts (1118.7 km/h; 695.1 mph). By October 1956, after an unusually short and trouble-free development period, the initial model entered service with the US Navy.

On 27 February 1979, the 2,960th and last Skyhawk was handed over (to the US Marine Corps) at Palmdale, where all but the initial 342 had been built. Thus ended the longest continuous manufacturing run

of any US military aircraft, although a start had already been made on conversion and updating programmes which are still producing almost 'new' Skyhawks. It was not until the mid-1960s, when the A-4 was making its name in the Vietnam War, that export orders began to arrive for Heinemann's bantamweight attack aeroplane.

Three major assemblies (the wing, front fuselage and rear fuselage) form the basic airframe. The fuselage is of all-metal semi-monocoque construction, and includes a detachable nosecone containing the integrated avionics pack, communications and IFF equipment. Ease of access for the maintenance crew is mirrored in the design of the cockpit for maximum pilot efficiency. The two halves of the fuselage are connected by just six bolts for ease of disconnection during engine changes, whilst the fin is an integral part of the rear component. Hydraulically-actuated air brakes are mounted in the sides of the fuselage,

behind the wing trailing edge.

So small is the Skyhawk's delta wing that no folding mechanism is required for stowage aboard carrier, thus reducing weight further. The stalky tricycle landing gear has no emergency back-up to its hydraulic systems, but can be released and will drop and lock under gravity in an emergency. Early-model aircraft were powered by a Wright J65 turbojet (licence-built Armstrong Siddeley Sapphire) which was introduced at 3493-kg (7,700-lb) thrust in the A-4A and uprated to 3856-kg (8,500-lb) thrust in the A-4B and A-4C. The A-4E introduced Pratt and Whitney's J52 engine at the last-mentioned rating, and this was increased to 4218-kg (9,300-lb) thrust for the A-4F. In 1970, the A-4M Skyhawk II was introduced, with a redesigned fin and rudder, braking parachute and modified canopy, plus yet a further and substantial improvement in power, to 5080-kg (11,200-lb) thrust.

Today, the Skyhawk's contribution to the defence of its home country is mainly in the areas of training and reserve forces. Well over 30 units are wholly or partly equipped with several models of A-4.

Oldest of these types, the A-4E introduced a further pair of weapon pylons, plus an improved navigation system (Doppler, TACAN and radar altimeter) compared with its predecessors. It retained the inflight refuelling capability (both receiver and 'buddy-buddy tanker') and provision for Martin AGM-12 Bullpup ASMs brought in with the A-4B, and further improved the A-4C's autopilot and bombing system. Pilots flying A-4Fs benefit from updated avionics in the distinctive spine 'hump' later added to some A-4Es, better flak protection and, for the first time, a zero/zero ejector seat. With a second seat under an extended canopy, the A-4E becomes the TA-4F, of which deliveries began in 1966. Finally the A-4M, whose more spectacular performance improvements (derived from the uprated engine) include 50 per cent better climb and 25 per cent shorter take-off runs, features originally applied to export aircraft. Not-

able are the APG-53A terrain-clearance radar, ASN-41 inertial navigation system and Elliott 546 head-up display, which with other equipment are reported to increase tactical effectiveness by some 30 per cent.

Armament
The A-4M can carry most of the Marine Corps inventory of weapons, including Mk 81 250-lb (113-kg) and Mk 82 500-lb (227-kg) bombs, gun pods, torpedoes and 5-in (127-mm) Zuni or 2-in (69.85-mm) Mighty Mouse rocket packs. Additionally, a Colt Mk 12 20-mm cannon is fitted in each wing root, and various ECM pods may be attached to complement the internal systems. Weapon attachment points are stressed to 1588 kg (3,500 lb) on the centreline, 1021 kg (2,250 lb) under the inner wings and 454 kg (1,000 lb) under the outer wings, but a typical Marine Corps close support mission involves the carriage of 1814 kg (4,000 lb) of ordnance 240 km (150 miles), allowing generous loiter time. The internal fuel capacity of 3032 litres (800 US gal) can be more than doubled by the addition of three 1137-litre (300-US gal) tanks to the centreline and inner wing pylons, giving a ferry range of over 3220 km (2,000 miles). The OA-4M, which partly equips three of the H&MSs, is optimized for forward air control.

In the US Navy, the Skyhawk in its TA-4J form is the standard pilot trainer and will remain so until the BAe/McDonnell Douglas T-45 Goshawk is fully de-

▲ For such a lightweight design, the Skyhawk can carry a remarkable amount of ordnance, as illustrated by this RNZAF A-4K. This ability has been enhanced by the Douglas-designed low-drag bomb racks and external stores.

▼ Israel has received five versions of the A-4 family, these receiving local modifications to increase survivability. The most obvious of these is the extended jetpipe to protect against heat-seeking missiles.

veloped. The TA-4J is similar to the Marine Corps' TA-4F, except that it has the downrated 3856-kg (8,500-lb) thrust J52-P-6 engine and some tactical systems deleted (missile firing, for example). Produced by TA-4F conversion as well as new manufacture, the TA-4J is flown by seven squadrons of Naval Air Training Command, whilst 10 support or refresher training units are also equipped at least in part by TA-4Js. Other variants in service are restricted to the well-known A-4Fs of the USN's Flight Demonstration Squadron (the 'Blue Angels') and the more shadowy EA-4F ECM trainers.

Of the eight other nations which bought Skyhawks only Argentina and Australia intended carrier operation: and of those, the latter has now scrapped its vessel and sold the aircraft. The Argentine air force was first, however, with contracts eventually totalling 50 A-4Bs and 25 A-4Cs to be modified by Lockheed Aircraft Service Co (LASCo) to A-4P standard, including installation of Ferranti ISIS D126R lead-computing weapon sights. In 1984, Argen-

tina claimed that the remaining Skyhawks, whose operating units had been reduced from four to two by accidents and war casualties, were equipped with Matra Durandal runway-cratering munitions and Matra R.550 Magic IR-homing AAMs for self-defence.

Argentine navy Skyhawks derive from the 16 A-4Bs converted to A-4Qs for operation from the carrier *Veinticinco de Mayo* and, again, a further 16 are claimed to be in prospect from Israel. Capable of carrying Bullpup ASMs and defensive AIM-9 Sidewinder AAMs, the original aircraft fired neither during minimal land-based participation in the 1982 conflict.

In contrast, Israel's Skyhawks have seen extensive use in Middle East wars, having formerly been the IDF/AF's prime attack aircraft. Deliveries comprised new A-4Hs, A-4Ns and TA-4H/Js, as well as A-4Es included in USN contracts: in all some 244 single-seat Skyhawks and 24 trainers. Earlier aircraft have undergone several stages of updating which makes their precise mark a matter of conjecture. Other notable local modifications included two 30-mm DEFA cannon instead of 20-mm weapons and a considerably extended jet-pipe for infra-red suppression in the face of heat-seeking missiles.

Exports

Elsewhere in the Middle East, Skyhawks used by Kuwait have been offered for disposal, despite delivery as recently as 1977-8 in response to a period of tension with Iraq which has now passed.

It is Australasia which is now becoming the centre of Skyhawk activity. Singapore has the largest fleet, accumulation of which began in 1972 when an order was placed for 40 A-4S aircraft to be produced from USN surplus A-4Bs. Confusingly given the local name Skywarrior, the aircraft were converted by LASCo in the USA and Singapore, and incorporate over 100 modifications, including a 3674-kg (8,100-lb) thrust J65-W-20 turbojet, a Ferranti lead-computing sight, a 30-mm cannon, spoilers and a brake parachute. A TA-4S trainer has also been produced, retaining full operational capability, and can be readily distinguished from US models by the fact that there are two entirely separate canopies for the pilots. Its fuselage is stretched by 71cm (28 in) to accommodate the additional cockpit.

In 1982, Singapore Aircraft Industries produced the first of an anticipated 40 or so A-4S-1 Skywarriors rebuilt from A-4Cs and around eight TA-4S-1s from more A-4Bs. These have new avionics, a complete rewiring, and underwing pylons of greater strength. Yet more changes may be in store for the original aircraft, following the decision for the experimental re-engining of two aircraft with the General Electric F404 turbofan. If successful, the modification will be applied to 41 Singaporean aircraft and offered to other operators by a GE-SAI-Grumman consortium.

Neighbouring Malaysia began equipping two Skyhawk squadrons with A-4PTMs from December 1984 onwards, the conversion work being undertaken by Grumman at St Augustine, Florida. Malaysian aircraft are formerly A-4Cs and A-4Ls (the latter an A-4C modified for the USN reserve with the A-4F avionics package) and have standards of updating lower than at first planned.

Elsewhere in the region, Indonesia bought 14 A-4Es and two TA-4H trainers from Israel in 1979 and a duplicate batch for a second squadron, formed in 1985.

Finally, New Zealand bought a squadron of A-4Gs and TA-4Gs in 1968, equipping them with AIM-9H Sidewinder AAMs for a secondary air-defence role in addition to the prime anti-shipping function. When a decision on new equipment became due, early in the 1980s, the RNZAF tested the General Dynamics F-16 Fighting Falcon, McDonnell Douglas F/A-18 Hornet and Northrop F-20 Tigershark, but then decided to buy Australia's surplus eight A-4Gs and two TA-4Gs and

▲ *The excellent visibility offered by the two seat, dual-control TA-4 trainer makes it an attractive proposition for Skyhawk users. The Royal Malaysian Air Force has had six A-4s stretched and updated for A-4 pilot training.*

▼ *Important in the US Navy's advanced training, the TA-4J has had a high workload, but has coped admirably. These machines have the old-style straight refuelling probes.*

to refurbish the enlarged fleet. The work, currently under way, involves new avionics, a revised cockpit layout, a chaff/flare dispenser and a braking parachute, and at a later stage could see the Skyhawk fitted with a sea surveillance radar (for which Ferranti Red Fox has been offered). It remains only for radar to be combined with the Singaporean F404-powered mode for the Skyhawk to re-emerge 35 years later after its conception as a completely transformed strike/aircraft able to challenge more costly new competitors on the market. Old soldiers never die; they just get new avionics.

A-4 Skyhawk in service units and example aircraft

Still constituting a considerable force within the US Marine Corps' air power, the Skyhawk (affectionately known as 'Scooter' or 'Tinker Toy') equips front-line attack units at both East and West Coast bases. As with other USMC types, the A-4 has fallen to the current fashion for low-visibility grey colours, as illustrated on this OA-4M forward air control (FAC) aircraft.

An A-4M from VMA-311 'Tomcats' at MCAS El Toro displays a low-visibility colour scheme.

US Marine Corps

VMA-211 (A-4M) El Toro, California
VMA-214 (A-4M) El Toro, California
VMA-233 (A-4M) Cherry Point, North Carolina

VMA-311 (A-4M) El Toro, California
VMAT-102 (A-4M) (TA-4F) Yuma, Arizona
H&MS-12 (TA-4F) Iwakuni, Japan
H&MS-13 (OA-4M) (TA-4F) El Toro, California
H&MS-14 (TA-4F) Cherry Point, North Carolina

H&MS-24 (TA-4F) Kaneohe Bay, Hawaii
H&MS-31 (OA-4M) (TA-4F) Beaufort, South Carolina
H&MS-32 (OA-4M) (TA-4F) Cherry Point, North Carolina

US Marine Corps Reserve

VMA-124 (A-4E) Memphis, Tennessee
VMA-131 (A-4E) Willow Grove, Pennsylvania

VMA-133 (A-4F) Alameda, California
VMA-142 (A-4F) Cecil Field, Florida
VMA-322 (A-4M) South

Weymouth, Maine
H&MS-42 (TA-4J) Alameda, California
H&MS-49 (TA-4J) Willow Grove, Pennsylvania

Though it was replaced within Navy attack units by the Vought A-7 some considerable time ago, the A-4 continues to form the major component in the advanced jet pilot training programme, in addition to Naval Reserve and test and evaluation duties. A variety of colour schemes are worn, some specifically to camouflage the aircraft and others, such as the high-visibility white and red scheme illustrated below on this Training Command TA-4J, to enable easy visual identification of the aircraft.

Adversary colours are frequently worn by A-4s engaged in air combat training.

Naval Air Training Command

VT-4 (TA-4J*) Pensacola, Florida
VT-7 (TA-4J) Meridian, Massachusetts

VT-21 (TA-4J) Kingsville, Texas
VT-22 (TA-4J) Kingsville, Texas
VT-24 (TA-4J) Chase Field, Texas
VT-25 (TA-4J) Chase Field, Texas
VT-86 (TA-4J*) Pensacola, Florida

FTS (A-4F) Pensacola, Florida ('Blue Angels')

experimental squadrons

US Navy Support, refresher and

VA-127 (TA-4J) Lemoore, California
VF-126 (TA-4J) Miramar, California
VC-1 (TA-4J*) Barbers Point, Hawaii

VC-5 (TA-4J*) Cubi Point, Philippines
VC-8 (TA-4J) Roosevelt Roads, Philippines
VC-10 (TA-4J) Guantanamo Bay, Cuba
VX-4 (TA-4J*) Point Mugu, California
FWS (TA-4J*) Miramar, California

Naval Air Reserve Force

VC-12 (TA-4J) Oceana, Virginia
VC-13 (TA-4J) Miramar, California

(*additionally operates other types of aircraft)

With an additional 10 Skyhawks purchased from the Royal Australian Navy, the RNZAF now has 22 A-4s, the new machines allowing for the formation of No. 2 Squadron; this unit is tasked with operational conversion training and the development of operational tactics and procedures. The entire fleet is to undergo major upgrading and modernization to extend its operational life, this including the fitment of new radar, navigation and attack systems.

Royal New Zealand Air Force

No. 2 Squadron
Re-formed: 11 December 1984
Base: Ohakea
Task: Reconnaissance,

conversion, development
Example aircraft: A-4G NZ6211, NZ6214, NZ6215, NZ6218; TA-4G NZ6255

No. 75 Squadron
Converted: 1970
Base: Ohakea
Task: Attack
Example aircraft: A-4K NZ6201, NZ6262, NZ6207, NZ6210; TA-4K NZ6251

One of the original batch of A-4Ks delivered to the RNZAF displays the standard sand and two-tone green camouflage.

The 40 Skyhawks procured by the RMAF represent a major upgrade for the air force's attack capability. All the machines are ex-US Navy examples, refurbished by Grumman, and redesignated as the A-4PTM/TA-4PTM (PTM = Peculiar To Malaysia). Of the 36 A-4PTMs, approximately 20 have an AGM-65 Maverick launch capability, while all of the machines are wired for the AIM-9 Sidewinder AAM. In addition to missiles, the Hughes Aircraft Angle Rate Bombing System is also fitted for the attack role.

Tentara Udara Diraja Malaysia

No. 6 'Naga' Squadron
Re-formed: 1985
Base: Kuantan
Task: Attack

No. 9 'Jebat' Squadron
Re-formed: 1986
Base: Kuantan
Task: Attack
Aircraft: As above

Aircraft: Drawn from A-4PTM M32-7 to M32-40; TA-4PTM M32-01 to 06

As with New Zealand, the RMAF Skyhawks are to be seen in a sand and two-tone green camouflage, and carry a small national insignia.

Republic of Singapore Air Force

No. 142 'Gryphon' Squadron
Formed: 1974
Base: Tengah
Task: Attack
Aircraft: A-4S and TA-4S (scrambled serials in range 601-683)

No. 143 'Phoenix' Squadron
Formed: 1975
Base: Tengah
Task: Attack
Aircraft: A-4S and TA-4S as above

No. 145 Squadron
Formed: 1982
Base: Tengah
Task: Attack

Aircraft: A-4S-1 and TA-4S-1 (scrambled serials in 901 series)

A fairly standard three-tone camouflage scheme on RSAF Skyhawks is brightened by prominent and colourful squadron insignia. This A-4S serves with No. 142 'Gryphon' Squadron.

Argentina made full use of its Skyhawk force, with both air force and navy, during the Falklands conflict, though their effectiveness was of limited value. Air force machines wear a sand and green camouflage with small national insignia on the rear fuselage and fin, while Navy aircraft wear the blue-grey and light grey scheme illustrated below. The prominent white codes identify this as an A-4Q of the 3ª Escuadrilla Aeronaval de Ataque. Note the Argentine flag represented on the rudder and upper fin.

Fuerza Aérea Argentina
V Grupo/V Brigada Aérea
Components: IV and V Escuadrones de Caza-Bombardeo
Converted: 1966
Base: BA General Pringles, Villa Reynolds
Task: Attack
Example aircraft: A-4P (A-4B) C-207, C-212, C-224; A-4P (A-4C) C-312, C-324

Comando de Aviacion Naval Argentina
3º Escuadra Aeronaval
Component: 3º Escuadrilla Aeronaval de Caza y Ataque
Converted: 1971
Base: Comandante Espora BAN, Puerto Belgrano
Task: Shipborne attack
Example aircraft: 0654 '3-A-301', 0655 '3-A-302', 0658 '3-A-305', 0661 '3-A-309', 0667 '3-A-314'

Purchase of the Skyhawk by Kuwait was intended to give its air force a specialized attack capability – most notably against targets in Iraq. Thirty-six aircraft were obtained, these wearing a suitable desert camouflage, though on delivery flights they wore United States national insignia. The current status of the KAF Skyhawk force is subject to conjecture, but it is believed that potential customers are being sought.

Al Quwwat al Jawwiya al Kuwait

Surviving 29 aircraft from 36 A-4KUs (801-830) and six TA-4TUs (881-886) withdrawn from use at Ahmad al Jabar AB in 1984, and offered for sale

Israel Defence Force/Air Force

Four squadrons in service at Eqron and elsewhere, flying aircraft with 'scrambled' serial numbers, such as
A-4E: 119, 216, 235, 610, 890
A-4H: 168, 274, 369, 632, 723
A-4N: 291, 323, 379 396, 398

Tentara Nasional Indonesia – Angkatan Udara

Skwadron Udara 11
Formed: 1980
Base: Maidun
Task: Attack
Example aircraft: A-4E (mod) TT-0401, TT-0404, TT-0408, TT-0411, TT-0412

Skwadron Udara 12
Formed: 1985
Base: Pakenbaru
Task: Attack
Example aircraft: A-4E none known

By far and away the biggest export customer for the Skyhawk has been Israel, the IDF/AF using this considerable force during its conflicts with Arab neighbours, most notably during the 1973 Yom Kippur war. Though the basic camouflage style has remained relatively unchanged over the years, the colours have moved from rich and dark to lightened tones, the current scheme being described as 'café au lait'. Squadron markings, when carried, are usually restricted to a fin badge or coloured rudder.

McDonnell Douglas A-4M Skyhawk cutaway drawing key

1 Fixed inflight-refuelling probe
2 Nose ECM recording and suppression aerials
3 Angle Rate Bombing System (ARBS) laser seeker head
4 Hinged nose compartment access door
5 Laser seeker system electronics
6 Electronics cooling air inlet
7 Pitot tube
8 Avionics access panel
9 APN-153(V) navigation radar
10 Lower TACAN aerial
11 Communications electronics
12 Cockpit front pressure bulkhead
13 Pressurization valve
14 Windshield rain dispersal air duct
15 Rudder pedals
16 Angle-of-attack sensor
17 Air conditioning refrigeration plant
18 Nosewheel door
19 Control system access
20 Cockpit floor level
21 Pilot's side console panel
22 Engine throttle
23 Control column
24 Instrument panel shroud
25 Head-up display (HUD)
26 Windscreen panels
27 AIM-9L Sidewinder air-to-air missile
28 Missile launch rail
29 D-704 flight refuelling pack containing 300 US gal (1135 litre)
30 Cockpit canopy cover
31 Face blind firing handle
32 Ejection seat headrest
33 Safety harness
34 McDonnell Douglas Escapac IG-3 zero-zero ejection seat
35 Anti-g valve
36 Cockpit insulation and fragmentation blanket
37 Rear pressure bulkhead
38 Emergency canopy release handle
39 Nose undercarriage leg strut
40 Steering linkage
41 Nosewheel
42 Leg shortening link
43 Hydraulic retraction strut
44 Emergency wind-driven generator
45 Port cannon muzzle
46 Intake gun gas shield
47 Port air intake
48 Boundary layer splitter plate
49 Self-sealing fuselage fuel cell, capacity 240 US gal (908 litres)
50 Fuel system piping
51 Canopy hinge cover
52 Starboard air intake duct
53 Fuel system gravity filler cap
54 UHF aerial
55 Electronics cooling air inlet
56 Engine-driven generator
57 Constant-speed drive unit
58 Bifurcated intake duct
59 Reel type ammunition magazine (200 rounds per gun)
60 Intake compressor face
61 Electrical system power amplifier
62 Engine accessory drive gearbox
63 Wing spar attachment fuselage double frame
64 Engine mounting trunion
65 Engine fuel system access panel
66 Pratt & Whitney J52-P-408 turbojet
67 Dorsal avionics bays
68 Compressor bleed air exhaust duct
69 Upper TACAN aerial
70 Starboard wing integral fuel tank (total wing tank capacity 560 US gal/2120 litres)
71 Wing tank access panels
72 Slat guide rails
73 Starboard automatic leading-edge slat (open)
74 Wing fences
75 Vortex generators
76 Starboard navigation light
77 Wing tip communications aerial
78 Aileron horn balance
79 Starboard aileron
80 Split trailing-edge spoiler (open position)
81 Starboard split trailing-edge flap (down position)
82 Anti-collision light
83 Cooling air exit louvres
84 Rear fuselage double frame break point
85 Engine firewall
86 Cooling air intake
87 VHF aerial
88 Upper fuselage stringers
89 Fin root dorsal fairing
90 Remote compass flux valve
91 Rear electronics bay cooling air inlet
92 Fin rib construction
93 Fin spar attachment joint
94 Rudder hydraulic jack
95 Artificial feel spring unit
96 Pitot tube
97 Fin tip ECM antenna housing
98 Externally-braced rudder construction
99 Fixed rudder tab
100 Tail navigation light
101 ECM antennas
102 Tailplane trim jack
103 Tailplane sealing plate
104 Elevator hydraulic jack
105 Tailpipe fairing
106 Port elevator
107 All moving tailplane construction
108 Elevator horn balance
109 Jet pipe exhaust nozzle
110 Brake parachute housing for 16-ft (4.88-m) diameter, ribbon type chute
111 Brake parachute release linkage
112 Insulated jet pipe
113 Electronics bay heat shield
114 Rear electronics bay, automatic flight control system (AFCS)
115 Port airbrake (open)
116 ATO rocket attachment hardpoints
117 Airbrake hydraulic jack

© Pilot Press Limited

168
167
166

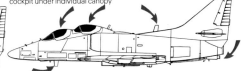

A-4C: all-weather **A4D-2N** model numbering 638 with terrain-clearance radar, autopilot, improved gyro system; A-4A/B/C retrofitted with 3856-kg (8,500-lb) thrust J65s

A-4E: two prototype and 497 production **A4D-5** aircraft; A-4C plus five pylons and 3856-kg (8,500-lb) thrust J52-P-6A, 27 per cent range improvement; some retrofitted with avionics 'hump'; transfers to Israel, thence Indonesia

A-4F: 139 built with avionics 'hump', spoilers, zero/zero seat and 4218-kg (9,300-lb) thrust J58-P-8A, of which 100 refitted with 4990-kg (11,000-lb) thrust J52-P-401; **EA-4F** is ECM-equipped

A-4N: 117 Israeli A-4H variants with Elliott HUD and improved avionics

A-4P: conversions of A-4B (50) and A-4C (25) for Argentine air force

A-4PTM: conversions of A-4C/L (34 by Grumman) for Malaysia

TA-4PTM: conversions of A-4C/L (six by Grumman) for Malaysia

A-4Q: conversions of A-4B (16) for Argentine navy

A-4S: conversions of A-4B (40 by LASCo) for Singapore; 3674-kg (8,100-lb) thrust J65-W-20, 30-mm Aden cannon, etc

A-4S-1: conversions of A-4C (about 40 by SAI) with new avionics and stronger pylons

TA-4S: conversions of A-4B (seven by LASCo) with second cockpit under individual canopy

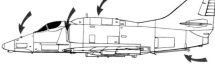

TA-4F: two-seat trainer ex **TA-4E**; two prototypes and 237 production; **ETA-4F** was ECM trainer

TA-4S-1: conversions of TA-4B (about 8 by SAI) with TA-4S seating

A-4T: offered to French navy (Super Etendard procured instead)

A-4Y: proposed A-4M update with strengthened landing gear and improved nav/attack equipment

plicity in overall design is reflected in the l cockpit, with a marked absence of er and arrays of computer-linked nics. At top is the head-up display unit associated display controls. The lower onsole covers performance and attitude, e the right-hand dials monitor fuel load communications.

4 Skyhawk variants

A-4G: 16 Australian A-4F versions
TA-4G: four Australian TA-4F versions
A-4H: 90 Israeli A-4F variants with 30-mm cannon, revised fin and braking parachute
TA-4H: 10 Israeli TA-4F trainer variants, plus single TA-4J conversion
TA-4J: 292 new (plus conversions from TA-4F) pilot trainers with weapon systems deleted and J52-P-6 engines
A-4K: 10 New Zealand A-4F variants with A-4H fin
TA-4K: four New Zealand TA-4F variants
A-4KU: 30 Kuwaiti A-4F variants
TA-4KU: six Kuwaiti TA-4F variants
A-4L: conversions (100) of A-4C for USN reserve with avionics 'hump'
A-4M: 158 Skyhawk IIs based on A-4F, featuring 5080-kg (11,200-lb) thrust J52-P-408A, A-4H fin and brake 'chute; **OA-4M** is USMC forward air control conversion of two-seat TA-4F

A: two **XA4D-1** prototypes with 3266-kg (7,200-lb) thrust -2 turbojets

: 18 pre-production **YA4D-1** aircraft, including 20-mm n, modified nose cone and three pylons; 146 production 1 aircraft had 3493-kg (7,700-lb) thrust J65-W-4/-4B engines
: 542 **A4D-2** aircraft with improved avionics, Bullpup ASM lity and inflight refuelling; **TA-4B** operational trainer has equipment removed, but remains single-seat

65-US gal (10-litre) liquid xygen converter (LOX) rrester hook (down osition)

120 Arrester hook hydraulic jack
121 Control cable runs
122 Inertial platform
123 Ventral pressure refuelling connection
124 Central hydraulic flap drive linkage
125 Port upper surface spoiler
126 Spoiler hydraulic jack

127 Ventral anti-collision light
128 Wing rib construction
129 Stringer construction
130 Port wing integral fuel tank (single tank tip-to-tip)
131 Rear spar

132 Port split trailing edge flap
133 Port aileron construction
134 Aileron trim tab
135 Tip fairing
136 Aileron horn balance
137 Wing tip antenna fairing
138 Port navigation light

139 LAU-10A Zuni rocket launcher
140 5-in (12.7-cm) folding fin rocket
141 AGM-12 Bullpup air-to-ground missile
142 Missile launcher rail
143 Outboard wing pylon (1,000 lb/454 kg capacity)
144 Port automatic leading edge slat (open)
145 Wing fences
146 Vortex generators
147 Aileron control rod linkage
148 Leading edge ribs
149 Wing centre spar
150 Main undercarriage hydraulic retraction jack
151 Undercarriage leg pivot mounting
152 Slat guide rail fuel sealing can
153 Port mainwheel
154 Mainwheel door
155 Position of landing lamp on starboard mainwheel door
156 Approach lights
157 Retractable catapult hook
158 Cranked wing front spar
159 Aileron servo control
160 Mk 12 20-mm cannon
161 Spent cartridge case and link ejector chutes
162 Mainwheel well
163 Centre-line pylon (3,575 lb/1622 kg) capacity
164 150-US gal (568-litre) fuel tank
165 Inboard wing pylon (2,240 lb/1016 kg) capacity
166 400-US gal (1514-litre) long-range fuel tank
167 Snakeye 500-lb (227-kg) retarded bomb
168 Mk 83 1,000-lb (454-kg) HE bomb

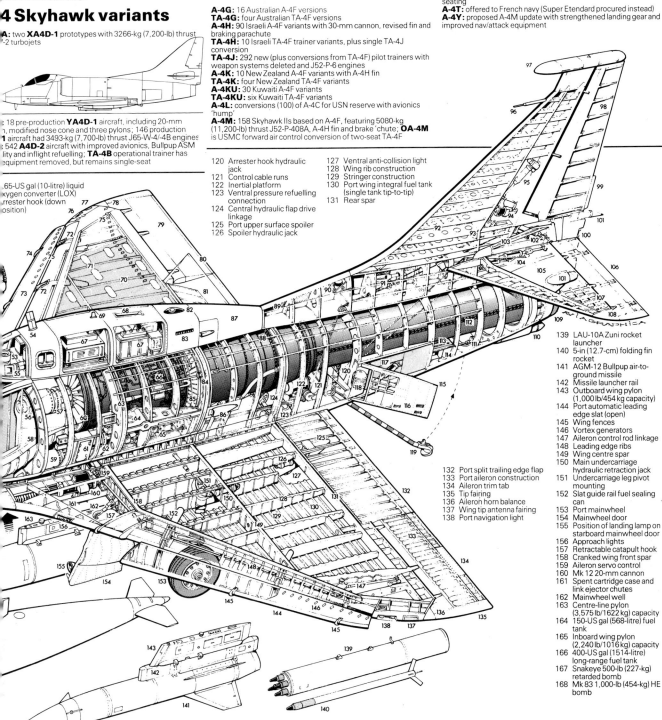

A-4 Skyhawk warload

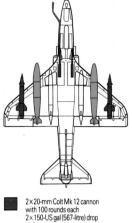

■	2×20-mm Colt Mk 12 cannon with 100 rounds each
	2×150-US gal (567-litre) drop tanks
■	2×Martin AGM-12 Bullpup ASMs

US Marine Corps attack

The Marine Corps continues to assign the Skyhawk to combat roles with free-fall and guided ordnance. The Skyhawk has also been equipped with the later Hughes AGM-65 Maverick ASM, and may fit AIM-9 Sidewinder AAMs on the outboard pylons.

■	2×20-mm Colt Mk 12 cannon with 100 rounds each
	2×450-US gal (1701-litre) drop tanks
	1×Douglas D-704 'buddy-buddy' pod

US Marine Corps inflight-refuelling

Skyhawks may operate as 'buddy-buddy' tankers in addition to receiving fuel via their fixed probes. The Douglas D-704 pod contains a 300-US gal (1135-litre) reservoir in addition to the hose-and-drogue unit.

■	2×20-mm Colt Mk 12 cannon with 100 rounds each
	2×450-US gal (1701-litre) drop tanks
	1×Mk 13 1,000-lb (454-kg) bomb

Argentine air force attack

Despite a bomb load reduced to a single 1,000-lb (454-kg) weapon, the British Mk 13, Argentine air force Skyhawks required the services of a KC-130 Hercules tanker to reach the Royal Navy Task Force in the Falkland Islands during the 1982 conflict. The American Mk 82 500-lb (227-kg) and Mk 83 1,000-lb (454-kg) bombs were also employed.

■	2×20-mm Colt Mk 12 cannon with 100 rounds each
	2×450-US gal (1701-litre) drop tanks
	6×500-lb (227-kg) Snakeye retarded bombs

Argentine navy attack

In the early stages of the 1982 Falklands War, naval Skyhawks planned to attack the RN Task Force from the carrier *Veinticinco de Mayo*. The aircraft could be bombed-up with six Snakeye weapons because of the shorter range, but the raid was cancelled as the result of insufficient wind for launching.

■	2×30-mm DEFA cannon with 150 rounds each
	2×LAU-10A Zuni rocket-launcher
	6×500-lb (227-kg) Snakeye retarded bombs

Israeli air force attack

Once the prime attack aircraft of the IDF/AF, the Skyhawk is armed with locally-built DEFA 30-mm cannon in place of the standard 20-mm weapon. The Zuni launcher pod holds four 5-in (127-mm) rockets. Some defence against heat-seeking missiles is provided by the extended jetpipe which reduces the infra-red signature.

Specification:

McDonnell Douglas A-4M Skyhawk

Wings

Span	8.38 m	(27 ft 6 in)
Area	24.16 m²	(260 sq ft)

Fuselage and tail unit

Accommodation: pilot on Douglas Escapac 1-C3 zero/zero ejector seat

Length overall (excluding probe)	12.27 m	(40 ft 3.5 in)
Height overall	4.57 m	(15 ft 0 in)
Tailplane span	3.44 m	(11 ft 3.5 in)

Landing gear

Retractable tricycle type with single wheels on all units

Wheel track	2.33 m	(7 ft 0.5 in)

Weights

Empty	4747 kg	(10,465 lb)
Normal take-off	11113 kg	(24,500 lb)
Maximum external load	3720 kg	(8,200 lb)
Internal fuel load	2011 kg	(4,434 lb)

Powerplant

One Pratt & Whitney J52-P-408A turbojet

Static thrust	5080 kg	(11,200 lb)

A-4 Skyhawk recognition features

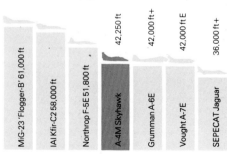

Short-span, moderately-swept main wing of cropped delta planform

Tricycle landing gear with long nose strut, giving a nose-high attitude

Long, angled inflight-refuelling probe on starboard side of fuselage

Prominent saddle fairing containing electronic equipment

Prominent fin tip ECM fairing

External stiffeners on rudder of high tailplane

Small cockpit area with excellent visibility over sharply tapered nose

Performance:

Maximum speed at 25,000 ft (7620 m)	Mach 0.9 or 543 kts	(1006 km/h; 625 mph)
Maximum speed at sea level	Mach 0.9 or 595 kts	(1102 km/h; 685 mph)
Combat radius with 1814 kg (4,000 lb) of ordnance	547 km	(340 miles)
Initial rate of climb at 10443 kg (23,000 lb)	8,440 ft (2573 m)	per minute
Take-off distance at 10433 kg (23,000 lb)	823 m	(2,700 ft)

Weapon load

- Grumman A-6E 8165 kg
- Vought A-7E 6804 kg+
- IAI Kfir-C2 5574 kg
- Jaguar 4725 kg / SEPECAT
- A-4M Skyhawk 4500 kg
- F-5E 3175 kg / Northrop

Service ceiling.

- MiG-23 'Flogger-B' 61,000 ft
- IAI Kfir-C2 58,000 ft
- Northrop F-5E 51,800 ft
- A-4M Skyhawk 42,250 ft
- Grumman A-6E 42,000 ft+
- Vought A-7E 42,000 ft E
- SEPECAT Jaguar 36,000 ft+

Speed at sea level

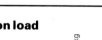

- Northrop F-5E Mach 1.64
- MiG-23 'Flogger-B' Mach 1.2 E
- SEPECAT Jaguar Mach 1.1
- Vought A-7E Mach 1.1
- IAI Kfir-C2 Mach 1.1 'clean'
- A-4M Skyhawk Mach 0.88
- Grumman A-6E Mach 0.8

Combat radius hi-lo-hi

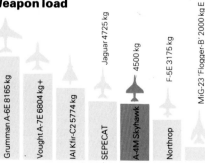

- Grumman A-6E 1627 km
- SEPECAT Jaguar (with external fuel) 1408 km
- IAI Kfir-C2 1186 km
- MiG-23 'Flogger-B' 900 km+
- Vought A-7E 885 km
- A-4M Skyhawk 620 km
- Northrop F-5E 222 km

Take-off run

- A-4M Skyhawk 2,730 ft
- MiG-23 'Flogger-B' 2,950 ft
- SEPECAT Jaguar 3,085 ft
- A-6E Intruder 3,890 ft+
- IAI Kfir-C2 (at maximum weight) 4,750 ft
- Vought A-7E 5,000 ft
- Northrop F-5E (at maximum weight) 5,700 ft

The DASSAULT-BREGUET SUPER ETENDARD

Super Etendard: shipborne striker

The combination of Super Etendard aircraft and Exocet missile was used with devastating effect during the Falklands conflict and in the Persian Gulf, but the combat successes of the Super Etendard cannot hide some serious deficiencies in performance, range and payload capability.

▲ *Selected in preference to a martime variant of the Anglo-French Jaguar, the Etendard, although quite fast, has a very poor radius of action when carrying weapons, and its selection was largely political.*

▼ *The catapult strop falls away from this Super Etendard of 17 Flottille as it launches from the carrier Clemenceau. 400-kg bombs are carried underwing, with a fuel tank under the belly. Super Etendards are seldom flown without auxiliary tanks of some sort.*

Two spectacularly successful missions during the 1982 Falklands War brought the Dassault-Breguet Super Etendard to the notice of the world. Wearing the insignia of Argentine naval aviation and armed with deadly Aérospatiale Exocet missiles, the Super Etendards sent two British vessels to the bottom of the cold South Atlantic. Subsequently, in warmer waters, the Gulf War has seen the same aircraft in Iraqi markings striking at tankers shipping Iranian oil, proving that it is, without doubt, a warplane of immense potential. As suggested by its name, the Super Etendard is a 'new-old' aircraft which originated in the 1950s, but was extensively remodelled two decades later. In service principally with France's naval air force, the Aéronavale, the Super Etendard is likely to remain in the front line until the end of the century.

As first conceived, the original Etendard was a land-based aircraft tendered to meet a French air force specification and (it was hoped) one issued by NATO for a light ground-attack aircraft. The putative local model was designated Mystère XXII and powered by two Turboméca Gabizo turbojets, whilst the NATO variant was the Mystère XXVI, with a single Bristol-Siddeley Orpheus. Becoming the Etendard II and Etendard VI respectively, they were joined by a private venture Etendard IV (née Mystère XXIV) which flew on the power of a SNECMA Atar engine for the first time on 24 July 1956. Air force interest waned and NATO chose the Fiat G91, yet the

Etendard IV was saved through its selection by the Aéronavale as France's next-generation embarked attack aircraft.

Seven development machines, fitted for catapult take-offs and arrested landings, were followed between 1961 and 1965 by 69 Etendard IVMs and 21 Etendard IVPs, the latter equipped for photo-reconnaissance. Today, a handful of Etendard IVMs remains in service at Hyères with 59 Escardrille de Servitude (59 S) in the land-based operational training role. The Etendard IVP variant, which has a secondary role carrying a Douglas inflight-refuelling 'buddy-buddy' pod beneath the fuselage, is still in operational service at sea, flown by 16 Flottille (16 F).

As the time approached for planning replacement of the Etendard, the Anglo-French SEPECAT Jaguar appeared the logical choice. Against competition from the McDonnell Douglas A-4 Skyhawk, LTV A-7 Corsair and even a navalized Dassault Mirage F.1, the Jaguar M (for Marine) progressed as far as carrier trials. But at this stage political considerations came to the fore, and the French government was persuaded by Dassault to buy from them. It was decided to modify the existing Etendard IVM to the new specificatio; the planned 'Super Etendard' would have considerable advantages of cost over its rivals in that there was 90 per cent commonality with the Etendard IVM model. It was hardly surprising, therefore, that the Dassault aircraft was chosen in

January 1973 as the navy's new combat aircraft.

Such were the changes introduced to the Super Etendard before the design was finalized that the aircraft flying today is 90 per cent different to its forebear. Existing only in single-seat form, the Super Etendard is a strike-fighter optimized for air-to-surface roles, but with air-to-air combat capability. A prime feature of the re-design is the new wing, fitted with double-slotted flaps and a modified drooping leading edge. This is mounted at the mid-fuselage position and swept back at 45 degrees, the thickness/chord ratio diminishing from 6 to 5 per cent between root and tip. Based on a two-spar torsion box covered by machined panels with integral stiffeners, the wing has outer sections which fold upwards to reduce span by 1.80 m (5 ft 10.9 in) when stowed aboard a carrier.

For simplicity, ailerons are inboard of the fold line, and they are powered by hydraulic, irreversible controls developed by Dassault. Drooping leading edges have extended chord ('dog tooth') on the fixed part of the wing, whilst the double-slotted flaps feature increased travel compared

with those of the Etendard IV. The technology invested in the wing stems from a requirement to maintain Etendard IV handling characteristics despite the increased weight of the 'Super'. When launched from a catapult, the Super Etendard may weigh up to 11900 kg (26,235 lb) some 1100 kg (2,425 lb) more than its predecessor. For landing the extra load is 300 kg (661 lb), at 8100 kg (17,857 lb). Wing performance, which translates directly into lifting capacity and landing/take-off speeds, is of paramount importance to carrier-based aircraft, and it is a measure of the improvement achieved by refinements that at a constant weight (7800 kg; 17,196 lb) the Etendard approaches for landing at 135 kts (250 km/h; 155 mph), whereas the Super Etendard's speed at this critical phase is only 125 kts (232 km/h; 144 mph).

The Super Etendard's fuselage is an all-metal semi-monocoque, its contours 'waisted' to conform to area rule. A Martin-Baker SEMMB CM4A lightweight ejection seat is provided for the pilot within an armoured, pressurized cockpit. Unusually for a naval aircraft, only medium-pressure tyres are fitted to the Messier-Hispano tricycle landing gear. This has the long-travel shock-absorbers associated with carrier landings, whilst for airfield operations a drag-chute may be deployed from a fairing at the intersection of the fin and all-moving tailplane

Performance improvements in the Super Etendard are additionally a product of the extra 500 kg (1,102 lb) of thrust obtained by moving up to the 8K50 version of SNECMA's Atar turbojet. Rated at 5000 kg (11,023 lb), this is basically the 9K50 as installed in the Mirage F.1 but with corrosion protection, and an augmented jetpipe fitted in place of the afterburner. More fuel-efficient than its predecessor, the Atar 8K50 in conjunction with larger underwing drop-tanks endows the Super Etendard with a greater radius of action than the Etendard IV. When fitted with a single AM.39 Exocet on the starboard

inner wing pylon, a 1100-litre (242-Imp gal) tank to port and a 600-litre (132-Imp gal) tank beneath the fuselage, the Super Etendard may operate up to 880 km (547 miles) from base. To this must be added the Exocet's range of 60-70 km (37-43 miles), or a far greater extension if the retractable inflight-refuelling probe is used.

Armament
In French service, the Super Etendard's weapon options begin with an AN 52 tactical nuclear weapon of 15-kiloton yield. Conventional armament includes two 30-mm DEFA 553 cannon fixed below the air inlets with 125 rounds apiece, and a variety of other ordnance on the four wing and single fuselage attachment points. In attack roles, typical loads would include four LR 150 rocket-launchers, each with 18 rockets of 68-mm (2.68 in) diameter; six 250-kg (551-lb) bombs; or four 400-kg (882-lb) bombs. For air defence of the Fleet, a Matra R.550 Magic heat-seeking AAM is fitted to each outer wing pylon in conjunction with a 600-litre centreline fuel tank, although it is possible to add two 1100-litre tanks inboard to give a maximum hi-hi intercept range of 1205 km (748 miles).

Vital to the aircraft in both types of mission (and one of the more obvious points of

▲ The Super Etendards loaned to Iraq have now been returned to France, replaced by Exocet-armed Mirage F1s. During their service they saw action against tankers in the Persian Gulf; one of the aircraft loaned is reported to have been lost.

▼ The Super Etendard was developed from the 1950s-vintage Etendard IV. A new nav/attack system was installed, but the rather thirsty SNECMA Atar 8C engine was retained. Despite its increased weight the Super Etendard's new wing does give improved handling.

difference from the Etendard IVM) is the Thomson-CSF/ESD Agave I-band monopulse radar mounted in the nose. Agave is optimized for naval use and can detect a large vessel at up to 111 km (69 miles) in air-to-surface search mode, or an aircraft at 28 km (17 miles) in the air-to-air mode. Other modes are available for air or surface tracking/ranging, ground mapping and designating a target for Exocet attack. Complementing Agave (and also a crucial aid over the featureless ocean) is a SAGEM-Kearfott ETNA nav/attack system, the main aspects of which are an SKS 602 inertial platform; a Thomson-CSF VE120 head-up display; a Crouzet 97 navigation display, armament control panel and selector box; a Crouzet 66 air data computer; a TRT radio altimeter; and LMT

TACAN. Aligned by laser before take-off, using data from the carrier's navigation system, ETNA is accurate to within about 2.2 km (1.4 miles) for each hour flown.

From 1988 onwards when the Super Etendard becomes operational with the Aérospatiale ASMP inertially-guided stand-off nuclear weapon. Rated at between 100 and 150 kilotons, ASMP has a range of up to 100 km (62 miles) and will be carried on the starboard inner wing pylon, balanced to port by a 1100-litre tank. In order to confuse enemy defences, the ASMP-armed Super Etendard is to mount a Philips-Matra Phimat chaff pod on the starboard outer position and a Matra Sycomor flare dispenser on the port outer position. The centreline position on such occasions will hold a 600-litre tank, increasing aircraft hi-lo-hi range to about 850 km (528 miles). In all, 53 Super Etendards will be modified to carry ASMP before the end of 1989.

In service

Development of the Super Etendard was considerably assisted by conversion of three Etendard IVMs. The first of these, which retained its old wing, flew on 28 October 1974; the second was similar, but had the complete nav/attack system; and the third was an Etendard IVM fuselage with the revised wing. After basic proving trials, the wing was removed from its testbed and fitted to the first prototype, transforming it into a definitive-standard aircraft, which first flew on 3 October 1975. Two years later, on 24 November 1977, the initial example of 71 production Super Etendards for the Aéronavale flew at Dassault's Bordeaux plant, deliveries following from 28 June 1978. The first operator was 11F, which accepted its initial aircraft on 4 September 1978 and first went to sea for a short proving cruise on 4 December of the same year. Because of cost escalation the projected 100 aircraft could not be funded, so only another two squadrons (14 and 17 Flottilles) were formed. The French navy thus retained the reconnaissance unit of Étendard IVPs and one of its two squadrons (12 F) of LTV F-8E(FN) Crusader interceptors to complement the Super Etendards.

Regular deployments are made by the Super Etendard to the decks of France's two 23,700-ton aircraft-carriers, Clemenceau and Foch. During one such tour off the Lebanese coast in support of the UN peace-keeping force, the Aéronavale went into action for the first time in more than two decades when four Super Etendards successfully attacked Druze militia gun emplacements on 22 September 1983. However, this was merely a footnote to the aircraft's debut in combat with Argentina's 2ª Escuadrilla Aeronaval de Caza y Ataque (2nd Naval Fighter-Attack Squadron) over a year before.

A component of 3ª Escuadra Aeronaval (3rd Naval Air Wing) at Puerto Belgrano, 2ª Escuadrilla had received five of its

planned 14 aircraft and five Exocets by the start of the Falklands War. Operating from Rio Grande, the Super Etendards mortally damaged the frigate HMS *Sheffield* on 4 May 1982 and the container ship MV *Atlantic Conveyor* on 25 May, two aircraft each launching a missile on each occasion. The fifth round was expended without result on 30 May, and the squadron took no further part in hostilities. Only later in 1982 did France resume aircraft and missile deliveries, and not until 18 April 1983 was the first landing of the type made aboard the Argentine aircraft-carrier *Veinticinco de Mayo*.

Iraq, with no carriers in its navy, became an unlikely Super Etendard user in 1983 when the 65th to 69th French naval aircraft were transferred, together with a large stock of Exocets. Apparently on loan for a term of two years, the aircraft were delivered in October 1983 after their pilots had been trained in France. War tactics then being employed were to sink or damage tankers carrying Iranian oil through the Persian Gulf, and so ruin the enemy's economy. Some success had already been gained by Exocets fired from Aérospatiale Super Frelon helicopters, and the Super Etendards were required to maintain the pressure at longer range.

The first admitted use of the aircraft by Iraq did not take place until 27 March

▲ *Seen at the moment of launch from the steam catapult on board* Foch *is a Super Etendard of 17 Flottille. The Aéronavale has three front-line Super Etendard units; 17 Flottille, based at Hyères, near Toulon, and 11 and 14 Flottilles at Landivisiau in Brittany.*

▼ *With an Exocet under the starboard wing, an Aéronavale Super Etendard takes the wire. The Super Etendards used in the attack on HMS* Sheffield *carried this weapon. Despite its shortcomings the Super Etendard has enjoyed a successful combat career.*

1984, when a Greek tanker was damaged. Thereafter, Super Etendards played a significant part in the 51 confirmed tanker attacks in the Persian Gulf during 1984. Perversely, viscous crude oil cushions a warhead explosion and is notoriously difficult to ignite, so that most tankers have escaped with repairable damage. After Mirage F.1s took over the Exocet role in February 1985, the remaining Super Etendards were stood-down in preparation for their return to France, one of the five reportedly having been lost and another damaged by a Sidewinder AAM. Few 'peacetime' aircraft can boast a combat record as lengthy as that of the Super Etendard at such a comparatively early stage in their careers, so Dassault's rejuvenated fighter-bomber, for all its faults, has been an effective carrierborne warplane.

Super Etendard in service units and example aircraft

Aéronavale (France)

11 Flottille
Base: Landivisiau
Converted: 4 September 1978
Task: maritime strike/attack and interception
Aircraft: nos 6, 10, 33, 37, 38, 39, 55, 61, 63, 71

This is a Super Etendard of 11 Flottille, whose land base is Landivisiau.

14 Flottille
Base: Landivisiau
Converted: 1 June 1979
Task: maritime strike/attack and interception
Aircraft: nos 13, 23, 25, 31, 32, 44, 47, 50, 58, 70

This Exocet-wielding Super Etendard belongs to 14 Flottille, the other Landivisiau unit.

17 Flottille
Base: Hyères
Converted: 5 September 1980
Task: maritime strike/attack and interception
Aircraft: nos 3, 4, 17, 24, 29, 30, 51, 52, 59, 64

17 Flottille, one of whose Etendards is seen here, was the final unit to form.

Comando de Aviación Naval Argentina
2ª Escuadrilla Aeronaval de Caza y Ataque

Base: Base Aerea Comandante Espora, Puerto Belgrano
Converted: 26 March 1981 (in France)
Task: maritime attack and interception
Aircraft: 0751 '3-A-201' to 0764 '3-A-214'

Argentina's Super Etendards are based at Puerto Belgrano, and can operate from the aircraft-carrier Veinticinco de Mayo. During the Falklands War the Super Etendards operated from Rio Grande and did not make their first carrier landings until after the war, in April 1983.

Performance:

Maximum speed at height	about Mach 1	
Maximum speed at low altitude	637 kts	1180 km/h (733 mph)
Service ceiling	45,000 ft	(13715 m)
Combat radius with Exocet and two fuel tanks hi-lo-hi	850 km	(528 miles)

Weapon load

- Grumman A-6E 8165 kg
- F/A-18 Hornet 7711 kg
- Vought A-7E 6804 kg +
- Sea Harrier 3629 kg
- Yak-38 'Forger' 3600 kg E
- Super Etendard 2100 kg

Service ceiling

- Sea Harrier 50,000 ft +
- F/A-18 Hornet 50,000 ft
- Super Etendard 45,000 ft
- Grumman A-6E 42,000 ft +
- Vought A-7E 42,000 ft
- Yak-38 'Forger' 40,000 ft E

Speed at high altitude

- F/A-18 Hornet Mach 1.8 +
- Super Etendard Mach 1
- Yak-38 'Forger' Mach 0.95 E
- Sea Harrier Mach 0.95
- Vought A-7E Mach 0.9
- Grumman A-6E Mach 0.8

Speed at low altitude

- F/A-18 Hornet Mach 1
- Super Etendard Mach 0.95
- Vought A-7E Mach 0.9
- Sea Harrier Mach 0.85
- Grumman A-6E Mach 0.85
- Yak-38 'Forger' Mach 0.8 E

Operational range (internal fuel)

- Vought A-7E 2300 km
- F/A-18 Hornet 2130 km
- Grumman A-6E 1627 km
- Super Etendard 1500 km
- Sea Harrier 1500 km
- Yak-38 'Forger' 1000 km

Dassault-Breguet Super Etendard warload

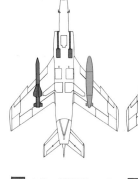

Anti-shipping (Exocet)

- 2×30-mm DEFA 552A cannon in the nose with 125 rounds per gun
- 1×AM.39 Exocet anti-ship missile on starboard inboard pylon
- 1×1100-litre (242-Imp gal) fuel tank on port inboard pylon

Nuclear strike

- 2×30-mm DEFA 552A cannon in the nose with 125 rounds per gun
- 1×ASMP cruise missile on starboard inboard pylon
- 1×1100-litre (242-Imp gal) fuel tank on port inboard pylon
- 1×Matra Phimat chaff and flare dispenser on starboard outboard pylon
- 1×Matra Sycomor ECM pod on port outboard pylon

Light attack

- 2×30-mm DEFA 552A cannon in the nose with 125 rounds per gun
- 2×400-kg (882-lb) bombs on outboard pylons
- 2×1100-litre (242-Imp gal) fuel tanks on inboard wing pylons

Air defence

- 2×30-mm DEFA 552A cannon in the nose with 125 rounds per gun
- 2×Matra 550 Magic IR-homing air-to-air missiles underwing
- 2×1100-litre (242-Imp gal) fuel tanks on inboard wing pylons

Anti-shipping (Exocet)

The Super Etendard is severely handicapped by its lack of range, and one Exocet is the most that can be carried on all but the shortest-range missions. This fuel/weapon combination was used by the Argentine Super Etendards for their attack on HMS *Sheffield*.

Nuclear strike

Both the ASMP cruise missile and the AN52 nuclear bomb have been mentioned as likely weapons for the Super Etendard in the future. Targets would primarily be tactical, with strategic targets being allotted to the ASMP-equipped Dassault-Breguet Mirage IVs of the 'Force de Frappe'.

Light attack

In the attack role up to four 400-kg bombs could be carried underwing, but this would not allow the carriage of the 1100-litre tanks which are so essential to boost the Super Etendard's unimpressive range. If external fuel was not required ECM and chaff pods might be more likely than extra bombs, to improve survivability and agility.

Air defence

The Super Etendard is considerably slower and less agile than the Vought F-8 Crusaders used as its primary self-defence asset by the Aéronavale, as well as having a shorter range. Without a dedicated air-to-air radar or gunsight the Super Etendard is not a vastly useful air-defence tool.

A Super Etendard of the Aéronavale fires it. deadly Exocet. In the Falklands war the Exocet/Super Etendard combination accounted for HMS Sheffield and Atlantic Conveyor.

Dassault-Breguet Super Etendard cutaway drawing key

1 Radome
2 Scanner housing
3 Flat plate radar scanner
4 Scanner tracking mechanism
5 Thomson-CSF/EMD Agave multi-mode radar equipment package
6 Refuelling probe housing
7 Retractable inflight-refuelling probe
8 Nav/attack avionics equipment
9 UHF aerial
10 Pitot head
11 Temperature probe
12 Refuelling probe retraction link and jack
13 Cockpit front pressure bulkhead
14 Instrument panel shroud
15 Windscreen panels
16 Head-up display
17 Control column
18 Rudder pedals
19 Cockpit section framing
20 Pressure floor level
21 Side console panel
22 Engine throttle lever
23 Radar hand controller
24 Nose undercarriage pivot fixing
25 Carrier deck approach lights
26 Nosewheel leg doors
27 Hydraulic steering jacks
28 Nosewheel forks
29 Nosewheel, aft retracting
30 Nose undercarriage leg strut
31 Rear breaker strut
32 Hydraulic retraction jack
33 Port engine air intake
34 Boundary layer splitter plate
35 Air conditioning system ram air intake
36 Cockpit sloping rear pressure bulkhead
37 Boundary layer spill duct
38 Pilot's Hispano-built Martin-Baker SEMMB CM4A ejection seat
39 Starboard engine air intake
40 Ejection seat headrest
41 Face blind firing handle
42 Cockpit canopy cover, upward hingeing
43 Canopy hinge point
44 Canopy emergency release
45 Air conditioning plant
46 Intake duct framing
47 Ventral cannon blast trough
48 Cannon barrel
49 Oxygen bottles (two)
50 Navigation and communications avionics equipment racks

51 Martin Pescador air-to-surface missile (Argentine aircraft only)
52 Martin Pescador guidance pod
53 Starboard external fuel tank
54 Equipment bay dorsal access panels
55 Fuel system inverted flight accumulator
56 Intake suction relief door
57 DEFA 30-mm cannon (two)
58 Ground power and intercom sockets
59 Ventral cannon pack access door
60 Ammunition magazine, 125 rounds per gun
61 Air system pre-cooler, avionics cooling air
62 Forward fuselage bag-type fuel tanks, total internal capacity 3200 litres (704 Imp gal)
63 Fuel tank access panels
64 Wing spar attachment main frames
65 Fuselage dorsal systems ducting
66 Avionics cooling air exit louvres
67 IFF aerial
68 Starboard wing integral fuel tank
69 Pylon attachment points
70 Matra 155 rocket launcher pack, 19×68-mm rockets
71 Leading edge dog-tooth
72 Leading edge flap control rod and links
73 Starboard leading edge flap, lowered
74 Aileron hydraulic actuator
75 Wing fold hydraulic jack
76 Outboard, folding wing tip panel
77 Strobe identification light
78 Starboard navigation light
79 Starboard wing tip folded position
80 Fixed portion of trailing edge
81 Starboard aileron
82 Aileron hinge control
83 Aileron/spoiler interconnecting link
84 Spoiler hydraulic actuator
85 Starboard spoiler, open
86 Double-slotted Fowler-type, flap down position
87 Rear fuselage bag-type fuel tanks
88 Rudder control cables
89 Engine starter housing
90 Compressor intake
91 Forward engine mounting bulkhead
92 Accessory gearbox drive shaft

93 Gearbox driven generators (two)
94 Engine accessory equipment
95 SNECMA Atar 8K-50 non-afterburning turbojet engine
96 Engine bleed air duct to air conditioning system
97 Rudder control cable quadrant
98 Fin spar attachment joint
99 Leading edge access panel to control runs
100 All-moving tailplane pitch trim control electric motor
101 Tailplane root leading edge aerodynamic notch
102 Elevator hydraulic actuator
103 Upper/lower fin segment joint
104 Tailplane sealing plate
105 Rudder hydraulic actuator
106 Tailfin construction
107 Starboard all-moving tailplane
108 Forward radar warning antenna
109 VOR aerial (Argentine aircraft only)
110 VHF aerial
111 Fin tip aerial fairing
112 Command telemetry aerial
113 Rudder
114 Rudder rib construction
115 Brake parachute housing, ground based operations only
116 Tailcone parachute door
117 Tail navigation and anti-collision lights
118 Rear radar warning antenna
119 Port elevator
120 Elevator rib construction
121 Elevator damper
122 Port all-moving tailplane construction
123 Engine exhaust nozzle
124 Jet pipe

125 Inflight-refuelling drogue, extended
126 Refuelling hose
127 Deck arrester hook, lowered
128 Arrester hook stowage fairing
129 Detachable tailcone frame and stringer construction
130 Rear fuselage break point, engine removal
131 Sloping fin spar attachment bulkhead
132 Engine bay heat shroud
133 Engine turbine section
134 Radar warning power amplifier
135 Fin spar and engine mounting bulkhead
136 Main engine mounting spigot
137 Aft avionics equipment bays, port and starboard
138 Port double-slotted Fowler-type flap
139 Flap rib construction
140 Flap shroud ribs
141 Inboard flap guide rail
142 Main undercarriage wheel bay
143 Main undercarriage leg pivot fixing
144 Flap hydraulic jack
145 Port spoiler

146 Spoiler hydraulic jack and control links
147 Outboard flap guide rail
148 Aileron rib construction
149 Port aileron
150 Port wing tip, folded position
151 Wing tip panel construction
152 Wing tip fairing
153 Port navigation light
154 Strobe identification light
155 Wing fold hydraulic jack
156 Wing fold hinge joints
157 Outboard leading edge flap segment
158 Matra 550 Magic air-to-air missile
159 Missile launch rail
160 Matra 155 18×68-mm rocket pack
161 Aileron hydraulic actuator

162 Outboard pylon attachment joint
163 Outboard stores pylon
164 Leading edge dog-toot
165 Machined wing skin/ stringer panel
166 Wing rib construction
167 Inboard pylon attachm joint
168 Inboard stores pylon
169 External fuel tank, 1100 litres (242 Imp gal)
170 Port mainwheel
171 Hydraulic multi-plate d brake
172 Torque scissor links
173 Main undercarriage leg strut
174 Hydraulic retraction jac

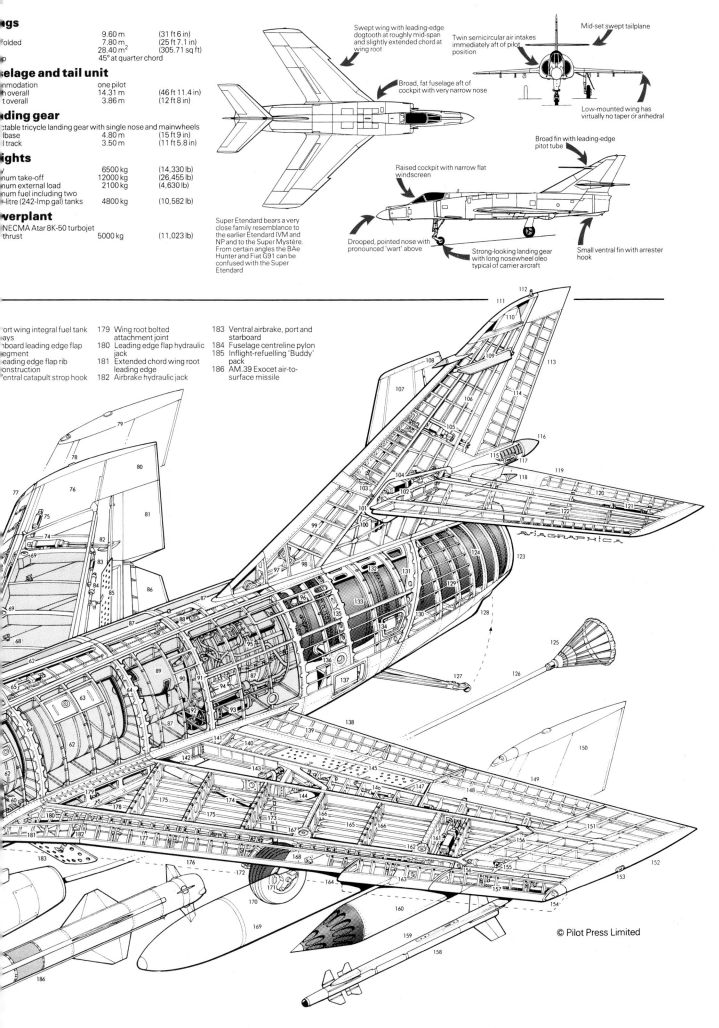

Specification: Dassault Super Etendard

Wings

folded	9.60 m	(31 ft 6 in)
	7.80 m	(25 ft 7.1 in)
	28.40 m²	(305.71 sq ft)
	45° at quarter chord	

Fuselage and tail unit

accommodation	one pilot	
length overall	14.31 m	(46 ft 11.4 in)
height overall	3.86 m	(12 ft 8 in)

Landing gear

retractable tricycle landing gear with single nose and mainwheels

wheelbase	4.80 m	(15 ft 9 in)
wheel track	3.50 m	(11 ft 5.8 in)

Weights

empty	6500 kg	(14,330 lb)
maximum take-off	12000 kg	(26,455 lb)
maximum external load	2100 kg	(4,630 lb)
maximum fuel including two 1100-litre (242-Imp gal) tanks	4800 kg	(10,582 lb)

Powerplant

one SNECMA Atar 8K-50 turbojet		
thrust	5000 kg	(11,023 lb)

Super Etendard recognition features

Swept wing with leading-edge dogtooth at roughly mid-span and slightly extended chord at wing root

Twin semicircular air intakes immediately aft of pilot position

Mid-set swept tailplane

Broad, fat fuselage aft of cockpit with very narrow nose

Low-mounted wing has virtually no taper or anhedral

Broad fin with leading-edge pitot tube

Raised cockpit with narrow flat windscreen

Super Etendard bears a very close family resemblance to the earlier Etendard IVM and NP and to the Super Mystère. From certain angles the BAe Hunter and Fiat G91 can be confused with the Super Etendard

Drooped, pointed nose with pronounced 'wart' above

Strong-looking landing gear with long nosewheel oleo typical of carrier aircraft

Small ventral fin with arrester hook

178 port wing integral fuel tank bays
179 Wing root bolted attachment joint
180 Leading edge flap hydraulic jack
181 Extended chord wing root leading edge
182 Airbrake hydraulic jack
183 Ventral airbrake, port and starboard
184 Fuselage centreline pylon
185 Inflight-refuelling 'Buddy' pack
186 AM.39 Exocet air-to-surface missile

inboard leading edge flap segment
leading edge flap rib construction
central catapult strop hook

© Pilot Press Limited

The DASSAULT MIRAGE IV

Dassault Mirage IV: France's big stick

The Mirage IV has equipped the nuclear strike squadrons of France's Force de Frappe since October 1964, providing her with the genuinely independent strategic nuclear deterrent that allowed her to leave NATO. Refurbishing and modifications to allow the aircraft to carry the new ASMP nuclear stand-off missile will allow the force to remain viable into the 1990s.

One of the more remarkable attributes of the strategic bombers designed during the 1940s and 1950s has been their unplanned longevity. The assumption during their drawing board gestation was that the cycle of replacement would remain at 10 years or so, and that something else would thus be along shortly to take over the role. Some new bombers did appear in the inventories of the more wealthy nations, but high costs resulted in the old equipment being refurbished for continued use. Aircraft designed for high-altitude operation underwent a profound change of mission profile with the adoption of under-the-radar penetration in the 1960s, also finding themselves carrying stand-off missiles as an alternative to free-fall nuclear bombs. Some, such as the Vickers Valiant and Boeing B-47, are long gone while others, the Myasischyev M-4 and Handley Page Victor for example, have been switched to other duties. The mighty Boeing B-52 continues to pack a tremendous strategic punch in USAF service and looks forward to many more years of use.

Unlike the three powers (the USA, USSR and UK) which preceded it into the nuclear 'club', France has possessed but one purpose-designed strategic jet bomber. Bearing the name of a world-famous series of combat aircraft, the Mirage IV has been a key element in the French nuclear armoury for 20 years. Now it is at the start of a new lease of life carrying a stand-off bomb, and ready to serve for a further decade: not bad for an aircraft intended to last for 10 years of smooth high-altitude flying.

Development

Designation and appearance confirm that the Mirage IV bomber is closely related to the Dassault Mirage III fighter. When development work was formally initiated in April 1957, Dassault was able to satisfy the official requirement by scaling-up the Mirage III some 50 per cent, doubling the wing area and weight, and adding a second afterburning SNECMA Atar engine. This aeroplane was at first regarded as an interim means of attaining strategic capability, for it had enough range only to reach 'the nearest NATO airfield' after attacking Soviet industrial targets from French bases. Next was to come a majestic bomber three times the size, although that programme was soon judged to be far beyond the available technical and financial means. Instead, France bought a dozen Boeing C-135F inflight-refuelling tankers with which to extend the range of its Mirage IVs.

The 'one-and-a-half-way' (some might even claim 'semi-suicide') mission thus became more survivable for the bomber's two-man crews. It was still a shorter distance from French airfields to Moscow than from (say) RAF Scampton, but this was by no means an unalloyed blessing. British subsonic bombers could enter Soviet airspace anywhere along its broad flanks, probably via the Baltic. French bombers would most likely have to fly through the dense air defences of the Central Front to reach their targets. Therefore, a supersonic aircraft was required: one which would fly through the SAM and fighter belt at high subsonic speed, then

▲ *An ASMP test round separates from the no. 1 Mirage IVP. The ASMP is powered by a liquid-fuelled ramjet and solid fuelled rocket booster. It has a range of between 80km (Mach 2/sea level) and 250 km (Mach 3/high altitude).*

▼ *The 300-kt ASMP cruise missile will eventually equip all 18 Mirage IVPs, but will also equip five Mirage 2000 Squadrons (75 aircraft), and two Flotilles of Super Etendards (12 aircraft).*

climb and accelerate to Mach 2 for a 'sprint' attack.

A low-mounted delta wing, swept at 60°, is a prominent common feature of Mirage III and IV. In the scaled-up aircraft, size made it possible for the engineers to build a wing with a thickness:chord ratio more suited to supersonic flight. This was 3.8 per cent at the root and 3.2 per cent at tips, compared with 4.5 per cent and 3.5 per cent in the Mirage III. Additionally, milled and tapered solid skins covered almost 95 per cent of the structure, making it possible to include integral wing tanks. As a further aid to maximum range, the fin too was built as a tank. The wings also inherited the Mirage III's system of split elevon controls with duplicated power operation, as well as air brakes similar to those of the fighter.

The air inlets mounted on each side of the fuselage feature half-cones (nicknamed 'souris', or mouse) which are moved according to aircraft speed in order to focus the shock wave at the optimum position on the inlet lip for pressure recovery. The engines are two Atar 09Ks rated at 4700-kg (10,362-lb) dry thrust and 6700-kg (14,771-lb) afterburning thrust. For take-offs at maximum weight, two groups of six JATO bottles are mounted beneath the wings. The pilot is seated well forward of the inlets in a cockpit air conditioned against the kinetic heating effects of sustained flight at Mach 1.8.

Armament

From a claustrophobic cockpit behind the pilot, naturally lit by only two small side windows, the navigator monitors equipment including CSF ground-mapping radar mounted in the aircraft's belly. Immediately behind the circular radome is a recess in the fuselage which matches the shape of the upper half of a 60-kiloton yield AN 22 nuclear weapon. Once freefall, this was modified from late-1967 for low-level 'lay down' delivery, and is parachute-retarded. Weight is around 750 kg (1,653 lb), or about half the mass when first deployed. The navigator operates the Thomson-CSF Type BF radar-warning receiver and doubtless also an undisclosed form of jamming equipment. For defence against heat-seeking SAMs, Philips-Matra Phimat flare dispensers may be fitted to each outer wing pylon. Inboard pylons will each accommodate a 2500-litre (550-Imp gal) drop tank.

The prototype Mirage IV flew on 17 June 1959, powered by Atar 09C engines and fitted with a tall, almost pointed fin. No. 02, which followed on 12 October 1961, was nearly to production standard in regard to external appearance, and was redesignated Mirage IVA. (Between the two first flights, on 13 February 1960, France had exploded its initial atomic weapon.) There were two more pre-series aircraft, of which No. 03 was fitted with a refuelling probe in the extreme nose for tanker trials and No. 04 reached full production standard with Atar 09K engines

and complete avionics. No. 03 was also equipped with Marconi Doppler, a Dassault computer and countermeasures equipment, and a SFENA autopilot.

The first 50 Mirage IVAs had been ordered in 1960, to be followed by a smaller batch of 12, and all were produced between December 1963 and November 1966. On 1 January 1964, the Commandant des Forces Aériennes Stratégiques (CoFAS) was formed within the Armée de l'Air to administer the strategic force. This rapidly gained the name Force de Frappe (strike force), but the less bellicose Force de Dissuasion was officially preferred. A squadron of Mirage IVAs was declared operational on 1 October 1964, and by 1 February 1966 nine squadrons were in being, each with four bombed-up ready-to-go aircraft. Less than six weeks later, France announced that it would leave the military structure of NATO at the end of 1966 and assume total responsibility for its own defence.

It was never practical for France to adopt the US system of maintaining an airborne alert force, so the compromise was adopted of each squadron having one aircraft at 15-minute readiness at all times. As silo-launched missiles were added to the

▲ *This Mirage IVA carries a retarded AN 22 nuclear weapon under its belly. One AN 22-equipped unit, EB 2/94 'Marne' at St Dizier, is to be retained alongside the ASMP carriers, EB 1/91 'Gascogne' and EB 2/91 'Bretagne'.*

▼ *Four Mirage IVs were equipped with CT-52 reconnaissance pods, which were similar in size and shape to the AN 22 nuclear bomb. This pod can carry a variety of vertical, forward and oblique cameras, and an infra-red linescan.*

inventory and progressively modernized, the number of Mirage squadrons was reduced to six in June 1976 and then to four in October 1983. Additionally, however, the OCU (Centre d'Instruction des Forces Aériennes Stratégiques [CIFAS] 329) operated a flight of four Mirage IVAs in the stratégique reconnaissance role. These four aircraft (from a total of 12 converted) were equipped from 1977 onwards with a CT 52 sensor pod of similar size and shape to the AN 22 weapon, and stowed in the same place. CT 52s have provision for vertical, oblique and forward cameras, such as three low-level Omera 35s and three high-level Omera 36s, plus a Wildt mapping camera. If IR linescan is required, a SAT Super Cyclone unit is fitted in place

of the Omera 36s.

These reconnaissance aircraft were to have been the only Mirage IVAs in operation after the extended retirement date of 1985. First signs that this would not be the case came in 1979 when it was revealed that 15 (later increased to 18) aircraft were being earmarked for modification to carry the Aérospatiale ASMP stand-off weapon, which received a development contract in April 1978. This is a missile 5.38 m (17 ft 8 in) long, powered by a kerosene-burning ramjet and a solid propellant launch booster. Range is in the order of 75 to 100 km (46 to 62 miles), and terrain-following flight to the target at Mach 3 is via a SAGEM inertial platform.

In order that the 150-kiloton warhead can be delivered accurately, the carrier aircraft's navigation system must feed the ASMP with position data up to the moment of launch. Several changes have had to be made in order that a 1950s aeroplane can 'talk' to a 1970s missile, whilst at the same time the Mirage IV's radar has required updating for increased accuracy. The belly radome now covers the scanner of a Thomson-CSF ARCANA (Appareil de Récalage et de Cartographie pour Navigation Aveugle) pulse-Doppler unit derived from the Iguane and VARAN systems which equip the Dassault-Breguet Atlantique 2 and Dassault-Breguet Gardian maritime surveillance aircraft respectively. Pulse-Doppler provides high-resolution mapping in all weathers to enable regular cross-checking to be made of the Mirage IV's own inertial system.

Although the ASMP is also to arm two other Dassault-Breguet designs, the Super Etendard and Mirage 2000N, the Mirage IV is the initial carrier, and so participated in early trials of the missile. First, the middle fuselage of the scrapped third Mirage IV prototype was used for static tests of the new centreline pylon on which the ASMP would be mounted. Following that, in 1981, Mirage IVA No. 8 made test drops of a dummy ASMP, whilst No. 4 started live launches in June 1983. Some problems manifested themselves with the combination rocket/ramjet, all of which were resolved by the time that missile proving was completed in mid-1985

Meanwhile, in 1982, No. 8 was con-

verted into the first prototype of the ASMP launcher version. Initially, the designation Mirage IVN (for Nucléaire) was used, but it was soon changed to Mirage IVP, indicating the role of Pénétration. In this new regime, the Mirage IV will abandon a dash to the target in favour of a hi-lo-hi mission profile over a 4000-km (2,485-mile) radius of action with inflight-refuelling. (So that it may also meet the demands of extended service, the tanker fleet is being converted to C-135FR standard.

Completed in October 1982, Mirage IVP No. 01 (née No. 8) was employed on Dassault trials before being handed over to the CEAM (Centre d'Expériences Aériennes Militaires) at Mont-de-Marsan on 1 July 1983. Because the Mirage IVP is a well-known airframe with new avionics, the CEAM evaluation team was unusual in being headed by an accomplished navigator rather than by a pilot. CEAM was unable to evaluate the revised ECM suite, as this was not available until Mirage IVP No. 02 (ex-Mirage IVA No. 28) flew in May 1983. The second aircraft was used mainly for Dassault trials whilst, released from CEAM, Mirage IVP No. 01 took over the ASMP launch programme.

Conversion

All 18 'production' Mirage IVPs are being converted by the Armée de l'Air's workshops at Aulnat/Clermont-Ferrand (the Atelier Industriel de l'Air). Arriving there in October 1983, the first was redelivered (to CEAM) in February 1985, and it is planned that the 18th (actually a re-work of Mirage IVP No. 02) will be completed in mid-1987. A full-scale overhaul and rewiring is part of the transformation process at Aulnat, but it could be that a further

▲ *Like many European air forces, l'Armée de l'Air has 'hardened' many of its airfields. To reduce the vulnerability of the Force de Frappe, its Mirage IVPs will be housed in Hardened Aircraft Shelters.*

▼ *This Mirage IVP carries as ASMP under its belly, and two underwing fuel tanks. The unit badge on the fin is that of CEAM; front-line aircraft will not carry any squadron insignia.*

rebuild will be necessary at a later stage: individual Mirage IVs have now flown almost 5,000 hours, and whilst an ultimate life of 7,500 hours is possible, a change of main spar at 6,500 hours might well be in prospect for any which reach that mark.

Only two of the original nine squadrons will be equipped to carry the ASMP, the first of which, EB 1/91 'Gascogne' at Mont-de-Marsan, declared its initial Mirage IVP operational on 1 May 1986. Deliveries of six to that unit were scheduled to be complete before the end of the year, allowing EB 2/91 'Bretagne' at Cazaux to begin conversion in December 1986. This, too, is receiving six, leaving the balance of six to go to CIFAS 328 for training. There remain just sufficient Mirage IVAs to provide an attrition reserve and keep one squadron in operation with the original AN 22 bomb – that honour going to EB 2/94 'Marne', which will fly from St Dizier, with a detachment at Cambrai, until the mid-1990s. Reduced to a third of its former size following the disbandment of three squadrons in 1976, two in 1983 and another as recently as October 1986, the Mirage IV fleet is re-mustering in the front line, endowed with a fresh lease of life. It is planned that the new era just beginning will last for 10 years, but that is what they said in 1964!

Dassault Mirage IVA in service

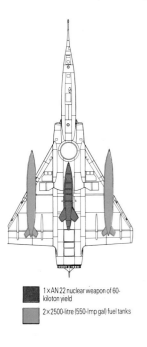
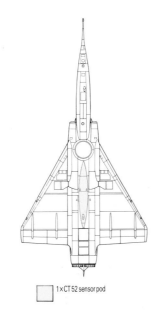

■ 1 × AN 22 nuclear weapon of 60-kiloton yield

■ 2 × 2500-litre (550-Imp gal) fuel tanks

□ 1 × CT 52 sensor pod

■ 1 × Aérospatiale ASMP 150-kiloton yield stand-off weapon

■ 2 × 2500-litre (550-Imp gal) drop tanks

□ 2 × Philips-Matra Phimat flare dispensers

Strategic bomber

The Mirage IVA entered service in 1964 as a strategic bomber, equipped with a free-fall nuclear weapon which was to be dropped from medium or high level after a Mach 2 sprint to the target. Low-level delivery was adopted in the second half of 1967 when a parachute-retarded weapon became available. By 1973 the AN 22 had been so refined that it weighed half the 1500 kg (3,307 lb) of the first French strategic air-dropped weapon. Despite large underwing tanks, refuelling from a Boeing C-135F tanker is included in a typical mission profile.

Strategic reconnaissance

A flight of four aircraft attached to the Strategic Air Force Training Centre (CIFAS) at Bordeaux has an operational role of long-range reconnaissance. In 1977 delivery was undertaken of five CT 52 pods, which are designed to fit in the recess originally provided for the AN 22 bomb. They are usually equipped with six high- or low-level optical cameras, plus a mapping camera, although a SAT Super Cyclope infra-red linescan system can be installed for low-altitude work. CIFAS is expected to retain its operational reconnaissance role after remaining squadrons re-equip with Mirage IVPs.

Stand-off strategic strike

In 1986, the Mirage IVP conversion gained operational status with a single ASMP weapon carried on a centreline pylon. ASMP is a Mach 3 missile, powered by a solid-propellant booster and kerosene-burning ramjet sustainer, which is guided to the target in terrain-following flight by an inertial navigation system. Its range of some 100 km (62 miles) means that the carrier aircraft is less at risk when attacking heavily defended targets. Phimat pods give protection against heat-seeking SAMs.

Dassault Mirage IVA in service

Armée de l'Air (French air force)

Mirage IVs of the Strategic Air Force formed the original cornerstone of France's independent nuclear deterrent, and will continue to play a vital role after introduction of ASMP-equipped Mirage 2000Ns to Tactical Air Command. Of the former 10 operating units (including the OCU), Escadron de Bombardement 'Beauvaisis' at Creil, EB 'Sambre' at Cambrai and EB 'Bourbonnais' at Avord all disbanded on 1 July 1976. They were followed by EB 3/91 'Cevennes' at Orange and EB 3/94 'Arbois' at Luxeuil both on 1 October 1983; and EB 1/94 'Gascogne' at Avord on 1 October 1986.

The Mirage IV fleet provides a pool of serviceable aircraft to operating units, none of which normally apply insignia. Production aircraft nos 2-62 are coded 'AA' to 'CI' in order, whilst no. 1 became a replacement 'AP'.

Escadron de Bombardement 1/91 'Gascogne'
Base: Mont-de-Marsan
Formed: 1 October 1964
Aircraft: Mirage IVP from 1 May 1986

Escadron de Bombardment 2/94 'Marne'
Base: St Dizier (det. Cambrai)
Formed: 1 October 1965
Aircraft: Mirage IVA

Escadron de Bombardement 2/91 'Bretagne'
Base: Cazaux
Formed: 1 December 1965
Aircraft: Mirage IVA (Mirage IVP from December 1986)

Escadron de Reconnaissance et de Instruction 1/328
Parent unit: CIFAS 328 'Aquitaine'
Base: Bordeaux
Formed: 15 July 1978
Aircraft: Mirage IVA/IVP

Huge 2500-litre (550-Imp gal) underwing fuel tanks extend the range of the mighty Mirage IV, and are a frequently-seen store. This Mirage IVA is not armed, nor does it have any EW pods under its outer wings, and it may be one of the CT-52 reconnaissance pod compatible aircraft.

Performance

Maximum speed at
36,000 ft (10975 m) Mach 2.2 1260 kts 2335 km/h (1,451 mph)
Normal penetration speed
Mach 1.8
Service ceiling   65,615 ft   (20000 m)
Combat radius with one ASMP
and inflight-refuelling   4000 km   (2,485 miles)
Time to 36,090 ft (11000 m)   4 minutes 15 seconds
Take-off distance not disclosed

Weapon load

- Rockwell International B-1B 29030 kg typical
- General Dynamics FB-111A 17000 kg
- Tupolev Tu-26 'Backfire' 12000 kg E
- Sukhoi Su-24 'Fencer' 11000 kg E
- Panavia Tornado GR.Mk1 9000 kg
- British Aerospace (HS) S.Mk 2 Buccaneer 7257 kg
- Dassault-Breguet Mirage IVA 4000 kg

Service ceiling

- Dassault-Breguet Mirage IVA 65,600 ft
- General Dynamics FB-111A 60,000 ft +
- Tupolev Tu-26 'Backfire' 55,000 ft
- Sukhoi Su-24 'Fencer' 54,135 ft E
- Rockwell International B-1B 50,000 ft E
- Panavia Tornado GR.Mk1 50,000 ft +
- British Aerospace (HS) S.Mk 2 40,000 ft + E

Maximum speed at high altitude

- Dassault-Breguet Mirage IVA Mach 2.2
- General Dynamics FB-111A Mach 2.2
- Panavia Tornado GR.Mk1 Mach 2.2 'clean'
- Sukhoi Su-24 'Fencer' Mach 2.18 E
- Tupolev Tu-26 'Backfire' Mach 1.92 E
- Rockwell International B-1B Mach 1.25 E
- British Aerospace (HS) S.Mk 2 Buccaneer Mach 0.85

Maximum speed at low altitude

- Sukhoi Su-24 'Fencer' Mach 1.2 E
- General Dynamics FB-111A Mach 1.1
- Dassault-Breguet Mirage IVA Mach 1.1 E
- British Aerospace (HS) S.Mk 2 Buccaneer Mach 0.92
- Panavia Tornado GR.Mk1 Mach 0.92
- Tupolev Tu-26 'Backfire' Mach 0.9 E
- Rockwell International B-1B Mach 0.8 E

Range

- Rockwell International B-1B 12000 km E
- Tupolev Tu-26 'Backfire' 11000 km E
- General Dynamics FB-111A 5000 km E
- Sukhoi Su-24 'Fencer' 3900 km E
- British Aerospace (HS) S.Mk 2 Buccaneer 3700
- Dassault-Breguet Mirage IVA 3200 km
- Panavia Tornado GR.Mk1 3000 km E

Mirage IV variants

Mirage IV: one prototype, powered by two 6000-kg (13,228-lb) thrust Atar O9Bs; span about 11.35 m (37 ft 2.9 in); world 1000-km (621-mile) closed circuit record 15 September 1960 at 982.1 kts (1820 km/h; 1,130.9 mph)
Mirage IVA: three pre-series and 62 production aircraft; first two with 6400 kg (14,110 lb) thrust Atar O9Cs and remainder with Atar O9Ks; shorter fin with braking parachute stowage at base, revised cockpit and forward fuselage contours; span 11.85 m (38 ft 10.5 in); strategic bomber with semi-recessed AN 22 weapon; strategic reconnaissance version with semi-recessed CT 52 sensor pod
Mirage IVN: upgraded version later redesignated Mirage IVP
Mirage IVP: ASMP stand-off weapon on centreline pylon; ugraded avionics, including Thomson-CSF ARCANA ground-mapping radar; two prototype and 18 'production' conversions
Mirage IV*: proposed RAF version to replace cancelled TSR-2 in 1965, with licensed production by BAC; two Rolls-Royce Spey 25R turbofans each of 9525-kg (21,000 lb) thrust; TSR-2 avionics and 0.61-m (2-ft) fuselage extension; rejected in favour of General Dynamics F-111K (also cancelled)

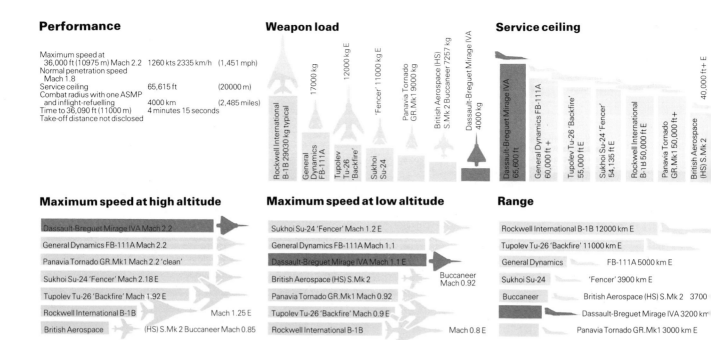

The Mirage IV is similar in many respects to the smaller Mirage III and Mirage 5 single-seat fighters; its under- and upper-surface airbrakes, for example, are almost identical. This aircraft is a late-series Mirage IVA.

Dassault Mirage IVP cutaway drawing key

1 Fixed inflight-refuelling probe
2 Refuelling pipe
3 Liquid oxygen converter
4 OMERA vertical strike camera
5 Pitot head, port and starboard
6 Nose avionics equipment compartment
7 Retractable refuelling spotlight
8 Temperature probe
9 Avionics equipment access door
10 Communications avionics equipment
11 Retractable landing/taxiing lamp
12 Lower VHF aerial
13 Front pressure bulkhead
14 Rudder pedals
15 Control column
16 Instrument panel
17 Pilot's instrument panel shroud
18 Knife-edged windscreen panels
19 Pilot's upward-hinging canopy cover
20 Ejector seat face blind firing handle
21 Martin-Baker (Hispano licence-built) Mk BM.4 ejector seat
22 Starboard side console panel
23 External canopy latch
24 Engine throttle levers
25 Cockpit pressure floor level
26 Periscope fairing
27 Port side console panel
28 Rear seat forward vision periscope
29 Navigator/bombardier's instrument console
30 Tactical navigation display
31 Upward-hinging rear cockpit canopy cover
32 Canopy operating jacks
33 Side window panels
34 Navigator/bombardier's ejector seat
35 External canopy latch
36 Weapons control panel
37 Nose landing gear pivot fixing
38 Hispano nose landing gear leg strut
39 Twin nosewheels, aft retracting
40 Hydraulic steering jacks
41 Nosewheel leg door
42 Retraction/breaker strut
43 Cockpit rear pressure bulkhead
44 Canopy emergency release
45 Battery
46 Elevon artificial feel control unit
47 Air conditioning system ram air intake
48 Movable inlet half-cone centrebody
49 Outline of nosewheel door, closed after cycling of landing gear
50 Port engine air inlet
51 Inlet duct framing
52 Centre-body frame construction
53 Heat exchanger and compressor air intakes
54 Air conditioning plant
55 Heat exchanger exhaust ducts
56 Centre fuselage avionics equipment bay
57 Avionics bay access hatch
58 Starboard engine air inlet
59 Navigation and weapons system avionics equipment
60 Forward fuselage centre-section bag-type fuel tanks
61 Boundary layer spill duct
62 Movable inlet centre-body screw jack
63 Screw jack drive electric motor
64 Inlet duct suction relief doors
65 Ventral radome, CSF navigation and attack radar
66 Fuselage flank bag-type fuel tanks
67 Fuel system piping
68 Inlet trunking
69 Centre fuselage fuel tanks
70 Fuel piping and control system access panels
71 IFF aerial
72 Starboard external fuel tank
73 Wing leading edge integral fuel tank
74 Starboard upper airbrake, open
75 Main landing gear leg pivot fixing
76 Elevon control linkages
77 Pylon attachment hard-points
78 Chaff/flare dispenser pod
79 Leading edge notch
80 Elevon control rod
81 Starboard navigation light
82 Radar warning antenna
83 Starboard outboard elevon
84 Elevon ventral hinge fairings
85 Outboard elevon hydraulic actuator
86 Starboard inboard elevon
87 Inboard elevon hydraulic actuator
88 Starboard wing panel integral fuel tank
89 Fuselage access panels
90 Fuel system inverted flight accumulators (two)
91 Main spar attachment fuselage double frame
92 Engine starter fairing
93 Compressor intake
94 Angled gearbox drive shaft
95 Accessory equipment gearbox
96 Engine fuel system equipment
97 SNECMA Atar 09K afterburning turbojet engine
98 Engine oil tank
99 Hydraulic reservoir
100 Engine bay dividing fireproof bulkhead
101 Starboard engine installation

Specification: Dassault Mirage IVP

Wings
	11.85 m (38 ft 10.5 in)
	78.0 m² (839.6 sq ft)
on leading edge	60°

Fuselage and tail unit
accommodation	pilot and navigator/electronics officer in tandem on Hispano-built Martin-Baker Mk 4 ejector seats
overall	23.50 m (77 ft 1.2 in)
overall	5.65 m (18 ft 6.4 in)

Landing gear
hydraulically retractable tricycle landing gear with four-wheel main and twin-wheel nose unit

Weights
take off	14500 kg (31,967 lb)
	31600 kg (69,666 lb)
external load (ASMP)	900 kg (1,984 lb)
fuel load	14000 litres (3,080 Imp gal)

Powerplant
SNECMA Atar 09K afterburning turbojets
thrust with afterburning 7000 kg (15,432 lb)

Mirage IV recognition features

- Large slender delta wing planform
- Door-type airbrakes close to wing roots
- Small windows above navigators cockpit
- Twin engines mounted side-by-side
- Sharply tapering pointed nose with slightly drooping and very substantial probe
- Long stroke nose landing gear set well back, just ahead of inlets
- Small semi-circular air inlets with prominent shock cones
- Broad based fin with slightly rounded fin tip
- Prominent fairing above jet-pipe
- ASMP missile, AN52 bomb or recce pack carried under fuselage faired into belly

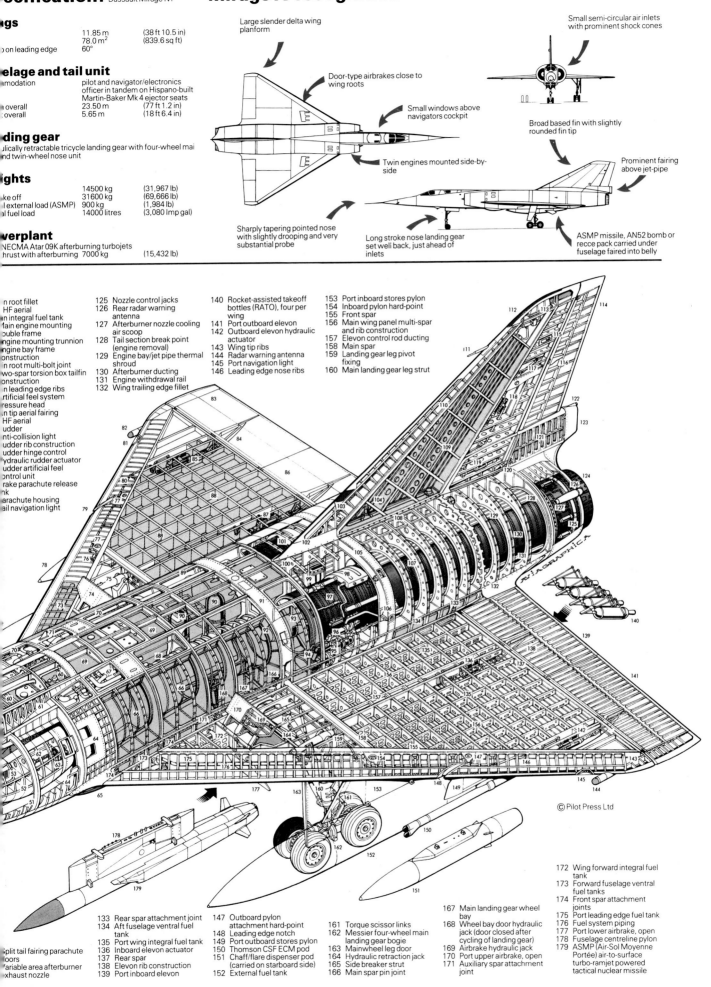

- n root fillet
- HF aerial
- n integral fuel tank
- Main engine mounting double frame
- engine mounting trunnion
- engine bay frame
- construction
- n root multi-bolt joint
- two-spar torsion box tailfin construction
- n leading edge ribs
- artificial feel system
- pressure head
- n tip aerial fairing
- HF aerial
- rudder
- anti-collision light
- rudder rib construction
- rudder hinge control
- hydraulic rudder actuator
- rudder artificial feel
- control unit
- brake parachute release
- link
- parachute housing
- tail navigation light
- 79
- 78

125 Nozzle control jacks
126 Rear radar warning antenna
127 Afterburner nozzle cooling air scoop
128 Tail section break point (engine removal)
129 Engine bay/jet pipe thermal shroud
130 Afterburner ducting
131 Engine withdrawal rail
132 Wing trailing edge fillet

140 Rocket-assisted takeoff bottles (RATO), four per wing
141 Port outboard elevon
142 Outboard elevon hydraulic actuator
143 Wing tip ribs
144 Radar warning antenna
145 Port navigation light
146 Leading edge nose ribs

153 Port inboard stores pylon
154 Inboard pylon hard-point
155 Front spar
156 Main wing panel multi-spar and rib construction
157 Elevon control rod ducting
158 Main spar
159 Landing gear leg pivot fixing
160 Main landing gear leg strut

133 Rear spar attachment joint
134 Aft fuselage ventral fuel tank
135 Port wing integral fuel tank
136 Inboard elevon actuator
137 Rear spar
138 Elevon rib construction
139 Port inboard elevon

- Split tail fairing parachute doors
- Variable area afterburner exhaust nozzle

147 Outboard pylon attachment hard-point
148 Leading edge notch
149 Port outboard stores pylon
150 Thomson CSF ECM pod
151 Chaff/flare dispenser pod (carried on starboard side)
152 External fuel tank

161 Torque scissor links
162 Messier four-wheel main landing gear bogie
163 Mainwheel leg door
164 Hydraulic retraction jack
165 Side breaker strut
166 Main spar pin joint

167 Main landing gear wheel bay
168 Wheel bay door hydraulic jack (door closed after cycling of landing gear)
169 Airbrake hydraulic jack
170 Port upper airbrake, open
171 Auxiliary spar attachment joint

172 Wing forward integral fuel tank
173 Forward fuselage ventral fuel tanks
174 Front spar attachment joints
175 Port leading edge fuel tank
176 Fuel system piping
177 Port lower airbrake, open
178 Fuselage centreline pylon
179 ASMP (Air-Sol Moyenne Portée) air-to-surface turbo-ramjet powered tactical nuclear missile

© Pilot Press Ltd

The SUKHOI SU-7

Sukhoi Su-7 'Fitter': Soviet Sledgehammer

Sukhoi's 'Fitter' may be deficient in range and weapon load, but its toughness, speed and handling make it a much-loved and useful ground-attack tool, albeit a thirsty one! The 'Fitter' has seen combat service in the Middle East and in the Indian sub-continent, and was not found wanting under combat conditions.

▲ *The Sukhoi Su-7 is thought to have been withdrawn from front-line service with Soviet Front Aviation, although it remains in use as an advanced trainer in substantial numbers in both single- and two-seat versions. It has been replaced in the front line by Su-17s.*

▶ *The 'Fitter' is heavy and somewhat brutish to fly, with handling similar to a Hunter with its powered controls disengaged! Nevertheless the 'Fitter' has gained a reputation as an acrobatic mount, and is popular with its pilots. This Czech Su-7 is seen at an air show.*

Over 30 years ago G. Kochyetkov, appointed chief test pilot to the recently reopened design bureau of Pavel O. Sukhoi, climbed aboard the S-1 prototype and made a successful maiden flight. Though conventional in appearance, and powered by a single jet engine, the S-1 bristled with new features. It was extremely large, and its afterburning turbojet was one of the most powerful flown at that time. The wing was swept back at the frightening angle of 62°, and the horizontal tail comprised one-piece 'slabs' with no separate elevators.

The S-1 (swept wing no. 1) had been designed, along with the rival I-380 by the MiG bureau, to shoot down the USAF's North American F-100 and other 'century series' supersonic fighters. Yet when the S-1's developments finally went into service as the Su-7B in 1959 they were used mainly in the tactical attack role, with bombs and rockets. By this time it had been realized in the West that 'Fitter', as it was called, was much bigger than the MiG-21 'Fishbed' and other counterparts. But further investigation appeared to show that it was really pretty useless. Examples were sold to India and Egypt, from which countries scathing comments were said to emanate. The gist of the criticism was 'It can carry fuel or bombs, but never both at the same time.' Statistics were produced to show that in full afterburner at low level (the kind of situation to be expected in any actual warfare) the internal tanks would go from brim-full to empty in about five minutes.

Today we know 'Fitter' much better. Gradually the West has begun to realize what has been repeatedly said for 50 years: the USSR has its own scale of priorities in aircraft design. In general this results in its combat aircraft being bigger than those in the West designed for the same job. This is because they are less fragile. There is not one 'No Step' notice on an Su-7. When the magazine *Air International* visited India in 1982 its editor was invited to try gymnasium pull-ups on an Su-7BM's long nose pitot boom, which on a Western fighter would result in expensive damage. Gradually the message penetrated that the USSR never puts anything into production unless it can do a real job, reliably and in the harshest conditions, and go on doing it.

The Su-7 was put into production in 1958, and through a series of fairly minor improvements remained in production until at least 1970. In 1967 one was seen with pivoted 'swing wings': Western intelligence dismissed this as a single experimental aircraft. There was much surprise when squadrons of these later versions were seen in the 1970s, still called 'Fitters' but with different suffix letters.

When the Su-7B entered service it had two devastatingly powerful cannon in the wing roots, and it could carry two drop tanks under the belly and either two bombs or two rocket pods under the wings. One obvious shortcoming was that, reflecting its original conception as a fighter, it was tied to long paved runways. Something had to be done about this, and to reduce the take-off run attachments were provided for two massive assisted take-off rockets under the rear fuselage. To reduce the landing run more powerful brakes were fitted, and the ribbon parachute under the rear fuselage was replaced by twin braking parachutes in a faired box under the rudder. There was no difficulty in fitting a larger low-pressure nosewheel tyre (the nosewheel doors were fitted with bulges), but the main wheels were housed tightly inside the wing and could not readily be enlarged. The solution was ingenious: massive sprung steel skids were attached beside the wheels to help the aircraft ride over soft ground. The result was the Su-7BKL.

Most of the production aircraft are of the Su-7BM type, with two extra wing pylons and a slightly more powerful engine (the original AL-7F engine having an afterburning thrust of 9000 kg/19,842 lb). Other improvements included Sirena 3 radar-warning receivers giving all-round coverage against enemy radars (or earlier Sirena installations covering the rear 120° only), an ejection seat able to be used at ground level (but not at speeds below 75 kts; 140 km/h; 87 mph), and larger steel panels on the fuselage adjacent to the gun muzzles to eliminate blast and flame damage. Quite late, around 1966, a tandem dual trainer version was introduced. Designated Su-7U and Su-7UM, this has been dubbed 'Moujik' by NATO and has even less internal fuel in order to accommodate the rear cockpit for the instructor. Unlike the arrangement in modern trainers both seats are at about the same level, so to give the instructor sufficient forward view

during landing a periscope is fitted. This is extended above the canopy at speeds below 325 kts (600 km/h; 373 mph). Surprisingly, the overall view from the rear cockpit is better than from the front.

There is little information on the early years of the Su-7B in Soviet Frontal Aviation service, but by the time it reached Egypt and India it was an extremely mature aircraft. Inevitably it was thought rather big for the job it did, and it was certainly demanding to fly. Despite the fact that it has fully powered controls, the forces the pilot must exert are extremely heavy. One Indian pilot described the task as being 'just like flying a Hunter with control power off, in the emergency manual mode'. Of course, this would never have been accepted by Boscombe Down in the UK or any other Western air force test centre, but the remarkable thing is that, almost to a man, 'Fitter' pilots love their aircraft. There are various reasons for this.

Perhaps the most obvious one is the type's sheer battleship-like strength. Time and again these aircraft have made belly landings on rough ground, or overshot the runway, with gear up or down, and simply been towed back, given an inspection and returned to the flightline! In its first publicized test, the Indo-Pakistan war of 1971, the Su-7 emerged with flying colours: in almost 1,500 sorties these tough machines dropped bombs, fired guns and rockets and took photographs (with a reconnaissance camera fitted in some examples behind the nose gear), and exceeded all expectations. Instead of falling off, the sortie rate increased throughout the two weeks of this war, stabilizing at six per pilot per day. Not one Su-7 was shot down in air combat, and two flew back to base after being hit by Sidewinder missiles whose warheads exploded (the rear end of one is in the IAF Museum).

All Su-7s have excellent traditional instruments, including a particularly good horizon, and a simple but reliable autopilot. The sharp sweepback allows the wing to be relatively thick and to have a

generous leading-edge radius, which in turn gives the aircraft forgiving flying qualities (in fact it has a very great deal in common with the English Electric Lightning). Perhaps the only basic drawback is the need for a long runway, especially on a hot day. The rockets are cumbersome and expensive, and most air forces do not use them. In consequence it takes about 2400 m (7,875 ft) to accelerate to the rotation speed of 195 kts (360 km/h; 224 mph). Once airborne, with gear retracted, the Su-7 accelerates rapidly even without afterburner, and can climb very quickly to its effective ceiling of around 39,000 ft (11,885 m).

On combat missions, however, the Su-7 stays 'on the deck'. Here, unlike the MiG-21, it can easily exceed Mach 1, under perfect control. Low-level supersonic flight is a routine part of Su-7 pilot conversion, and the Indian air force used to fly 'sonic salutes' with perfect formations at special parades and ceremonies. One of the chief reasons for the old Sukhoi's enduring popularity is the way it can be hauled round the sky. It needs tremendous physical effort, and afterburner has to be used to avoid speed bleeding off too much in really violent manoeuvres, but a well-flown Su-7 is a match for almost anything at low level. Despite the grave drawback that its afterburner needs six or seven seconds to light up after being selected,

▲ Brute force and ignorance – the afterburning Lyulka turbojet delivers a staggering amount of thrust, giving the 'Fitter' a superb low-level dash capability. The aircraft may be big and crude by Western standards, but it is fast, tough and dependable.

▼ The Indian Air Force probably has more combat experience with the Su-7 than any other operator. Their Sukhois are now being replaced by locally built SEPECAT Jaguars, which will give improved capability.

whereas that of the Tumanskii engines of advanced MiG-21s comes in with a bang instantly, a clean Su-7 can usually outfly a MiG-21 in virtually every respect in a practice dogfight. This has been demonstrated many times, and the feeling of superiority gives the Sukhoi pilot such elation he forgets that he is perspiring from the manual effort and from the fact the cockpit has heating but no cooling!

While low-level manoeuvrability is outstanding, so is stability in shallow dive attacks. Several user air forces have claimed the Su-7 family to be the most accurate aircraft in their inventory in making attacks on surface targets with guns and unguided rockets. The Indian air force, which probably has more actual combat experience with these early 'Fitter' versions than any other, noted that for nine consecutive years squadrons

equipped with the Su-7BM succeeded in winning trophies for the highest proficiency in bombing or gunnery, the latter being the coveted Arjuna Trophy contested by virtually every fighter unit in the service. This is despite the fact that many of the other squadrons were equipped with later aircraft fitted with radar, fire-control computers and advanced all-weather navigation systems. Indeed many former Su-7 pilots regret that they have been posted to squadrons which have re-equipped with such machines as the MiG-23, SEPECAT Jaguar, Dassault-Breguet Mirage 2000 and MiG-29, because they would welcome the chance to climb once more into the old Sukhoi.

Su-7BM and Su-7BKL fighters continue to soldier on with some air forces, along with Su-7UM trainers. In the Egyptian air force they remained more consistently operational than the later swing-wing Su-20s. By 1982 all Egyptian aircraft of Soviet origin were at a low ebb, but the old Sukhois were considered such a valued and popular asset that since then great efforts have been made not only to restore all available examples to front-line service (many parts for both the engine and airframe being made at the Helwan factory complex), but also to update them with improved radio navaids, head-up display sights and other equipment. This has involved collaboration of many companies in the USA, the UK and elsewhere, which have been requested not to issue news releases on this work.

Training

This appreciation of the original fixed-wing 'Fitters' exceeds that shown in the USSR, where the type is believed to have been withdrawn from Frontal Aviation combat regiments. This is not so much because the type is no longer thought of value, but merely reflects the wealth of newer tactical aircraft with which Frontal Aviation has been re-equipped. At the same time, not much is ever thrown away, and in the USSR some hundreds of single- and two-seat Su-7s continue to serve as advanced trainers, especially for air-to-ground gunnery and weapon delivery.

In almost all advanced weapons schools the two-seaters are used purely for conversion to type and for instrument-flight training, and they are also used to some degree for conversion to the later swing-wing 'Fitter' variants. Actual training with ordnance is done with single-seaters. Missions seldom involve much high-altitude flight, though it is worth noting that at 39,000 ft (11885 m) and above the Su-7BM can exceed Mach 1 in level flight with tanks and bombs on the pylons. At all heights there is no problem in handling the aircraft at any speed, the only exception being that, lacking lateral trim, care has to be taken if stores separate asymmetrically. Bringing an aircraft back with a bomb on one outer pylon only is very tiring. With plenty of height in hand it is possible to demonstrate

the simplicity of the straight unaccelerated stall: the aircraft merely begins to drop like a stone, and recovers to level flight after firm forward stick.

Probably at least half the Su-7s still in use spend most of their time being flown, at no mean cost in fuel, purely for pleasure. It is a most enjoyable aerobatic aircraft, though plenty of sky is needed and all such flying has to be manual. Should the pilot become disoriented or lose the horizon, the autopilot has a special mode (usable within 60° pitch or bank) which automatically restores the aircraft to level flight. Possibly some of the updates performed on Egyptian Su-7s have improved the ability to maintain full attitude information at all times, and in particular to overcome a previous limitation in pitch stability which made it impossible to use more than about three-quarters of the internal fuel capacity.

A point not made previously is that the basic shape of these early 'Fitters', with 62° of wing sweep, automatically gives the air-

▲ Two Czechoslovakian 'Fitters' roar into the air. Czechoslovakia is thought to have three 'Fitter' regiments, although it remains to be seen whether all will be retained following the introduction of the Su-25 'Frogfoot'.

craft the high wing loading and short span needed for good stability and modest gust response when making an attack at full throttle at sea level. Egyptian pilots say they would rather fly for an hour at full throttle at desert level in an Su-7 (if that were possible) than three minutes in a Dassault Mirage, McDonnell Douglas Phantom or General Dynamics F-16. On the other hand a penalty of this acute fixed sweep is inability to carry heavy weapons loads, partly on the score of long field length and partly because so little span is available for pylons. These problems were addressed in the variable-geometry successor generation of these extremely popular battlewagons.

Sukhoi Su-7 in service

Algeria
Two squadrons, each equipped initially with 10 Su-7BMs, entered service in about 1969. It is believed that one squadron has been disbanded or re-equipped.
Example aircraft: 339

Czechoslovakia
From 1965 (?) three fighter/ground-attack squadrons or regiments were equipped with an initial complement of about 60 single- and two-seat Su-7s. All are still thus equipped in 1985.
Example aircraft: 5604, 5623

Egypt
Some 120 single-seaters, plus a few Su-7UM two-seaters, were supplied from late 1964. In 1985 one Su-7 fighter/ground-attack regiment survives at Katamia air base, with aircraft progressively restored to operational status and upgraded with new equipment. All aircraft are accommodated in hardened shelters.
Example aircraft: (Su-7BM) 7025, 7649, 7664; (Su-7UM) 7904, 7912 (Arabic numerals)

India
About 140 Su-7s, including some 12 Su-7UMs, entered Indian service from March 1968. The original squadrons were No. 26, No. 32 'Thunderbirds', No. 101 'Falcons', No. 108, No. 221 'Falcons' and No. 222 'Killers'. All saw action against Pakistan in December 1971. The identity of the bases used by the surviving squadrons is classified.
Example aircraft: (Su-7BM) B744 to about B860; (Su-7UM) about U1350 to U1360

Poland
About 220 aircraft were delivered from 1965, and in 1985 five fighter/ground-attack regiments are operational with 160 Su-7BM and/or Su-7BKL single-seaters plus 15-20 Su-7UMs. It is thought that in-service numbers are falling sharply.

USSR
The initial service-test units were formed in 1959, fully operational Frontal Aviation combat regiments equipping from 1961. About 2,000 aircraft were delivered, of which an estimated 130 remain with FA operator units in 1985. Some aircraft have been retrofitted with KM-1 rocket-boosted zero/zero seats.

Afghanistan
Some 48 Su-7BMs were supplied from 1970, without Su-7UM two-seaters, forming the equipment of two fighter/ground-attack squadrons at Shindand. Since the Soviet occupation of 1979 these aircraft have seen prolonged action and suffered considerable attrition.

Hungary
The Su-7 entered service with the Hungarian air force, possibly in 1967, some 35 aircraft equipping one regiment. This regiment was believed by the US Department of Defense to be slated for deactivation during 1985.

Iraq
It is believed that the 'Fitter' entered Iraqi service in 1968, deliveries amounting to some 95 aircraft (including some Su-7UM trainers) to equip three regiments. It is possible that some 60 are still serviceable after intensive and protracted combat operations against Iran. No details of units or bases are available.

North Korea
Some 30 or more aircraft were delivered from about 1966, but only one regiment with 20 aircraft remains.

Romania
The 'Fitter' entered Romanian service after 1967. US Department of Defense assessments omit any reference to Romanian Su-7 units, but British sources claim one regiment with some 35 Su-7BMs.

South Yemen
It is believed that a few Su-7s serve alongside a larger number of swing-wing Su-22s, though US sources do not mention Su-7s in this air arm.

Syria
The 'Fitter' entered Syrian service before 1970. Current US estimates indicate that one 'squadron' is operational with 18 aircraft, though British sources indicate that there is one regiment of 60 aircraft including some Su-7UMs. Syria lost more than 20 'Fitters' in the October 1973 war with Israel, but these were quickly replaced by the USSR.

Vietnam
The 'Fitter' entered service with Vietnamese air force units in about 1970. The current total is one regiment with 30 aircraft (US sources) or one regiment with 40 Su-7s and Su-22s (British sources).

Performance:

Maximum speed at 40,000 ft (12200 m)	Mach 1.6 (917 kts)	1699 km/h (1,056 mph)
Maximum speed at sea level	Mach 1.1 (730 kts)	1352 km/h (840 mph)
Service ceiling	49,700 ft	(15150 m)
Maximum range with four drop tanks	1450 km	(900 miles)
Combat radius, hi-lo-hi with typical bombload and fuselage tanks	345 km	(215 miles)
Initial rate of climb	29,900 ft (9120 m) per minute	
g limits	+7.5/-4.0	
Take-off ground run	2400 m	(7,875 ft)

Weapon load

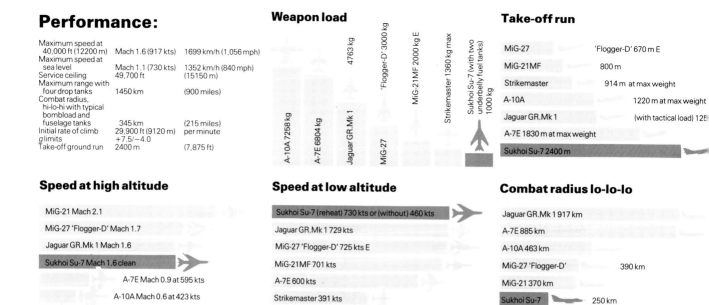

A-10A 7258 kg
A-7E 6804 kg
Jaguar GR.Mk 1 4763 kg
MiG-27
'Flogger-D' 3000 kg
MiG-21MF 2000 kg E
Strikemaster 1360 kg max
Sukhoi Su-7 (with two underbelly fuel tanks) 1000 kg

Take-off run

MiG-27	'Flogger-D' 670 m E
MiG-21MF	800 m
Strikemaster	914 m at max weight
A-10A	1220 m at max weight
Jaguar GR.Mk 1	(with tactical load) 125
A-7E	1830 m at max weight
Sukhoi Su-7 2400 m	

Speed at high altitude

- MiG-21 Mach 2.1
- MiG-27 'Flogger-D' Mach 1.7
- Jaguar GR.Mk 1 Mach 1.6
- Sukhoi Su-7 Mach 1.6 clean
- A-7E Mach 0.9 at 595 kts
- A-10A Mach 0.6 at 423 kts
- Strikemaster Mach 0.68 at 418 kts

Speed at low altitude

- Sukhoi Su-7 (reheat) 730 kts or (without) 460 kts
- Jaguar GR.Mk 1 729 kts
- MiG-27 'Flogger-D' 725 kts E
- MiG-21MF 701 kts
- A-7E 600 kts
- Strikemaster 391 kts
- A-10A 381 kts

Combat radius lo-lo-lo

- Jaguar GR.Mk 1 917 km
- A-7E 885 km
- A-10A 463 km
- MiG-27 'Flogger-D' 390 km
- MiG-21 370 km
- Sukhoi Su-7 250 km
- Strikemaster (with max weapon load) 233 km

Specification: Sukhoi Su-7BM

Wings
Span	8.93 m	(29 ft 3.6 in)
Area	27.60 m^2	(297.09 sq ft)
Sweep	62°	

Fuselage and tail unit
Accommodation	pilot only	
Length overall	17.37 m	(57 ft 0 in)
Height overall	4.57 m	(15 ft 0 in)

Landing gear
Retractable tricycle landing gear with a single wheel on each unit

Weights
Empty	8620 kg	(19,004 lb)
Maximum take-off	13500 kg	(29,762 lb)
Maximum take-off (some air forces)	14800 kg	(32,628 lb)
Maximum external load (seldom fully exploited)	4000 kg	(8,818 lb)
Internal fuel load	2353 kg	(5,187 lb)

Powerplant
One Lyul'ka AL-7F-1 afterburning turbojet		
Static thrust with afterburning	10000 kg	(22,046 lb)

Su-7 recognition features

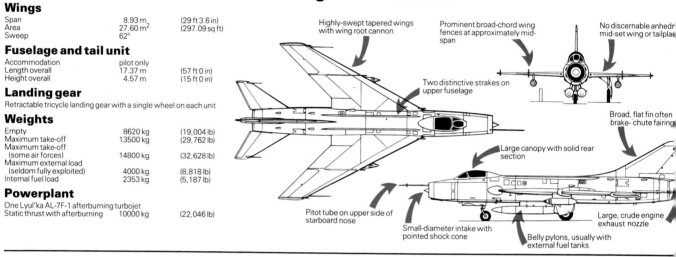

Highly-swept tapered wings with wing root cannon

Prominent broad-chord wing fences at approximately mid-span

No discernable anhedr mid-set wing or tailpla

Two distinctive strakes on upper fuselage

Broad, flat fin often brake-chute fairing

Large canopy with solid rear section

Pitot tube on upper side of starboard nose

Small-diameter intake with pointed shock cone

Belly pylons, usually with external fuel tanks

Large, crude engine exhaust nozzle

Sukhoi Su-7 variants

S-1: original 1954 Sukhoi prototype, flown 1955
S-2: area-ruled prototypes with AL-7F engine
S-22: production prototypes with further refinements
Su-7B: initial production version, NATO **'Fitter-A'**
Su-7BKL: rough-field model with wheel/skid main gears, larger nose gear tyre, rocket boost for take-off and twin braking parachutes
Su-7BM: main production version with previous alterations (often without skids) and AL-7F-1 engine, improved ejection seat and variable degrees of avionics updating

Su-7BM (improved): Egyptian (and possibly other) Su-7BMs are being upgraded by fitting newer or additional avionics items; no new designation

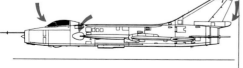

Su-7U and Su-7UM: corresponding tandem dual-control versions with reduced internal fuel and rear instructor cockpit, NATO **'Moujik'**

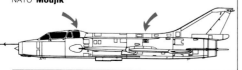

Sukhoi Su-7MBK 'Fitter-A' cutaway drawing key

1. Pitot tube
2. Pitch vanes
3. Yaw vanes
4. Engine air intake
5. Intake centre-body
6. Radome
7. Ranging radar scanner
8. ILS aerial
9. Radar controller
10. Weapon release ballistic computer
11. Retractable taxiing lamp
12. SRO-2M 'Odd-Rods' IFF aerials
13. Intake suction relief doors
14. Intake duct divider
15. Instrument access panel
16. Su-7U 'Moujik' two-seat operational training variant
17. Armoured glass windscreen
18. Reflector sight
19. Instrument panel shroud
20. Control column

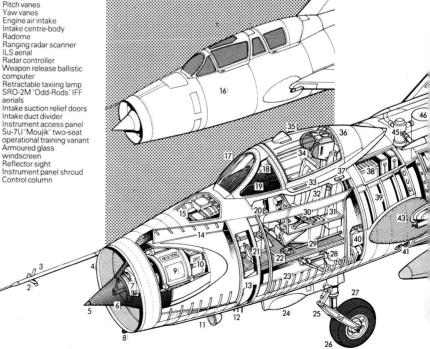

khoi Su-7 warload

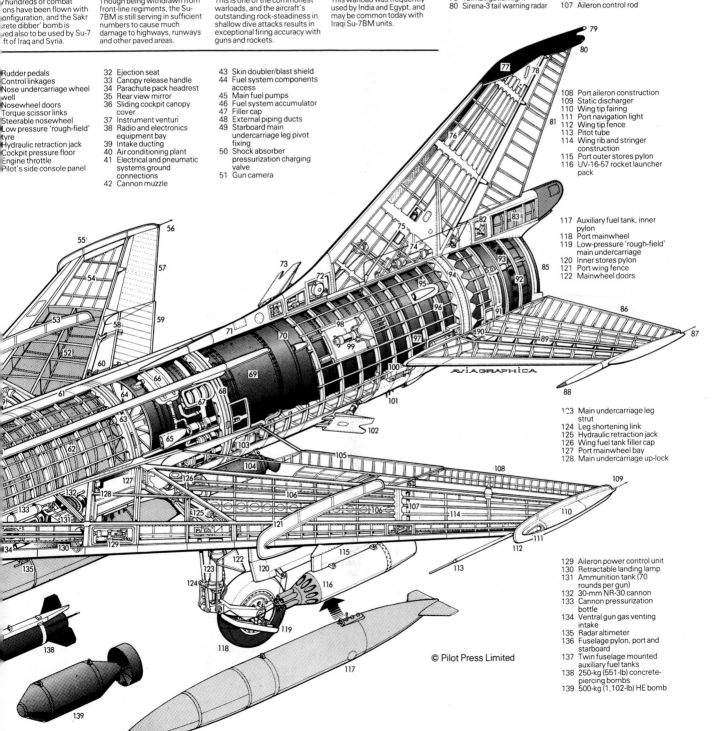

2×30-mm NR-30 cannon with 70 rounds per gun
2×triple 100-kg (220-lb) Sakr crete dibber' bomb
2×1200-litre (264-Imp gal) fuselage drop tanks

2×30-mm NR-30 cannon with 70 rounds per gun
2×250-kg (551-lb) S-24 concrete-piercing bombs
2×1200-litre (264-Imp gal) fuselage drop tanks

2×30-mm NR-30 cannon with 70 rounds per gun, four UV-16-57 launchers each with 16 57-mm (2.24-in) rockets
2×1200-litre (264-Imp gal) fuselage drop tanks

2×30-mm NR-30 cannon with 70 rounds per gun
2×500-kg (1,102-lb) FAB-500 GP bombs
2×1200-litre (264-Imp gal) fuselage drop tanks

ti-airfield (ypt)

y hundreds of combat ons have been flown with onfiguration, and the Sakr crete dibber' bomb is ved also to be used by Su-7 ft of Iraq and Syria.

Anti-airfield (Warsaw Pact)

Though being withdrawn from front-line regiments, the Su-7BM is still serving in sufficient numbers to cause much damage to highways, runways and other paved areas.

Alternative hard-target attack

This is one of the commonest warloads, and the aircraft's outstanding rock-steadiness in shallow dive attacks results in exceptional firing accuracy with guns and rockets.

Alternative ground attack

This warload was frequently used by India and Egypt, and may be common today with Iraqi Su-7BM units.

Rudder pedals
Control linkages
Nose undercarriage wheel well
Nosewheel doors
Torque scissor links
Steerable nosewheel
Low pressure 'rough-field' tyre
Hydraulic retraction jack
Cockpit pressure floor
Engine throttle
Pilot's side console panel

32 Ejection seat
33 Canopy release handle
34 Parachute pack headrest
35 Rear view mirror
36 Sliding cockpit canopy cover
37 Instrument venturi
38 Radio and electronics equipment bay
39 Intake ducting
40 Air conditioning plant
41 Electrical and pneumatic systems ground connections
42 Cannon muzzle

43 Skin doubler/blast shield
44 Fuel system components access
45 Main fuel pumps
46 Fuel system accumulator
47 Filler cap
48 External piping ducts
49 Starboard main undercarriage leg pivot fixing
50 Shock absorber pressurization charging valve
51 Gun camera

52 Starboard wing integral fuel tank
53 Starboard wing fence
54 Outer wing panel dry bay
55 Wing tip fence
56 Static discharger
57 Starboard aileron
58 Flap guide rail
59 Starboard slotted flap
60 Flap jack
61 Fuselage skin plating
62 Fuselage fuel tank
63 Wing/fuselage attachment double frame
64 Engine compressor face
65 Ram air intake
66 Engine oil tank
67 Bleed air system 'blow-off' valve
68 Fuselage break point, engine removal
69 Lyulka AL-7F-1 turbojet
70 Afterburner duct
71 Fin root fillet
72 Autopilot controller
73 Starboard upper airbrake, open
74 Rudder power control unit
75 Artificial feel unit
76 Tailfin construction
77 VHF/UHF aerial fairing
78 RSIU (very short wave fighter radio) aerial
79 Tail navigation light
80 Sirena-3 tail warning radar

81 Rudder
82 Brake parachute release tank
83 Brake parachute housing
84 Parachute doors
85 Engine exhaust nozzle
86 Port all-moving tailplane
87 Static discharger
88 Tailplane anti-flutter weight
89 Tailplane construction
90 Pivot mounting
91 Tailplane limit stops
92 Variable area exhaust nozzle flaps
93 Nozzle control jacks
94 Fin/tailplane attachment fuselage frame
95 Afterburner cooling air intake
96 Rear fuselage frame and stringer construction
97 Insulated tailplane
98 Airbrake housing
99 Hydraulic jack
100 Tailplane power control unit
101 'Odd-Rods' IFF aerials
102 Port lower airbrake, open
103 Engine accessories
104 Jettisonable JATO bottle
105 Port slotted flap
106 Port wing integral fuel tanks
107 Aileron control rod

108 Port aileron construction
109 Static discharger
110 Wing tip fairing
111 Port navigation light
112 Wing tip fence
113 Pitot tube
114 Wing rib and stringer construction
115 Port outer stores pylon
116 UV-16-57 rocket launcher pack

117 Auxiliary fuel tank, inner pylon
118 Port mainwheel
119 Low-pressure 'rough-field' main undercarriage
120 Inner stores pylon
121 Port wing fence
122 Mainwheel doors

123 Main undercarriage leg strut
124 Leg shortening link
125 Hydraulic retraction jack
126 Wing fuel tank filler cap
127 Port mainwheel bay
128 Main undercarriage up-lock

129 Aileron power control unit
130 Retractable landing lamp
131 Ammunition tank (70 rounds per gun)
132 30-mm NR-30 cannon
133 Cannon pressurization bottle
134 Ventral gun gas venting intake
135 Radar altimeter
136 Fuselage pylon, port and starboard
137 Twin fuselage mounted auxiliary fuel tanks
138 250-kg (551-lb) concrete-piercing bombs
139 500-kg (1,102-lb) HE bomb

AVIAGRAPHICA

The SUKHOI SU-24

Su-24 'Fencer': Soviet Striker

The Sukhoi Su-24 is the first modern interdictor and deep strike aircraft to enter service with the Soviet air force. Initially assigned mainly to the strategic role, 'Fencer' is now replacing the Yak-28 'Brewer' as a reconnaissance and ECM platform. With external fuel tanks the 'Fencer' can range over most of Western Europe from bases inside the Soviet Union.

▲ A Sukhoi Su-24 'Fencer-C' with wings at intermediate sweep and carrying a pair of 3000-litre (660-Imp gal) fuel tanks under its wing glove pylons. The photograph has been unaccountably censored to obscure the Soviet stars under the wings.

▶ Lack of triangular fairings on the fin and engine intakes identify this aircraft as a 'Fencer-B'. This aircraft was probably photographed in the circuit at Templin, during the type's first deployment outside the Soviet Union in 1979.

The Sukhoi Su-24 'Fencer' is probably the most feared aircraft in current Soviet service, since it represents a major threat to NATO and a major erosion of the West's technological lead over the USSR. Probably inspired to some extent by the General Dynamics F-111, the Su-24 is, however, much more than a carbon copy of the older American design.

Designed from the outset as a replacement for the Yak-28 'Brewer' and Ilyushin Il-28 'Beagle' in the tactical bombing, reconnaissance and electronic warfare roles, the new aircraft also offered a sufficiently long range for it to be a suitable replacement for the Tupolev Tu-16 'Badger' and Tu-22 'Blinder'.

While General Dynamics with the F-111 and Panavia with the Tornado optimized their swing-wing attack aircraft for a long subsonic radius of action, increasingly fuel capacity at the expense of engine power, the Sukhoi OKB (design bureau) went all out for high-speed penetration, without recourse to afterburner. No concessions were made to providing any kind of 'fighter' capability, and the Su-24 probably compares more closely with the BAC TSR.2 and F-111 than the Panavia Tornado.

Sukhoi produced the Su-7IG, essentially a modified Su-7 hastily fitted with variably-geometry outer wing panels, which was probably originally intended purely as a technology demonstrator for the 'swing wing'. The type showed sufficient advantages over the fixed-wing 'Fitter' to be taken on to form the basis of the swing-wing Su-17 and Su-22 'Fitter'.

It also provided a clear indication of the advantages offered by the variable-geometry wing, and of the problems involved. No insurmountable structural or aerodynamic problems were encountered, and the improved take-off performance, penetration speed, low-level ride and subsonic range encouraged the Sukhoi design bureau to start work on a new variable-geometry strike aircraft, while gaining valuable production experience with the interim Su-17 'Fitter' family.

A prototype Su-24 'Fencer' probably made its maiden flight during 1969 or 1970, and the intelligence agencies of the West became aware of the aircraft during 1971. By 1974 the aviation press were referring to the 'Sukhoi Su-?' by its NATO codename 'Fencer', and the chairman of the US Joint Chiefs of Staff described it as "the first modern Soviet fighter to be developed specifically as a fighter-bomber for the ground attack mission".

In service

By 1975 the aircraft was in squadron service, some sources suggesting that an evaluation unit at Chernaykhovsk, on the Soviet Baltic coast, received its first aircraft in November 1974. Unconfirmed reports stated that a handful of aircraft briefly visited Soviet air bases in East Germany during 1975, but right up to the 1980s it was rare for 'Fencers' to be allowed outside Soviet territory.

A second regiment formed at Lusatia as part of the 16th Air Army during the summer of 1976, and the 'Fencer' force continued to build up. The first deployment of a full 'Fencer' regiment outside the Soviet union took place in July 1979, when a unit was based at Templin, north of Berlin, for operational evaluation. It was not until 1982, however that a 30-aircraft regiment was based permanently in East Germany.

NATO finally stopped using the erroneous Sukhoi Su-19 designation during 1980, the new Su-24 designation first being used in the Fiscal Year 1981 US Department of Defense annual report.

By this time there were about 400 'Fencers' in Europe, with two regiments having formed in Tukums, Latvia, near the Gulf of Riga, and with others at Starokonstantinov and Gorodok in the Ukraine. Between 110 and 130 aircraft were based in the Soviet Far East.

In 1984, the Su-24 received its 'baptism of fire', being used in anger against the Mujahideen in Afghanistan during the offensives against the Panjshir Valley. The aircraft flew from Termez, inside the Soviet Union, where they were co-located beside a regiment of Tupolev Tu-16 'Badgers'. Over Afghanistan the aircraft were mainly used for area bombing from medium level, but some reports suggest that a few precision attacks, using laser-guided bombs, may also have been carried out.

In 1984, 10 years after it had entered service, the Su-24 began to be more regularly encountered outside the Soviet Union. A 'Fencer-C' became the first Su-24 to be intercepted and photographed when the Swedish air force encountered one over the Baltic. The following year four 'Fencers' participated in a flypast over a major military parade in Prague. Interestingly, these are the only examples of the

type to be photographed wearing a standard disruptive tactical camouflage; all other released photographs show a light grey and white colour scheme.

By the beginning of 1987, according to the Pentagon, 770 'Fencers' were in service in the strike role, more than 450 of them being assigned to what were loosely described as strategic missions. A further 65 'Fencers' are thought to be in service as reconnaissance and electronic warfare platforms, and it is believed that the Baltic Fleet air force of the AV-MF (Soviet Naval Aviation) has received its first squadron of 'Fencer-E' dual-capable fighter-bomber/reconnaissance aircraft.

New 'Fencer' regiments are thought to be based at Debrecen in Hungary; Sagan and Szprotawa in western Poland; and in East Germany at Neuruppin, north-west of Berlin, Brand, south of Berlin, and at Grossenhain, north of Dresden. Because the Su-24 is such a capable machine it will probably never be offered for export, even to the most faithful Warsaw Pact nations.

As a consequence of the latter policy, any technical analysis of the 'Fencer' must rely largely on speculation, and occasional tit-bits gleaned from information and photographs released by Western intelligence agencies. 'Fencer' has been photographed frequently enough for estimates of its size to be reasonably accurate, but assessments of its performance, warload, mission equipment and even powerplant vary enormously.

The Su-24 is about the same size as the F-111, with a 'spread' wingspan some 2 metres (6 ft) shorter at 17.5 metres (57 ft 5 in), and being about the same length at 22 metres (72 ft 2 in). Most Western sources suggest that the aircraft has a significantly

▼ An interesting view of a 'Fence-B' with wings at minimum sweep, and with its distinctive airbrakes deployed. The aircraft has eight pylons fitted, two in tandem on the centreline, two on the fuselage shoulders, and four on the wings and wing roots.

▼ This new photograph of 'Fencer-D' shows off the type's kinked fin leading edge and extended nose to advantage. 'Fencer-D' is optimized for the strategic role and is equipped for inflight-refuelling from the new Il-76 'Midas' tanker.

lower empty weight, and a smaller internal fuel load. Maximum all-up weight, however, is similar to that of the F-111, representing a significantly larger weapon load.

The 'Fencer's' two-man crew sit side-by-side, as in the F-111, but almost certainly on conventional upward-firing ejection seats, not in any complex and unreliable escape capsule. The rather narrow fuselage width probably makes the cockpit a little cramped and 'chummy' by Western standards, but it does allow both crew members a good view ahead of the aircraft. A large, heavily-framed, upward-hinging clamshell canopy covers the cockpit, and access is by means of external ladders.

As far is is known, all 'Fencer' variants have a powerful pulse-Doppler navigation and attack radar, with a separate terrain-following or terrain-avoidance radar. Whether 'Fencer' is capable of 'hands-off' automatic terrain-following flight is unknown at present, but there seems little reason why the appropriate technology would not have been obtained.

The nav/attack system is held to be in the same class as that fitted to many Western aircraft, although it may not be quite as sophisticated as those fitted to the F-111 and Tornado. Nonetheless, Lieutenant General Donald R. Keith, one-time US Army Deputy Chief of Staff for Research, Development and Acquisition, credited 'Fencers' with having "the capability to deliver ordnance in all weather within 65 metres of its target". This blind, first-pass, fully automatic attack capability makes 'Fencer' a very different machine from the aircraft it is replacing. A modern head-up display is almost certainly fitted.

Although no details are known of the 'Fencer's' defensive and weapons aiming systems, the plethora of bumps, bulges and flush dielectric panels seem to tell their own story. Comprehensive active ECM equipment is carried, augmented by an omni-directional passive radar warning receiver, probably of the type known as Sirena 3.

'Fencer-A' and 'Fencer-B' were the initial production versions, and were equipped to a much lower standard than later variants. 'Fencer-C', introduced in 1981, featured small fairing on the fin and engine intakes, which probably serve an electronic warfare system. Additional sen-

sors were added under the nose, and the simple nose probe was replaced by a complex multiple fitting.

The next variant, the 'Fencer-D', had a lengthened nose and reverted to simple single nose probe. Most Western sources agree that the aircraft is the first 'Fencer' variant to be capable of inflight-refuelling from the new Ilyushin Il-76 'Midas' tanker now entering service. The leading edge of the tailfin is extended forward, giving a slightly kinked appearance, but the small inlet or missile guidance radome is retained at the base of the fin. A fairing aft of the nose almost certainly contains a stabilized electro-optical sensor, probably similar to the American 'Pave Tack' system fitted to the F-111F.

The main inboard pylons are enlarged to incorporate huge overwing aerodynamic fences, and these are though to be associated with the new AS-14 'Kedge' missile. No photographs have been released of the latest two 'Fencer' variants, which are now thought to be a multi-sensor reconnaissance platform and anti-ship strike aircraft for the Soviet navy, known as 'Fencer-E', and an electronic warfare aircraft provisionally known as 'Fencer-F'.

Some analysts have speculated that a variant, equipped with a long-range, pulse-Doppler, look-down/shoot-down air-to-air radar, might be developed as an ultra-long range interceptor to replace the Tu-128 'Fiddler'.

Performance

Little is known about what powers the 'Fencer'. Most sources have guessed that the 11204-kg st Lyulka AL-21F-3 fitted to the Su-17 family is the most likely engine. This thirsty turbojet does not seem ideal for long-range low-level strike aircraft, however, and a turbofan seems a more logical choice. One distinguished analyst suggested that putting the AL-21 in 'Fencer' would have been like putting Avons in the Tornado. He went on to speculate that the 11453-kg st Tumanskii R-29B of the MiG-27 family was a more likely choice of engine.

The engine need not be familiar one, anyway; a new one may have been developed for the aircraft, or it could use a pair of the new-generation Tumanskii R-32B turbofans used by the record-breaking Sukhoi P.42, a variant of the new Su-27 'Flanker' interceptor. The thrust rating of the 'Fencer's' engines may have been over-estimated and an engine in the same 8165 kg class as the TF-30 of the F-111 might be fitted. In this case a version of the Tumanskii R-33D turbofan fitted to the MiG-29 'Fulcrum' might be suitable.

Each new 'Fencer' variant has had a slightly different rear fuselage, possibly for aerodynamic reasons, but perhaps indicating powerplant changes. Whatever the powerplant, Western sources credit the Su-24 with a radius of action of between 1300 and 1578 km nautical miles in a hi-lo-lo-hi mission with a 3175-kg (7,000-lb)

warload, considerably greater than that of the F-111 with a similar load. This gives 'Fencer' the ability to attack NATO forces in any part of Europe, except perhaps in Spain and Portugal. With inflight-refuelling the 'Fencer' is an even more worrying problem, able to carry a huge warload even further afield.

'Fencer' has eight external stores pylons, with single swivelling pylons under the outer wing panels, large wing with glove pylons, and four hardpoints under the fuselage. These have a combined capacity in excess of 10866 kg (24,000 lb), and an enormous variety of stores can be carried. The wing glove pylons and two of the underfuselage pylons are 'plumbed' for the the carriage of 3000 litres (660 Imp gal) external fuel tanks, which can extend the 'Fencer's' radius of action.

A range of bombs can be carried, including straightforward free-fall weapons, retarded and cluster bombs, runway penetrating devices and laser-guided bombs as well as chemical or nuclear weapons. Sophisticated stand-off guided missiles can be carried, including the AS-7 'Kerry', the

AS-10 'Karen', the AS-12 'Kegler' and the AS-14 'Kedge'. A six-barrel Gatling-type gun of unknown calibre is carried in a fairing on the starboard side of the forward fuselage, with a similar fairing to port housing either the ammunition feed mechanism or a chaff/flare gun.

The 'Fencer' is built like a battleship, crammed with sophisticated avionics, and can carry a large and deadly warload to targets all over Europe. It can deliver its deadly punch with unerring accuracy, making fully automatic, blind, first-pass attacks in all weathers.

▼ The 'Fencer' is optimized for use from rough, semi-prepared airstrips. The nosewheel incorporates built-in mudguards, and each of the undercarriage units is fitted with twin low-pressure tyres for optimum soft-ground performance.

▲ The Su-24 'Fencer-C' is a well-equipped powerful strike aircraft and is capable of making automatic, blind, first-pass attacks with deadly accuracy. Large internal fuel tanks and turbofan engines give a long radius of action.

Su-24 'Fencer' in service

'Fencer' has not been offered for export, even within the Warsaw Pact. Estimates of the number of 'Fencers' in service range from 645 to over 750, and production is continuing at a rate of about 10 per month. Approximately 450 are assigned to the strategic role, and 'Fencers' are known to serve with individual regiments based at Chernyakhovsk, Gorodok, Staro Konstantinov, Templin and Tukums, and with regiments of the Legnica and Vinnitsa air armies.

This Frontal Aviation Su-24 'Fencer-B' wears an unusual camouflage colour scheme. Most 'Fencers' are two-tone grey.

An Su-24 'Fencer-C' of Frontal Aviation with its wings at intermediate sweep. Eight weapons pylons are clearly visible, as are the fairings covering the cannon and ammunition feed system.

An Su-24 'Fencer-C' of the Soviet air force. The 'Fencer-C' has now been in service for six years.

Specification: Su-24 'Fencer-C' (estimated)

Wings
Span, 16° sweep	17.50 m	(57 ft 5 in)
68° sweep	10.50 m	(34 ft 5.4 in)
Sweep	16°, 45° and 68°	
Area, 16° sweep about	47.0 m²	(505.9 sq ft)
68° sweep about	42.5 m²	(457.5 sq ft)

Fuselage and tail unit
Accommodation	pilot and systems operator side-by-side on KM-1 ejector seats	
Length overall, excluding probe	21.29 m	(69 ft 10.2 in)
Height overall	6.00 m	(19 ft 8.2 in)
Tailplane span about	8.25 m	(27 ft 0.8 in)

Landing gear
Hydraulically retractable tricycle landing gear with twin-wheel main and nose units
Wheel track	4.00 m	(13 ft 1.5 in)
Wheelbase	7.25 m	(23 ft 9.4 in)

Powerplant
Believed to comprise two Lyul'ka AL-21F (possibly AL-21F-3) turbojets
Dry thrust, each	7800 kg	(17,196 lb)
Afterburning thrust, each	11200 kg	(24,692 lb)

Weights
Empty equipped	19000 kg	(41,888 lb)
Maximum take-off	41000 kg	(90,390 lb)
Maximum external load	11000 kg	(24,251 lb)
Internal fuel	10400 kg	(22,928 lb)

Su-24 'Fencer' recognition features

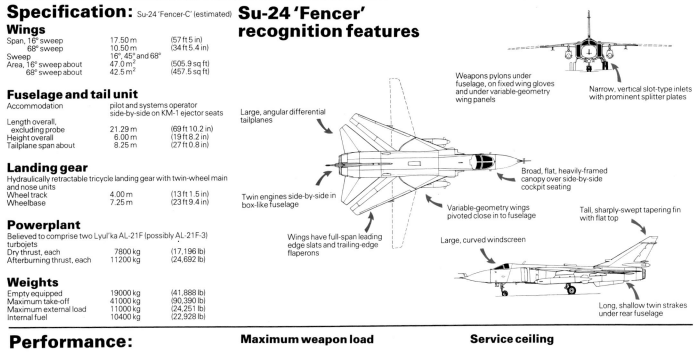

Weapons pylons under fuselage, on fixed wing gloves and under variable-geometry wing panels

Narrow, vertical slot-type inlets with prominent splitter plates

Large, angular differential tailplanes

Twin engines side-by-side in box-like fuselage

Wings have full-span leading edge slats and trailing-edge flaperons

Broad, flat, heavily-framed canopy over side-by-side cockpit seating

Variable-geometry wings pivoted close in to fuselage

Large, curved windscreen

Tall, sharply-swept tapering fin with flat top

Long, shallow twin strakes under rear fuselage

Performance:

Maximum cruising speed at sea level	112 kts	208 km/h (129 mph)
Hovering ceiling out of ground effect	3,200 ft	(975 m)
Hovering ceiling in ground effect	5,000 ft	(1525 m)
Maximum range with standard fuel load	1230 km	(764 miles)
Initial rate of climb	2,020 ft	(616 m) per minute

Maximum weapon load

- General Dynamics F-111F 11340 kg
- Sukhoi Su-24 'Fencer' 11000 kg E
- McDonnell Douglas F-15E Eagle 10705 kg
- Panavia Tornado GR.Mk 1 9000 kg
- Grumman A-6E Intruder 8165 kg
- SEPECAT Jaguar 4763 kg
- Mikoyan-Gurevich MiG-27 'Flogger-D' 4000 kg E
- Nanchang Q-5 'Fantan' 2000 kg

Service ceiling

- General Dynamics F-111F 60,000 ft
- McDonnell Douglas F-15E Eagle 60,000 ft+
- Sukhoi Su-24 'Fencer' 54,100 ft E
- Mikoyan-Gurevich MiG-27 'Flogger-D' 52,500 ft E
- Nanchang Q-5 'Fantan' 52,500 ft
- Panavia Tornado GR.Mk 1 50,000 ft+
- SEPECAT Jaguar 50,000 ft+E
- Grumman A-6E Intruder 42,400 ft

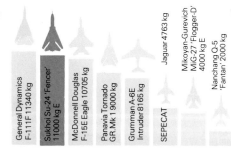

Maximum speed at high altitude

- McDonnell Douglas F-15E Eagle Mach 2.5+
- General Dynamics F-111F Mach 2.4
- Panavia Tornado GR.Mk 1 Mach 2.2 'clean'
- Sukhoi Su-24 'Fencer' Mach 2.18 E
- Mikoyan-Gurevich MiG-27 'Flogger-D' Mach 1.7 E
- SEPECAT Jaguar Mach 1.6
- Nanchang Q-5 'Fantan' Mach 1.12
- Grumman A-6E Intruder Mach 0.8

Maximum speed at sea level

- McDonnell Douglas F-15E Eagle Mach 1.23
- General Dynamics F-111F Mach 1.2
- Sukhoi Su-24 'Fencer' Mach 1.2 E
- Panavia Tornado GR.Mk 1 Mach 1.2
- SEPECAT Jaguar Mach 1.1
- Mikoyan-Gurevich MiG-27 'Flogger-D' Mach 1.1 E
- Nanchang Q-5 'Fantan' Mach 0.99
- Grumman A-6E Intruder Mach 0.85

Combat radius hi-lo-hi (external fuel)

- Grumman A-6E Intruder 1627 km
- General Dynamics F-111F 1480 km
- Panavia Tornado GR.Mk 1 1390 km
- McDonnell Douglas F-15E Eagle 1200 km+
- Mikoyan-Gurevich MiG-27 'Flogger-D' 950 km E
- Sukhoi Su-24 'Fencer' 950 km E
- SEPECAT Jaguar 852 km
- Nanchang Q-5 'Fantan' 690 km E

Su-24 'Fencer' warload

 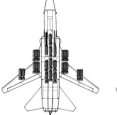  

1×30-mm six-barrel cannon in port underfuselage fairing
1×unidentified gun or multi-sensor weapons delivery/designation system in starboard underfuselage fairing
4×AS-14 'Kedge' tactical ASM on underfuselage pylons
2×3000-litre (660-Imp gal) tanks under wing glove pylons
2×AA-8 'Aphid' AAMs under outboard underwing pylons for self defence

1×30-mm six-barrel cannon in port underfuselage fairing
1×unidentified gun or multi-sensor weapons delivery/designation system in starboard underfuselage fairing
22×FAB-500 free-fall 500-kg (1,102-lb) bombs on underwing and underfuselage pylons

1×30-mm six-barrel cannon in port underfuselage fairing
1×unidentified gun or multi-sensor weapons delivery/designation system in starboard underfuselage fairing
4×500-kg (1,102-lb) laser-guided bombs on underwing and glove pylons

1×30-mm six-barrel cannon in port underfuselage fairing
1×unidentified gun or multi-sensor weapons delivery/designation system in starboard underfuselage fairing
1×TN-1000 series retarded nuclear bomb on centreline pylon
4×3000-litre (660-Imp gal) tanks under wing gloves and fuselage
1×AA-8 'Aphid' AAM under port outboard pylon
1×unidentified ECM pod under starboard outboard pylon

1×30-mm six-barrel cannon in port underfuselage fairing
1×unidentified gun or multi-sensor weapons delivery/designation system in starboard underfuselage fairing
6×AS-10 'Karen' EO-guided solid-propellant tactical ASMs on underwing, glove and fuselage pylons

All-weather precision attack ('Fencer-C')

The AS-14 'Kedge' is a large tactical ASM similar in appearance to the smaller AS-7 'Kerry', and is thought to be carried also by the MiG-27, Su-17 and Su-25. About 4.0 m (13.1 ft) long, the AS-14 has a range of 40+ km (25+ miles) and a large warhead. Guidance is by an electro-optical homing system similar to that employed by the smaller, shorter-ranged AS-10 'Karen'. Various air-to-air missiles can be carried for self-defence, possibly including the AA-7 'Apex' and AA-10 semi-active and active radar homing weapons.

Conventional maximum-effort bombing ('Fencer-C')

The Su-24 can carry up to 11000 kg (24,250 lb) of bombs under its wings and fuselage. FAB-500s can be carried in pairs and triplets but this heavy and high-drag load places a severe limit on combat radius and take-off performance. A less than maximum bombload would usually be carried to allow the carriage of defensive ECM pods, AAMs or fuel tanks. Virtually the whole range of Warsaw Pact free-fall and guided weapons can be carried by 'Fencer'.

Precision attack ('Fencer-C')

Various types of laser-guided bomb are thought to have been used by Su-24s involved in attacks on the resistance forces in Afghanistan. These weapons can be released in a shallow dive, or can be tossed or lobbed. A new generation of laser-guided bombs is thought to be on the point of entering service to augment and eventually to replace the current 'Paveway' type weapons based on the standard Warsaw Pact FAB-250, 500, 750 and 1000 bombs.

Strategic strike ('Fencer-D')

A single nuclear weapon is carried for a single target, and few strike sorties would be expected to encompass more than one target. Comprehensive navigation and attack avionics give a genuine all-weather capability. On a hi-lo-hi profile a radius of 1200+ km (745+ miles) should be possible, even without inflight-refuelling. The 'Fencer-D' has a retractable refuelling probe in place of the fixed probe fitted to earlier variants, and may be capable of flying with a 'buddy' refuelling pod.

Precision anti-armour attack ('Fencer-C')

The AS-10 'Karen' is a missile in the same class as the US Maverick, albeit with advanced electro-optical homing. It is, however, of similar configuration to (and possibly developed from) the earlier command guidance AS-7 'Kerry'. In essence the AS-10 can be considered a smaller version of the AS-14 'Kedge'. The AS-7 itself can also be carried by the 'Fencer'.

Su-24 'Fencer' variants

'Fencer-A': Su-24 initially thought to be designated Su-19, but Su-24 designation used since US DOD annual report for Fiscal Year 1981; Su-19 designation probably erroneous even for prototypes; 'Fencer-A' probably used only by initial trials unit; squared-off rear-fuselage box enclosing afterburner nozzles; small brake parachute fairing; possibly powered by Lyulka AL-21F-3 turbojets each rated at 11200 kg (24,692 lb) st with afterburning

'Fencer-E': multi-role reconnaissance and anti-ship strike aircraft for AVMF; one squadron in service with Baltic Fleet by beginning of 1987; comprehensive internal sensor fit including SLAR, IR linescanners and optical cameras; provision for anti-shipping missiles underwing; interim reconnaissance variant may have been converted 'Fencer-A' or 'Fencer-B' with pod-mounted or palletized recce package
'Fencer-F': provisional NATO Air Standards Co-ordinating Committee reporting name for dedicated electronic warfare, ECM and defence suppression variant of 'Fencer-D' intended as 'Brewer-E' replacement

'Fencer-B': initial production strike variant; larger brake parachute fairing probably indicates increased all up weights; rear fuselage 'dished' between jet pipes, possibly indicating change of powerplant; Tumanskii R-29B, R-32B or R-33 are most likely powerplants; this variant used by unit which deployed to Templin during 1979
'Fencer-C': advanced strike variant thought to have entered service in 1981; fitted with more advanced avionics, externally distinguished by new multiple probe fitting on nose of aircraft, and by triangular fairings on the wing-root gloves and on the tailfins; these probably serve an active ECM system, but are similar in shape to the missile guidance blisters found on the nose of 'Flogger-D' and 'Flogger-J'; first encountered in 1984, by Swedish interceptor over the Baltic; probably most numerous variant in service

An unusual view of a Soviet crew boarding their 'Fencer-D'. No built-in steps are provided, so external ladders are used.

'Fencer-D': thought to have entered service in 1983, the 'Fencer-D' was first identified in the West during 1986; optimized for strategic duties and fitted with retractable or removable inflight-refuelling probe for use with new Ilyushin Il-76 'Midas' tanker; simple nose probe with pitch/yaw vanes; nose lengthened by 0.75 m (29.5 in) forward of windscreen, possibly accommodating new radar; lower tailfin chord increased, giving kinked leading edge; wingroot glove pylons integral with large overwing fences; electro-optical sensor in fairing behind nose landing gear bay

© Pilot Press Ltd

67
57
56
55
54
51
117

29
27
28
26
21
25
31
32
33
22
24
20
19
23
8
18
17
7
16
5
8
9
3
4
6
15
2
1
10
14
13
11
12

Sukhoi Su-24 'Fencer'
away drawing key

Pitot head
Air data sensor probes
Radome
Navigation and weapons system radar scanner
Terrain-following and avoidance radar
Scanner tracking mechanism
Radar mounting bulkhead
Dynamic pressure probes, port and starboard
Radar equipment modules
Nose undercarriage pivot fixing
Levered suspension nosewheel leg
Twin nosewheels aft retracting
Mudguard

14 Hydraulic steering unit
15 Electrical system equipment
16 Cockpit floor level
17 Rudder pedals
18 Control column
19 Instrument panel shroud
20 Windscreen panels
21 Cockpit canopy cover, upward-hinging
22 Weapons systems officer/ navigator's 'zero-zero' ejection seat
23 Pilot's ejection seat
24 Cockpit rear pressure bulkhead
25 Avionics equipment bay
26 Canopy hinge point
27 Starboard engine air intake
28 Communications aerial

29 Forward ESM aerials, port and starboard
30 Boundary layer spill duct
31 Boundary layer splitter plate
32 Intake ramp bleed air holes
33 Port engine air intake
34 Intake variable area ramp doors
35 Airbrake hinge fairing
36 Airbrake hydraulic jack
37 Port airbrake/mainwheel door, open position
38 Main undercarriage stowed position
39 Intake suction relief door
40 Forward radar warning antenna
41 Forward fuselage fuel tanks, total internal capacity around 13,000 litres (2,860 Imp gal)
42 Dorsal spine fairing, cable and systems ducting
43 Wing sweep control screw

jacks
44 Screw jack hydraulic motors and gearboxes
45 Gearbox interconnection
46 Air conditioning system ram air intake
47 Wing pivot box carry-through
48 Starboard wing pivot bearing
49 Fixed wing root glove section
50 Leading edge slat segments, open
51 Starboard swivelling pylon
52 Pylon pivot mounting
53 Starboard wing integral fuel tank
54 Wing fully forward (16° sweep) position
55 Starboard navigation light
56 Wing tip fairing
57 Static discharger
58 Starboard double-slotted 'Fowler-type' flap, down

60 Flap guide rails
61 Wing glove sealing plates
62 Starboard engine bay venting air intake
63 Starboard wing full (68°) sweep position
64 Starboard wing intermediate (45°) sweep position
65 Su-24 'Fencer-D' ventral view
66 Air data sensor unit ('Fencer-C' only)
67 Pitot head with yaw and pitch vanes
68 Ventral laser marked target seeker aperture
69 Starboard side cannon bay, 23-mm rotary-type multi-barrel cannon
70 Port side ammunition stowage and feed system
71 Wing glove pylon extended to upper surface fence
72 Fuselage stores pylons
73 Starboard all-moving tailplane
74 Radar directing antenna associated with air-to-surface weapons

antenna
82 Rudder hydraulic actuator
83 Brake parachute housing
84 Parachute housing rear conical fairing
85 Engine exhaust nozzle shroud
86 Variable area afterburner nozzle
87 Port all-moving tailplane
88 Static dischargers
89 Tailplane pivot fixing
90 Tailplane hydraulic actuator
91 Afterburner ducting
92 Fixed ventral fin, port and starboard
93 Engine accessory equipment gearbox
94 Wing root housing sealing plates
95 Lyulka afterburning turbofan engines
96 Port engine bay venting air intake
97 Wing glove sealing plates
98 Port wing pivot bearing
99 Rear fuselage fuel tanks
100 Port roll control spoilers
101 Port wing fully swept position

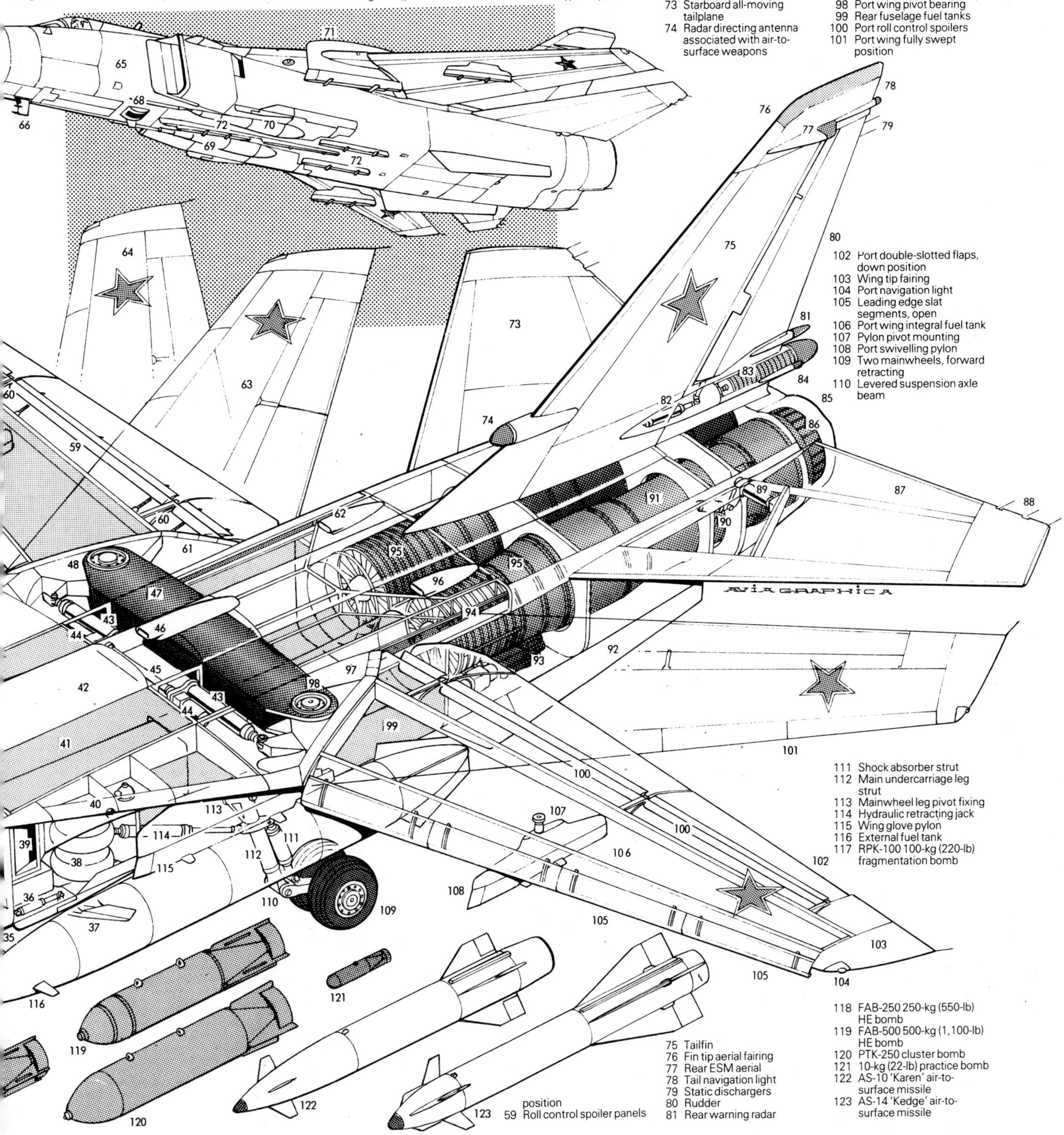

102 Port double-slotted flaps, down position
103 Wing tip fairing
104 Port navigation light
105 Leading edge slat segments, open
106 Port wing integral fuel tank
107 Pylon pivot mounting
108 Port swivelling pylon
109 Two mainwheels, forward retracting
110 Levered suspension axle beam

111 Shock absorber strut
112 Main undercarriage leg strut
113 Mainwheel leg pivot fixing
114 Hydraulic retracting jack
115 Wing glove pylon
116 External fuel tank
117 RPK-100 100-kg (220-lb) fragmentation bomb

75 Tailfin
76 Fin tip aerial fairing
77 Rear ESM aerial
78 Tail navigation light
79 Static dischargers
80 Rudder
81 Rear warning radar

59 Roll control spoiler panels

position

118 FAB-250 250-kg (550-lb) HE bomb
119 FAB-500 500-kg (1,100-lb) HE bomb
120 PTK-250 cluster bomb
121 10-kg (22-lb) practice bomb
122 AS-10 'Karen' air-to-surface missile
123 AS-14 'Kedge' air-to-surface missile

AViAGRAPHICA

The MIKOYAN-GUREVICH MIG-27 FLOGGER

Attack 'Floggers': MiG's duck-nose

Derived from the MiG-23 fighter series, the attack 'Floggers' are in service in large numbers around the world. Their use of existing design makes them a cheap solution to the problem of providing a capable attack craft for many air forces, while the Soviet Union and India have fitted advanced avionics to make them a state-of-the-art striker.

The basic design of the MiG bureau's Ye-231 original swing-wing prototype was undertaken primarily in order to create a new air-combat fighter for the V-VS (Soviet air force) and Warsaw Pact air forces. With a Tumanskii R-27 engine, fully variable inlets and nozzle and no less than 5,750 litres (1,265 Imp gal) of internal fuel it emerged as an extremely capable and formidable aircraft able to operate by night or bad weather from rough austere strips and shoot down almost anything in the sky. It has been built in extremely large numbers, with over 2,600 in Soviet service and about as many again in the hands of WarPac and export customers.

In theory, just as the Panavia Tornado IDS can shoot down other aircraft, so can the MiG-23M and more powerful MiG-23MF attack ground targets. It was obvious that for tactical attack missions a somewhat different aircraft would ideally be needed, and in about 1971 the MiG bureau was formally ordered to build prototypes of such an aircraft. It was given the service designation MiG-27, which is unusual because odd numbers had previously been reserved for fighters and the MiG-27, like the equally inappropriately designated General Dynamics F-111, is not a fighter but an attack machine.

Designation of the Ye-numbered prototypes is not known, but they probably flew in 1972. From these stemmed three significantly different sub-families: the MiG-23BM, the MiG-23BN and the MiG-27. Oddly, the hybrid MiG-23 versions did not precede the fully customized MiG-27 attack aircraft but followed it. To a considerable degree the MiG-27, the true attack version, is the one produced with urgency for the FA (Frontal Aviation) of the V-VS, while the MiG-23BM and MiG-23BN were hybrids for export customers.

Called 'Flogger-D' by NATO, the MiG-27 was first seen after it had entered service with the GSFG during 1974. It differed in almost every part from the MiG-23MF, apart from the wings and tail, but the chief alterations concerned the engine installation and the nose.

Whereas the fighter's engine installation had to be designed for high efficiency over a wide spread of Mach numbers and altitudes, the attack aircraft was hardly ever to fly at supersonic speed or at any considerable height. Most of its life is spent at high power toting heavy attack loads at the lowest possible altitude to escape detection by hostile radars, and the variable inlets and nozzle of the fighter thus became heavy extras that were no longer worth their considerable cost. Accordingly the entire propulsion system was redesigned, though without significantly altering the thrust figures for the engine. According to an Indian brochure the MiG-27M is powered by an R-29-300 afterburning turbojet, quoted at the extraordinarily low maximum thrust in full afterburner of 8130 kg (17,923 lb), but generally believed to be in the order of 11500 kg (25,353 lb). The increase in afterburning thrust is only 43.75 per cent (compared with 55.9 per cent for the R-29B used in the MiG-23 series), resulting largely from the needs of subsonic cruise and greater fuel economy. For reasons not yet clear, the designers decided that the sides of the inlets should

◀ *The MiG-23BN 'Flogger-H' is in service with most of the Warsaw Pact air forces, exemplified by this Czech machine. The MiG-23BN features the large splitter plates of the interceptor variants, while adding the 'duck nose' of the MiG-27.*

▲ *With wings at minimum sweep, a MiG-27 is caught on final approach. The six-barrelled cannon is clearly visible, as is the folded ventral fin. The MiG-27 has a much shorter and simpler exhaust nozzle than the MiG-23. Note the cluster of weapons pylons.*

be bulged out, whereas in the MiG-23 fighter versions the sides are straight and vertical. The complex variable geometry of the inlets was eliminated, the new bigger inlet being simple and fixed as in the SEPE-CAT Jaguar and General Dynamics F-16. In the same way the small afterburner terminates in a short pipe and two-position nozzle well forward of the trailing edges of the tail surfaces.

Equally profound alterations were made ahead of the inlets, and in fact hardly any part of the structure or equipment in the forward fuselage is the same as that of the MiG-23MF. To suit the totally different needs of the low-level attack mission the suite of sensors carried in the nose was completely rethought.

Externally the most obvious change is that the big radar has gone, and the nose has a distinctive wedge shape known to Soviet pilots as the *utkanos* (duck nose). Broad in plan view, it is slim and has almost triangular taper in side elevation, all the taper being on the top while the bottom line is straight. This gives a much better pilot view, a factor further improved by raising the seat and increasing the height of the rear-hinged canopy and, in particular, the depth of the windshield and quarter-light panels giving the view ahead. The result is that the angular view downward is changed from 8° below the horizontal for the fighter (with a typcial pilot) to no less than 20° in the MiG-27. To protect the pilot against ground fire large plates of armour were scabbed on each side of the cockpit, and further extra armour was added internally. The weight of these slabs almost counterbalanced the reduced moment arm of the shorter nose without the radar, the rest of the counterbalancing being provided by the smaller and shorter afterburner and nozzle.

Full details of the MiG-27 sensors are still not known in the West, despite the fact that on several occasions since October 1984 examples of attack 'Floggers' have been publicly displayed at Nasik in India.

To rub salt in the wound, the stencilling detailing all equipment on the Indian aircraft is in English! Suffice to say that the basic kit of sensors in the original MiG-27 includes a laser ranger and marked-target seeker, terrain-avoidance radar, large Doppler radar for navigation, radar altimeter (duplicated and linked to the autopilot and terrain-avoidance subsystem) and a modern HUD sight. Almost all attack versions in Soviet service also have the small blisters (on each side of the lower edge of the forward fuselage, just ahead of the nosewheel door hinges) for the target-illuminating and beam-riding requirement of the important attack ASM known to NATO as AS-7 'Kerry'.

Avionics

All MiG-27s have extremely comprehensive avionics systems. These include autopilot and linked automatic flight-control system, VHF and UHF communications radio (inclung the RISU-5 VHF operating in the 100-150 MHz waveband, and a special radio for communication with local ground forces), the SRZO-2 IFF (called 'Odd Rods' by NATO on account of the rod aerials of three different lengths) mounted under the nose, the SOD-57M air-traffic control transponder which automatically

▲ *Latest version of the attack 'Flogger' is the MiG-27M 'Flogger-J'. This is a HAL-built example, displaying the leading edge root extensions and revised nose characteristic of the variant. Indian aircraft carry two extra sensors under the nose.*

▼ *'Flogger-D' is the original version of the MiG-27, with bullet fairings mounted above the glove pylons. Hundreds are in service with Frontal Aviation in the battlefield strike and attack role. Note the slightly bulged intake.*

enhances the radar signature on friendly surveillance screens, the ARL-5 data link, ARK-10 radio compass which also incorporates a simple DME function, a TACAN type radio beacon navigation aid, and comprehensive weapon-control interfaces into which the pilot inserts ballistics plugs corresponding to the actual weapons loaded on each pylon on each mission. Thereafter the weapon control automatically feeds the HUD sight with the correct launch parameters and symbology for accurate release of each weapon.

Not least of the onboard avionics are the comprehensive EW systems. Full details are not yet known, especially in relation to the remarkable array of avionic items inside the leading edges of the fixed wing gloves and the inboard ends of the pivoting

outer wings. Early MiG-27s had two for-ward-projecting dielectric pods (in the leading edge of the left and right gloves, about halfway from the root to the junc-tion with the outer wings). It was generally supposed that the left pod housed either an ECM jammer or an IR seeker, while that on the right glove was said to have a missile-guidance function. Other aerials inside the leading edge, with flush glassfibre skins, include the forward-hemisphere receivers in the SO-69 (Sirena 3 or 3M) RWR system, which gives an audio and visual (flashing light) warning if the aircraft is illuminated by a hostile radar, and in the Sirena 3M version the pilot is additionally given the direction of the hostile threat. The aerials covering the rear hemisphere in the SO-69 system are on each side at the top of the fin.

To match the high weights at which the MiG-27 operates to the soft unpaved strips it would exclusively use in wartime the MiG bureau redesigned the landing gear to have increased 'flotation'. In the case of the nose gear the best answer was to increase the wheel and tyre diameter, and this has resulted in blisters appearing in the left and right nose-gear doors (or, in some versions, a complete bulged door assembly lower than the rest of the fuselage undersurface). The bigger tyres are no longer covered by the mudguard, which instead is mounted only to the rear as in a bicycle.

As for the main gears, there was no way increased-diameter wheels and tyres could be accommodated in the existing bay, but at the cost of bulging the fuselage outwards laterally it was found possible to make the wheels and tyres significantly wider. This enabled tyre pressure to be approximately halved, multiplying 'footprint area' by almost five and enabling the MiG-27 to operate from typical sod fields in temper-ate climates. The bulge is not very notice-able except when looking up at the MiG-27 from below. It has only a minor effect on drag and aircraft performance. The promi-nent downward facing flush disc aerials of the fighter, on each side of the front of the ventral fin, are eliminated.

On the other hand new appurtenances appeared on each side of the rear fuselage in the MiG-27, and though these were widely hailed as 'assisted take-off rocket attachments' they are in fact simply bomb racks. Each normally carries an FAB-250

GP bomb of 551lb, though bigger stores have been seen here, and the starboard rear-fuselage pylon sometimes carries an active ECM jammer pod. The heaviest loads can be carried by the fuselage pylons, and while that on the centreline is plumbed for an 800-litre (176-Imp gal) tank it can also carry stores or groups up to a total mass of 920kg (2,028lb). The flanking pylons on the fighter are close alongside on the fuselage, but in the MiG-27 they were moved far outboard under the inlet ducts, which also made the pylons vertical instead of inclined. These can each take groups of stores up to 1000kg (2,205lb), such as tandem pairs of FAB-250s. As in the fighters, the gloves and the swing wings provide for four further pylons, though those under the outer wings are fixed and cannot be used if the wings are to be swept. These are normally restricted to 800-litre tanks, used for ferrying. The glove pylons, which are directly behind and below the bullet-shaped avionics fairings on the lead-ing edges, are each rated at 1000kg. Not all pylons are normally loaded simulta-neously, though there is reason to believe that the Western estimates of 4000kg (8,818lb) maximum weapon load is an underestimate (until 1983 the guess was only 3000kg/6,614lb).

One further important change distin-guished the MiG-27 from the fighter. In place of the GSh-23L twin-barrel gun a completely new six-barrel rotary cannon was installed, believed to have the same 23-mm calibre as the older weapon. With much higher firing rates, the new gun is better matched to use against ground tar-gets, and the capacity of the magazine is believed to be at least 700 rounds, com-pared with 200-220 for the fighter. The

new gun is recessed into the underside of the fuselage in the usual location.

Chronologically the next variant was the hybrid MiG-23BM (an unconfirmed designation) called 'Flogger-F' by NATO. This combined the nose, cockpit, armour and landing gear of the MiG-27 with the rest of the airframe of the fighter. It is widely used by export customers. It was followed by the MiG-23BN 'Flogger-H', which adds the missile guidance radar blis-ters on each side of the nose, and this is even used by the Soviet FA and other War-Pac forces as well as by India. Latest of the attack versions is the MiG-27M 'Flog-ger-J', which differs from the MiG-27 in having a modified nose with additional and upgraded sensors, wing-root extensions, kinked taileron trailing edge and no glove bullet aerials. MiG-27Ms made under licence by Hindustan Aeronautics have twin sensor blades, thicker than normal blade aerials, projecting obliquely down from under the nose. Their function has not yet been identified, despite the fact that on this version, called Bahadur (valiant), all external descriptive stencils are in English.

▲ *India is the largest non-Soviet user, utilizing both MiG-23BMs and MiG-27s. This is one of the former, which differ from other MiG-23s by having short exhaust nozzles (but still retaining the large splitter plates). The MiG-23s were assembled by HAL at Nasik.*

▼ *Typical of the MiG-23BM and BNs supplied to many nations, this Czech MiG-23BN displays the landing light which folds down from the engine inlet. The MiG 23BN 'Floggger-H' is distinguished by the two small missile guidance blisters each side of the nosewheel doors.*

MiG-23VM, MiG-23BN and MiG-27 in service

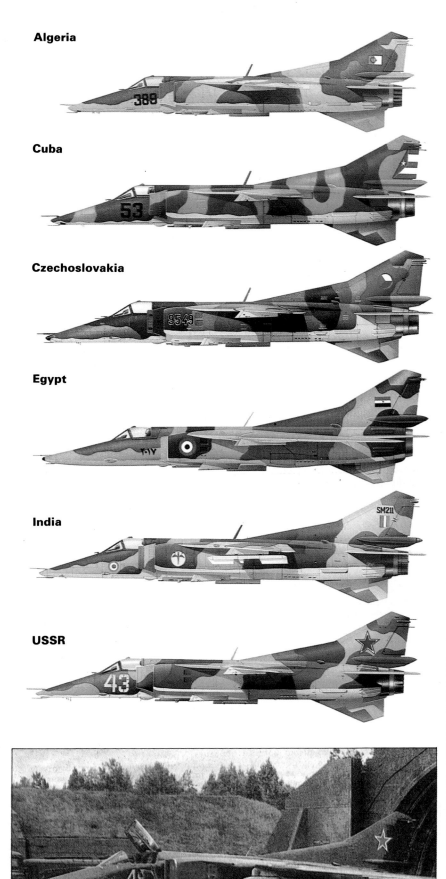

Algeria

Cuba

Czechoslovakia

Egypt

India

USSR

Algeria
Forty MiG-23BM 'Flogger-Fs' are disposed in two squadrons for attack duties. Known serials include 383, 388 and 389.

Bulgaria
An unknown number (40?) of attack-configured MiG-23s are in service, thought to be the MiG-23BN 'Flogger-H' variant.

China
At least one example of the MiG-23BM was delivered to China for test and evaluation from Egypt, perhaps as an offset for the supply of Shenyang F-7s.

Cuba
Some 25 MiG-23BMs were supplied to update the ground-attack element, which had previously flown MiG-17s. These MiG-23s have been recently augmented by the delivery of an unknown number of MiG-27s. Known MiG-23BM serials include 53 and 710.

Czechoslovakia
This Warsaw Pact country has been supplied with at least 30 'Flogger-Fs' and more recently an unknown number of updated 'Flogger-Hs'. These are thought to be based at Pardubice. Known serials include 8025 and 9549.

East Germany
Two squadrons of 'Flogger-Fs' were supplied for the ground-attack role, recently supplemented by a further squadron operating the MiG-27 'Flogger-D'

Egypt
This country was originally supplied with two squadrons of MiG-23BM, but it is thought that all have been passed on to China and the USA.

Ethiopia
Two squadrons of MiG-23s are flown, and at least six of the aircraft are MiG-23BMs. These have been involved in the civil war raging between government forces and Eritrean guerrillas. The Eritreans claimed 16 MiG-23s destroyed in an airfield attack, and some of these may have been ground-attack variants.

India
India is the largest foreign operator, with 80 'Flogger-Fs' in service with Nos 10, 220 and 221 Sqns. These were delivered in knock-down form to the MiG complex at Nasik for HAL to assemble. This factory is now turning out the MiG-27M 'Flogger-J', the first of which entered service with No. 227 Sqn in January 1986. Planning calls for 200 to be built, adding to a small number supplied from Soviet sources.

Iraq
Some 80 'Flogger-Fs' have been delivered, and these have seen much action against Iran during the long Gulf War.

Libya
The large and disparate Libyan air force operates some 20 'Flogger-Fs', which serve alongside various Sukhoi and Western types on ground-attack duties.

North Korea
Little is known of the North Korean air force, but it is believed that a small number of ground-attack MiG-23s have entered service since better relations with Moscow were resumed.

Poland
Poland has a large ground attack force spearheaded by 50 MiG-27s. A further 60 MiG-23BM/BN 'Flogger-F/H' aircraft bolster this force.

Syria
Some 60 'Flogger-Fs' were supplied to Syria, and several of these were lost during the fighting against Israeli jets over the Bekaa Valley in 1982. No doubt these losses have been made good by Moscow, and judging by the regard in which the Soviets hold this Arab nation, MiG-27s are likely to have been supplied. Known serials include 2017 and 60130 (MiG-23BM).

USA
Some Egyptian 'Floggers' were supplied to the US Air force for evaluation and dissimilar air combat purposes. These are based within the vast Nellis ranges in Nevada. At least one has been lost while in USAF service.

USSR
Frontal Aviation employs over 700 MiG-27 'Flogger-D/Js' as a major component of the battlefield strike and attack forces. Several MiG-23BN 'Flogger-Hs' have been seen in Soviet use, and these have appeared in Afghanistan, some of them wearing Afghan air force markings. MiG-27s have been seen at a test site near the Black Sea in conjunction with carrier deck trials, suggesting that a naval attack version may go to sea aboard the new Soviet nuclear carrier. Known serials include 34, 43 (MiG-23BN) and 07, 41, 53, 62 (MiG-27).

Vietnam
Over 100 of all versions of the MiG-23 have been delivered, including an unknown number of ground-attack variants. These may have seen limited action in Kampuchea.

Many of the Soviet aircraft deployed close to NATO are housed in hardened shelters. This MiG-27 'Flogger-D' undergoes maintenance outside its shelter.

MiG-27 variants

Ye-231: prototype with Lyulka AL-7F-1 afterburning turbojet, first flown in late 1966; no radar or armament, but paved the way for the MiG-23 and MiG-27 series

MiG-27 'Flogger-D': initial production version of the dedicated attack model with redesigned engine installation (R-29-300 engine plus fixed inlets and a short simple nozzle), new forward fuselage, modified landing gear and revised armament (including a six-barrel rotary cannon)

MiG-23BM 'Flogger-F': hybrid fighter-bomber version with the nose, cockpit, landing gear, armour and other features of the MiG-27 matched to the engine installation; centre/rear fuselage, pylons and gun of the MiG-23

MiG-23BN 'Flogger-H': upgraded hybrid type similar to the MiG-23BM but with missile-guidance blisters on each side of the nose; some earlier aircraft were retrofitted to this standard

MiG-27M 'Flogger-J': upgraded attack variant similar to the MiG-27 but with wing root extensions, modified nose featuring extra sensors, and glove bullet fairings deleted

HAL Bahadur: licence-built MiG-27M for the Indian air force, generally similar to the 'Flogger-J' but with twin projecting blade fairings beneath the nose, and other small modifications

Close-up of the 'Flogger-D' nose reveals 'Swift Rod' ILS aerial, laser marked-targ seeker, 'Odd Rods' IFF aerial, terrain-avoidance radar and missile guidance bli

Mikoyan-Gurevich MiG- 27M 'Flogger D/J' cutaway drawing key

1. Pitot head
2. Radar antenna fairing
3. Weapons system ranging-only radar unit
4. 'Swift Rods' ILS aerial
5. Laser marked target seeker
6. Ventral navigation and terrain-following radar
7. Radar mounting bulkhead
8. 'Odd Rods' IFF aerials
9. Radar altimeters
10. Temperature probe
11. Avionics equipment, navigation and weapons systems equipment
12. Nose compartment construction
13. Avionics equipment access doors, port and starboard
14. Dynamic pressure probe (q-feel)
15. Instrument access panel
16. Air data probes, instrumentation system
17. Forward pressure bulkhead, armoured
18. Ventral doppler antenna
19. Blade aerial
20. Lateral radar antenna, port and starboard
21. Nosewheel steering mechanism
22. Levered axle beam shock absorber
23. Twin nosewheels
24. Nosewheel spray/debris guards
25. Nose landing gear leg strut
26. Nosewheel doors
27. Hydraulic retraction jack
28. Angle of attack transmitter
29. Cockpit armoured pressure floor
30. Rudder pedals
31. Instrument panel
32. Control column
33. Instrument panel shroud
34. Armoured glass windscreen panels
35. Pilot's head-up display
36. UV-16-57 rocket launcher
37. 57-mm folding fin aircraft rocket (FFAR)
38. Upward-hingeing cockpit canopy cover
39. Electrically-heated rear view mirror
40. Ejection seat headrest
41. Pilot's 'zero-zero' ejection seat
42. Canopy external latch
43. Seat pan firing handles
44. Engine throttle and wing sweep control levers
45. Port side console panel
46. Cockpit side panel external armour plating
47. Armoured rear pressure bulkhead
48. Ground test panel
49. Nose landing gear wheel bay
50. Electrical system equipment
51. Canopy hydraulic jack
52. Canopy hinge point
53. Starboard engine air intake
54. ADF sense aerial
55. Avionics equipment, navigation and communications systems
56. Boundary layer spill duct
57. Boundary layer splitter plate
58. Avionics equipment cooling air inlet
59. Fixed geometry engine air inlet
60. Retractable landing/taxiing lamp, port and starboard
61. Inlet duct framing
62. Control rod runs
63. Ventral cannon ammunition magazine
64. Inlet duct stores pylon, port and starboard
65. Ground power and intercom sockets
66. Inlet suction relief doors
67. Wing leading edge root extension ('Flogger-J')
68. Forward fuselage fuel tanks
69. Electronic countermeasures equipment
70. Wing glove stores pylon
71. Weapons management system electronics
72. Centre section fuel tank
73. SO-69 'Sirena-3' radar warning and suppression aerials
74. Wing glove pylon attachment
75. Screw jack wing sweep rotary actuator
76. Twin hydraulic motors
77. Control rod runs
78. Dorsal spine fairing
79. Wing sweep control central combining gearbox
80. Wing pivot box integral fuel tank
81. VHF aerial
82. Wing pivot box carry-through unit (welded steel construction)
83. Starboard wing sweep control screw jack
84. Electronic warfare equipment
85. Wing glove section 'Flogger-D'
86. Missile control radar directing antenna ('Flogger-D'); television camera on port wing glove
87. Jettisonable fuel tank 800-litre (176-Imp gal) capacity
88. FAB 250 250-kg (551-lb) HE general purpose bomb
89. Twin bomb carrier/ejector rack
90. Bomb rack wing glove pylon
91. Starboard 'Sirena-3' radar warning and suppression aerials
92. Extended chord saw-tooth leading edge
93. Starboard wing pivot bearing
94. Non-swivelling-jettisonable wing pylon (wing restricted to forward swept position)
95. Pylon attachment joint
96. Fixed portion of leading edge
97. Starboard wing integral fuel tank
98. Leading edge flap hydraulic actuator
99. Leading edge flap operating linkage
100. Starboard leading edge flap segments, down position
101. Starboard navigation light
102. Wing tip fairing
103. Static discharger
104. Full-span three-segment plain flap, down position
105. Starboard wing intermediate (45-degree sweep) position
106. Starboard wing full (72-degree sweep) position
107. Two-segment spoilers/lift dumpers, open
108. Spoiler hydraulic actuators
109. Flap hydraulic jack
110. Flap mechanical interconnect and disengage mechanism
111. Wing root housing
112. Wing glove flexible-seal
113. Fin root fillet construction
114. Dorsal fuel tank
115. Engine intake compressor face
116. Wing root housing sealing plates
117. Rear fuselage fuel tanks
118. Tailplane control spring linkages
119. Afterburner duct cooling air scoop
120. Artificial feel control units
121. Control system hydraulic accumulators
122. Artificial feel and autopilot controls
123. Fin spar attachment joint
124. Tailplane trim controls
125. Tailfin construction
126. Fin leading edge ribs
127. Starboard all-moving tailplane
128. Remote compass transmitter
129. Short-wave ground control communications aerial
130. Fintip UHF aerial fairings
131. ILS aerial
132. ECM aerial
133. 'Sirena-3' tail warning radar antenna
134. Tail navigation light
135. Static discharger
136. Rudder
137. Honeycomb core construction
138. Rudder hydraulic actuators, port and starboard
139. Brake parachute housing
140. Parachute release linkage
141. Split conic fairing parachute doors
142. Simplified two-position (on-off) afterburner nozzle
143. Fixed tailplane tab
144. Honeycomb core trailing edge panel
145. Static discharger
146. Port all-moving tailplane construction
147. Afterburner nozzle pneumatic control jacks (six)
148. Tailplane pivot bearing
149. Tailplane hydraulic actuator
150. Airbrake (four) upper and lower surfaces
151. Airbrake hydraulic jacks
152. Afterburner duct heat shroud
153. Ventral fin, folded (landing gear down) position
154. Ventral fin down position
155. Rocket Assisted Take-Off bottle (RATO) for rough/ short field operations
156. Screw jack ventral fin actuator

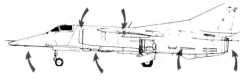

Specification: Mikoyan-Gurevich MiG-27M — MiG-27 recognition features

Wings
, at 16° sweep	14.25 m	(46 ft 9 in)
, at 72° sweep	8.17 m	(26 ft 9.7 in)
ep, manually controlled at 16°, 45° or 72°		
, gross at 16° sweep	27.25 m²	(293.33 sq ft)

selage and tail unit
ommodation	pilot only seated on an ejector seat	
th overall	16.00 m	(52 ft 5.9 in)
ht overall	4.50 m	(14 ft 9.2 in)
lane span	5.75 m	(18 ft 10.4 in)

nding gear
actable tricycle type with single-wheel main units and twin
eel nose unit
el track	2.87 m	(9 ft 5 in)
elbase	6.15 m	(20 ft 2.1 in)

eights
ty	10790 kg	(23,788 lb)
nal take-off, clean	15500 kg	(34,172 lb)
mum take-off	20100 kg	(44,313 lb)
imum external load	4000+ kg	(8,818+ lb)
nal fuel load	5750 litres	(1,265 Imp gal)

werplant
Tumanskii R-29-300 afterburning turbojet
c thrust, dry	8000 kg	(17,637 lb)
in afterburner	11500 kg	(25,352 lb)

Large dogtooth in wing leading edge is apparent at medium and maximum sweep positions

Bullet fairings extend from leading edge of wing glove on some aircraft

Complicated landing gear and chisel nose give ungainly appearance

Nose probe offset to starboard

Small fixed splitter plate forward of inlet

Long, chisel-shaped 'duck' nose

Short non-variable exhaust nozzle

The MiG-27 is most easily confused with the MiG-23, from which it is derived. The most notable difference is the chisel nose, others being the small splitter plate and simple exhaust nozzle. At speed and distance the MiG-27 could be taken for a number of Western attack types, such as the F-111, Tornado or Jaguar. The characteristic 'MiG' fin with large dorsal fillet is the most notable feature.

Long-strut nose landing gear mounts large, low-pressure tyres

Large, six-barrelled rotary cannon under belly

Large ventral fin folds horizontally during ground and circuit operations

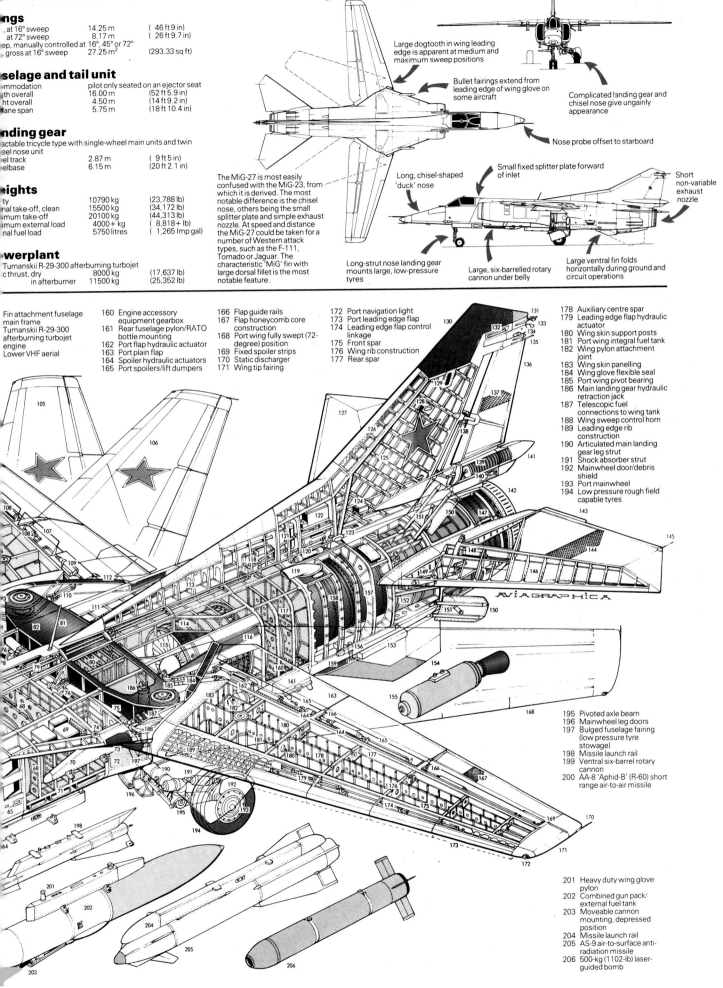

Fin attachment fuselage main frame
Tumanskii R-29-300 afterburning turbojet engine
Lower VHF aerial

160 Engine accessory equipment gearbox
161 Rear fuselage pylon/RATO bottle mounting
162 Port flap hydraulic actuator
163 Port plain flap
164 Spoiler hydraulic actuators
165 Port spoilers/lift dumpers

166 Flap guide rails
167 Flap honeycomb core construction
168 Port wing fully swept (72-degree) position
169 Fixed spoiler strips
170 Static discharger
171 Wing tip fairing

172 Port navigation light
173 Port leading edge flap
174 Leading edge flap control linkage
175 Front spar
176 Wing rib construction
177 Rear spar

178 Auxiliary centre spar
179 Leading edge flap hydraulic actuator
180 Wing skin support posts
181 Port wing integral fuel tank
182 Wing pylon attachment joint
183 Wing skin panelling
184 Wing glove flexible seal
185 Port wing pivot bearing
186 Main landing gear hydraulic retraction jack
187 Telescopic fuel connections to wing tank
188 Wing sweep control horn
189 Leading edge rib construction
190 Articulated main landing gear leg strut
191 Shock absorber strut
192 Mainwheel door/debris shield
193 Port mainwheel
194 Low pressure rough field capable tyres

195 Pivoted axle beam
196 Mainwheel leg doors
197 Bulged fuselage fairing (low pressure tyre stowage)
198 Missile launch rail
199 Ventral six-barrel rotary cannon
200 AA-8 'Aphid-B' (R-60) short range air-to-air missile

201 Heavy duty wing glove pylon
202 Combined gun pack/ external fuel tank
203 Moveable cannon mounting, depressed position
204 Missile launch rail
205 AS-9 air-to-surface anti-radiation missile
206 500-kg (1102-lb) laser-guided bomb

AVIAGRAPHICA

MiG-27 warload

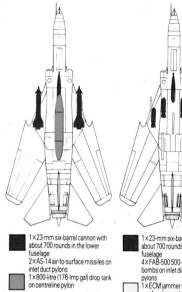
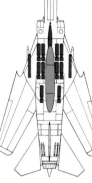

■ 1×23-mm six-barrel cannon with about 700 rounds in the lower fuselage
■ 2×AS-14 air-to-surface missiles on inlet duct pylons
■ 1×800-litre (176-Imp gal) drop tank on centreline pylon

■ 1×23-mm six-barrel cannon with about 700 rounds in the lower fuselage
■ 4×FAB-500 500-kg (1,102-lb) bombs on inlet duct and glove pylons
□ 1×ECM jammer pod on starboard rear fuselage pylon

■ 1×23-mm six-barrel cannon with about 700 rounds in the lower fuselage
■ 2×AS-7 'Kerry' air-to-surface missiles on inlet duct pylons
■ 2×AA-8 'Aphid' IR-homing air-to-air missiles on inlet duct pylons
■ 1×800-litre (176-Imp gal) drop tank on centreline pylon

■ 1×23-mm six-barrel cannon with about 700 rounds in the lower fuselage
■ 2×GSh-23 23-mm twin-barrel cannon pods on glove pylons
■ 10×OFAB-250 250-kg (551-lb) fragmentation bombs, four carried on each inlet duct pylon with one each on the rear fuselage pylons
■ 1×800-litre (176-Imp gal) drop tank on centreline pylon

■ 1×23-mm six-barrel cannon with about 700 rounds in the lower fuselage
■ 2×TN-1200 tactical nuclear bombs on inlet duct pylons
■ 1×800-litre (176-Imp gal) drop tank on centreline pylon
□ 1×ECM jammer pod on starboard rear fuselage pylon

■ 1×23-mm six-barrel cannon with about 700 rounds in the lower fuselage
■ 10×BETAB-250 250-kg (551-lb) rocket retarded/boosted runway penetrators, six carried on the glove pylons and four on the inlet duct pylons
□ 1×ECM jammer pod on starboard rear fuselage pylon

Hard target (missile)
The AS-14, previously called by NATO the AS-X-14 and not yet given a published NATO name, is the biggest of the ASMs carried by the MiG-27 and variants. It can probably be carried on the inlet duct pylons, but has been seen only on the glove pylons. Range is estimated at 32 km (20 miles).

Hard target (bomb)
Several types of 500-kg (1,102-lb) bomb are in common use with Frontal Aviation, though the MiG-27 naturally tends to carry types offering lower aerodynamic drag than the flat-nosed, parallel-sided patterns. No details are yet available on Soviet ECM pods.

Precision attack
The AS-7 is a widely used ASM offering precision attack capability. Laser-guided bombs can also be carried for this kind of attack. AS-8 'Aphids' or AA-2 'Atolls' can be carried to provide a measure of self-defence.

Soft target
The gun pods carried on the glove pylons contain twin-barrel cannon which can be tilted down to about 14° for attack on surface targets, so avoiding the need for the carrying aircraft to sustain a dive to very low levels. The fragmentation bombs can be replaced by various kinds of 55-mm (2.16-in) rockets.

Interdiction
Frontal Aviation has very large numbers of both nuclear (N and TN) and also fuel/air explosive (FAE) devices, most of which could knock out any NATO air base with a single detonation. The heaviest weapons in these categories are issued to Sukhoi Su-24 regiments.

Counter-air
The BETAB 'concrete dibber' device strongly resembles the French Durandal pavement penetrator, and like that weapon is first slowed horizontally by a braking rocket and, after being tilted nose-down, is accelerated into the runway by a rocket of very high thrust.

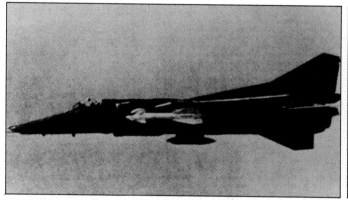

Several air-to-surface missiles can be carried by the MiG-27, the most usual being the AS-7 'Kerry'. This missile is the larger AS-14, and it is likely that the underfuselage pod is a camera for test work.

Among the more unusual weapons carried by the MiG-27 is the gun pod carried on the glove pylon. Each pod contains a twin-barrelled GSh-23 cannon, which can be depressed to 14° for ground strafing.

Performance:

Maximum speed, at altitude	Mach 1.7; 975 kts; 1807 km/h	(1,123 mph)
Maximum speed, at sea level	Mach 1.1; 726 kts 1345 km/h	(836 mph)
Service ceiling	52,495 ft	(16000 m)
Combat radius on a lo-lo-lo sortie with two AA-2 missiles, four 500-kg bombs and one drop tank	390 km	(240 miles)
Ferry range with three drop tanks	2500 km	(1,550 miles)
Take-off distance to clear 15-m (50-ft) obstacle at AUW of 15700 kg (34,612 lb)	800 m	(2,625 ft)

Maximum weapon load
- Vought A-7E Corsair II 6804 kg+
- SEPECAT Jaguar GR.Mk 1 4535 kg
- MiG-27 'Flogger-D' 4000 kg E
- Dassault Breguet Mirage 5 4000 kg+
- British Aerospace Harrier
- Sukhoi Su-17 'Fitter-C' 3175 kg+ E
- MiG-21 MF GR.Mk 3 3629 kg
- 'Fishbed-J' 2000 kg E

Service ceiling
- Sukhoi Su-17 'Fitter-C' 59,050 ft E
- Dassault-Breguet Mirage 5 55,775 ft
- Mikoyan-Gurevich MiG-27 'Flogger-D' 52,500 ft E
- British Aerospace Harrier GR.Mk 3 51,200 ft
- SEPECAT Jaguar GR.Mk 1 50,000 ft+ E
- MiG-21MF 'Fishbed-J' 50,000 ft
- Vought A-7E Corsair II 42,000 ft E

Maximum speed at optimum height
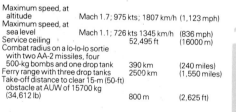
- Dassault-Breguet Mirage 5 Mach 2.2 'clean'
- MiG-21MF 'Fishbed-J' Mach 2.1 'clean'
- Sukhoi Su-17 'Fitter-C' Mach 2.09 E
- Mikoyan-Gurevich MiG-27 'Flogger-D' Mach 1.7 E
- SEPECAT Jaguar GR.Mk 1 Mach 1.6
- Vought A-7E Corsair II Mach 1.04
- British Aerospace Harrier GR.Mk 3 Mach 0.85 E

Maximum speed at sea level
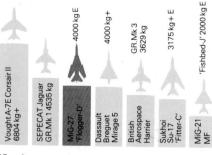
- Dassault-Breguet Mirage 5 Mach 1.13 'clean'
- Mikoyan-Gurevich MiG-27 'Flogger-D' Mach 1.1 E
- SEPECAT Jaguar GR.Mk 1 Mach 1.1
- Mikoyan-Gurevich MiG-21MF 'Fishbed-J' Mach 1.06
- Sukhoi Su-17 'Fitter-C' Mach 1.05 E
- British Aerospace Harrier GR.Mk 3 Mach 0.96
- Vought A-7E Corsair II Mach 0.91

Combat radius hi-lo-hi with stated weapon load

- Dassault-Breguet Mirage 5 1300 km with 907 kg
- Vought A-7E Corsair II 885 km with 1814 kg
- SEPECAT Jaguar GR.Mk 1 852 km with 1814 kg
- MiG-27 'Flogger-D' 700 km with 1140 kg and one tank E
- Sukhoi Su-17 'Fitter-C' 630 km with 2000 kg E
- MiG-21MF 'Fishbed-J' 370 km with 1000 kg
- Harrier GR.Mk 3 333 km with 1995 kg

The TUPOLEV TU-16

Tupolev Tu-16 'Badger'

Tupolev's classic Tu-16 'Badger' was in the first generation of Soviet bombers, and like its turboprop 'big brother', the 'Bear', is still going strong after 35 years of flight. A large array of variants perform a myriad of tasks for the Soviet Union, while China is still building the aircraft to fulfil its strategic bomber role.

In the early days of Soviet jet bomber development, what could be accomplished depended squarely on the engines available. In the early 1950s the Mikulin engine KB (construction bureau) came up with a new axial type of turbojet designated AM-3 (service designation RD-3). The only unusual thing about it was its great size: at a stroke it roughly doubled the thrust of Soviet turbojets. The famous aircraft OKB (experimental construction bureau) of A.N. Tupolev tore up earlier plans and quickly schemed a new swept-wing bomber to use two of these big engines. Secrecy was so high its OKB designation of Tu-88 was replaced on the drawings and documents by a cryptic 'Type N'.

The prototype began a brilliantly successful flight-test programme in the hands of N.S. Rybko in early 1952. A second and slightly more powerful prototype followed a few months later, and before the end of 1952 the big Tupolev had been picked (by a wide margin) over the rival Ilyushin Il-46 and been accepted for production. A nationwide manufacturing plan was organized, though there was only one assembly line. By 1959 about 2,000 of the type had been delivered, and it is conceivable that a few more may have been built subsequently. In addition, since 1968 about 150 bombers closely resembling the original Soviet model have been made in China, where production is continuing!

Even more remarkably, many parts of these aircraft can be traced straight back to the wartime Boeing B-29, a copy of which was produced in the USSR as the Tu-4. This was developed via the Tu-80 into the impressive Tu-85, last of the piston-engined bombers, and the fuselage of the Tu-85 was the starting point for the Tu-88 and, considerably stretched, the Tu-95 (NATO 'Bear'). Changes in the jet bomber include use of a new alloy and thicker skin, and a new centre section cut away on each side to accommodate the buried engines. The latter were arranged to bolt on to two very strong frames of chrome-steel, each with a hinged and bolted lower arc so that the engines could be changed downwards. Each of the massive wings was bolted on near the top of the frame at the two main spars, leaving room under the wing for the large hinged engine access doors. The engines were given plain inlets of a nearly circular shape, with flattish tops, the duct curving in towards the engines. The jet pipes were toed slightly out again (sustained flight is possible at maximum weight on one engine turning at maximum continuous revolutions).

Each wing is swept at first 42° and then, over most of the span, at 35°. There are track-mounted slotted flaps driven via electric actuators and ballscrew jacks, and manual geared-tab ailerons. There was no obvious place for the main landing gears. Tupolev's team studied the B-47 'bicycle' arrangement but rightly considered that this had many shortcomings. To avoid cutting open the highly stressed wing skins, and probably having large blisters in any case, the decision was taken to fold each gear backwards from the main wing box

into completely unstressed fairing boxes projecting behind the wing. Even though gross weight was much less than that of the Tu-85 the gears were made in the form of four-wheel bogies, the first in the USSR. This spread the weight for soft pavements, and also reduced weight and retracted drag.

As in the previous Tu-4 derived bombers, there is a pressurized crew compartment forming the nose, plus a small pressurized compartment for the tail gunner. In the main compartment, entered via a ventral door with pull-down ladders, are armoured seats for two pilots side-by-side and a radio operator/gunner looking through a rear sighting dome. In the original (and many later) versions there is a station for a navigator/bombardier in a glazed nose. In the tail compartment are stations for two gunner/observers, one in the tail and the other using left and right sighting blisters. The rear compartment has its own ventral hatch, there being no pressurized tunnel between the compart-

Tu-16 in service

China

Production of the Xian H-6 continues in China, and current estimates suggest that at least 150 are in service. Most serve with the air force on bombing and missile-carrying duties, but a small number are believed to be used in the anti-shipping role by the navy.

Egypt

Some 25 'Badger-Gs' were supplied to the Egyptian air force, complete with AS-5 'Kelt' missiles, and these saw limited action against Israel, including several 'Kelt' launches. Many aircraft are now unserviceable, and some may have been supplied to Iraq. During the 1970s several Soviet reconnaissance 'Badgers' flew with Egyptian markings.

Indonesia

Indonesia was supplied with two squadrons of 'Badger-Bs' with AS-1 'Kennel' missiles for anti-ship attack. The 22 survivors were placed in storage and are no longer used.

Iraq

Eight 'Badger-Gs' have been supplied to Iraq, and these may have been augmented by some aircraft from Egypt. Tu-16s have seen limited action against Iran, with alleged 'Kelt' launches.

USSR

Over 800 'Badgers' are believed still to be in service with both navy and air force, forming the backbone of the attack, reconnaissance and electronic warfare force.

V-VS (air force)

Some 285 Tu-16s are employed for bombing ('Badger-A and -B') and missile attack ('Badger-G and -G (Modified)'), the latter carrying AS-5 or AS-6 missiles. 'Badgers' have been employed on the bombing campaign against guerrillas in Afghanistan. Support forces include 20 'Badger-As' converted for tanking duties, 15 strategic reconnaissance aircraft (including the dedicated Sigint platform 'Badger-K') and 90 'Badger-H and -J' electronic warfare aircraft.

AV-MF (navy)

Serving alongside the more capable Tu-22 and Tu-26, around 240 Tu-16s are employed on anti-shipping duties. Most 'Badger-Bs' and -Gs' have been updated to 'Badger-G (Modified)' standard with AS-6 capability, matched by the 'Badger-C' which is also in large-scale service. Some 75 tankers serve this large fleet, and various Photint/Sigint/ECM platforms ('Badger-C, -E and -F' etc) account for a further 80 airframes.

China's long-range bombing assets rest on the Xian H-6, which is similar to the 'Badger-A' with only minor differences. The later H-6 IV is a missile carrier, with refinements to the nose radome, intakes and avionics.

Xian H-6 of the Chinese air force wearing anti-flash white and low-visibility insignia, and carrying the C-601 missile.

Egyptian Tu-16 'Badger-G' seen carrying the AS-5 'Kelt' missile.

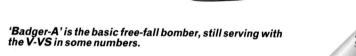

'Badger-B' with AS-1 'Kipper' as it appeared with the Indonesian air force.

'Badger-A' is the basic free-fall bomber, still serving with the V-VS in some numbers.

'Badger-G Modified' of the AV-MF, complete with AS-6 'Kingfish' missile.

Tu-16 variants

'Badger-A': original free-fall bomber version; normal conventional bombload is 9000 kg (19,842 lb) and normal fuel capacity 44900 litres (9,877 Imp gal)

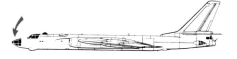

'Badger-A variant': bomber converted as inflight-refuelling tanker with weapons bay revised for one or three fuel tanks, and refuelling hose unreeled from right wingtip, exiting via Day-Glo red/white striped rigid pipe; hose is picked up by a reception socket on the left wingtip of the receiver, the two aircraft thereafter flying together with the hose looped between them

'Badger-A variant': a different form of tanker conversion uses a British-style hose drum unit carrying a hose of larger diameter, with a large drogue end. This is compatible with the M-4, Tu-22, Tu-22M/26, Tu-95, Tu-126 and Tu-142.

Xian H-6: very similar to 'Badger-A', this aircraft is in production at Xian in the People's Republic of China; it has different avionics, including a large drum-type chin radar, no fixed gun, and an anti-nuclear white overall paint scheme; the **H-6 IV** is the subvariant optimized for the anti-ship role with C601 missiles

'Badger-B': equipped to launch from underwing pylons and (initial part of trajectory) guide two AS-1 'Kennel' cruise missiles; large fully retractable guidance radar bin under centre fuselage; missiles removed, but aircraft continue in aviation armies as a free-fall bomber

'Badger-C': anti-ship version, with no internal weapon bay but large recess and special attachments and umbilical connectors for single large AS-2 'Kipper' turbojet-powered supersonic cruise missile on centreline; no glazed nose, nav/bombardier station or nose gun, but giant 'Puff Ball' nose radar; first seen 1961 and still in service with AV-MF Northern, Black Sea, Baltic and Pacific Fleets

'Badger-C (Modified)': similar to 'Badger-C' but converted to launch highly supersonic AS-6 'Kingfish' cruise missiles from two wing pylons; AS-2 capability retained

'Badger-D': Elint version; giant nose radar resembling that of 'Badger-C', enlarged chin radar and three passive receiver antenna blisters along underside (one is retractable), with receiver equipment inside weapons bay; formerly flown with Egyptian markings, now used only by AV-MF

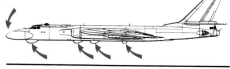

'Badger-E': multi-sensor photographic/Elint conversion of 'Badger-A', with bomb bay occupied by camera pallet and two additional passive receiver radomes under fuselage, that at the rear being larger

'Badger-F': EW platform basically similar to 'Badger-E' but w... deep wing pylons carrying unidentified avionics pods (various interpreted as passive Elint receivers 'seeing' to front and rea also as communications links for telemetry and guidance of c missiles launched from friendly surface platforms and possibl aircraft)

'Badger-G': equipped to launch (and initially to guide) two A 'Kelt' rocket-powered cruise missiles carried on underwing py whilst retaining free-fall bombing capability; most serve in ant role with AV-MF but several supplied to Iraq where the missile have been used in the war against Iran

'Badger-G (Modified)': major rebuild for launching AS-6 'Kingfish' long-range highly supersonic cruise missiles from tw wing pylons; chin radar replaced by giant target acquisition an initial guidance radar under the belly; unknown 'inverted-T' de on tip of nose, thought to be associated with stabilizing aircraf exact attitude for missile launch; in service with AV-MF Black S Northern and Pacific Fleets

During the late 1960s and early 1970s, several Soviet aircraft flew with Egyptian markings, including this 'Badger-F' Elint platform.

Seen in its typical operational environment, this Tu-16 turns away from its RAF pursuer. The fuselage bulges and pods on the wing pylons identify it as a 'Badger-F', used for cataloguing NATO defences.

Tupolev Tu-16 'Badger' cutaway drawing key

1 Radome, 'Badger-C' & 'D'
2 Weapons ranging and search radar scanner
3 Radar navigator/bombardier's seat
4 Windscreen wipers
5 Pitot head
6 Windscreen panels
7 Cockpit eyebrow windows
8 Instrument panel shroud
9 Navigation radome
10 Pilot's seat
11 Co-pilot's seat
12 Cockpit roof escape hatches
13 Glazed nose section, all variants except 'C' & 'D'
14 Optically flat sighting window
15 Fixed forward firing NR-23, 23-mm cannon on starboard side only
16 Navigator/bombardier's seat
17 Navigation radome
18 'Towel-rail' aerial
19 Astrodome observation hatch
20 Forward gunner's swivelling seat
21 Cabin side window panels
22 Ventral entry/exit hatch
23 Extending boarding ladder
24 Retractable landing/taxiing lamps, port and starboard
25 Nose landing gear leg strut
26 Twin nosewheels, aft retracting
27 Nosewheel doors
28 Nose landing gear hydraulic jack
29 Electronics equipment racks, port and starboard
30 HF blade antenna
31 Remotely controlled dorsal gun turret
32 Twin NR-23, 23-mm cannon

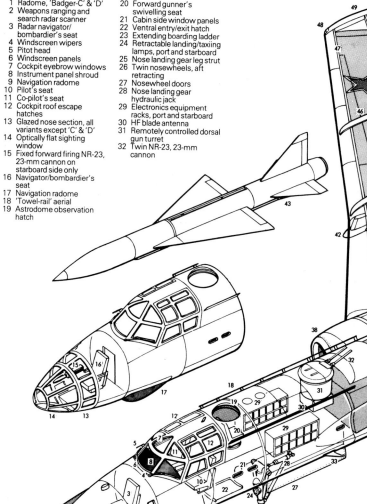

Tupolev Tu-16 'Badger'

'Badger-J': dedicated high-power ECM jammer, with large flat-plate passive receiver antennas projecting outboard of square-cut wingtips, with additional wingtip pods housing front/rear-facing spiral helix antennas, the whole covering all known or expected hostile emitter wavelengths; computer power management supplying large active jammer installation in former weapon bay, with its own separate cooling system, emitting to front and/or rear via antenna groups inside the linear canoe radome along centreline

'Badger-K': Elint version with two teardrop radomes inside and forward of former weapon bay, with four small pods on struts along centreline ahead of rear radome; nose resembles that of 'Badger-A'

'Badger-L': probable designation of new AV-MF variant seen in 1986, painted white; nose glazed and fixed gun retained, but tip of nose carries forward-facing thimble radome; chin radar replaced by different type with large rotary strip antenna inside flat dish radome; 'Standard of excellence' insignia, first time on AV-MF aircraft; some have new (VHF?) blade antenna above cockpit

...ger-H': stand-off (or possibly escort) ECM platform, equipped ...wide-waveband electronic jammers, with teardrop radomes ...d of and behind original weapon bay; the latter bay is occupied ...me 9000 kg (19,842 lb) of chaff, automatically sized to match ...eived hostile emitter threats, and cut to length before being ...ensed via aft-facing chutes (each for a particular size of chaff); ... access hatch aft of weapon bay; two blade antennas aft of ...pon bay; retains original bomber nose and chin radar

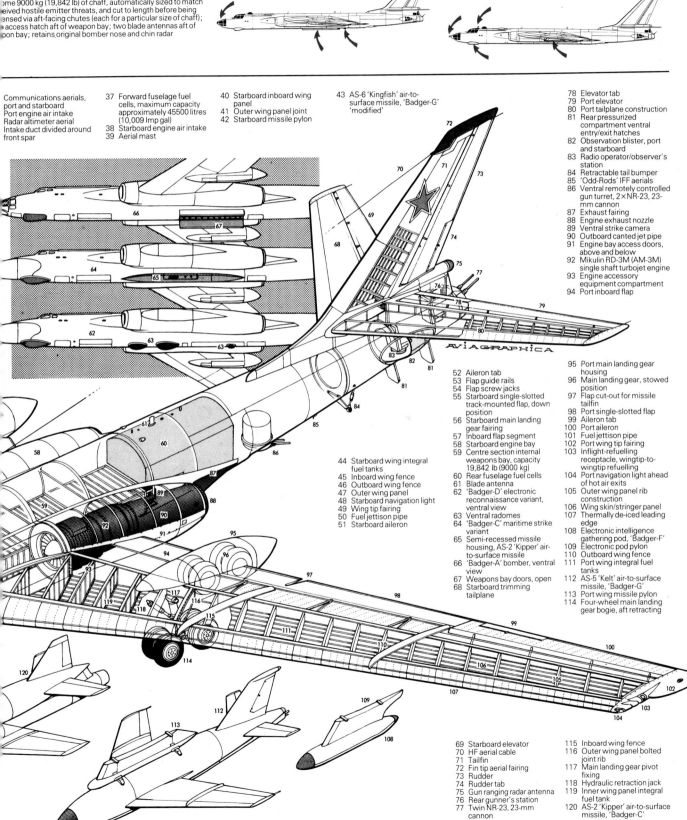

1 Communications aerials, port and starboard
2 Port engine air intake
3 Radar altimeter aerial
4 Intake duct divided around front spar

37 Forward fuselage fuel cells, maximum capacity approximately 45500 litres (10,009 Imp gal)
38 Starboard engine air intake
39 Aerial mast
40 Starboard inboard wing panel
41 Outer wing panel joint
42 Starboard missile pylon
43 AS-6 'Kingfish' air-to-surface missile, 'Badger-G' 'modified'

44 Starboard wing integral fuel tanks
45 Inboard wing fence
46 Outboard wing fence
47 Outer wing panel
48 Starboard navigation light
49 Wing tip fairing
50 Fuel jettison pipe
51 Starboard aileron

52 Aileron tab
53 Flap guide rails
54 Flap screw jacks
55 Starboard single-slotted track-mounted flap, down position
56 Starboard main landing gear fairing
57 Inboard flap segment
58 Starboard engine bay
59 Centre section internal weapons bay, capacity 19,842 lb (9000 kg)
60 Rear fuselage fuel cells
61 Blade antenna
62 'Badger-D' electronic reconnaissance variant, ventral view
63 Ventral radomes
64 'Badger-C' maritime strike variant
65 Semi-recessed missile housing, AS-2 'Kipper' air-to-surface missile
66 'Badger-A' bomber, ventral view
67 Weapons bay doors, open
68 Starboard trimming tailplane

69 Starboard elevator
70 HF aerial cable
71 Tailfin
72 Fin tip aerial fairing
73 Rudder
74 Rudder tab
75 Gun ranging radar antenna
76 Rear gunner's station
77 Twin NR-23, 23-mm cannon

78 Elevator tab
79 Port elevator
80 Port tailplane construction
81 Rear pressurized compartment ventral entry/exit hatches
82 Observation blister, port and starboard
83 Radio operator/observer's station
84 Retractable tail bumper
85 'Odd-Rods' IFF aerials
86 Ventral remotely controlled gun turret, 2×NR-23, 23-mm cannon
87 Exhaust fairing
88 Engine exhaust nozzle
89 Ventral strike camera
90 Outboard canted jet pipe
91 Engine bay access doors, above and below
92 Mikulin RD-3M (AM-3M) single shaft turbojet engine
93 Engine accessory equipment compartment
94 Port inboard flap

95 Port main landing gear housing
96 Main landing gear, stowed position
97 Flap cut-out for missile tailfin
98 Port single-slotted flap
99 Aileron tab
100 Port aileron
101 Fuel jettison pipe
102 Port wing tip fairing
103 Inflight-refuelling receptacle, wingtip-to-wingtip refuelling
104 Port navigation light ahead of hot air exits
105 Outer wing panel rib construction
106 Wing skin/stringer panel
107 Thermally de-iced leading edge
108 Electronic intelligence gathering pod, 'Badger-F'
109 Electronic pod pylon
110 Outboard wing fence
111 Port wing integral fuel tanks
112 AS-5 'Kelt' air-to-surface missile, 'Badger-G'
113 Port wing missile pylon
114 Four-wheel main landing gear bogie, aft retracting

115 Inboard wing fence
116 Outer wing panel bolted joint rib
117 Main landing gear pivot fixing
118 Hydraulic retraction jack
119 Inner wing panel integral fuel tank
120 AS-2 'Kipper' air-to-surface missile, 'Badger-C'

AVIAGRAPHICA

The TUPOLEV TU-26

Tu-22 and Tu-26: Baltic Bogeys

Of all the Soviet aircraft emerging in recent years, none have caused more consternation to the West than the two giant supersonic Tupolev bombers, the 'Blinder' and its formidable offspring, the 'Backfire'.

Among the wealth of previously unknown aircraft which flew past during the 1961 Aviation Day display in Moscow were no fewer than 10 examples of a giant supersonic bomber, one of them carrying under its fuselage a large stand-off missile. Ever since this family and its successors have posed problems to the West, not least because it seems they were difficult to assess correctly. The original type, given the NATO reporting name 'Blinder', was for a long time said to have a range of 2250 km (1,400 miles). It was thus widely held to be some kind of failure, completely overlooking the fact that the USSR does not buy failures!

The history of this design goes back to the early 1950s when, spurred on by the USAF Convair B-58 programme, Tupolev and Ilyushin vied with each other to build better supersonic bombers. In 1956 a Western delegation was shown the latest prototype, a remarkable machine with bogie landing gears folding into the fuselage, which also housed the engines inside the tail end, fed via giant ducts from inlets near the cockpit. What was not explained was that this, the Tu-98, had already been overtaken by a much bigger and more powerful Tupolev, which probably flew in 1959. Known to the design bureau as the Tu-105, the new bomber was quickly accepted for service as the Tu-22. It was this machine that burst on a shocked world in 1961, NATO giving it the name 'Beauty'. Later, in conformity with the belief such names must never sound praiseworthy, the name was changed to 'Blinder'.

Production during the 1960s totalled about 250. This modest figure becomes more meaningful when it is considered that the Tu-22 was a very big aircraft, 50 per cent longer than the UK's V-bombers and even heavier than the rival B-58 (of which the USAF never had more than 80). The design was noteworthy for the mounting of the twin afterburning turbojets, Koliesov VD-7s of 30,865-lb (14000-kg) thrust each, above the rear fuselage on each side of the fin. This resulted in excellent engine efficiency and left most of the giant circular-section fuselage available for fuel, with further tankage in the wings, which were sharply swept at 45°. In typical Tupolev style the bogie main landing gears retracted backwards into large fairings projecting aft of the trailing edges. The fairings can also house strike cameras and large dispensers for chaff/flare cartridges.

Performance

As in the B-58, the crew comprises three men in tandem. The navigator has a downward-ejecting seat immediately behind the giant main radar, and windows enable him to aim bombs visually. The systems engineer also manages the 23-mm cannon barbette in the tail, with its own radar; he too can eject downwards. The pilot sits on the centreline at the front of a dorsal spine fairing, his seat ejecting upwards. Amidships is the weapon bay, which can be configured for 10 500-kg (1,102-lb) bombs and many other kinds of load.

Most of the Tu-22s went to the VVS (air force) air armies, nearly all being of the 'Blinder-B' type in which the radar is enlarged and the weapon bay modified to carry a recessed cruise missile (NATO designation AS-4 'Kitchen') which can deliver a large nuclear or HE warhead up to 460 km (286 miles) at over Mach 2. It is estimated that 135 of this version are in Soviet service, tasked mainly against NATO navies (not only ships but also their home bases). Libya is thought to have had 24, some of which have made free-fall bombing missions in Chad and Tanzania. Iraq has nine, which have been used sporadically in the war against Iran.

'Blinder-C' is a reconnaissance aircraft believed to serve mainly with the AV-MF (naval aviation), about 20 being operational today. These are packed with reconnaissance and electronic intelligence equipment, and they operate mainly over the Black Sea and Mediterranean from the Ukraine and over the Baltic from Estonia. 'Blinder-D' is a trainer, which apparently retains the existing crew cockpits and

▲ Seen on take-off, this Tu-22 demonstrates the rearward retracting undercarriage, which 'somersaults' as it retracts into the trailing edge fairing. The aircraft is a 'Blinder-C', as evidenced by the six camera ports in the bomb bay and various dielectric panels underneath.

▼ A large number of 'Blinders' are still in Soviet service, yet it is easy to overlook the impact the type could have on a future conflict. This example display the unique arrangement for the giant engines. It is unsusual in not having a refuelling probe fitted.

weapons capability but has an extra instructor cockpit immediately behind and above the standard pilot's position. This is used by the USSR and Libya.

In service the Tu-22 must, like the B-58, have proved costly to operate. The fact that it has served for 20 years, more than twice as long as its USAF rival, shows that it is a valued weapon system fully matured in service, though of course it needs a long and strong runway. When variable-geometry 'swing wings' became all the rage in the early 1960s the Soviet TsAGI organization went into high gear studying the application of the technology both to new and to existing aircraft. The latter included two types which, after prolonged study, led to production of greatly modified swing-wing versions. One was the tactical Sukhoi Su-7; the other was the giant Tu-22.

There is some evidence the Tu-22IG (variable geometry) prototype flew in 1968. This aircraft is believed to have been an existing Tu-22 incorporating new wings with pivoting outer panels having full-span slats, and with the minimum of other changes. What this change accomplished may be guessed by looking at the known figures for the Su-7IG, which in aerodynamic terms was very closely similar: the swing-wing aircraft carried twice the bombload over a combat radius 30 per cent greater using runways only half as long!

In July 1970 a US satellite photographed the prototype of a new swing-wing bomber outside the Kazan factory where the Tu-22s had been made, and it was given the NATO name 'Backfire'. Eventually an estimated 12 pre-production aircraft were tested. US intelligence states that 'one squadron' of similar aircraft entered service with the V-VS. In fact the basic service unit is the regiment, larger than a Western squadron, and in any case no firm information has been published on whether this initial version was put into limited production beyond the dozen or so examples. In any case 'Backfire-A', as the type is called, differed from the Tu-22 in having engines inside the fuselage, fed through giant ducts from side inlets midway between the wing

and cockpit. How far the rest of the aircraft resembled the Tu-22 is unknown publicly, but in the SALT 2 talks the 'Backfire' was quoted by Soviet negotiators as the Tu-22M, showing the kinship.

It has been suggested in the West that the main-gear fairings 'caused excessive drag', but this is probably just as unfounded as the assertion that the swing-wing 'Backfire' was needed because the Tu-22 failed to fulfil 'the long-range strategic bombing role for which it has been intended'. In fact the flight performance of the Tu-22 was known in the fullest detail long before any commitment to production, and the aircraft in service have always done all that was expected of them. It is only sensible to keep on introducing improvements, and in fact the decision had been taken as early as 1970 to develop the swing-wing aircraft further.

Development

The obvious difference, spotted in satellite imagery in 1973, is that the landing-gear fairings are absent. Another change is that the outer wings have increased span. The fuselage is also redesigned with an oval section, the pressurized cabin accommodating a crew of four seated two-by-two all with upward-ejecting seats. There are many other changes including a new weapon bay, provision for two wing pylons and a row of stores attachments under the engine inlet ducts. The tail bar-

▲ Libya is one of two export nations for the Tu-22, the other being Iraq. These two are seen in 1977 during their delivery flight, with old-style national insignia. Libyan 'Blinders' have seen action against Chad and Tanzania on free-fall bombing missions.

▼ A Tu-26 'Backfire-B' intercepted over the Baltic. This example is fitted with weapon racks under the inlet duct, which may be used for decoy missiles and other aids for defence penetration. Several types of tail-warning radar fairing have been noted.

bette has twin guns, and a totally new electronic warfare suite is installed. The new main landing gears pivot inwards, the bogies lying in the bottom of each side of the fuselage under the wing. There are various other changes, including redesign of the tips of both the wings and tailplanes.

At a rough guess, compared with the Tu-22 the redesigned aircraft (called 'Backfire-B' by NATO, and believed to have the service designation Tu-26) has double the wing lift at low speeds and a cruising aerodynamic efficiency 35 per cent greater, in each case with wings at minimum sweep 20°. The pilot can select any sweep angle to a maximum of 65°, adopted only for brief dashes at Mach numbers which at high altitude can reach an estimated 1.92. Compared with the Tu-22 the unrefuelled combat radius is almost doubled, from 3100 km (1,925 miles) to at least 5500 km (3,420 miles).

At the same time, the range of missions

and loads has been vastly increased. In the conventional bombing role 'Backfire-B' can carry a typical load of 12000 kg (26,455 lb), including almost every large store in the inventory of the V-VS and AV-MF. Both the long-established types of supersonic cruise missile can be carried, as shown in separate warload diagrams, while there are probably many possible ways of loading the fuselage external racks though details have not been made public.

In 1980 the US Department of Defense, which is the source of most new fact (and guesswork) on Soviet weapons, reported a 'Backfire-C'. This is said to have deep engine inlets of wedge type, sloping not in the horizontal but in the vertical plane, as do those of the Mikoyan-Gurevich MiG-25 and MiG-29. This could indicate either a higher dash Mach number or, possibly, a wish to reduce radar cross section. Certainly, the original inlets appear to be bad from the 'stealth' point of view, whereas most of the rest of the aircraft is excellent. At the time these aircraft were designed this was probably not given any more consideration than it was with contemporary Western bombers. Today reducing the observability of all combat aircraft is seen to be a prime requirement. Not much can be done to an existing aircraft beyond the application of special paints which are electrically conductive and have thickness chosen to minimize radar reflectivity. A more fundamental modification involves reskinning in radar-absorbent materials, but ideally this also requires alteration of the underlying structure. All this is probably being progressively introduced to the USSR's 'Backfire' forces.

Production of 'Backfire-B', and possibly the alleged 'Backfire-C' model, has averaged about 30 per year from the Kazan factory for the past 12 years. About 200 are in service with V-VS medium bomber units, while the other 160 or so serve with the AV-MF. The NATO estimate is that two-thirds of the total force are in the Western USSR, tasked against NATO but with the ability to cover targets from the Indian Ocean to North America, while the other one-third is in the Far East operating over

the Sea of Japan and Pacific. It has been suggested that the total force will probably level off at about 400, subsequent production being for attrition only. In passing, it has been hinted that attrition has been extremely low.

In service

As the most formidable large Soviet warplane of its day, 'Backfire' naturally caused alarm in the Pentagon, just as did the Tupolev Tu-95 'Bear' and Myasishchyev M-4 'Bison' 30 years ago. In the same way, it has apparently been difficult for analysts to view these aircraft objectively, there being sustained wild assertions that this was a strategic bomber and missile carrier aimed at the USA. In fact, like the B-58 and earlier Boeing B-47, 'Backfire' is not a strategic aircraft, though with inflight-refuelling it certainly could attack the USA should such a thing be ordered. All the important targets in that country have for the past 25 years been covered by Soviet land- and submarine-launched ballistic missiles, and manned bombers have different things to do.

The obvious thing that strategic missiles cannot hit are ships, because they move about. NATO's warships are thus the primary target for the 'Backfires', and nearly all the examples of these aircraft inter-

▲ The primary weapon for the 'Backfire' and missile-equipped 'Blinder' is the AS-4 'Kitchen', carried under the belly. This 'Backfire-B' is fitted with wing pylons just outboard of the undercarriage fairing for the carriage of two further 'Kitchens'.

▶ The air forces of Norway and Sweden are no strangers to the mighty 'Backfire', these giants often being intercepted around Scandinavia. This Royal Norwegian air force F-16A keeps tabs on a 'Kitchen'-toting 'Backfire-B', serving to illustrate the size of this bomber.

cepted by NATO, Japanese and Swedish fighters (a matter of 180 occasions in the past three years) have belonged to the AV-MF. Several have carried training missiles under the centreline, but no pictures have become available showing loads carried in the other locations. Another feature not photographed but repeatedly reported, and fairly logical, is that the internal weapon bay can house a large multi-sensor reconnaissance pallet. There appear to be three bay configurations. In the free-fall mode the bay carries bombs, mines or other stores, and has normal doors. When carrying a cruise missile the doors are replaced by others shaped to fit round the recessed missile. In the reconnaissance mode the doors are removed, the pallet fitting the available aperture.

American reports have suggested that decoy missiles are being developed to assist such aircraft to penetrate hostile airspace. Again this is logical, because several US companies have specialized in such products for 30 years. There is no reason for such vehicles to be large unless they have to fly a long way after release, and they are likely to be among the loads carried on the external racks.

Speed at low level has been said to be supersonic, but this is doubtful. Wing flexure is high on this aircraft, and especially with a weapon load it is very unlikely that a 'Backfire' at low level would exceed 520 kts (964 km/h; 599 mph). Despite this, 'Backfire' remains a very formidable adversary, in a class absent from Western air forces and navies.

Tu-22 and Tu-26 in service

Iraq

A dozen Tu-22 'Blinder-Bs' were initially supplied to Iraq in 1974, and these have seen some use during the long-running war with Iran on conventional bombing missions, as well as against Kurdish insurgents. Around nine are thought to be still in use, the Iranians claiming at least one aircraft shot down over Tehran in 1981. Known serials include 10, 11, 12 and 22.

Libya

Some 24 Tu-22 aircraft were delivered during the mid-1970s, comprising mostly 'Blinder-B' bombers but also an unspecified number (perhaps two) of 'Blinder-D' trainers. Some of the bombers may also be configured for reconnaissance missions. Libyan aircraft have seen action over Tanzania in support of Uganda and more recently a single aircraft carried out an attack on the French-held airfield at N'Djamena in Chad after simulating the flight path of a civil airliner. Libyan aircraft are likely to often fly with Soviet crew.

USSR

The 'Blinder' and 'Backfire' series is in widespread use with Soviet forces, mostly as air-to-surface missile carriers, although some aircraft are employed on conventional bombing and electronic tasks. Production of the Tu-26 is believed to be about 30 units per year, with an eventual force level of over 400 aircraft envisaged.

Long-range Aviation (Aviatsiya Dal'nevo Deistviya)

The Tu-26 'Backfire-B/C' is the mainstay of this service with over 130 (perhaps as many as 200) in service, carrying either AS-4 missiles or conventional bombs. The AS-15 cruise missile has long been tipped as a replacement for the AS-4 carried by 'Backfires', but no details have yet been released. Reports suggest that up to 70 of these aircraft are based in the Far East, with the rest facing NATO in the West. The small number of 'Backfire-A' development aircraft may still be in service. The Tu-22 in ADD service numbers some 150, of which several are 'Blinder-D' trainers. Approximately 15 'Blinders' have been modified for Sigint/ECM tasks, the rest employed on bombing and missile duties. The Tu-22 is one of the types that has been reported on free-fall bombing missions over Afghanistan.

Naval Aviation (Aviatsiya Voenno-Morskoyo Flota)

The Tu-26 'Backfire-B/C' is the prime anti-ship strike aircraft for the Soviet navy, carrying up to three AS-4 'Kitchen' missiles for striking large and valuable surface targets. Some 120 are in service, mainly based around the Baltic Sea, with 30 based in the Far East. The Tu-22 serves in smaller numbers, with around 35 'Blinder-Bs' used for anti-ship missile and other conventional attacks. The specialist 'Blinder-C' is a maritime reconnaissance and Elint platform which flies exclusively with the AV-MF. Estimates vary as to how many are in service, but 20 seems a likely number.

Tu-22 'Blinder-B' of the Iraqi air force.

Tu-22 'Blinder-B' wearing the colours of the Libyan air force.

Tu-22 'Blinder-C' of the Soviet AV-MF, used for maritime reconnaissance.

Tu-26 'Backfire-B' of the AV-MF, carrying an AS-4 'Kitchen' anti-ship missile.

This maritime strike 'Backfire' shows the tail warning radar and gun turret to good advantage. The huge size of the jet exhausts are readily apparent.

This AV-MF 'Backfire-B' is equipped with the inlet duct weapons rack, which can carry defensive loads as well as free-fall weapons.

Specification: Tupolev Tu-22 'Blinder'
(estimated)

Wings

Span	23.75 m	(77 ft 11 in)
Sweep	approximately 45° on outer panel leading edge	

Fuselage and tail unit

Accommodation	Crew of three in tandem	
Length overall	40.53 m	(132 ft 11.7 in)
Height overall	10.67 m	(35 ft 0 in)

Landing gear

Type	Main units have rearwards retracting four-wheel bogies. Twin-wheel nose unit also retracts rearwards	
Wheelbase	13.73 m	(45 ft 0 in)
Wheel track	8.72 m	(28 ft 7.3 in)

Weights

Maximum take-off	83915 kg	(185,000 lb)

Powerplant

Designation	two Koliesov VD-7	
Type	afterburning turbojets	
Thrust	14,000 kg	(30,865 lb)

Tu-22 'Blinder' recognition features

Sharply-swept, compound taper, high aspect ratio wings

Large engines mounted on each side of tail

Landing gear nacelles project beyond wing trailing edge

Smoothly tapering sharp pointed nose contours

Wide-track landing gear units with nacelles

Tail warning radar and gun turret mounted at base of tail

Hump-backed fuselage

Small canopy causes little break in fuselage lines

Distinctive refuelling probe on top of nose

Large double axle mainwheel bogie

Tu-22 and Tu-26 warload

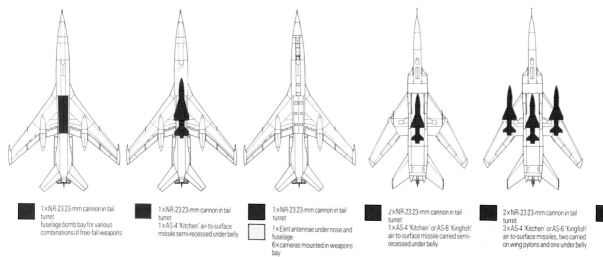

■ 1 × NR-23 23-mm cannon in tail turret	fuselage bomb bay for various combinations of free-fall weapons

■ 1 × NR-23 23-mm cannon in tail turret	1 × AS-4 'Kitchen' air-to-surface missile semi-recessed under belly

■ 1 × NR-23 23-mm cannon in tail turret	? × Elint antennae under nose and fuselage 6 × cameras mounted in weapons bay

■ 2 × NR-23 23-mm cannon in tail turret	1 × AS-4 'Kitchen' or AS-6 'Kingfish' air-to-surface missile carried semi-recessed under belly

■ 2 × NR-23 23-mm cannon in tail turret	3 × AS-4 'Kitchen' or AS-6 'Kingfish' air-to-surface missiles, two carried on wing pylons and one under belly

■ 2 × NR-23 23-mm cannon in tail turret	various combinations of bomb external wing racks, inlet racks internal bomb bay

'Blinder-A' free-fall bombing

'Blinder-A' can carry up to around 10000 kg (22,046 lb) of stores in the fuselage weapons bay. These can be either nuclear or conventional devices. Both the Libyans and Iraqis have used their aircraft on bombing missions, the aircraft believed to be 'Blinder-Bs' with missile capability deleted.

'Blinder-B' missile attack

This configuration is aimed mainly at naval targets, either high-priority surface vessels (such as carriers) or ports. The 'Blinder-B' has bomb bay doors specially modified to accommodate the AS-4 missile which has either a nuclear or conventional warhead. The tail gun is radar-controlled.

'Blinder-C' maritime reconnaissance

These 'Blinders' serve the Soviet navy on long-range reconnaissance patrols, particularly in the Baltic and Black Seas. The mass of dielectric panels indicates that they are equipped for electronic surveillance of Western ships, and may possess active jamming capability.

'Backfire-B' missile attack

The usual configuration seen by NATO interceptors is a single 'Kitchen'. The 'Backfire' has comprehensive ECM and ECCM suites, and development is under way of a decoy missile system to assist penetration by strategic systems. The bomb bay doors are specially modified for missile carriage.

'Backfire-B' short-range missile attack

For maximum effort against naval targets, the 'Backfire' carries three missiles, each with a 1000-kg (2,205-lb) conventional or nuclear warhead, the latter yielding up to 350 kilotons. Maximum range of the missile is some 440 km (270 miles) at high altitude.

'Backfire-B' free-fall bombing

Up to 12000 kg (26,455 lb) of free-fall stores can be carried, including nuclear weapons and naval mines. Aircraft with internal stores have conventional bomb bay doors fitted. A reconnaissance pod can be carried in the bomb bay with cameras, SLAR and IR linescan. Elint and jamming may also exist.

Specification: Tupolev Tu-26 'Backfire-B'

(estimated)

Wings

Span, minimum sweep	34.45 m	(113 ft 0.3 in)
maximum sweep	26.21 m	(86 ft 0 in)
Area	170.0 m²	(1,830 sq ft)
Sweep limits (quarter-chord line)	20° to 65°	

Fuselage and tail unit

Accommodation	pilot and co-pilot, plus two systems operators, all seated on ejector seats
Length overall (with probe extended)	42.50 m (139 ft 5.2 in)
Height overall	10.06 m (33 ft 0 in)

Landing gear

Retractable tricycle landing gear with four-wheel main bogies and twin-wheel nose unit

Weights

Empty	54000 kg	(119,050 lb)
Internal fuel	57000 kg	(125,663 lb)
Maximum take-off	122500 kg	(270,066 lb)

Powerplant

Two afterburning turbofans (probably Kuznetsov NK-144 variants)
Thrust rating, each 20000 kg (44,092) or more

Tupolev Tu-26 'Backfire' recognition features

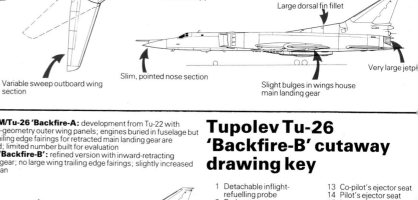

Thick fixed wing centre-section

Large air inlets give rectangular section fuselage

Sharply-swept, low-set tailplane

Large wing fence near wing pivot point

Side-by-side cockpit has full width canopy

Large dorsal fin fillet

Very large jetpipe

Variable sweep outboard wing section

Slim, pointed nose section

Slight bulges in wings house main landing gear

Tu-22/Tu-26 variants

Tu-22 'Blinder-A': initial version with conventional fuselage bomb bay for free-fall weapons
Tu-22 'Blinder-B': missile-carrying version, with bomb bay doors able to take recessed AS-4 'Kitchen' ASM with nuclear or high-explosive warhead; a larger radar and inflight refuelling boom were fitted

Tu-22M/Tu-26 'Backfire-A': development from Tu-22 with variable-geometry outer wing panels; engines buried in fuselage but wing trailing edge fairings for retracted main landing gear are retained; limited number built for evaluation
Tu-26 'Backfire-B': refined version with inward-retracting landing gear; no large wing trailing edge fairings; slightly increased wing span

Tu-22 'Blinder-C': maritime reconnaissance version with six camera windows in bomb bay. Extra dielectric panels on aircraft suggest an electronic reconnaissance capability
Tu-22 'Blinder-D': trainer version with raised second cockpit behind the standard pilot's position

Tu-26 'Backfire-C': refined propulsive system with steeply-raked wedge inlets similar to those on MiG-25; other advances as yet undocumented

Tupolev Tu-26 'Backfire-B' cutaway drawing key

1 Detachable inflight-refuelling probe
2 Radome
3 'Down-Beat' bombing and navigation radar scanner
4 Radar equipment bay
5 Cockpit front pressure bulkhead
6 Pitot head, port and starboard
7 Angle of attack transmitter
8 Rudder pedals
9 Control column
10 Instrument panel shroud
11 Windscreen panels
12 Cockpit roof escape hatches
13 Co-pilot's ejector seat
14 Pilot's ejector seat
15 Instrument consoles
16 Blade aerial
17 Navigator/bombardier and electronics systems officer's ejector seats
18 Rear cockpit side window panel

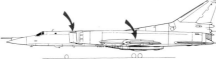

erformance

Tupolev Tu-22 'Blinder'
imum speed
ch 1.4 or
2 knots 1487 km/h; 924 mph at 40,025 ft (12200 m)
ice ceiling 60,040 ft (18300 m)
unrefuelled
ombat radius 3100 km (1,926 miles)

olev Tu-26 'Backfire-B'
imum speed at
a level Mach 0.9 595 kts; 1102 km/h (685 mph)
imum speed at high
tude Mach 1.92 1100 kts; 2039 km/h (1,267 mph)
ice ceiling at least 60,000 ft (18290 m)
imum unrefuelled
ombat radius 5470 m (3,399 miles)
y range 14000 km (8,699 miles)

Weapon load

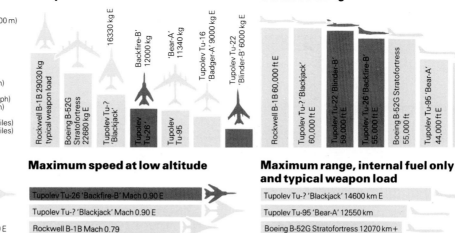

Service ceiling

aximum speed at optimum gh altitude

polev Tu-? 'Blackjack' Mach 2.10 E
polev Tu-26 'Backfire-B' Mach 1.92 E
polev Tu-22 'Blinder-B' Mach 1.50 E
ckwell B-1B Mach 1.25
polev Tu-16 'Badger-A' Mach 0.93
eing B-52G Stratofortress Mach 0.90
polev Tu-95 'Bear-A' Mach 0.89

Maximum speed at low altitude

Tupolev Tu-26 'Backfire-B' Mach 0.90 E
Tupolev Tu-? 'Blackjack' Mach 0.90 E
Rockwell B-1B Mach 0.79
Boeing B-52G Stratofortress Mach 0.77
Tupolev Tu-22 'Blinder-B' Mach 0.75 E
Tupolev Tu-16 'Badger-A' Mach 0.75 E
Tupolev Tu-95 'Bear-A' Mach 0.75 E

Maximum range, internal fuel only and typical weapon load

Tupolev Tu-? 'Blackjack' 14600 km E
Tupolev Tu-95 'Bear-A' 12550 km
Boeing B-52G Stratofortress 12070 km+
Rockwell B-1B 12000 km
Tupolev Tu-22 'Blinder-B' 5500 km E
Tupolev Tu-26 'Backfire-B' 5470 km E
Tupolev Tu-16 'Badger-A' 4800 km E

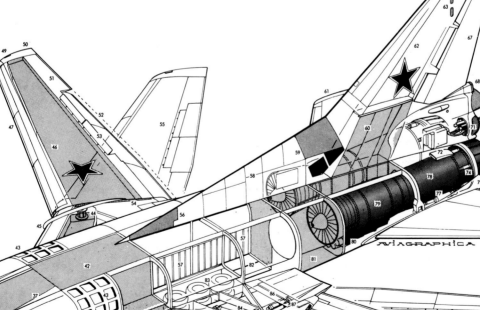

The SAAB VIGGEN A.J.37

Viggen: Swedish Thunderbolt

With a deafening roar an aircraft climbs above the trees and hurtles skywards. The mighty Saab Viggen goes to work again, providing a truly awesome capability to Swedish air power through its operation in several key military roles.

A unique combination of strongly-armed neutrality and military self-sufficiency has resulted in Sweden producing a remarkable series of warplanes at least equal to the combat equipment of the major alliances, namely NATO and the Warsaw Pact. This high degree of sophistication has been necessary in order to meet the prime requirement of national defensive strategy, that is to say, deterring the superpowers from allowing any conflict between them to overspill onto Swedish territory. As a buffer state between two powerful, ideologically-opposed power blocs, Sweden is faced with an immense defensive task.

Naturally, it has been the Swedish Aeroplane Company (Svenska Aeroplan Aktiebolag, or Saab) which has been responsible for developing aircraft to meet the exacting demands of the Svenska Flygvapen, (Swedish air force). In the jet era, Saab produced the J 29 Tunnan, J 32 Lansen and J 35 Draken before turning its attention to the multi-role Viggen. Apart from the obvious requirement of being able to operate in a northern European environment, sometimes within the Arctic Circle, these fighters have additionally been deployed to the Swedish network of dispersal airfields. Often centred on what seems to be no more than a straight stretch of road,

these emergency strips have set the aircraft designers the tough problem of combining high combat speeds and weapons loads with STOL performance.

With few aircraft produced anywhere in the world have such dissimilar characteristics been so successfully combined as in the Viggen. Like its immediate predecessor, the Draken, it was an aircraft of unusual configuration when first revealed, the large foreplanes (canards) being complemented by a wing of highly distinctive planform. Arguably, this was as intended, for first thoughts on a Draken replacement were made as long ago as May 1952, three years before the Draken's first flight, using the metaphorical 'clean sheet of paper'. Firm proposals began to emerge in the late 1950s, and after some hesitation and one false start, the programme was set in motion by a Flygvapen order of February 1961.

Development

In the methodical Swedish approach to defence, the aircraft is but one part of a complete weapon system, involving parallel development of armament and support equipment. System 37 was the number of the new project, and the prime component was Flygplan 37 (Aircraft 37). This received the popular name, Viggen

▼ *Roaring off after a commendably short take-off run, this brace of AJ 37s make full use of the powerful RM8A powerplant in an airframe that allows excellent handling characteristics at both high and low speeds.*

▲ *Over a period of nearly three decades, the Saab 37 Viggen concept has developed and matured until it is now a truly multi-role aircraft. The Swedish air force relies almost exclusively on the Viggen for front-line duties, and will continue to use the various models for many years to come.*

(loosely translated as 'Thunderbolt') and emerged as a single-seat machine with the design flexibility necessary for adaptation to no less than four combat roles, plus room for a second seat in the conversion-trainer model. The most recent addition to this family, an air superiority fighter designated JA 37, represents such a significant advance on the first generation of Viggens that it warrants mention at another time, except to record that the 100th of 149 on order was delivered in August 1985.

Despite the appearance of being heavily-built, the Viggen has an airframe remarkably light for its strength (it is stressed for up to 12g) thanks to imaginative use of honeycomb panels and metal bonding. The fuselage is of all-metal con-

struction, employing light forgings and heat-resistant plastics bonding, plus titanium in areas requiring particular strength, such as the engine firewall. Wings use honeycomb structures for control surfaces, comprising trailing-edge flaps to the delta foreplane and elevons on the main wing which may be operated in unison or differentially. The fin is built on similar lines, except for the unusual addition of a hinge at the base, so that it can be folded.

Great effort has been expended on ensuring ease of servicing for the Viggen, so that maintenance times are reduced and a high sortie rate can be sustained during hostilities. Important considerations in this respect are that half Flygvapen personnel are conscripts who have only 11 months to learn their duties, and 80 per cent of wartime personnel (men and women) will be drawn form the reserves. For three reasons, there is easy ground-level access to many internal components, including the radar, and provision for the rear fuselage to be removed entirely for a rapid engine change.

Performance

Whilst the canard configuration provides high lift for take-off from confined spaces, short landing is made possible in part by the landing gear design. Built by Motala Verkstad, this can accommodate high rates of sink (up to 5 m/16.4 ft per second) associated with the deliberately heavy, no-flare landing procedure employed, and is fitted with a Dunlop anti-skid system. The main oleos are shortened during retraction so that they occupy less room, and carry two wheels in tandem. Pressurized to 14.8 bars (215 lb/sq in), the wheels are arranged in this manner to fit into the thin wing.

However, it is the Viggen's engine which is the key component in provision of its impressive performance. The designation Volvo Flygmotor RM8A (Reaktionmotor, or jet engine, 8A) fails to reveal the fact

that the Viggen is powered by a licence-built version of the Pratt & Whitney JT8D, whose other applications include the Boeing 727 and McDonnell Douglas DC-9. Whilst basically a civilian engine, the RM8 has been extensively modified for Swedish military use by the addition of afterburners and thrust-reversers designed and built in Sweden. A switch included in the landing gear mechanism activates the thrust reverser doors as soon as the nosewheel touches the runway, and exhaust is deflected forwards through three annular slots in the rear fuselage. In normal flight the slots are kept open to reduce drag, but when closed, they produce a supersonic nozzle for the exhaust gases during high-speed flight.

Swedish defensive strategy does not require aircraft to have inflight refuelling provision, so the Viggen relies on internal tankage. The tanks are located one in each wing and on each side of the fuselage, plus single fitments behind the pilot and above the engine. The turbofan design of the RM8 allows for efficient use of fuel in the cruise, whilst the powerful afterburner is cut-in for take-off, climb and combat acceleration. Use must be undertaken with care, for the entire fuel capacity is sufficient for only seven minutes' flight at full throttle. Great emphasis was placed during the Viggen's design period on maximum automa-

▲ *Towed from dispersal before flying commences, this Viggen displays the highly distinctive camouflage worn by the majority of Viggens in operational use. The tandem-wheel main landing gear units are built to wishstand a sink rate of 5 m (16.4 ft) per second on landing.*

▼ *The basic Viggen platform has proved highly adaptable, with each model having a primary and secondary mission capability. In addition, a wide range of ordnance can be carried on up to nine external hardpoints, this AJ 37 carrying four rocket packs and a fuel drop tank.*

tion of systems to ease the pilot's workload and to allow him to concentrate on the most vital aspects of the mission. This is particularly true in the case of the radar, which is integrated to a considerable extent with the navigation, display and digital computer-based data processing subsystems. Produced by Swedish firm L.M. Ericsson, the PS-37/A radar is a multi-mode, I/J-band, monopulse unit in which long range is achieved through high output power. Comprising 13 replaceable modules, almost all solid-state, the PS-37/A is claimed to be highly resistant to natural and enemy-generated interference. Its facilities include search, target acquisition, air-target ranging, surface-target ranging, obstacle warning, fixed point

radar navigation and terrain mapping. The addition of one further module provides terrain-following capability, but the Flygvappen has not confirmed that aircraft in service have received this modfication.

Radar data is supplied to the pilot's head-up and head-down displays, along with information from other systems essential to flight. The Marconi HUD also provides the pilot with steering cues as an aid to navigation; acts as an aid for accurate alignment of short landings in conjunction with the onboard microwave scanning beam blind landing system; and is an optical weapon sight. Complementing the usual cockpit instrumentation is the head-down screen, upon which may be shown the radar picture and the important flight parameters. The two displays can be merged so that the pilot does not have to refer elsewhere when scanning his radar screen. Remaining equipment includes a Philips air-data computer linked to a digital fire-control system; a radar altimeter; a Decca 72 Doppler; and a comprehensive ESM/radar warning system. The cockpit is pressurized and air-conditioned.

Four different models of first-generation Viggen serve the Flygvapen, the first and most numerous being the AJ 37. Signifying a primary attack (A) role with secondary fighter (Jagt) capability, the AJ 37 is cleared to carry up to 7000 kg (15,432 lb) of ordnance or fuel on its three fuselage and four wing attachment positions. Missiles form the primary AJ 37 armament, and were originally the Saab Rb 04E anti-ship weapon and the Saab Rb 05. The latter is essentially a general-purpose air-to-surface missile, but it is also claimed to have air-to-air capability in certain, undisclosed circumstances. Up to three Rb 04s can be carried (one under each wing and one on the centreline) but two is the more normal fit.

Recently, the TV-guided Hughes AGM-65A/B Maverick ASM (designated Rb 75) has been adapted to the Viggen, whilst in 1982, development was authorized of the Saab-Bofors RBS 15F anti-ship missile for eventual application to the aircraft. Performing in its secondary, interceptor role, the AJ 37 may be equipped with Rb 24 and Rb 28 versions of the American AIM-9 Sidewinder and AIM-4 Genie AAMs. Other armament includes free-fall bombs, four pods each with six 135-mm (5.3-in) rockets, and a British Aden 30-mm cannon pod.

Two reconnaissance (Spaning) Viggens have been produced, of which the SH 37 is for radar surveillance via a modified version of the PS-37. Fuselage shoulder pylons carry a long-range camera to starboard and (normally) a Red Baron infrared linescan and night photography pod to port. More clearly a photographic aircraft, the SF 37 Viggen has nose radar deleted in favour of high- and low-altitude and infrared cameras, although it still retains provision for the shoulder position pods of its sister aircraft.

Finally, pilot conversion to the Viggen is via the two-seat Sk 37 (Skol, or school), identified by its taller fin and larger ventral fin as well as the additional cockpit. Fitting of the new rear seat for the instructor has decreased fuel capacity, so the Sk 37 flies with the centreline drop-tank which is now invariably seen on all models of Viggen.

Seven prototypes were involved in the first-generation Viggen programme, these (of which the last was a trainer) making their maiden flights from 8 February 1967 onwards. Production deliveries of AJ 37s began in June 1971, and 110 of this model were built. First to equip was No. 7 'Skaraborgs' Wing (Skaraborgs Flygflottilj F7) at Satenas, which comprises two attack squadrons (1 and 2 Attackflygdivisionen). One AJ 37 was converted to an SH 37, and this flew on 10 December 1973, 26 production aircraft following from June 1975 onwards. There were also 26 SF 37s, the first flying on 21 May 1973; and 18 production Sk 37s, delivered from June 1972, although the prototype had flown two years before, on 2 June 1970. Series manufacture of these four types thus totalled 180, the last of which (an SF 37) was completed on 1 February 1980, but some prototypes appear to have been 'productionized' for service, and a few SH 37s have been given SF 37 camera noses.

Losses of the initial Viggen series are

▲ Dedicated to the overland reconnaissance role, the SF 37 model has a revised nose profile to accommodate a suite of cameras, sensors and registration equipment. This model has a 24-hour, high- or low-altitude reconnaissance capability with 180° photograpic coverage.

▼ The unique 'double delta' configuration of the Viggen features flapped foreplanes ahead of a very large main wing. Acting in combination, this configuration produces highly effective STOL characteristics which allow operations from extremely short strips.

approaching 30, despite which the aircraft is highly respected by both Swedish pilots and their foreign guests. Powerful and manoeuvrable, with a well-appointed cockpit which is positively spacious compared with that of some fighters, the attack and reconnaissance Viggen is destined to be retained in the Flygvapen front line until the closing years of the century. Even now, an unusual new duty is being considered for some in the form of an airborne early-warning pod which will relay its information to ground stations for interpretation. A decision on the programme is expected in 1987 for possible deployment three years later. When the AJ, SF and SH 37 Viggens are at last withdrawn, their replacement, will be the JAS 39 Gripen, now in its development phase.

Viggen in service units and example aircraft

Västgöta Flygflottilj F6

Converted: 1976
Base: Karlsborg
Task: attack

Squadrons: 1 Attackflygdivisionen (AJ 37); 2 Attackflygdivisionen (AJ 37)
Aircraft: 37022 '22', 37085 '43', 37088 '46', 37104 '17', 37107 '20'

Refuelling and last-minute checks for an F6 AJ37 Viggen, with the pilot ready to taxi out for another sortie.

Skaraborgs Flygflottilj F7

Converted: 1971
Base: Satenas
Task: attack

Squadrons: 1 Attackflygdivisionen (AJ 37); 2 Attackflygdivisionen (AJ 37)
Aircraft: 37029 '29', 37059 '59', 37071 '02', 37083 '05'

This F7 AJ37 Viggen sits at Satenas airfield before being hangared.

Bravala Flygflottilj F13

Converted: 1976
Base: Bravalla
Task: surveillance/reconnaissance
Squadron: 1 Spaningsflygdivisionen (SF/SH 37)
Aircraft: (SH 37) 37901 '01', 37914 '27'; (SF 37) 37952 '04', 37961 '12', 37962 '14'

Externally similar to the AJ37, the SH37 maritime surveillance model can carry various external pods. This F13 SH37 is distinguished by the fin-mounted unit crest and the white fin tip.

Halsinge Flygflottilj F15

Converted: 1975
Base: Soderhamn
Task: attack (and OCU)
Squadrons: 1 Attackflygdivisionen (AJ 37); 2 Attackflygdivisionen (AJ 37/Sk 37)
Aircraft: (AJ 37) 37007 '07', 37078 '23', 37082 '27'; (Sk 37) 37801 '69', 37815 '54'

The four-colour upper surface camouflage is very effective when the aircraft is operating at low altitude. High-visibility codes are worn, as on this AJ37 of F15 at Soderhamn.

Blekinge Flygflottilj F17

Converted: 1977
Base: Ronneby
Task: surveillance/reconnaissance
Squadrons: 2 Spaningsflygdivisionen (SF/SH 37)
Aircraft: (SH 37) 37908 '69', 37913 '59', 37925 '53'; (SF 37) 37954 '68', 37972 '56'

Set for a joint take-off from Ronneby, an SF37 and SH37 illustrate the different nose profiles, with the SF37 containing a variety of reconnaissance equipment in the revised nose. No radar is carried in this model, hence the slender contours.

The Sk37 dual-control trainer is easily identified by the raised rear cockpit occupied by the instructor. Note the periscopes on the canopy framing.

Norrbottens Flygflottilj F21

Converted: 1979
Base: Lulea-Kallax
Task: surveillance/reconnaissance
Squadrons: 1 Spaningsflygdivisionen (SF/SH 37)
Aircraft: none identified

Like F17, the aircraft of F21 are split between the SF37 and SH37 reconnaissance models, both operating within one division. This is one of the SF37 overland reconnaissance aircraft.

Specification: Saab AJ 37 Viggen

Wings
Span	10.60 m	(34 ft 9.3in)
Area	46.00 m²	(495.16 sq ft)

Fuselage and canard unit
Accommodation	pilot only in Saab ejector seat	
Length overall	16.30 m	(53 ft 5.7 in)
Height overall	5.80 m	(19 ft 0.3 in)
Foreplane span	5.45 m	(17 ft 10.6 in)

Landing gear
Tricycle retractable landing gear with twin-wheel nose and main units
Wheelbase	5.60 m	(18 ft 4.5 in)
Wheel track	4.76 m	(15 ft 7.4 in)

Weights
Empty	not disclosed	
Maximum take-off	20500 kg	(45,195 lb)
Maximum external load	6000 kg	(13,227 lb)
Internal fuel load	not disclosed	

Powerplant
One Volvo Flygmotor RM8A (Pratt & Whitney JT8D-22) reheated turbofan
Static thrust	11800 kg	(26,015 lb)

Viggen recognition features

Viggen variants

AJ 37 Viggen: all-weather attack model with secondary interception capability; 110 built

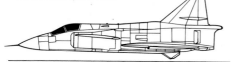

JA 37 Viggen: second-generation interceptor; 149 in production
SF 37 Viggen: armed photographic reconnaissance model of AJ 37 with camera nose; 26 built

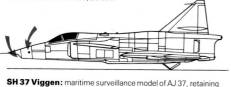

SH 37 Viggen: maritime surveillance model of AJ 37, retaining radar; 26 built
Sk 37 Viggen: dual-control trainer variant of AJ 37 with same length, but taller fin; 18 built

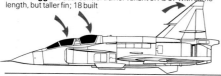

Saab 37X: designation for proposed export version in late 1960s
Saab 37E: 'Eurofighter' version of JA 37, offered to Belgium, Denmark, Netherlands and Norway, but rejected in favour of F-16 Fighting Falcon
A 20: attack-optimized JA 37 variant, offered to Sweden; not adopted

These views of the SK 37 cockpits (front cockpit at right, rear below) illustrate the uncluttered layout. The engine instruments are visible in the front cockpit to the pilot's right, while the control column has several control functions grouped together. Note the rear-view mirrors on the rear canopy framing.

Saab AJ 37 Viggen cutaway drawing key

1 Pitot tube
2 Radome
3 Radar scanner
4 LM Ericsson PS-37/A attack radar equipment
5 Angle of attack transmitter
6 Radome withdrawal rails
7 Front pressure bulkhead
8 Flush aerial
9 Forward avionics equipment bay
10 Nose undercarriage wheel bay
11 Nosewheel doors
12 Cockpit floor level
13 Rudder pedals
14 Control column
15 Instrument panel
16 Instrument panel shroud
17 Frameless curved windscreen panel
18 Head-up display
19 Canopy arch
20 Cockpit canopy cover
21 Canopy, open position
22 Pilot's rear view mirrors
23 Starboard air intake
24 Seat arming lever
25 Ejection seat headrest
26 Saab 'zero-zero', rocket-powered ejection seat
27 Safety harness
28 Canopy external latch
29 Radar hand controller
30 Engine throttle lever
31 Port side console panel
32 Nose undercarriage pivot fixing
33 Underfloor control runs
34 Landing/taxiing lamp

35 Torque scissor links
36 Twin nosewheels, forward retracting
37 Shock absorber leg strut
38 Hydraulic steering jack
39 Port air intake
40 Intake lip aerodynamic notch
41 Boundary layer splitter plate
42 Cockpit rear pressure bulkhead
43 Ejection seat launch rails
44 Canopy hinge point
45 Forward fuselage bag-type fuel tank
46 Boundary layer spill duct
47 Intake duct framing
48 Port canard foreplane
49 Centre fuselage avionics equipment bay
50 Electro-luminescent formation lighting strip
51 Ventral access hatch
52 Jettisonable external fuel tank
53 Port lateral stores pylon, fixed
54 Temperature probe
55 Air system ground connection
56 Oxygen servicing point
57 Foreplane spar attachment joint
58 Spar attachment main frame
59 Dorsal avionics equipment bay
60 Starboard canard foreplane rib construction

61 Foreplane leading edge
62 SK 37 Viggen, two-seat tandem trainer variant
63 Student pilot's cockpit
64 Instructor's raised cockpit
65 Forward vision periscopes
66 Enlarged area fin
67 Starboard canard flap
68 Cooling air spill ducts
69 SSR transponder aerial
70 Anti-collision light
71 Air conditioning plant
72 Heat exchanger air exhaust
73 Air system heat exchanger, port and starboard
74 Oxygen bottle
75 Fuselage lateral fuel tank
76 Engine intake centre-body
77 Gas turbine starter
78 Constant speed drive unit
79 Lower fuselage lateral avionics bay
80 Emergency ram air turbine, deployed position
81 Canard flap honeycomb construction
82 Hydraulic reservoirs
83 Canard flap hydraulic actuator

84 Engine intake compressor face
85 Ventral accessory equipment gearbox
86 Electro-luminescent formation lighting strips
87 Volvo Flygmotor RM8A afterburning turbofan engine
88 Fuselage integral main fuel tank
89 Main engine mounting
90 Cooling air scoop
91 Engine bleed air pre-cooler
92 Engine oil cooler, fuel cooled
93 Fuel system recuperators
94 Fuel system piping
95 ADF aerial

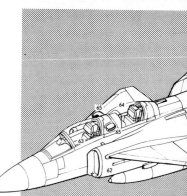

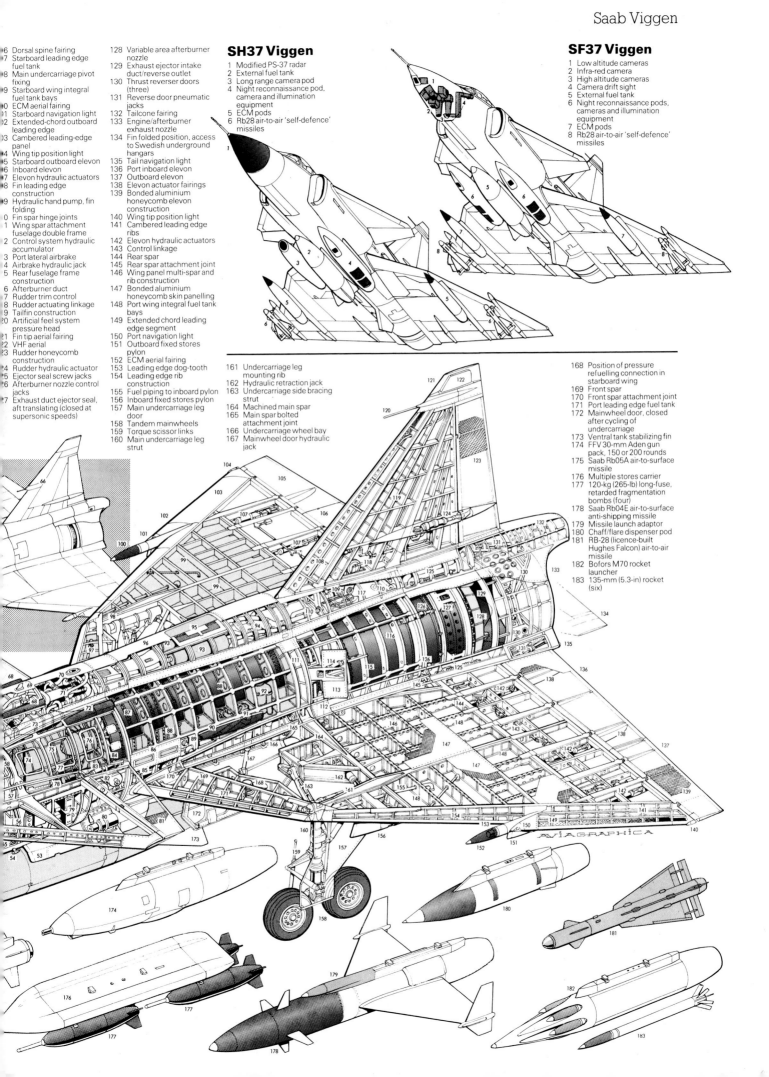

6 Dorsal spine fairing
7 Starboard leading edge fuel tank
8 Main undercarriage pivot fixing
9 Starboard wing integral fuel tank bays
0 ECM aerial fairing
1 Starboard navigation light
2 Extended-chord outboard leading edge
3 Cambered leading-edge panel
4 Wing tip position light
5 Starboard outboard elevon
6 Inboard elevon
7 Elevon hydraulic actuators
8 Fin leading edge construction
9 Hydraulic hand pump, fin folding
0 Fin spar hinge joints
1 Wing spar attachment fuselage double frame
2 Control system hydraulic accumulator
3 Port lateral airbrake
4 Airbrake hydraulic jack
5 Rear fuselage frame construction
6 Afterburner duct
7 Rudder trim control
8 Rudder actuating linkage
9 Tailfin construction
20 Artificial feel system pressure head
21 Fin tip aerial fairing
22 VHF aerial
23 Rudder honeycomb construction
24 Rudder hydraulic actuator
25 Ejector seal screw jacks
26 Afterburner nozzle control jacks
27 Exhaust duct ejector seal, aft translating (closed at supersonic speeds)

128 Variable area afterburner nozzle
129 Exhaust ejector intake duct/reverse outlet
130 Thrust reverser doors (three)
131 Reverse door pneumatic jacks
132 Tailcone fairing
133 Engine/afterburner exhaust nozzle
134 Fin folded position, access to Swedish underground hangars
135 Tail navigation light
136 Port inboard elevon
137 Outboard elevon
138 Elevon actuator fairings
139 Bonded aluminium honeycomb elevon construction
140 Wing tip position light
141 Cambered leading edge ribs
142 Elevon hydraulic actuators
143 Control linkage
144 Rear spar
145 Rear spar attachment joint
146 Wing panel multi-spar and rib construction
147 Bonded aluminium honeycomb skin panelling
148 Port wing integral fuel tank bays
149 Extended chord leading edge segment
150 Port navigation light
151 Outboard fixed stores pylon
152 ECM aerial fairing
153 Leading edge dog-tooth
154 Leading edge rib construction
155 Fuel piping to inboard pylon
156 Inboard fixed stores pylon
157 Main undercarriage leg door
158 Tandem mainwheels
159 Torque scissor links
160 Main undercarriage leg strut

161 Undercarriage leg mounting rib
162 Hydraulic retraction jack
163 Undercarriage side bracing strut
164 Machined main spar
165 Main spar bolted attachment joint
166 Undercarriage wheel bay
167 Mainwheel door hydraulic jack

SH37 Viggen

1 Modified PS-37 radar
2 External fuel tank
3 Long range camera pod
4 Night reconnaissance pod, camera and illumination equipment
5 ECM pods
6 Rb28 air-to-air 'self-defence' missiles

SF37 Viggen

1 Low altitude cameras
2 Infra-red camera
3 High altitude cameras
4 Camera drift sight
5 External fuel tank
6 Night reconnaissance pods, cameras and illumination equipment
7 ECM pods
8 Rb28 air-to-air 'self-defence' missiles

168 Position of pressure refuelling connection in starboard wing
169 Front spar
170 Front spar attachment joint
171 Port leading edge fuel tank
172 Mainwheel door, closed after cycling of undercarriage
173 Ventral tank stabilizing fin
174 FFV 30-mm Aden gun pack, 150 or 200 rounds
175 Saab Rb05A air-to-surface missile
176 Multiple stores carrier
177 120-kg (265-lb) long-fuse, retarded fragmentation bombs (four)
178 Saab Rb04E air-to-surface anti-shipping missile
179 Missile launch adaptor
180 Chaff/flare dispenser pod
181 RB-28 (licence-built Hughes Falcon) air-to-air missile
182 Bofors M70 rocket launcher
183 135-mm (5.3-in) rocket (six)

AVIAGRAPHICA

Saab Viggen warload

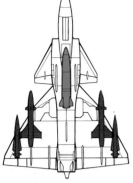
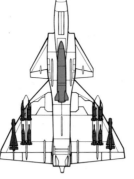
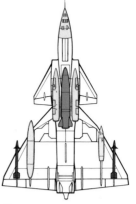
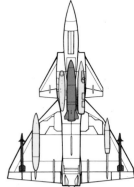

- 2 × Saab-Bofors Rb04E anti-ship missiles on inner wing pylons
- 2 × Saab-Bofors Rb05A air-to-surface missiles on outer fuselage pylons
- 2 × ECM 'bullet' fairings (one at the dogtooth of each wing leading edge)
- 1 × auxiliary fuel tank on fuselage centreline pylon

AJ 37 attack

With defence of the Baltic approaches of primary concern to Sweden, this configuration allows extended time on station and the versatility of attacking sea or land targets. The Rb05A missiles also have a limited air-to-air capability.

- 2 × Saab-Bofors Rb05A air-to-surface missiles on outer fuselage pylons
- 4 × Bofors M70X low-drag rocket packs (six 135-mm/5.3-in projectiles per pack) on the four underwing pylons
- 2 × ECM 'bullet' fairings (one at the dogtooth of each wing leading edge)
- 1 × auxiliary fuel tank on fuselage centreline pylon

AJ 37 ground attack

Mission flexibility, a high payload and the ability to operate from dispersal sites close to the front line mean the ground-attack AJ37 can provide a very effective back-up to ground forces defending Swedish territory. The rockets are much larger than usual.

- 2 × Rb28 air-to-air missiles on outboard wing pylons
- 2 × multiple stores carriers (each with four Virgo M/71 120-kg/265-lb fragmentation bombs) on inboard wing pylons
- 2 × ECM 'bullet' fairings (one at the dogtooth of each wing leading edge)
- 1 × auxiliary fuel tank on fuselage centreline pylon

AJ 37 fighter-bomber

The Viggen's excellent low-level performance and manoeuvrability allow for an effective bombing role, this being backed-up with air-defence armament to oppose enemy interceptors. Again, the awesome power of the Viggen ensures it an excellent survivability factor in the face of enemy fire.

- 2 × Saab-Bofors Rb24 air-to-air missiles on outboard wing pylons
- 2 × Red Baron multi-sensor reconnaissance pods on outboard fuselage pylons
- 1 × SATT AQ31 ECM jammer pod on inner starboard wing pylon
- 1 × Philips BOX 9 chaff and flare dispenser on inner port wing pylon
- 7 × cameras (including a data-camera) for multi-purpose photography in nose reconnaissance housing
- 2 × ECM 'bullet' fairings (one at the dogtooth of each wing leading edge)
- 1 × auxiliary fuel tank on fuselage centreline pylon

SF 37 armed overland reconnaissance

All-weather photo-reconnaissance SF 37s are extremely versatile, with the nose package having four vertical or oblique low-level cameras, one vertical long-range high-altitude camera, one infra-red camera and an air-data camera which records aircraft course, altitude and position. Augmented by the night cameras and illumination from the Red Baron pods, the SF 37 can detect camouflaged targets and provide 180° photo-coverage.

- 2 × Saab-Bofors Rb24 air-to-air missiles on outboard wing pylons
- 1 × Red Baron multi-sensor reconnaissance pod on port fuselage pylon
- 1 × long-range camera pod on starboard fuselage pylon
- 1 × SATT AQ31 ECM jammer pod on inner starboard wing pylon
- 1 × Philips BOX 9 chaff and flare dispenser on inner port wing pylon
- 2 × ECM 'bullet' fairings (one at the dogtooth of each wing leading edge)
- 1 × nose-mounted camera linked to the radar display
- 1 × nose-mounted air-data camera
- 1 × auxiliary fuel tank on fuselge centreline pylon

SH 37 maritime surveillance

Primary responsibility for the Swedish air force SH 37s is the surveillance, detection and identification of seaborne units operating in the waters off the Swedish coast. The nose-mounted radar display can be photographed at any time, and registration equipment allows for detailed coverage of subjects at sea.

From the outset of design, the Viggen had to feature relatively easy maintenance procedures as much of the Swedish air force personnel are short-term conscripts. These requirements have been met and the Viggen can achieve excellent turnaround and overhaul times, thus enhancing operational capability. This machine displays the large tail fin folded to port and the main radar housing with nose radome removed immediately ahead of the cockpit.

Performance

Maximum speed at 36,100 ft (11000 m)	Mach 2 (1,146 kts)	2124 km/h (1,320 mph)
Maximum speed at 330 ft (100 m)	Mach 1.2 (793 kts)	1470 km/h (914 mph)
Service ceiling	60,000 ft	(18290 m)
Maximum range	not disclosed	
Combat radius with six Mk 82 500-lb (227-kg) bombs	476 km	(296 miles)
Climb to 32,810 ft (10000 m)	1 minute 40 seconds	
g limit	+12 (ultimate)	
Take-off distance	400 m	(1,312 ft)

Weapon load

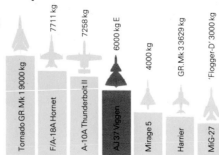

- Tornado GR Mk 1 9000 kg
- F/A-18A Hornet 7711 kg
- A-10A Thunderbolt II 7258 kg
- AJ 37 Viggen 6000 kg E
- Mirage 5 4000 kg
- Harrier GR.Mk 3 3629 kg
- MiG-27 'Flogger-D' 3000 kg

Combat radius lo-lo-lo

- Tornado GR.Mk 1 700 km E
- Mirage 5 650 km with 1000-kg payload
- F/A-18A Hornet 600 km E on attack mission
- AJ 37 Viggen 500 km + with external payload
- A-10A Thunderbolt II 463 km with 20-min reserves
- MiG-27 'Flogger-D' 390 km with 2900-kg payload
- Harrier GR.Mk 3 370 km with external payload

Speed at sea level

- Tornado GR.Mk 1 Mach 1.2
- Mirage 5 Mach 1.13 clean
- AJ 37 Viggen Mach 1.1+
- MiG-27 'Flogger-D' Mach 1.1 E clean
- F/A-18A Hornet Mach 1
- Harrier GR.Mk 3 Mach 0.95+
- A-10A Thunderbolt II Mach 0.58 clean

Take-off run

- Harrier GR.Mk 3 305 m at max weight
- AJ37 Viggen 400 m E
- F/A-18A Hornet 428 m
- MiG-27 'Flogger-D' 670 m E clean
- Tornado GR.Mk 1 885 m E
- A-10A Thunderbolt II 1220 m at max weight
- Mirage 5 1600 m at max weight

Combat radius hi-lo-hi

- Tornado GR.Mk 1 1390 km with 3629-kg load
- Mirage 5 1300 km with 1000-kg load
- F/A-18A Hornet 1065 km on attack mission
- AJ 37 Viggen 1000 km + with external load
- A-10A Thunderbolt II 998 km with 20-min reserves
- MiG-27 'Flogger-D' 950 km E with external fuel
- Harrier GR.Mk 3 666 km

GLOSSARY

AAA	Anti-Aircraft Artillery
AAM	Air-to-Air Missile
ACM	Air Combat Manoeuvre
AFB	Air-Force Base
AFRes	Air Force Reserve
ANG	Air National Guard
AHRS	Attitude and Heading Reference System
ALARM	Air-Launched Anti-Radiation Missile
ALCM	Air-Launched Cruise Missile
ARM	Anti-Radiation Missile
ASM	Air-to-Surface Missile
ASMP	Air-Sol Moyenne-Portee (medium range surface-to-air)
AMRAAM	Advanced Medium-Range Air-to-Air Missile
AV-MF	Soviet Naval Aviation
BW	Bomber Wing
CBU	Cluster Bomb Unit
CILOP	Conversion in Lieu Of Procurement
CITS	Central Integrated Test System
COMED	COmbined Map and Electronic Display
CRT	Cathode Ray Tube
DARIN	Display, Attack, Ranging and Inertial Navigation
DME	Distance-Measuring Equipment
ECM	Electronic CounterMeasures
Elint	Electronic intelligence
EMP	Electro-Magnetic Pulse
EO	Electro-Optical
ESM	Electronic Support Measures
EVS	Electro-optical Viewing System
EW	Electronic Warfare
FLIR	Forward-Looking Infra-Red
GP	General Purpose
GSFG	Group of Soviet Forces in Germany
HARM	High-speed Anti-Radiation Missile
HUD	Head-Up Display
HUDWAS	Head-Up Display and Weapon-Aiming System
IFF	Identification Friend or Foe
ILS	Instrument Landing System
INS	Inertial Navigation System
IOC	Initial Operational Capability
IR	Infra-Red
IRCM	Infra-Red CounterMeasures
JATO	Jet-Assisted Take-Off
LID	Lift-Improvement Device
LLLTV	Low-Light-Level TV
LRMTS	Laser Ranger and Marked-Target Seeker

MCAS	Marine Corps Air Station
NAS	Naval Air Station
NAVWAS	NAVigation and Weapon-Aiming System
NWDS	Navigation and Weapons Delivery System
OAS	Offensive Avionics System
OCU	Operational Conversion Unit
OTEAF	Operational Test and EvaluAtion Force
PGM	Precision-Guided Munition
Photint	Photographic intelligence
QRA	Quick-Reaction Alert
RAAF	Royal Australian Air Force
RDT&E	Research, Development, Test and Evaluation
RIO	Radio Intercept Officer
RNAS	Royal Naval Air Station
RWR	Radar Warning Receiver
SAC	Strategic Air Command
SACEUR	Supreme Allied Commander EURope
SACLANT	Supreme Allied Commander AtLANTic
SAM	Surface-to-Air Missile
SAR	Search And Rescue
SEAM	Sidewinder Expanded-Acquisition Missile
SIOP	Single Integrated Operational Plan
SLEP	Service Life Extension Program
SNOE	Smart Noise Operation Equipment
SOR	Specific Operational Requirement
SRAM	Short-Range Attack Missile
Tacan	Tactical Air Navigation
TAC	Tactical Air Command
TERCOM	TERrain COntour Matching
TFR	Terrain Following Radar
TFS	Tactical Fighter Squadron
TFW	Tactical Fighter Wing
TFX	Tactical Fighter, eXperimental
TISL	Target Indicator System - Laser
TRAM	Target Recognition and Attack Multi-Sensor
TRIM	Trails, Roads, Interdiction Multi-sensor
TTTE	Trinational Tornado Training Establishment
UHF	Ultra High Frequency
VG	Variable Geometry
VHF	Very High Frequency
VOR	VHF Omni-directional Range
VTAS	Visual Target-Acquisition System
VTOL	Vertical Take-Off and Landing
V-VS	Soviet air force
WAC	Weapon-Aiming Computer
WSO	Weapons System Officer